The Korean War

A Historical Dictionary

Paul M. Edwards

*Historical Dictionaries of War,
Revolution, and Civil Unrest, No. 23*

The Scarecrow Press, Inc.
Lanham, Maryland, and Oxford
2003

SCARECROW PRESS, INC.

Published in the United States of America
by Scarecrow Press, Inc.
A Member of the Rowman & Littlefield Publishing Group
4720 Boston Way, Lanham, Maryland 20706
www.scarecrowpress.com

PO Box 317
Oxford
OX2 9RU, UK

British Library Cataloguing in Publication Information Available

Library of Congress Cataloging-in-Publication Data

Edwards, Paul M.
    The Korean War : a historical dictionary / Paul M. Edwards.
        p. cm. — (Historical dictionaries of war, revolution, and civil unrest ; no. 23)
    Includes bibliographical references.
    ISBN 0-8108-4479-6 (alk. paper)
        1. Korean War, 1950–1953—Dictionaries. 2. Korea—History—1864–1910—
    Dictionaries. 3. Korea—History—20th century—Dictionaries. I. Title. II. Series.
    DS918 .E363 2003
    951.904'2'03—dc21   2002070848

*To
Frank Kelley,
friend*

Contents

Foreword

For many, but not all those concerned, the Korean War has sadly become a forgotten war. It is not hard to grasp why. Despite enormous sacrifices in human and material terms, no party—neither North Korea nor South Korea, China, Russia, nor the United States and its allies—achieved its goals. The war ended in a stalemate, about where it had begun, not much to be proud of. But what a stalemate it was!

It permitted South Korea to concentrate on reconstruction and launch an impressive economic "miracle." It allowed other neighbors, including Japan, to go about their business more or less normally. It gave the great powers a salutary lesson in humility so that there were few other hot wars aside from the Vietnam War. This long period of semi-peace/semi-war known as the Cold War finally ended, ushering in a new era in which all parties put the economy first and in which, by the way, United Nations intervention (under the aegis of the United States of America as often as not) is a common occurrence.

So the Korean War was certainly not just a messy, inconclusive war that should be forgotten. It was, for all its ambiguities, a decisive war whose long-term benefits have yet to be counted. Thus, the more we know about it, the better. This volume is a further contribution.

Like other historical dictionaries in this series of war, revolution, and civil unrest, this book covers the war in several ways. The people, places, and events, including the battles and other engagements, are dealt with in detail in the dictionary section. But in some ways, the bibliography is the key, since it opens the door to the growing literature that dwells more on specifics of the Korean War.

The Korean War: A Historical Dictionary was written by Paul M. Edwards whose contact with the war goes back to 1953 when he served in Korea with the 7th Division. His writing on the war spans several decades, during which he produced several dozen articles. Over the past decade, he has written books on the whole war, on specific phases (Inchon Landing, Pusan Perimeter), on one of the outstanding leaders (Matthew Ridgway), and also on films, poetry, and a bibliography.

Dr. Edwards has taught and is teaching history, including that of the Korean War. This was certainly ample training for the compilation of a historical dictionary that brings together the many facets of a war he does not want the world to forget.

Jon Woronoff
Series Editor

Acknowledgments

A composite research work like a dictionary cannot be completed without relying on the works of hundreds of other authors who have produced monographs, books, and reference works. I owe a great debt of gratitude to many such authors, too many to be acknowledged, but especially to the excellent work of Harry G. Summers Jr., Michael J. Variola, Stanley Saddler, James I. Matray, and John Quick. My thanks to Graceland University that made available the resources of the Center for the Study of the Korean War, and to Tom Rives of the Central Plains Region National Archives located in Kansas City, Missouri.

A variety of individuals have also been supportive and have lent their peculiar talents to this endeavor. Special thanks to Joni Wilson who contributed her extraordinary talent as a copy reader, to Gregory Madison Edwards, Pamela Peck, Cindy Roberts, Laura Lane, and Randy Hallauer. Appreciation to Bradley whose "what'ya doing?" kept me asking the same question. As always my deepest gratitude to my wife, Carolynn, and to Nash (a real sit-at-your-feet type cat) for their patience.

Reader's Notes

Several decisions have been made about the individual listings in order to make the dictionary as friendly as possible.

The People's Republic of China (PRC) is the official name of the nation that joined in the conflict in Korea, but it is also identified as Communist China. When possible the official name is used. The other China that is located on the island of Taiwan is officially the Republic of China (ROC), but it is also referred to as "Nationalist China." The southern portion of Korea is officially the Republic of Korea (ROK) but is often called South Korea. The northern portion is officially the Democratic People's Republic of Korea (DPRK), but is also identified, sometimes even in official documents, as North Korea. When any of these nations are referenced (in boldface type) the reader should seek them under their official name.

The same confusion exists when referring to the military arms of these nations. The troops of the People's Republic of China are often listed as the People's Liberation Army (PLA), the Chinese Volunteers Army (CVA), or even more common, Communist Chinese Forces (CCF). The military force of the Democratic People's Republic of Korea is identified as North Korean People's Army (NKPA), yet the various branches are generally referred to as North Korean. On those occasions when it is necessary to refer to both the Democratic People's Republic of Korea and the People's Republic of China they are combined under the heading "communist."

Names listed in the dictionary and bibliography use the traditional last name first for English spellings. In listing Korean, Japanese, and Chinese names those spellings common during the course of the war are used. Sometimes Orientals use an adopted name in memory of a national hero and in cases where both names are used they are identified in brackets. Because most Westerners have difficulty identifying the proper order of Korean, Japanese, and Chinese names, these names are listed as they are spoken (the premier of North Korea is found as Kim Il-Sung) without regard for Western order. Because of the variance of diacritical identity used in efforts at transliteration, names are identified only by breaks, allowing the item to be spelled in the English fashion.

As there are so many military people identified, it is important to be consistent when assigning rank. I have used the generally preferred system of listing the rank of the individual at the time being discussed.

Thus while Colonel Puller later rose to the rank of general, the action in which he is discussed happened when he was still a colonel, and he is listed by that rank.

Dates can be confusing because of the time difference between Korea and the United States and other allies. Therefore the times and dates are used as they were in the location about which the comment is made. Entries that focus on the United States use the time and date according to United States time; an entry about Korea uses the time and date in Korea.

Entries appear in alphabetical order and are cross-referenced. Cross-reference entries that can provide additional information appear in **bold.**

It was impossible to list all the people and events related to the Korean War. In establishing priorities a substantially larger portion of the space available has been allocated to the United Nations, the United States, United Kingdom, and the Republic of Korea. This is due, in part, to the imbalance of the historical records available. Despite the end to the Cold War and the opening of some Soviet archives there is still much that is unknown. In determining which individuals to identify it has been necessary to list high-ranking officers, civilian administrators, and diplomats. This is the nature of historical memory and in no way should be seen as lessening the contribution of the men and women who fought the war. The selection process was difficult and both the names listed, and those not listed, were placed in their categories after considerable consideration. The final selection, of course, is the responsibility of the author.

Wherever possible the appropriate gender terms have been used, preferring "service men and women" to servicemen. But there are some occasions when such an adjustment is either too difficult or misleading. Both men and women served in Korea, and it is the author's intent to acknowledge their contribution.

The bibliography tries to list important (and some less important but popular) works. It would be impossible to identify them all, especially articles and monographs that are now difficult to locate. Any item published after 1 December 2001 is not included. Most of the items listed can be found in a public or university library either on the shelves or by inter-library loan. A few, however, will be more difficult to locate.

Abbreviations and Acronyms

AAA	Antiaircraft artillery
ACR	United States Navy armored cruiser
AD	Destroyer tender
ADCOM	Advance Command and Liaison Group in Korea
Adm	Admiral
AE	United States Navy ammunition ship
AF	Stores ship
AFB	Air Force base
AFFE	Army Forces Far East
AGC	United States Navy amphibious command ship
AH	Hospital ship
AKA	Also known as
AKR	United States Navy vehicle cargo ship
AM	United States Navy minesweeper
AMS	Army Map Service
AMS	United States Auxiliary Motor Minesweeper
ANC	Amphibious Construction Battalion, United States Navy
ANZAC	Australian/New Zealand Army Corps
AO	Oiler
AOG	Gasoline tanker
AP	Armor piercing
AP	United States Navy transport
APA	United States Navy attack transport
ARSV	Army reconnaissance scout vehicle
Arty.	Artillery
ATR	Ocean-going tug
B	Bomber
BAR	Browning Automatic Rifle
BB	Battleship
BN	Battalion
BOQ	Bachelor officer quarters
Brig	Brigade
Btry	Battery
CA	Heavy cruiser
Capt	Captain, United States Army

CAPT	Captain, United States Navy
CAS	Close air support, United States Navy
Cav	Cavalry
CCF	Chinese Communist Forces
CCP	Chinese Communist Party
CCS	Combined Chiefs of Staff
CDR	Commander
CG	Commanding General
CIA	Central Intelligence Agency
CIB	Combat Infantryman Badge
CinC	Commander in Chief
CINCFE	Commander in Chief, Far East
CincPac	Commander in Chief, Pacific Fleet Area
CINCUNC	Commander in Chief, United Nations Command
CJCS	Chairman of the Joint Chiefs of Staff
CL	Light cruiser
CNO	Chief of Naval Operations
CO	Commanding Officer
Co	Company
CofS	Chief of Staff
COIN	Counter-insurgency
Col	Colonel
Comdr	Commander
COMO	Commander
CONUS	Continental United States
CP	Command Post
CPVA	Chinese People's Volunteers Army
CSA	Chief of Staff, United States Army
CTF	Commander Task Force
CTG	Commander Task Group
CVA	United States Navy attack aircraft carrier
CVE	Aircraft carrier escort
CZ	Combat Zone
DA	Department of the Army
DCM	Distinguished Conduct Medal
DD	Destroyer
DFC	Distinguished Flying Cross
DFM	Distinguished Flying Medal, British
Div	Division
DivArty	Division artillery
DL	United States Navy frigate

DMS	Highspeed minesweeper
DMZ	Demilitarized Zone
-do	Korean suffix for island
DOD	Department of Defense
DOW	Died of wounds
DPRK	Democratic People's Republic of Korea
DSC	Distinguished Service Cross
DSM	Distinguished Service Medal, British
DSU	Distinguished Unit Citation
DUKW	United States amphibious 2½-ton truck (also called Duck)
EM	Enlisted man
Eng	Engineer
ENS	Ensign
EUSAK	Eighth United States Army in Korea
ETA	Estimated time of arrival
ETD	Estimated time of departure
F	Fighter
FA	Field artillery
FEAF	Far East Forces
FEC	Far East Command
FECOM	Far East Command
FIFIK	Fifth United States Air Force in Korea
G-1	Personnel section of division or higher staff
G-2	Intelligence section of division or higher staff
G-3	Operations and training of division or higher staff
G-4	Logistics section of division or higher staff
G-5	Civil section of a division or higher staff
Gen	General
GHQ	General headquarters
GI	Government issue, slang for soldier
GO	General orders
HE	High explosives
HEAT	High-explosive anti-tank
Hist Sec	Historical section
HMAS	His/Her Majesty's Australian Ship
HMCS	His/Her Majesty's Canadian Ship
HMNZS	His/Her Majesty's New Zealand Ship

HMS	His/Her Majesty's Ship
HNMS	His/Her Netherlands Majesty's Ship
How	Howitzer
HQ	Headquarters
ICRC	International Committee of the Red Cross
IFS	Inshore fire support
Inf	Infantry
JCS	Joint Chiefs of Staff
J-1	Joint staff personnel section
J-2	Joint staff intelligence section
J-3	Joint staff operations section
J-4	Joint staff logistic section
J-5	Joint staff civil affairs section
KATCOM	Korean Augmentation Troops, Commonwealth
KATUSA	Korean Augmentation Troops, United States Army
KCOMA	Korean Communication Zone
KIA	Killed in action
KMAG	Korean Military Advisory Group, United States
KMC	Korean Marine Corps, Republic of Korea
KSC	Korean Service Corps
KSM	Korean Service Medal
LCDR	Lieutenant commander
LCVP	Landing craft, vehicle, personnel
LSD	Landing ship, dock
LSM	Landing ship, medium
LSMR	Landing ship, medium (rocket)
LST	Landing ship, tank
LSV	Landing ship, vehicle
Lt	Lieutenant, United States Army
1st Lt	First lieutenant, United States Army
2nd Lt	Second lieutenant, United States Army
LT	Lieutenant, United States Navy
Lt. Col	Lieutenant colonel, United States Army
LTGEN	Lieutenant general, United States Army
LTJG	Lieutenant Junior Grade, United States Navy
LVT	Landing vehicle, tracked
MAAG	Military Assistance Advisory Group

MAC	Military Armistice Commission
MAG	Marine Aircraft Group
Maj	Major
MAJGEN	Major general
MASH	Mobile Army Surgical Hospital
MATS	Military Air Transport Service
MAW	Marine Aircraft Wing
MG	Machine gun
MIA	Missing in action
MiG	Mikoyan–Gurevich Soviet-made jet
MIS	Military Intelligence Service
MLR	Main line of resistance
MSF	Navy minesweeper (steel-hulled)
MSR	Main supply route
MSTS	Military Sea Transport Service
NAS	Naval air station
NATO	North Atlantic Treaty Organization
NAVFE	Naval Forces Far East
NCO	Non-commissioned officer
NK	North Korea
NKPA	North Korean People's Army
NNRC	Neutral Nations Repatriation Commission
NNSC	Neutral Nations Supervisory Commission
NSC	National Security Council
OCMH	Office of the Chief of Military History
OJCS	Office of the Joint Chiefs of Staff
OP	Observation post
OpNav	Office of Naval Operation
Opns	Operations
PF	Frigate
PLA	People's Liberation Army, North Korea
Plt	Platoon
POL	Petroleum, oil, and lubricants
POW	Prisoner of war
PRC	People's Republic of China
PT	Motor patrol boat
PVA	People's Volunteer Army
QM	Quartermaster Corps

R&R	Rest and recuperation
RAAK	Resist America and Aid Korea Movement
RADM	Rear admiral
RAF	Royal Air Force, British
RAN	Royal Australian Navy
Recon	Reconnaissance
RCN	Royal Canadian Navy
RCT	Regimental combat team
Regt.	Regiment
-ri	Korean suffix for town
RN	Royal Navy
RNZN	Royal New Zealand Navy
ROC	Republic of China
ROK	Republic of Korea
ROKA	Republic of Korea Army
ROKN	Republic of Korea Navy
RM	Royal Marines, British
RMC	Royal Army Medical Corps
ROK	Republic of Korea, South Korea
S-1	Adjutant, personnel
S-2	Intelligence officer
S-3	Operations and training officer
S-4	Supply officer
-san	Korean suffix for mountain
SAAF	South African Air Force
SANACC	State–Army–Navy–Air Force Coordinating Committee
SAR	Special action report
SCAP	Supreme Commander for the Allied Powers
SEAL	Sea Air Land (Team)
SEATO	Southeast Asia Treaty Organization
SecDef	Secretary of Defense
SecState	Secretary of State
SHAPE	Supreme Headquarters Allied Powers Europe
Sitrep	Situation report
SP	Self-propelled
SS	Submarine
TAC	Tactical Air Command
TACP	Tactical air control party
TADC	Tactical air direction center

TE	Task element
TF	Task force
T/O&E	Table of organization and equipment
UDT	Underwater demolition team
UN	United Nations
UNC	United Nations Command
UNCMAC	United Nations Command Military Armistice Commission
UNCURK	United Nations Commission for the Unification and Rehabilitation of Korea
UNTOCK	United Nations Temporary Commission on Korea
US	United States
USA	United States Army
USAF	United States Air Force
USAFIK	United States Armed Forces in Korea
USMC	United States Marine Corps
USN	United States Navy
USNS	United States Naval ship (in service)
USS	United States Ship
USSR	Union of Soviet Socialist Republics
VADM	Vice admiral
VFM	Marine fighter squadron
VHF	Very high frequency
VMFN	Marine night fighter squadron
VMO	Marine observation squadron
VMR	Marine transport squadron
VP	Patrol squadron
VT	Variable time fuse
WAAC	Women's Auxiliary Army Corps
WAC	Women's Army Corps
WAF	Women in the Air Force
WAVE	Women Accepted for Volunteer Emergency service, United States Navy
WD	War diary
WIA	Wounded in action
WP	White phosphorus
YMS	Motor minesweeper

| ZI | Zone of Interior, the United States |
| ZULU | United States, Zone of Interior |

Maps

Photographs

Chronology

1882	Korean–American Treaty of friendship and commerce.
1908	United States recognizes Japan's primacy in Korea and Manchuria.
1910	Korea annexed by Japan.
1919	Provisional Korean government established. Syngman Rhee leaves Korea for political reasons.

1943

15 Aug.	U.S. General Order Number One temporarily divides Korea at 38th Parallel.
1 Dec.	Cairo Declaration promises Korean independence "in due course."

1945

24 July	President Harry Truman asks for Russian help against Japan at Potsdam Conference.
6 Aug.	Atomic bomb dropped on Japanese city of Hiroshima.
8 Aug.	Soviet Union declares war on Japan and invades Manchuria and Korea.
2 Sept.	Japan's formal surrender.
8 Sept.	United States troops land at Jintsen near Seoul, Korea.
9 Sept.	United States accepts Japanese surrender in Korea south of the 38th Parallel.
16 Nov.	Fleet Admiral Ernest King testifies before Congress that the rapid demobilization of the navy meant they could no longer fight a major war.

1946

8 May	Joint Soviet–American commission adjourns failing to reach agreement on Korean reunification.

1947

17 Sept.	United States refers Korean independence to United Nations.
14 Nov.	United Nations resolution to remove troops from Korea after national elections.
	United Nations approves creation of Temporary Commission on Korea (UNTCOK) to supervise national elections.

1948

24 Jan.	Soviets refuse to permit UNTCOK into northern Korea.
2 Feb.	North Korean People's Army (NKPA) begins.
8 Apr.	President Truman withdraws most U.S. troops from Korea.
10 May	Republic of Korea (ROK) elections held.
15 Aug.	Republic of Korea (ROK) established, Syngman Rhee first president.
9 Sept.	Democratic People's Republic of Korea (DPRK) claims jurisdiction over all Korea.
16 Sept.	National Security Council Directive 30, on the use of atomic weapons, approved.
12 Dec.	United Nations recognizes Republic of Korea as only legitimate government, calls for withdrawal of occupation troops.
31 Dec.	Soviets withdraw troops.

1949

8 Apr.	Russia vetoes Republic of Korea admission to United Nations.
29 June	U.S. troops withdraw from Republic of Korea and Korean Military Advisory Group (KMAG) remains.
25 Aug.	First Soviet atomic bomb is detonated.

1950

12 Jan.	Secretary of State Dean Acheson proclaims Korea and Taiwan outside America's Far East security zone.
25 June	Democratic People's Republic of Korea attacks the Republic of Korea with estimated 135,000 troops and 150 tanks.
	United Nations Security Council orders Democratic People's Republic of Korea to stop the attack.

United Nations Security Council calls for end of aggression. Republic of Korea replies with army of about 98,000 men.

26 June United Nations Ambassador John J. Muccio orders embassy personal and dependents evacuated from Korea.

27 June President Truman authorizes United States air and naval support of Republic of Korea south of 38th Parallel.

United States 5th Air Force planes shoot down first enemy plane near Seoul.

United Nations adopts United States resolution asking members to aid Republic of Korea.

28 June British forces in Japanese waters placed under United States command.

29 June Seoul falls, destroyed Han River bridge traps many in Republic of Korea Army without an escape route.

Members of 507th Anti-Aircraft Artillery Battalion down enemy plane.

President Harry Truman authorizes sea blockade of the Korean coast.

First U.S. casualties of the Korean War when five from 507th are wounded.

First Naval bombardment when USS *Juneau* fires a salvo on the east coast.

3rd Bomber Group hits Heijo Airfield near Democratic People's Republic of Korea capital of Pyongyang.

British Royal Navy and Royal Australian Navy attack warships to NAVFE.

30 June Democratic People's Republic of Korea 3rd Div. crosses Han River.

President Harry Truman commits United States troops to support the United Nations demand.

President Truman extends Public Law 599 extending the draft until 9 July 1951.

1 July First United States Task Force Smith arrives in Korea.

2 July Only naval battle fought between United States and the Democratic People's Republic of Korea, when USS *Juneau* destroys attacking DPRK torpedo boats near Chumuunjin.

	President Truman rejects Chiang Kai-shek's offer of troops.
3 July	First United Nations carrier strike when planes from the USS *Valley Forge* hit airfields near the Pyong-yang–Chinnampo area in Democratic People's Republic of Korea.
5 July	Task Force Smith (1st Bn, 21st Regt. 24th Infantry Div.) defeated by Democratic People's Republic of Korea 4th Div. in battle of Osan, the first land engagement.
6–8 July	34th Infantry Regiment of the 24th Division delays advancing North Korean People's Army at Osan.
7 July	United Nations Command created and given to General Douglas MacArthur.
8 July	Troops from the 3rd Bn, 34th Regt, 24th Infantry Div. defeated at Chosin.
10 July	Planes of the 5th Air Force hit North Korean People's Army tanks at Pyongtaek.
10–18 July	25th Infantry Div. moves to Korea from Japan.
12 July	Eighth United States Army given ground operations assignment in Korea.
13 July	Lt. General Walton "Johnny" Walker takes command of ground forces in Korea.
	United States and Republic of Korea form line along Kum River.
	B-29s bomb the port city of Wonsan, Democratic People's Republic of Korea.
	The Pusan Base Command is replaced by the Pusan Logistical Command.
	Indian Prime Minister Jawaharlal Nehru urges United States and Soviet United Nations to contain fighting in Korea.
13–16 July	Battle of the Kum River, 19th and 34th Infantry of 24th Infantry Division delays North Korean People's Army at the river.
13–24 July	On west coast, North Korean People's Army 6th Div. drives south capturing Chonju.
18 July	8th Cavalry Regiment (leading unit of the First Cavalry Division) lands at Pohang.
19 July	President Harry Truman authorizes Secretary of Defense to mobilize the reserves and national guard including marines.

19–20 July	Battle of Taejon where members of the 24th Infantry Division defended the town.
20 July	Taejon is taken by North Korean People's Army.
20–21 July	First major holding action achieved by Republic of Korea Army 3rd Division.
20–30 July	Eighth and 5th Cavalry Regiments defeated at Yong-dong. 27th Regiment of the 25th Infantry Division defeated in first action.
24 July	Fifth United States Air Force relocates in Korea.
25 July	29th RCT is defeated near Chinju and 3rd Battalion nearly destroyed.
	USS *Princeton* removed from storage.
25–30 July	North Korean People's Army defeats 19th Regt, 24th Infantry Division and captures Chinju.
26 July	8th Army orders withdrawal to prepare positions near Pusan.
29 July	General Walton Walker is said to have issued "Stand or Die" order.
31 July	9th Regiment, 2nd Infantry Division lands in Pusan.
	General Douglas MacArthur visits Taiwan to discuss island defense.
1 Aug.	Jacob Malik, Soviet delegate, returns to United Nations as president of Security Council.
2 Aug.	First Provisional Marine Brigade lands at Pusan, attached to 25th Infantry Division.
	Marines moved to Masan.
3 Aug.	Eighth Army completes second "adjustment" and establishes Naktong Perimeter defense line anchored in the west at the Naktong River.
4 Aug.	First aeromedical evacuation of United Nations troops by Marine VMO-6 helicopters.
5 Aug.–19 Sept.	First battle of the Naktong Bulge.
7–14 Aug.	Labeled Task Force Kean, the 25th Infantry Division supported by the Marine Brigade makes the first United States counterattack.
8 Aug.	Tanks land in Pusan.
10 Aug.	First bombing raid on Rashin.
	United States IX Corps activated and ordered to Korea.
	President Harry Truman approves active duty for 28th, 40th, 43rd, and 45th National Guard Div. and the 196th and 278th Regimental Combat Teams.

14 Aug.	USS *Pickerel*, a submarine, begins covert operations against Democratic People's Republic of Korea.
15–20 Aug.	Battle of Bowling Alley, United Nations victory near Taegu.
16 Aug.	72nd (Medium) and two 2nd Infantry Division tank companies arrive.
	United Nations X Corps activated in Japan.
17 Aug.	Massacre of American prisoners at Hill 303 near Waegwon.
18–22 Aug.	Republic of Korea Army 3rd and 8th Divisions stop the North Korean People's Army 8th, 12th, and 5th in their movement down the eastern Kyonju corridor toward Pusan.
25 Aug.	Major General William F. Dean taken prisoner.
26 Aug.	X Corps reactivated.
29 Aug.	British 27th Brigade lands at Pusan.
4 Sept.	Marine Brigade withdrawn from Pusan for Inchon invasion.
15 Sept.	Inchon landings, 1st Marines and 7th Infantry Division land.
16–19 Sept.	United Nations breaks the Naktong Perimeter line.
17 Sept.	Kimpo Airfield captured.
25 Sept.	Chinese People's Liberation Army warns that China will not allow the Americans to come to the Chinese border.
	Joint Chiefs of Staff authorize United Nations action north of 38th Parallel.
26 Sept.	USS *Brush* hits mine off Tanchon, 19 casualties.
27 Sept.	General MacArthur given permission to cross the 38th Parallel.
	Seoul recaptured; Syngman Rhee and General Douglas MacArthur enter Seoul.
	Joint Chiefs of Staff issue directive prohibiting airstrikes beyond Yalu River.
29 Sept.	USS *Magpie* (minesweeper) hits mine and is destroyed off Chuksan, Democratic Republic of Korea.
30 Sept.	USS *Mansfield* hits mine with 32 casualties.
	Republic of Korea troops cross 38th Parallel.
2 Oct.	People's Republic of China premier Mao Tse-tung tells Indian ambassador K. M. Pannnikar that it will enter the war if United States troops approach the Yalu River.

7 Oct.	United Nations authorizes action north of the 38th Parallel.
9 Oct.	First Cavalry Division crosses 38th Parallel.
11 Oct.	Republic of Korea 3rd Division occupies Wonsan.
	General Douglas MacArthur demands immediate North Korean People's Army surrender.
13 Oct.	Communist Chinese Forces begin crossing Yalu River to prepare for entering war.
15 Oct.	President Harry Truman and General Douglas MacArthur meet on Wake Island for talks.
19 Oct.	Pyongyang, Democratic People's Republic of Korea capital, is occupied.
20 Oct.	187th Airborne reinforced (674th FA Bn.) jumps at Sukchon north of Pyongyang.
25 Oct.	CCF troops hit ROK 6th Division.
26 Oct.	First Marine Division accomplishes administrative landing at Wonsan.
1 Nov.	21st Infantry Regt. and 24th Infantry Division reach the northernmost point where it captured Chonggodo about 18 miles from the Yalu River.
1–6 Nov.	CCF 39th Army opens China's first phase offensive.
4 Nov.	Intensified bombing of communication routes to Yalu River.
5–17 Nov.	Third Infantry Division lands at Wonsan.
7 Nov.	General Douglas MacArthur asks permission to follow Chinese planes across the Manchurian border.
8 Nov.	B-29s hit Yalu River bridges at Sinuiju.
	First all-jet combat occurs when an F-80 Shooting Star shot down a MiG-15 over Sinuiju.
16 Nov.	Harry Truman declares a state of emergency.
21 Nov.	U.S. 17th Regiment, 7th Infantry Division reaches Hyesanjin at the source of the Yalu River.
25 Nov.	United Nations "final offensive" begins at Chongchon River.
26–30 Nov.	United States 2nd Infantry Division and 25th Infantry Division are defeated as Communist Chinese Force attacks and 8th Army begins retreat in the west.
27 Nov.	Task Force MacLean/Faith is defeated east of the Chosin Reservoir.
27–30 Nov.	1st Marine Division and 7th Infantry Division are attacked by four Communist Chinese Force armies at Chosin Reservoir.

28 Nov.	President Harry Truman hints atomic bomb could be used if necessary.
	Task Force Kingston (elements of the 7th Infantry Division) reaches Yalu River at Singaipajin.
28–29 Nov.	Battle of Kunu-re where the Communist Chinese Force defeats the U.S. 2nd Infantry Division.
30 Nov.	First Canadian Korean War briefing.
30 Nov.–11 Dec.	Retreat from Chosin Reservoir, 1st Marine Division fights through Communist Chinese Force to 3rd Infantry Division lines holding the port city of Hungnam.
3–7 Dec.	Task Force 90 (Amphibious Force Far East) evacuates troops from Hungnam.
11 Dec.	United Nations naval forces begin the evacuation of troops at Hungnam.
14 Dec.	United Nations passes a cease-fire resolution.
15 Dec.	United Nations establishes Imjin River line of defense just north of Seoul.
20 Dec.	Press censorship imposed by United Nations Command over all Allied journalists in Korea.
21 Dec.	7th Infantry Division sails from Hungnam to Pusan.
22 Dec.	Army issues third involuntary recall of reserve officers.
23 Dec.	General Walton Walker killed in jeep accident.
	People's Republic of China's Chou En-lai rejects Cease-fire Group proposal.
24 Dec.	Last of X Corps, and refugees, taken from Hungnam.
26 Dec.	General Matthew Ridgway assumes command of Eighth Army.
30 Dec.	MiG 15 jets attack United Nations planes over Democratic People's Republic of Korea.
31 Dec.	Republic of China launches third phase operation.

1951

3 Jan.	Communist Chinese Force and North Korean People's Army continue offensive.
4 Jan.	Seoul is abandoned.
5 Jan.	Inchon is abandoned.
7–14 Jan.	General Ridgway stabilizes United Nations lines near the 38th Parallel.

25 Jan.	United Nations counteroffensive, Operation Thunderbolt, moves out as General Ridgway begins operations.
1 Feb.	United Nations resolution to end the war in Korea.
	Battle of Twin Tunnels, combined United Nations force attacks Communist Chinese Forces.
5–24 Feb.	Operation Roundup as X Corps advances on central front.
11–12 Feb.	People's Republic of China forces attack at Hoengsong inflicting heaviest American losses of the war, 2nd Infantry Division, 7th Infantry Division, and 187th RCT.
14 Feb.	French Battalion and 23rd RCT stop People's Republic of China attack on Chipyong-ni in defense of Wonju line.
16 Feb.	Beginning of the siege of Wonson harbor by Task Force 95 (United Nations Blockade and Escort Force) that lasts a record blockade of 861 days.
21 Feb.	Republic of Korea First Marine Regiment joins United States First Marine Division as its fourth regiment.
21 Feb.–7 Mar.	General Ridgway's Operation Killer moves forward to drive People's Republic of China forces north of Han River.
	IX Corps limited success in clearing communists from the Chipyong-ni mountain area.
7 Mar.–4 Apr.	Eighth Army's Operation Ripper pushes across the Han River, Chunchon recaptured, Line Idaho reached.
18 Mar.	Seoul taken again by United Nations Command.
22 Mar.	Operation Courage moves United Nations Command to position just south of 38th Parallel.
23 Mar.	Operation Tomahawk, 187th Airborne supported, drop near Munsan-ni.
24 Mar.	General Douglas MacArthur issues "pronunciamento" in which he demands the surrender of all communist forces.
29 Mar.	People's Republic of China rejects Douglas MacArthur's demands and issues orders for renewed fighting.
1–22 Apr.	Operations Rugged and Dauntless drive a dozen miles north of Line Kansas.

5 Apr.	Representative Joseph Martin reads (on the floor of the House) Douglas MacArthur's letter calling for victory in Korea.
7 Apr.	President Harry Truman fires General Douglas MacArthur.
11 Apr.	General Matthew Ridgway commands FECOM.
15 Apr.	General James Van Fleet takes command of Eighth Army.
19 Apr.	General MacArthur begins congressional hearings.
22 Apr.	People's Republic of China begins spring offensive, drive through Line Kansas, head toward Seoul. Americans begin system of rotation of troops after specific time in Korea.
24–25 Apr.	British Commonwealth troops supported by United States medium tanks stop communists at Kapyong Valley.
25 Apr.	First Battalion, Gloucestershire Regiment, annihilated.
28 Apr.	Joint Chiefs of Staff authorize bombing bases in Manchuria if CCF planes threaten security of United Nations forces on the ground.
30 Apr.	Republic of China and North Korean People's Army pull back from the attack to regroup.
3 May–25 June	Douglas MacArthur hearing conducted before joint committee of Armed Services and Foreign Relations.
4 May	The Douglas bill authorizes four marine divisions and places the marine commandant as a member of the Joint Chiefs of Staff.
10 May–5 June	Communist Chinese Force begins Second Spring Offensive with "May Massacre."
20 May	Communist Chinese Force offensive stops after reaching 30 miles. Operation Strangle is a massive campaign of air interdiction by FEAF and navy and marine planes.
31 May	State Department representative George F. Kennan meets with Jacob A. Malik, Soviet delegate to the United Nations on possible cease-fire discussions.
6 June	Operation Detonate where United Nations resumes attack, regains Line Kansas and the Wyoming Bulge.
10–16 June	Battle for the Punchbowl.
12 June	USS *Walke* is hit by mine near Hungnam.

13 June	General James Van Fleet ordered from Washington to stop offensive and wait for armistice negotiations. United Nations forms a Main Line of Resistance and character of Korean War changes from mobile to static.
19 June	President Harry Truman signs Universal Military Training and Service Act extending draft to 1 July 1955 and lowers draft age to 18.
23 June	Soviet Union delegate Jacob Malik proposes truce talks in radio broadcast.
30 June	Acting on orders, General Matthew Ridgway broadcasts a United Nations willingness to negotiate.
2 July	Communists agree to cease-fire discussions at Kaesong.
10 July	Truce talks begin at Kaesong.
14 July	Korean Service Corps established by Republic of Korea.
1 Aug.–18 Sept.	Battle of Bloody Ridge.
5 Aug.	Talks suspended by United Nations citing North Korean People's Army in area.
10 Aug.	Talks resume.
22 Aug.	Talks suspended by Communist Chinese Forces because of troop violation.
8 Sept.	Japanese Peace Treaty signed in San Francisco.
13 Sept.	Battle for Heartbreak Ridge begins.
21 Sept.	Operation Summit is first helicopter deployment of a combat unit.
3–23 Oct.	United Nations Offensive to correct a "sag" along I Corps and X Corps lines. Five United Nations divisions involved in savage fighting.
7 Oct.	Negotiating parties agree to move talks to Panmunjom.
15 Oct.	Kojo amphibious landing ploy.
25 Oct.	Peace talks resume at Panmunjom. Winston Churchill replaced Clement Attlee as British prime minister following Labour Party defeat.
12 Nov.	Operation Ratkiller begins to destroy guerrillas in South Korea.
12 Nov.–8 May	Offensive operations come to a halt as Eighth Army begins "active defense."
27 Nov.	Truce talks continue at Panmunjom. Cease-fire line agreed upon.

30 Nov.	Rare air battle between Soviet MiG and United Nations F-86s.
30 Nov.–Apr.	Stalemate on Main Line of Resistance.
5 Dec.	45th Infantry Division replaces First Cavalry at front.
18 Dec.	Exchange of prisoner-of-war lists.

1952

1 Jan.	General Lemuel Shepherd named commandant of U.S. Marine Corps.
2 Jan.	United Nations prisoner-of-war exchange proposal.
3 Jan.	Communist Chinese Forces reject prisoner-of-war exchange proposal.
8 Jan.	Communists reject voluntary repatriations.
10–15 Feb.	Operation Clam Up.
18 Feb.	Koje-do prison camp riots.
	Soviet Union charges United States with germ warfare.
27 Feb.	Democratic People's Republic of Korea charges United States with germ warfare.
13 Mar.	Second riot at Koje-do prison camp.
17 Apr.	Presidential Executive Order extends enlistment for nine months.
21 Apr.	USS *St. Paul* has magazine fire, 30 crew members die.
28 Apr.	Japanese occupation officially ends.
7 May	General Francis T. Dodd captured in Koje-do POW riots.
11 May	General Francis T. Dodd is released.
12 May–12 June	General Haydon Boatner replaces General Charles Colson at Koje-do. Riots end.
	General Mark Clark assumes Far East Command from General Matthew Ridgway.
22 May	Major General William K. Harrison replaces Admiral C. Turner Joy as senior negotiator.
26 May	Syngman Rhee declares martial law in Pusan.
22 June	Lloyd–Alexander mission to Tokyo.
23 June	General Clark orders bombing of NK hydroelectric power plants.
1 July	Operation Homecoming releases civilian internees.
11 July	Bombers raid Pyongyang.
5 Aug.	Rhee elected president again.
6 Aug.	A hanger fire on USS *Boxer* kills eight.

12–25 Aug.	Marines capture Bunker Hill (Hill 122) near Panmunjom and hold it against large communist force.
21 Aug.	Korean Communication Zone established.
30 Aug.	Ocean-going tug *Sarsi* is sunk by mines off Hungnam.
1 Oct.	Cheju-do prisoner-of-war uprising.
6–15 Oct.	Battle of White Horse, Republic of Korea heavy casualties on Communist Chinese Forces.
7 Oct.	The second United States Air Force Superfortress disappears over the Japanese Sea. Soviets suspected.
8 Oct.	Final prisoner-of-war compromise rejected by communists.
9 Oct.	Beginning of Operation Cherokee that lasts until 1 July 1953.
14–25 Oct.	Operation Showdown. Battle of Sniper Ridge. 7th Infantry Division battles Communist Chinese Forces near right end of Iron Triangle.
24 Oct.	Dwight Eisenhower says he will go to Korea if elected.
26 Oct.	Battle of the Hook.
4 Nov.	Dwight D. Eisenhower elected president of the United States.
15 Nov.	Ellis O. Briggs replaces John J. Muccio as United States ambassador to the Republic of Korea.
18 Nov.	United States and Soviet planes clash over Task Force 77 near naval complex at Vladivostok.
2–5 Dec.	President-elect Dwight Eisenhower visits Korea as promised in campaign.
25 Dec.	Hill 812 held after heavy assault by NKPA. Chinese repelled from T-Bone Hill.

1953

20 Jan.	Eisenhower replaces Truman as commander-in-chief. John Foster Dulles replaces Secretary of State Dean Acheson.
22 Jan.	40th Infantry Division replaces 24th Infantry Division on line.
25 Jan.	Operation Smack, assault on Spud Hill by 31st Infantry Regiment.
2 Feb.	Eisenhower's speech "Unleashed" Chiang.

8 Feb.	General Maxwell Taylor replaces James Van Fleet as Eighth Army commander.
15 Feb.	Two Soviet MiGs violate Japanese airspace.
1 Mar.	Planes from Task Force 77 destroy hydroelectric plant.
5 Mar.	Soviet Premier Joseph Stalin dies.
15 Mar.	Georgi Malenkov voices support for cease-fire.
17 Mar.	Communist Chinese Forces assault Little Gibraltar (Hill 355), turned back.
23–24 Mar.	Battles of Old Baldy and Pork Chop complex.
28 Mar.	Kim Il-Sung of the Democratic People's Republic of Korea and Peng The-huai of Communist Chinese Forces agree to prisoner-of-war exchange.
30 Mar.	Peace talks resume at Panmunjom.
11 Apr.	Operation Little Switch approved.
16–18 Apr.	Battle of Pork Chop Hill.
20 Apr.	Exchange of sick and wounded prisoners of war in Operation Little Switch.
26 Apr.	Talks at Panmunjom resume.
13 May	Raid on Toksan Dam by 58th Fighter–Bomber Wing.
22 May	Plans for Operation Everready approved.
	Secretary of State John Foster Dulles warns China that the United States may use atomic weapons if the current United Nations prisoner of war proposal is rejected.
25 May	Syngman Rhee announces his government will not accept any agreement that leaves Korea divided.
4 June	Communists accept major portions of United Nations proposal.
10 June	Outpost Harry, United States troops hold out against assault by Communist Chinese Forces.
11–16 June	Communist Chinese Forces attack drives Republic of Korea positions back.
15 June	USS *Princeton* launches largest number of sorties from a single carrier (184).
18 June	Syngman Rhee releases 27,000 POWs who refuse repatriation. Communist Chinese Forces break off truce talks.
25 June	Communist Chinese Forces launch a major attack against Republic of Korea positions.

30 June	General Hoyt Vandenberg replaced by General Nathan Twining as air force chief of staff.
6–10 July	7th Infantry Division ordered to withdraw from Battle of Pork Chop Hill after five days of fighting.
10 July	Talks resume after United Nations assures Communist Chinese Forces the Republic of Korea will accept cease-fire.
13–20 July	Marines overrun Outposts Berlin–East Berlin.
14 July	United Nations 555th Field Artillery Bn. is overrun. 187th Airborne RCT to Korea.
24–25 July	Communist Chinese Forces launch heavy attack on The Hook, United Nations holds.
25 July	Pilots of Task Force 77 set new record with 600 sorties in 24 hours.
27 July	Cease-fire signed, effective 2200 hours.
28 July	First meeting of the Armistice Commission.
29 July	United States Air Force Superfortress is shot down by Soviet fighters over Sea of Japan.
4 Sept.	Repatriation of prisoners starts at Freedom Village at Panmunjom.
6 Sept.	Operation Big Switch, when last of 3,597 POWs are released.

1954

10 Jan.	United Nations Command in Korea goes on full alert when Democratic People's Republic of Korea threatens to interfere with the release of communist prisoners of war.
26 Jan.	Senate ratifies United States–Republic of Korea Mutual Defense Treaty.
1 Feb.	Neutral Nations Reparations Commission dissolves.
26 Apr.	Opening of the fifth Geneva Conference on the reunification of Korea and other Asian matters.
10 Sept.	United States Navy minesweeping operations in Korean waters are concluded.

1955

2 Feb.	President Dwight Eisenhower states that the Korean conflict started because the United States was not clear about its intention to protect South Korea.

Introduction

The Korean War was a watershed event. In many respects it was the culmination of the emerging war of words between the Eastern Bloc and the West. And yet in some ways it was the beginning of the end of the communist threat. The war resulted in large numbers of killed and wounded and almost led to a far greater conflagration. It was also a serious testing time for the fledgling United Nations. The suffering and destruction in both North and South Korea were particularly acute and took decades to recover from. The war was also a heavy burden on the major communist powers: the People's Republic of China and the Soviet Union. The Democratic People's Republic of Korea was particularly traumatized by the events and the People's Republic of China has only recently given the war either public or policy consideration. And, for reasons that are still difficult to understand, it has been largely ignored by the popular press, limited in consideration by the academic world, and primarily ignored by the American people.

Korea—The Place

Korea is the approximate shape of the American state of Florida and slightly larger in territory than the state of Kansas. Unified Korea occupies 85,246 square miles of land. In some ways it can be better understood as an island, for it has 5,400 miles of coast line and is primarily influenced by the sea. Several significant ports lie on the shallow Yellow Sea—Inchon, Chinnampo—and on the much deeper and more violent Japanese Sea—Rashin, Hungnam, Wonsan, and Pohang. Perhaps the most significant port, Pusan, is located on the Strait of Korea. The nation is divided east and west by mountains and the watershed lies close to the east coast. What are identified as plains are limited to about 15 percent of the area and heavy forests cover large areas concentrated in the southeast and northwest. Most of the agriculture is found along the west coast and, after the division, in the Republic of Korea. What industrialization there was in Korea before the war was located in the north, in the Democratic People's Republic of Korea. The weather is difficult, ranging from the extremes of 110 in the summer to 40 F degrees below zero in the winter. Harsh winds coming down from Siberia bring heavy snow.

Geographically Korea is at the crossroads of Asia, 120 miles from the Japanese islands, 75 miles south of the Russia port city of Vladivostok. It shares an 850-mile border with the People's Republic of China and 75 miles of border with the former Soviet Union. Transportation, especially in the 1950s, was difficult. The roads that existed at the time tended to move north and south and were concentrated around the cities of Pusan and Seoul. Movement across Korea, even though it averaged little more than 200 miles in some places, was hampered by ancient mountains that rose sharply from the eastern coast. Rail transportation centered around the few major cities and was limited and undependable. On the east coast the mountains often came so close to the sea that tunneling was necessary for any kind of transportation system.

The population of Korea at the outbreak of war was about 30 million, with the smaller share, about 9 million, living in the north. Population was sporadic and tended to be located in pockets near the plains and along the coast lines. The heaviest population centers were in the southern portions of the Republic of Korea.

Korea—The History

Korea's beginnings as a nation are lost in a legend in which a creator god, called Tangun, mated with a maiden who had been transformed from a bear. What appears to be fact is that people from Manchuria and Mongolia moved onto the peninsula somewhere around the third millennium BCE. The first recorded history lists the Chinese Han Dynasty as establishing colonies in northern Korea in the second century BCE. From the second century BCE to 600 CE Korea was divided into three kingdoms. The northernmost, including parts of Manchuria, was called Koguryo. The second, Paekche, was along the Han River basin and Sillia lay in the southeastern corner of present-day Republic of Korea. The country was unified under the Chinese T'ang Dynasty in 668. Korea was in *suzerain* status to the Chinese Empire, a tributary but autonomous, which continued until the 20th century. This unified Korea lasted nearly 1,300 years until in 1945 the nation was once again divided

The Koryo Dynasty, from which Korea gets its name, was formed in 935. Under the Koryos the nation both grew and suffered from foreign invasion. Finally in 1392 General Yi Song-gye overthrew the pro-Mongol king and seized the government. The Yi Dynasty brought Confucianism to Korea, fought the Japanese on several occasions, and finally fell to the

Manchu Dynasty in 1644. Known as the Hermit Kingdom, Korea resisted contact with foreigners.

American attempts to open trade led them to Korea in 1866 when the crew of the *General Sherman* was massacred near present-day Inchon. In response the USS *Wachusett* and a task force went aground on 10 June 1871 and took Seoul. It was some time later, in May of 1882, that an agreement of mutual friendship and trade treaty, the Treaty of Chemulpo, was signed between Korea and the United States. But the United States did not offer much help and a Korean appeal to the Chinese for aid led the Japanese to send a sizable force that eventually led to the Sino–Japanese War of 1894–1895 and a quick victory for Japan.

Russia became interested in Korean minerals and timber and in 1903 unsuccessfully tried to divide Korea along the 38th Parallel, recognizing Japanese occupation south of the line and assuming control north. The rivalry led to the Russo–Japanese War of 1904 and the Russian defeat gave Japan prominence and control. The Korean independence movement petitioned President Theodore Roosevelt to interfere in the negotiations and provide for Korean independence. This was not done and President Roosevelt lent his help to the Treaty of Portsmouth (New Hampshire) that opened the way for the Japanese annexation of Korea as a colony in 1910.

The question of independence suffered a deadly blow with the Japanese annexation of Korea. The Japanese rule was harsh and led to several attempts at revolt. Many Korean nationalists were forced into exile. In April 1919 a Korean Provisional Government was established in Shanghai. Syngman Rhee, already in exile in the United States, was named its president.

Hoping to take advantage of the Allied victory following World War I, Rhee—then a student and a favorite of Woodrow Wilson when they were at Princeton at the same time—used the Treaty of Chemulpo in 1882 to petition President Wilson. He claimed the United States had a moral obligation to seek Korean independence. The petition was ignored.

The whole question of Korean independence was an agenda full of many expectations and ambitions. Following the Japanese attack on the United States, the provisional government under Syngman Rhee petitioned Washington to recognize it as the legal government in return for aid in the war. The State Department position was that it was not the role of the United States to impose on the people of Korea a government they had not requested. A government, in fact, that had been out of Korea since 1911. But there were other reasons not the least of which was an awareness of Soviet interest in Korea. The United States realized it might need the Soviets to enter the war against Japan. Generalissimo Chiang Kai-shek, the leader of the Republic of China, was also concerned, petitioning Washington and London to join him in support of Korean independence.

The Cairo Conference in December 1943 issued a statement supporting Korean independence in "due time." But there was a feeling in the State Department that the Korean people were not yet ready to govern themselves. This was reaffirmed at the Potsdam Conference and agreed to by the Soviet Union. Part of the agreement used the 38th Parallel as a line for occupation, granting Russia the area to the north and the United States the area to the south.

The occupation of Korea occurred shortly after the end of World War II. Soviet troops invaded Korea on 11 and 12 August and by 14 August were along the 38th Parallel. At the time General John Hodge was still in a state of preparation and it was not until 9 September that the 6th, 7th, and 40th Infantry Divisions arrived to receive the Japanese surrender. While the United States appeared to see the occupation as temporary the Soviet Union began the fortification of the 38th Parallel almost immediately.

The Joint Chiefs of Staff, in September 1947, decided that Korea was not worth protecting and urged the withdrawal of the two divisions still stationed there. The State Department agreed, and it was planned. The best solution seemed to rest with the United Nations (UN) and on 17 September of that year the question was placed on the UN agenda. A Temporary Commission on Korea was established and despite lack of cooperation from the Soviets an election was held in May of 1948. The Republic of Korea (South) elected Syngman Rhee. On 15 August 1948 the United States withdrew most of its troops and in June 1949 the 5th Regimental Combat Team was withdrawn, leaving only the 500-man Korean Military Advisory Group.

The Belligerents

Affairs in Korea, even before the war, reflected an intense and violent struggle between north and south. The conflict was in part the result of growing ideological differences and, in part, the vacuum created by the collapse of Japan's colonial empire and the eventual intervention of long-term rivals China and Russia and a new player, the United States. The struggle was intensified, unfortunately, by the fact that once again Korea was used as a pawn between warring giants as it had been for thousands of years. The Chinese, Japanese, and Russians had all invaded the Hermit Kingdom with national interests in mind. As World War II came to an end the Soviet Union saw the control of Korea as significant to their global ambitions. This time Korea was caught in the middle of the Cold War alliances of east and west. What many saw as a civil war had every possibility of becoming World War III.

On the one side of the national conflict was the Democratic People's Republic of Korea under the leadership of the communist-trained Kim Il-Sung. The North had a long historical association with the Soviet Union and many of its military leaders were combat trained in the Soviet Army. On 9 September 1948 the new government took up business at Pyongyang. The Soviet ambassador was the first to be recognized.

On the other side of the unification question was the newly formed Republic of Korea under the leadership of the nationalist Syngman Rhee. The conflict cast a wider shadow and while the extent of the Soviet Union's involvement is not as yet fully understood there is no doubt that Joseph Stalin was involved in the planning and execution of the war Kim Il-Sung began. Historically the Soviet Union saw Korea as a buffer zone and the source of friendly ports. When the Soviet Union recognized Kim Il-Sung as the leader of North Korea on 3 October 1945 the stage was set for the development of a communist government. Russian-trained communists took key positions in the Interim People's Committee. After failing to take part in the United Nations–sponsored elections, the Democratic People's Republic was formed on 8 September 1948 and by Christmas of the same year Soviet occupation troops were withdrawn.

American occupation troops had arrived shortly after the end of the war. Uninterested in a prolonged commitment they urged the United Nations to act and supported the decision to conduct elections. After the formation of the Republic of Korea and the election of Syngman Rhee as president, the United States withdrew its occupation forces.

When the North Koreans attacked, the United States reacted and within a few days air, sea, and ground forces were involved. Once the United Nations resolution passed, calling on its members to come to the aid of the Republic of Korea, several nations lent their support to the cause. The result of the UN resolution was that every North Atlantic Treaty Organization (NATO) nation, with the exception of Iceland, contributed aid to the UN Command. During the course of the war more than 10,000 NATO nation soldiers were wounded and 3,000 killed. Despite this contribution the United States sent more troops to the NATO assignment than it did to Korea.

The final nation involved was the People's Republic of China though the involvement was never official. Those who fought in Korea did so under the banner of the Chinese People's Volunteers Army.

The Beginning of the War

The war began early on Sunday morning 25 June 1950 as elements of the North Korean People's Army (NKPA) crossed the 38th Parallel supported by Russian T-34 tanks. It was unexpected both in terms of timing and intensity. The troops of the Republic of Korea (South) were not yet well enough trained or equipped to meet the challenge and they retreated. The NKPA moved quickly, took the Korean capital at Seoul, then crossed the Han River and west on to the Kum River, then south to Taejon and Taegu.

President Harry Truman approved the evacuation of dependents and authorized the use of air support for the protection of evacuees. He ordered the 7th Fleet into the Taiwan Strait. Within two days the United Nations adopted a resolution, proposed by the United States, calling on the troops of the Democratic People's Republic of Korea to withdraw. The North Korean People's Army moved farther south and President Truman authorized General Douglas MacArthur to send ground troops. By 4 July 1950 Task Force Smith was in Osau and in battle. Despite the presence of the Americans, the North Koreans continued to move south.

Lieutenant General Walton H. Walker, who commanded Eighth United States Army, was assigned to Korea. The 24th Infantry Division, commanded by General William Dean, was the first into action and took much of the brunt. They delayed the NKPA at the Kum River. The Fifth Air Force was relocated to Korea and was able to further delay, though it could not stop, the advancing communist force.

By the end of July 1950 the United Nations took a stand along the Naktong Perimeter as it consolidated its forces: the American First Cavalry Division, the Second Infantry Division, 24th Infantry Division, 25th Infantry Division, the First Marine Brigade, and five Republic of Korea infantry divisions.

Phase One—The United Nations Involvement

Almost immediately following the appeal to the United Nations, member nations began to send troops and supplies. The British were the first to respond with military forces, placing its ships, which had been in Japanese waters, under command of the United Nations.

Harry S. Truman had a strong opinion about the failure at Munich believing that if the League of Nations had acted against Germany it might have required a small war at the time, but it would have avoided the tragedy of World War II. In the argument provided, North Korea replaced Germany and the Communist Party the Nazi movement, and the United Nations was the only means of stopping communist expansion.

South Korea became the "far away nation" that required the actions of concerned nations if it, and eventually the world, was to be spared. The aggression in Korea was also an important testing ground of American and United Nations resolve to stop communist expansion. What is more, the aggression seemed to be a test for the newly implemented National Security Council document #68, September 1950, that decreed the United States would come to the aid of any nation that fought communism.

Phase Two—Inchon and the Yalu

On 15 September 1950, after expanding his forces and establishing a route of supply, General MacArthur put into operation a plan he had considered right from the beginning. Operation Chromite was an amphibious landing at the west coast port of Inchon. It was a risky and serious endeavor but bore the marks of those events that had made the general famous during World War II. In preparation he formed X Corps and placed it under the command of General Edward (Ned) Almond. His force consisted of the Seventh Infantry Division (army) and the First Marine Division. Moving around the southern tip of Korea, X Corps landed on the morning of 15 September 1950 and within a few days had taken Inchon and Kimpo Airfield. By October Seoul had been taken and returned to President Syngman Rhee.

In the meantime Eighth Army had broken out of the perimeter and moved north at a rapid pace. Cut off from supplies and communication the NKPA retreated, or faded into the population, and by early October the United Nations forces were together again at the 38th Parallel. In many respects the war might have ended at this point. But the opportunity seemed ripe to take all of Korea and restore it as a unified nation. Authorized by the Joint Chiefs of Staff, and quickly by the United Nations, both UN and Republic of Korea troops crossed over the 38th Parallel and moved north. Eighth Army headed up the west side of the mountains and X Corps, having been moved by sea to the port of Wonsan, moved up the east side. Conditions were such that communication was difficult between the two forces. By Thanksgiving elements of the 17th Infantry Regiment (army) reached the Yalu River.

Phase Three—The Chinese Enter

The People's Republic of China had warned that if UN troops crossed the 38th Parallel it would enter the war. But MacArthur assured Truman that this would not happen. By mid-October 1950 there had been clashes with Chinese troops and some prisoners taken. Then, on 23 November nearly 200,000 Chinese attacked. They had crossed the frozen Yalu and gathered strength during November. The UN Command was hit hard. Walker began to withdraw, evacuating troops by sea whenever possible.

In the east X Corps was swamped. Fighting a desperate retreat, army and marine personnel pulled out under the pressure of heavy Chinese attacks and weather that had dropped to nearly 40 degrees below zero. As the army and marines retreated to the port of Hungnam the navy began an evacuation which, by Christmas eve, had removed nearly 100,000 UN and Republic of Korea troops and almost that many refugees. By Christmas the port had been destroyed and the majority of the UN forces headed for Pusan and other ports along the coast. Seoul was abandoned once again on 3 January 1951.

Phase Four—Hill War and the Long Debate

General Walton Walker died in a jeep accident toward the end of December 1950. His replacement, General Matthew B. Ridgway, arrived on Christmas day and began the process of rebuilding Eighth Army and restoring its morale. Seoul was recaptured and on 27 March 1951 Eighth Army had reached the 38th Parallel. In Operation Rugged, Ridgway's men established Line Wyoming and Line Kansas that would be the primary Main Line of Resistance (MLR) for the rest of the war.

The first few months of the war resembled World War II with armies massed in mobile conflicts. The second part of the war was fought under conditions that more reflected the fighting of World War I. That is, it was fought by greatly reduced forces in battles limited to specific locations. Early in 1952 most of the territorial rights had been decided and in early November 1952 the United Nations Command adopted a defensive policy. The new war was fought in accordance with the UN goals of limited expectation. The battles were limited to hills and the size of the units involved were often no more than companies. Success or failure at the conference table was reflected in the success or failure in the field. Peace negotiation continued as hill after hill was added to the list of fiercely contested areas: Bloody Ridge, Heartbreak Ridge, Old Baldy, and Pork Chop. At the negotiations table little separated the major powers other than the question of prisoner repatriation.

Phase Five—Armistice and Cease-Fire

Shortly after the death of Joseph Stalin on 5 March 1953, the communists returned to the negotiation table and agreed to the screening of prisoners, by a neutral nation, to determine to which country they wished to be returned. The changing international environment was reflected in the numerous peace proposals offered. But it was agreement on prisoner-of-war (POW) exchange that made the Armistice possible. What produced the final agreement is a little hard to define. Certainly it would include the death of Joseph Stalin and the Soviet's domestic concerns, President Dwight D. Eisenhower's hint at the use of atomic weapons, and the finally achieved control over the still aggressive Syngman Rhee. The Armistice was signed by General William K. Harrison and eventually General Mark Clark for the United Nations, Marshal Peng The-huai for the Republic of China, and Marshall Kim Il-Sung and General Nam Il for North Korea. The Republic of Korea did not sign the agreement. Twenty-three Allied soldiers preferred to remain in communist hands. The larger numbers of (North) Koreans and the much smaller numbers of (South) Koreans who refused to be repatriated created future friction between the two Koreas.

Costs of the War

The Korean War was very expensive in terms of human life. It is difficult to provide casualty figures because the word is used in so many different ways. The most accurate figures for American casualties are 33,629 killed in action; 20,617 killed in war-related but non-battle deaths; and 103,284 wounded who required hospitalization. This figure would be more, if counting the slightly wounded. The figures for the Republic of Korea are 59,000 killed and 291,000 wounded plus enough civilian casualties to bring this figure to nearly three million. The UN figures are lumped into nations largely involved and nations with a small contingent. The British Commonwealth Forces—which include Australia, United Kingdom, Canada, and New Zealand—suffered 1,263 killed and 4,817 wounded. Belgium, Colombia, Ethiopia, France, Greece, the Netherlands, Philippines, South Africa, Thailand, and Turkey lost 1,800 killed with 7,000 wounded.

The casualties suffered by the Democratic People's Republic of Korea and the People's Republic of China are even harder to determine because these figures are closely guarded by the nations involved. The best estimates place the number at about 500,000 killed in action and another million wounded.

Korea itself was also a major casualty and some areas, fought over four or five times during the course of the war, were virtually destroyed. Some villages were wiped out and Seoul, the nation's capital, primarily flattened. Railways, communication, the whole infrastructure of the nation, hydroelectric plants, factories, civic buildings, even farms and rice paddies were destroyed.

Consequences of the War

The war in Korea solidified the Cold War positions for a good portion of the world, probably even more than the loss of China to the communists, the Soviet's expanding role in Eastern Europe, the Berlin Airlift, or the Soviet Union's entrance to the atomic age. It was an important period in American and world history. There were lessons to be learned both in its victories and in its failures.

British Prime Minister Winston Churchill felt that the rearming of the United States was the most significant outcome of the Korean War. Certainly the beginnings of the arms race can be traced to the rather sudden awareness that the Soviet Union posed a definite threat to national security. There were significant operational lessons as well, and military preparation, logistics, mobilization, and a code of conduct for prisoners of war all underwent considerable refinement as a result of the events experienced in Korea. Yet, the Eisenhower administration, which took credit for getting out of Korea, downplayed the importance of ground troops and placed more and more of its defense expectations in the air force and nuclear deterrence.

Interestingly many people considered the political condition that brought about the war a series of aberrations from which little was to be learned in terms of policy and procedure. At the time the danger imposed by communist expansion supported Senator Joseph McCarthy's charges of communists in government. The subversive nature of communist activities was the only excuse that many could find for America's losses in Korea.

While not the first war that America lost, the lack of a distinct victory had its effects in shaping the second half of the 20th century. The United Nations action in Korea did contain the expansion of communism and the fact that a stand was taken most probably slowed the aggressive tendencies of the Soviet Union. The war was highly significant in the reconstruction of Japan, both in terms of an accelerated peace treaty, and because of the economic opportunities the war presented.

The Americans who fought in Korea were to suffer considerable criticism where even the courage and commitment of the soldier was questioned. Concerns based in stories of brainwashing, bug-outs, desertions, and traitors were rampant and greatly exaggerated. The moral fiber of the generation was questioned and "soft Americans" were compared to the fine fighting men of World War II. Some of this can be understood when it is realized how minor was the impact of the Korean War on the homefront. Unlike World War II, the draft imposed on very few, and there was no need for rationing or shortages. The nation continued to experience an economic boom

General MacArthur was right, of course, for there is no substitute for victory. The lack of victory either on 27 July 1953 or in the half-century since then has never set well with the American people.

Korea Today

Today the Demilitarized Zone remains, heavily guarded, to separate the two areas. The unification the Koreans fought so hard to achieve has not been accomplished. The tragedy is, of course, that the war gave birth to two different kinds of exclusive politics, both of which base fear of the other as the key to their political authority. Yet, the Korean language remains primarily pure, there are few ethnic or religious minorities that have been disturbed, and the culture remains unique to the nation. Families divided by the parallel remain divided. So, while considerable time has passed since the cease-fire was accepted, most of the bitterness and hostility remain.

The Democratic People's Republic of Korea (North) has not kept up economically with the Republic of Korea. It is hindered by the harshness of the government and by the cult of personality. It is one of the few (with Cuba) that still maintains the prominence of the communist economic system. Today, as this is being written, North Korea still suffers from shortages and poverty.

The Republic of Korea has grown economically due in part to aid from the United Nations, United States, and Japan. American forces in large number remain in Korea to assure compliance with the cease-fire agreement. The Republic of Korea government has gone through several changes, and in the latter part of the 1980s, fierce demonstrations brought changes that have made the government more accountable. Although recently efforts have been made at reconciliation and closer relations between the two Koreas, the results are still uncertain.

The Republic of Korea has maintained the memories of the war in terms of monuments and celebrations. In 2001, the government of the Republic of Korea provided medals of commemoration to American veterans who fought in the war, and delivered them in a series of celebrations held in a wide variety of American cities. The Democratic People's Republic of Korea has been less vocal in its commemoration, but has erected memorials to several events and battles. The presence of the Demilitarized Zone keeps the war in the thinking of the people of these two nations, and tension along the line grows and diminishes in a rhythm of political expectations. The People's Republic of China has allowed discussion of the Korean War to reappear in the recent decade, as its leaders increasingly point to it for lessons to be learned and victories to be enjoyed.

THE DICTIONARY

–A–

A-FRAME. A traditional load-carrying device peculiar to Korea. Using these wooden backpacks, designed like the letter A with straw shoulder straps, Koreans could carry large loads for long distances over difficult terrain.

ACE. The unofficial title given for destroying five enemy aircraft. There were 40 aces identified during the Korean War. The **United States Navy** and the **United States Marines** each had one ace and the **United States Air Force** 38. On 20 May 1951 Captain James Jabara (Air Force) became the first jet ace in history. Captain Joseph C. McConnell was the leading jet ace with 16 **MiGs** destroyed. Information about pilots from the **People's Republic of China**, the **Democratic People's Republic of Korea**, and the **Soviet Union** is limited but some sources identify Soviet pilot Ivan N. Kozhedub and Chinese airmen Li Han, Chang Chi-wei, and Wang Hai as aces.

ACHESON, DEAN G. (1893–1971). Born in Middletown, Connecticut, Acheson took a degree in law, served in a variety of jobs with the **State Department**, and succeeded **Secretary of State George C. Marshall** in 1947. He was instrumental in the design of the **Truman Doctrine** as well as the **Marshall Plan** and in the formation of the **North Atlantic Treaty Organization (NATO)**. As secretary of state he defined the expectations of the Korean War. He was influenced by a strong suspicion of the **United Nations** and was directed by belief in a Europe-first policy. He felt that America's first response to events in Korea should be to regain the political status quo, but later affirmed the need to liberate all of Korea. He was replaced, in January 1953, by **John Foster Dulles**. Acheson later served as an advisor to Presidents John F. Kennedy and Lyndon B. Johnson. He died on 12 October 1971. Some historians suggest he encouraged the communist attack when, in his January 1950 address to the National Press Club, he excluded Korea from America's defense perimeter. But he was only stating what the **Joint Chiefs of Staff** had already determined.

    Acheson–Morrison Meeting (11 September 1951). This meeting between **Secretary of State Dean G. Acheson** and **Herbert Morrison**, the British Foreign Secretary, resulted from the failure of the **cease-fire** talks on 23 August 1951. **Great Britain** was against any action that would expand into a war with the **People's Republic of China**. Morrison routinely protested any action that he felt would drive the communist government in China further into the **Soviet** camp. Morrison also voiced Great Britain's objection to the suggested use of **Japanese** troops in Korea.

Acheson's National Press Club Speech. On 12 January 1950, **Secretary of State Dean Acheson** responded to his critics by addressing the National Press Club. He was under considerable fire from Congress both because of the communist takeover of China and because of the **Korean Aid Bill of 1949–1950**. He was interested in showing that the **Republic of Korea** had an excellent chance to resist communism if the **United States** provided aid. But, he also acknowledged that Korea lay outside the United States perimeter of defense. His statements, which were a significant articulation of America's Asian policy, were most likely not a cause for the invasion by the **North Korean People's Army**.

ACTIVE DEFENSE STRATEGY (12 November 1951). CINCUNC General **Matthew B. Ridgway** instructed **Eighth United States Army** Commander General **James Van Fleet** to limit the size and aggressiveness of his command's activities. Van Fleet was to inflict maximum casualties while limiting his operations to small unit attacks and defense. The effort was to maintain a reasonable battle line (**Main Line of Resistance**) that had been identified by negotiations. This policy was to become the *de facto* military position and, while the nations involved used military action to pursue their negotiations, the lines in Korea became more static.

AD SKYRAIDER. A single-engine propeller attack plane developed for the **United States Navy** in 1945 that saw service during the Korean War. It was capable of carrying a large bomb load, could reach a speed of 365 miles per hour, and had a range of 1,500 miles. It was armed with two 20mm cannons and adapted to carry rockets.

ADVANCE COMMAND AND LIAISON GROUP IN KOREA. Following the invasion by the Democratic People's Republic of Korea, President **Harry Truman** authorized a survey team to go to Korea to determine what needed to be done. General **Douglas MacArthur** established a group headed by Brigadier General **John H. Church** that departed for Korea on 27 June 1950. As this was being organized MacArthur received word he had been given control of military activities in Korea. He then changed the name of the survey group to the **Advance Command and Liaison Group in Korea (ADCOM)** and expanded its mission to include control of the **Korean Military Advisory Group (KMAG)**. On 28 June 1950 General John Church reported that it would be necessary to commit at least two combat teams of American troops. MacArthur made a quick trip to Korea on 29 June but took no action toward requesting troops. Church reaffirmed the immediate need on 30 June, after which MacArthur asked for authority to commit United States forces. General Church remained in Korea during the first few days. On 3 July the **United States Forces in Korea (USFIK)** was activated under General **William Dean**. On 13 June the Church group returned to Tokyo.

ADVISORS, MILITARY. *See* KOREAN MILITARY ADVISORY GROUP.

AERIAL COMBAT. Perhaps the most celebrated aspect of the Korean War was the aerial combat, some of which occurred for the first time between jets. Most aerial combat occurred over the **Democratic People's Republic of Korea** between Soviet-built **MiG-15** Fagot jets and **United States Air Force F-86 Saberjets**. United Nations pilots were instructed not to cross into **Manchuria** thus providing the enemy a place of sanctuary. Soviet/Chinese pilots were instructed not to fly over South Korea or the coastal waters thus providing some sanctuary for United Nations pilots. The two planes involved in the majority of air action were reasonably matched. The MiG had a better climb rate but the F-86 had some speed advantage. Other planes were involved, of course; in fact a British **Royal Navy** pilot shot down a MiG-15 from a propeller-driven **Seafury**.

AGENDA CONTROVERSIES. On 26 July 1951, at the 10th meeting of the **cease-fire** negotiations group, the **United Nations** and communist representatives finally agreed on an agenda of five items. The items were the adoption of an agenda, determination of a **demarcation line**, a cease-fire arrangement including supervisory support for the carrying out of the agreement, relations concerning **prisoners of war**, and recommendations to the governments. These items were a compromise between the United Nations' nine-point proposal that the communists rejected and the communists' proposal that the United Nations did not accept.

AGENDA ITEM I. The process of adopting an agenda was the result of a great deal of compromise. An agenda was finally accepted on 26 July 1951.

AGENDA ITEM II. *Demarcation Line and Demilitarized Zone.* In November 1951 a **United Nations** proposal recommended a line based on the existing combat line. The United Nations suggested a one-month time period for acceptance. While both parties agreed on the battle line with a **Demilitarized Zone (DMZ)** of four kilometers, the agreement was not reached within the established deadline. However, since neither side pushed the issue, the provisional line and DMZ became the *de facto* line. Other than a few adjustments made during the last weeks of fighting, the line was the same at the end of the war.

AGENDA ITEM III. *Cease-Fire Arrangements and Inspection Provisions.* The **United Nations** proposed a plan that would prevent military buildup following the **cease-fire**. The plan called for the creation of a **Military Armistice Commission (MAC)** as a supervisory body that was free to travel through all of Korea. This item was not acceptable to either the **People's Republic of China** or the **Democratic People's Republic of Korea**. On 3 December the **Communist Chinese Forces (CCF)** presented a proposal that called for no troop replacement. During February 1952 considerable negotiations occurred that led to an acceptable proposal. The last major drawback on this item was the People's Republic of China insistence that the **Soviet Union** be a part of the inspection team. The communists later dropped this demand in return for United Nations withdrawal of its plan to impose limitations on airfield rehabilitation. *See also* AIRFIELD REHABILITATION CONTROVERSY.

AGENDA ITEM IV. *Repatriation of Prisoners of War.* Prisoner exchange was the critical item on the agenda. The disagreement was simple: the **United Nations** wanted **voluntary repatriation**, and the communists wanted **required repatriation**. By May 1952, despite several efforts to work out prisoner exchange, the issue was deadlocked. Several plans were put forth and finally the United Nations agreed to the **V. K. Krishna Menon prisoner-of-war settlement proposal** that called for a **neutral nations repatriation commission**. The proposal was rejected by the **People's Republic of China** and the **Democratic People's Republic of Korea** on 3 December 1952. In February 1953 General **Mark W. Clark** proposed an exchange of sick and wounded prisoners. The communists agreed and in April **Operation Little Switch** was underway. Several proposals and counter proposals dragged on until both sides agreed to a plan that called for prisoner screening by the **Neutral Nations Repatriation Commission**. The commission would provide 120 days of custody. Those prisoners who refused repatriation would become civilians. A six-month limit was imposed on the amount of time a prisoner could be held.

AGENDA ITEM V. *Referral of Political Questions.* The **People's Republic of China** wanted a provision that called for the withdrawal of all foreign troops (clarified to mean non-Korean) from Korea. The **United Nations** did not agree, thinking this was not a proper item for discussion in a **cease-fire**. Both sides agreed to establish an agenda item that would consider recommendations to the countries involved. Following a breakdown in the talks, the communists proposed a plan that was adopted fairly quickly. It called for a postwar political conference within three months of the nations involved to negotiate the question of troop withdrawal.

AID MEN. *See* COMBAT MEDICAL PERSONNEL.

AIRBORNE SUPPLY OPERATIONS. Because of the fluid nature of the war, resupply by air became very important. The 315th Air Division, **Combat Cargo Command** provided the planes, and preparation and drops were made by the 234th Army Quartermaster Airborne Supply and Packaging Company (later identified as the 8081st Army Unit). Despite the large amount of logistical support provided by Combat Cargo Command, they suffered less than a 3 percent loss of supplies.

AIRBORNE TROOP OPERATIONS. There were only two airborne operations during the Korean War. The **187th Airborne Regimental Combat Team** made two drops, one at **Sukchon** on 20 October 1950 and one at **Munsan-ni** on 23 March 1951. During most of the period, members of the airborne teams fought as infantry. On several occasions individuals were dropped behind the enemy lines.

AIRCRAFT. *See* AIR FORCE, DEMOCRATIC PEOPLE'S REPUBLIC OF KOREA; AIR FORCE, PEOPLE'S REPUBLIC OF CHINA; AIR FORCE, REPUBLIC OF KOREA; AIR FORCE, UNITED NATIONS. *See also* individual aircraft by name or number.

AIRCRAFT CARRIER. Following World War II a number of aircraft carriers were put into mothballs, and when war broke out in 1950 the **United States Navy** had seven attack carriers (CVA), four light carriers (CVE) and four escort carriers (CVE). At the end of the war 34 carriers were in service. Serving in tours they were assigned primarily to **Task Force 77**, the Seventh Fleet Striking Force, or **Task Force 95**, the Blockading and Escort Force. During the war 275,912 navy and marine sorties were flown. *See also* AIRCRAFT CARRIERS, COMMONWEALTH; AIRCRAFT CARRIERS, UNITED STATES.

AIRCRAFT CARRIERS, COMMONWEALTH. **Great Britain** and the Commonwealth nations provided aircraft carriers that served alongside **United States** ships during the Korean War. These include the **Australian HMAS** *Sydney*, **Great Britain**'s **HMS** *Glory*, **HMS** *Ocean*, **HMS** *Theseus*, and **HMS** *Triumph*.

AIRCRAFT CARRIERS, UNITED STATES. Eleven American fleet **aircraft carriers (CVA)** served in Korea, many on more than one occasion. They included the **USS** *Antietam* (CVA 36), **USS** *Boxer* (CVA 21), **USS** *Bon Homme Richard* (CVA31), **USS** *Essex* (CVA 9), **USS** *Kearsarge* (CVA 33), **USS** *Lake Champlain* (CVA 39), **USS** *Leyte Gulf* (CVA 2), **USS** *Oriskany* (CVA 34), **USS** *Philippine Sea* (CVA 47), **USS** *Princeton* (CVA 37), and **USS** *Valley Forge* (CVA 45). Each carrier embarked 24 **Carrier Air Groups** with a total of 100 squadrons composed of variations of 38 **F4U Corsairs** squadrons, 35 **F9F Panther** squadrons, 23 **AD Skyraider** squadrons, and 4 **F2H Banshee** squadrons. There were also several **CVL (Light)** and **CVE (Escort)** carriers that served primarily on the west coast. They include USS *Bairoko* (CE 115), **USS** *Badoeng Strait* (CVE 116), **USS** *Bataan* (CVL 29), USS *Rendova* (CVE 114), and **USS** *Sicily* (CVE 118).

AIRCRAFT DESIGNATION, PEOPLE'S REPUBLIC OF CHINA. *See* AIRCRAFT DESIGNATION, SOVIET UNION.

AIRCRAFT DESIGNATION, SOVIET UNION. All **Soviet** aircraft from the Korean War period were designated by a designer's name and a model number. Therefore the **MiG** indicated planes produced by Artem Mikoyan and Mikhail Gurevich. The **Yak** was the designation for fighter planes designed by Aleksandir Sergeivich Yakovlev.

AIRCRAFT DESIGNATION, UNITED STATES AIR FORCE. After 1946 aircraft were designated by a functional category followed by a number consecutively applied in each category. A suffix was used to identify changes in model or design. The air force designations used during the Korean War were B-**bomber**, C-cargo and transport, F-fighter, L-liaison, and R-**reconnaissance**.

AIRCRAFT DESIGNATION, UNITED STATES NAVY. After 1946, naval aircraft were designated by a first letter functional category, a second letter manufacturer code, with intervening numbers used to indicate design and model changes. The following were the functional categories during the Korean War: A-attack, F-fighter, H-**helicopter**, U-utility, P-patrol, PB-patrol bomber, and R-transport. The manufacturer designations were D-Douglas, F-Grumman, H-McDonnell, M-Martin, O-Lockheed (former), S-Sikorsky, U-Chance Vought, V-Lockheed (current) and Y-Consolidated. Thus AD would be the first attack plane produced by Douglas after 1946. The **F9F** is the ninth Grumman fighter.

AIRCRAFT LOSSES, UNITED NATIONS. During the war the **United Nations** (including the United States and the **Republic of Korea)** lost 147 aircraft (78 were **F-86** Sabre jets) in air combat primarily to **MiG-15s**. The air losses for the **People's Republic of China** and the **Democratic People's Republic of Korea** were 950 aircraft (792 MiG-15s) in aerial combat with Allied aircraft.

AIRFIELD REHABILITATION CONTROVERSY. The **United Nations** was concerned about the **People's Republic of China** and the **Democratic People's Republic of Korea** rebuilding or revitalizing their airfields after the **cease-fire** was signed. This discussion was considered under **Agenda Item III**. The United Nations finally gave way on this point in return for the communists dropping their demand that the **Soviet Union** serve on the **Neutral Nation Inspection Team**. *See also* AGENDA ITEM III.

AIRFIELDS, COMMUNIST. The majority of the **Communist Chinese Air Force (CCAF)** planes were based in Manchuria, primarily in the area known as Antung. The distance involved, and the relative short range of **MiG-15s** limited their activities to the northwestern portions of Korea in an area identified as **MiG Alley**. The CCAF provided very little close ground support or aerial interdiction.

AIRFIELDS, JAPAN. United Nations air activity operated from airfields in Japan and Korea. Those in Japan were located at Hokkaido, Misawa, Matsushima, Yokota, Tachikawa, Komaki, Itami, Miho, Bofu, Iwakuni, Ashiya, Itazuki, Tsuiku, and Brady. Two bases on Okinawa, Kadena and Naha, were also used.

AIRFIELDS, KOREA. During the war, the air force constructed or improved 55 bases that were identified by numbers. These were identified by a number. The more important of the fields were K-1 Pusan West, K-2 Taegu, K-3 Pohang, K-5 Taejon, K-6 Pyongtaek, K-8 Kumsan, K-10 Chinhae, K-13 Suwan, K-14 **Kimpo**, K-15 Seoul, K-18 Kangnung, K-24 Pyongyang, K-37 Taegu West, K-40 Cheju-do Island, K-46 Hoengsong, K-47 **Chunchon**, and K-55 Osan.

AIR FORCE, DEMOCRATIC PEOPLE'S REPUBLIC OF KOREA (NORTH KOREAN AIR FORCE, NKAF). At the beginning of the war the **NKAF** consisted of 180 Soviet-built propeller-driven aircraft. They were commanded by Major General Wang Yong, a Soviet-trained and experienced combat pilot. The NKAF was active during the early months of the war attacking several airfields, strafing ground troops at **Chongju**, and attacking formations of B-26 bombers inflicting damage. Attacks on Democratic People's Republic of Korea airfields nearly destroyed the NKAF. Later in the war primary air resistance came from the **People's Republic of China**.

AIR FORCE, PEOPLE'S REPUBLIC OF CHINA (CHINESE COMMUNIST AIR FORCE, CCAF). The **Chinese Communist Air Force (CCAF)** entered the war on 1 November 1950. At that time they possessed 650 planes but the number quickly increased to 1,050 planes. A year later it reached its peak with 22 air divisions consisting of 1,830 planes, 1,000 of them jets. As well as increasing in size the CCAF pursued a definite modernization policy concentrating on defense against bombers rather than participating in air-ground support of troops. While separate figures are not available, the **People's Republic of China** and the **Democratic People's Republic of Korea** suffered the loss of approximately 950 aircraft (792 MiGs) in dogfights with **United States** pilots.

AIR FORCE, REPUBLIC OF KOREA. When war began there was no ROK Air Force (ROKAF). It was established on 10 October 1950 and consisted, at that time, of 39 pilots and 10 American T-6 trainers. By 1953 the Republic of Korea Air Force held a few **F-51 Mustangs** but it was never an active force during the war.

AIR FORCE, UNITED NATIONS. The United Nations Air Force was made up of elements from several contributing nations. The vast majority were from the **United States (United States Air Force)**, but **Great Britain (Royal Air Force)**, **Australia (Royal Australian Air Force)**, **South Africa**, **Belgium**, and **Greece (Royal Hellenic Air Force)** provided planes and pilots. Land-based planes flew 44,873 **sorties** during which they lost 152 planes to enemy fire. *See also* NAVAL AIR.

AIR FORCE, UNITED STATES (USAF). The air force had only been independent since 1947, yet it played a major role in the Korean War. The air force responded to four significant responsibilities: air operations over the **Republic of Korea** (ROK) in support of **United Nations** ground forces; operations over the **Democratic People's Republic of Korea** (DPRK) to neutralize communist forces; the deep interdiction bombing campaigns against major military and industrial targets; and the combined support of search and rescue. More than 1,250,000 men and women served in the air force in Korea. *See also* BOMBER COMMAND; COMBAT CARGO COMMAND; FIFTH AIR FORCE; JAPAN AIR DEFENSE FORCE.

AIR LIFT. *See* MILITARY AIR TRANSPORT COMMAND.

AIR MEDAL. The Air Medal was issued during the Korean War in the name of the president of the **United States** for single acts of merit or heroism. It was given for acts considered in a lesser degree than those awarded the **Distinguished Flying Cross**. Second awards are represented with an **oak leaf cluster** (gold star for navy and marines).

AIR NATIONAL GUARD (ANG). Organized as a separate reserve component of the **United States Air Force** in 1947, its role was poorly defined, and equipment and training were limited. Unprepared to serve in combat as units, the ANG assumed a variety of support roles, and many ANG personnel were deployed as individuals to combat units. During the Korean War more than 45,000 ANG personnel served.

AIR PRESSURE STRATEGY. The **United States Air Force (USAF)**, only a few years old, was seeking an independent role to be played in Korea. It defined its mission more in terms of bombing than in support of ground troops. The plan was to bomb targets of economic importance that would raise the cost of continuing the war. General **Mark W. Clark** considered an increased air attack in June 1952 thinking it might bring the communists back to the armistice table without amassing a large number of **United Nations casualties**. The first wave of attacks was from 11 July 1952 to 27 August 1952. A second set of targets was the dams that controlled water and thus rice production. By June 1953 the air pressure campaign had done about all that it could. The next step, if one were to be taken, was to attack **Manchuria** or to use **nuclear weapons**.

AIR RECONNAISSANCE. *See* RECONNAISSANCE.

AIR RESCUE. *See* RESCUE.

ALEMAN PLAN. *See* MEXICAN PRISONER-OF-WAR SETTLEMENT PROPOSAL.

ALEXANDER–LLOYD MISSION OF JUNE 1952. While **Great Britain** provided strong support from the initial days of the Korean War, it was concerned that the **United States** was moving too fast. It believed that increased pressure on the **People's Republic of China** might expand the war. There were rumors as well that the **Republic of China** was influencing American policy. Minister of Defence Lord Alexander and Minister of State for Foreign Affairs Selwyn Lloyd went to Tokyo and to Korea to discuss their concerns with American authorities. General **Mark Clark** rejected Britain's suggestion that there be a British representative assigned to the United Nations Command's delegation to the armistice talks, but he supported their request that there be a British representative to the general's staff. British Prime Minister **Winston Churchill** appointed Major General Stephen N. Shoesmith to the position. The mission, and the representation, appears to have eased the British concern.

ALMOND, EDWARD M. (1892–1979). Born in Luray, Virginia, he graduated from Virginia Military Institute and entered the army just before World War I. He served with the 4th Infantry Division, was wounded, and received the **Silver Star Medal**. During World War II he commanded the only "black" division, the 92nd Infantry in Italy. When the war broke out in Korea he was chief of staff to General **Douglas MacArthur**. MacArthur named Edward Almond to command **X Corps** at the **Inchon Landing**, and he maintained command during the advance and retreat at **Chosin Reservoir** and the evacuation from **Hungnam**. He continued to command **X Corps** after it came under **Eighth United States Army** and until July 1951 when he returned to the United States as commandant of the Army War College. He retired on 1 January 1953. He served as president of Virginia Military Institute from 1961 to 1968 and died on 11 June 1979. A difficult and highly controversial officer, both his role and that of X Corps have been the subject of considerable inquiry.

AMPHIBIOUS FORCE FAR EAST (TASK FORCE 90). This significant subordinate command of **United States Naval Forces Far East (NAVFE)** provided for both amphibious landings and the constant threat of amphibious attacks. Responsible for landings at **Pohang** (18 July 1950), **Inchon** (15 September 1950), **Wonsan** (25 October 1950), and the **Hungnam evacuation** (December 1950), it also harassed with feints against **Kojo** (October 1950) and simulated landing of the **Eighth Regimental Combat Team**. Identified as Task Force 90 it also provided fire support along the coast.

AN HO-SANG (1902–1999). He was a highly influential member of **Syngman Rhee**'s Liberal Party who was largely responsible for the National Assembly constitutional revision in 1952. At one time he served as minister of education. Following Rhee's reelection, however, the Jokchong faction, which An Ho-Sang represented, was purged. He continued to be active in national campaigns and to represent the right-wing nationalists. He opposed the armistice at the end of the war. After the Korean War he continued to be active in national politics.

ANDREWES, WILLIAM G. (1899?–1974). When war broke out **Great**

Britain sent those ships that were already in the area and placed them under Admiral Andrewes. This task force consisted of two cruisers, a carrier, two destroyers, and three frigates. Supportive of the **United States**, Andrewes played an essential role in the sea war. He was promoted to vice-admiral and departed Korea in April 1951.

ANGLO–AMERICAN MILITARY AND POLITICAL CONSULTATION OF JULY 1950. In the 1950s **Great Britain** was suffering severe economic distress. While it supported the **United States** and the **United Nations** in Korea it was concerned that the war in Korea would draw funds necessary to provide for stability in Europe. Without encouragement from the United States, Britain's Foreign Minister **Ernest Bevin** pressed for concessions that would bring an end to the war. One suggestion was that the United States withdraw its support for the **Republic of China** in return for the **People's Republic of China** withdrawing north of the 38th Parallel. The United States response was a firm "no consideration" sent by Secretary of State **Dean G. Acheson** on 10 June 1950. The British ceased their efforts in this regard though they continued to warn against any action that would force the hand of the People's Republic of China. The conversations did reaffirm America's determination to maintain the primacy of the Anglo–American partnership.

ANGLO–INDIA FIVE POINT PLAN. *See* PRISONER-OF-WAR QUESTION.

ANTI-AIRCRAFT ARTILLERY (AAA). Eight divisional anti-aircraft artillery weapons units were deployed in Korea. In addition, individual units of the 10th AAA Group and the 507th AAA–AW Battalion were involved. Since neither the **People's Republic of China** nor the **Democratic People's Republic of Korea** was committed to aerial interdiction or ground support, the majority of AAA units in Korea operated in support of ground troops. The divisional AAA units were equipped with "quad 50s" (four-barrel .50 caliber machine guns mounted on half-tracks) and motorized 37mm and 40mm guns. The 90mm guns of the 10th AAA Group were used as artillery. The communist forces had available a variety of guns that proved to be effective. Those used the most were the Soviet-built 85mm and 37mm cannons.

ANTI-GUERRILLA. *See* COUNTERINSURGENTS.

ANTI-WAR SENTIMENT DURING KOREAN WAR. While public support for the Korean War was fairly high at the beginning, it declined as the war continued. In June 1950 there was a 75 percent support for the action. By the time the **People's Republic of China** entered the conflict in November 1950 it had dropped to 50 percent. There was a small rally after the evacuation from **Hungnam** when the level of support returned to about 50 percent. By the 1952 election less than 33 percent agreed that the United States should be in Korea. After **Dwight Eisenhower**'s return from his visit to Korea in December 1952, public support dropped to 25 percent. President **Harry Truman** was blamed for the United States involvement and his public approval rating dropped as low as any president to that time.

ANZUS TREATY. See AUSTRALIA, NEW ZEALAND, UNITED STATES.

ARAB–ASIAN PEACE INITIATIVES. During the Korean War peace initiatives by Arab–Asian nations played an important role in limiting the expansion of the war. These nations, while not dominant, could muster enough votes to have an effect on **United Nations** discussion and legislation. The first major effort was in December 1950 and led to the creation of the **United Nations Cease-Fire Group**. The second, in the fall of 1952, would provide much of the substance for the eventual POW agreement. See also AGENDA ITEM IV; MENON PRISONER-OF-WAR PROPOSAL; PERUVIAN PRISONER-OF-WAR PEACE PROPOSAL.

ARGENTINA. On 5 October 1950 Argentina offered canned and frozen meat for the troops under the **United Nations Command**.

ARGYLL AND SUTHERLAND HIGHLANDERS REGIMENT. The first battalion of this regiment, embarking with the first battalion of the Middlesex Regiment, formed the British **27th Brigade** that arrived from Hong Kong on 29 August 1950. They formed a part of the **Naktong Perimeter** defense line. Later in the war they were incorporated into the **British Commonwealth Division**.

ARMISTICE. The **United Nations** delegates to the negotiations were Vice Admiral **C. Turner Joy** and after 22 May 1952 Lieutenant General **William K. Harrison Jr.** Representatives from the **Republic of**

Korea Army were major generals **Paik Son-Yup**, after October 1951 **Lee Hyung Keun**, after February 1952 **Yu Jai Hyung**, after April 1953 **Choi Duk Shin**. The **North Korean People's Army (NKPA)** representatives were General **Nam Il** and Premier Marshal **Kim Il-Sung**. The **People's Republic of China** was represented by Marshal **Peng The-huai**.

The fighting came to a halt by a cease-fire that was an agreement among the **United Nations Command (UNC)**, the North Korean People's Army (NKPA) and the Chinese Communist Forces (CCF) on 27 July 1953. The agreement had taken more than two years. Following overtures by the United States, the talks began on 10 July 1951 at **Kaeson**. The negotiations moved on 25 October 1951 to **Panmunjom**. The negotiations were bitter, hostile, and often boycotted by one side or the other. On 28 March 1953, shortly after the death of **Joseph Stalin**, an exchange of prisoners was agreed to that took place from 20 April to 3 May 1953. A significant difficulty in the later stages of the negotiations was the opposition expressed by the Republic of Korea. **Syngman Rhee's** objections were so deep he tried to prevent an armistice by releasing nearly 25,000 North Korean prisoners of war on 18 June 1953 and threatening to continue the war on his own. After considerable pressure from the United States, and the promise of a long-term economic and military treaty, he agreed not to block further efforts.

The final agreement provided for an armed truce, a **Demilitarized Zone** between the **Democratic People's Republic of Korea** and the **Republic of Korea**, and the exchange of all prisoners. It was finally signed by Marshall **Kim Il-Sung** and General **Nam Il** of the NKPA, Marshal **Peng The-huai** of the CCF, UNC commander General **Mark Clark** and Lieutenant General **William K. Harrison**. No representative of the Republic of Korea signed the agreement. Representatives still meet at Panmunjom to discuss violations of the treaty.

The communists indicated that if senior officers signed the **cease-fire** correspondents from the Republic of Korea and the **Republic of China** would be prevented from attending. While General **Mark Clark** was not happy about it, he agreed to allow the senior delegates to sign the armistice and then the primary commander General Mark Clark, Premier **Kim Il-Sung** and Commander **Peng The-huai** would sign at their headquarters. The United Nations representative complained that the signing building had only a north door and thus the representative would need to pass through communist territory to sign the document. Finally a south entrance was constructed. During the meeting in which the signing occurred, 18 copies in English and 12 each in Korean and Chinese were provided, and none of the delegates spoke to one another.

ARMOR. When the Korean War broke out, the **United States** only had available the light **M-24 Chaffee** reconnaissance tank and some old M15a half tracks. The **Republic of Korea** had no armor at all. Shortly the U.S. **Sherman** medium tanks from Tokyo manned by World War II tank veterans called from headquarters units there. The **Democratic People's Republic of Korea (DPRK)** had available 120 Russian-made **T-34** tanks. Because of this the DPRK dominated the opening days of the war. By late August of 1950 the United States had nearly 500 tanks (M-46 Patton) in six medium tank battalions. Great Britain also sent an armored unit with 45 British Cromwell and **Centurion** tanks. After the early tank battles in July and August of 1950, armor in Korea returned to its primary role in support of infantry.

ARMOR, DEMOCRATIC PEOPLE'S REPUBLIC OF KOREA. The **North Korean People's Army** used, almost exclusively, the T-34 tanks supplied by the **Soviet Union**.

ARMOR, PEOPLE'S REPUBLIC OF CHINA. The Soviet-made **T-34 tank** was the main armor used by the **Communist Chinese Forces**. It weighed 35 tons and could reach 34 miles per hour. The tank mounted an 85mm gun and two 7.62mm machine guns. The heavier tank, Joseph Stalin III, was never provided to any satellite or allied nations. Tanks were significant in the beginning months of the war but the increase in Allied air power made them less effective as the war continued.

ARMOR, UNITED NATIONS. When the war broke out, the **United States** had no tanks in Korea or the Far East that were a match for the **Soviet Union**'s **T-34**. There were eventually some **M-24s** (light reconnaissance) with a 76mm cannon. In September the United Nations effort was supported by **M-26 Pershing** tanks fitted with a 90mm cannon. The World War II tank, the **Sherman**, fitted with a 76mm gun, became the standard tank in Korea. It was lighter than the T-34 but had the advantage of being maneuverable. Some of the heavy **Centurion III**s from **Great Britain** were used.

ARMORED VESTS. Body armor came into use in Korea as a result of lessons learned during World War II. The vests were made of pads of basket-weave nylon overlapping armor plates made of laminated plastic. It could stop most fragments at three feet or more and the full thrust of a **bayonet**. Standardized as the M-1951 they were widely available to most troops of the army and marines.

ARMY. This term is used in several ways: it is synonymous with ground troops; a military unit commanded by a lieutenant general or general and composed of two **corps** or more; members of the military who belong to the **United States Army** as opposed to being **marines, navy,** or **air force** personnel. *See also* ARMY, UNITED STATES; EIGHTH ARMY; UNITED STATES ARMY.

ARMY–AIR FORCE CLOSE SUPPORT CONTROVERSY. This conflict was between diverse policies fed by inter-service rivalry. The **United States Army** felt the newly created **United States Air Force** (USAF) was too independent and neglected its role of ground support in favor of tactical strategic bombing. The army, led in this case by Lieutenant General **Edward M. Almond**, wanted close air support of the type provided by the marine air wings. The USAF favored strikes that isolated the enemy and destroyed its means for waging war. In an effort to work it out, a series of close support experiments was attempted. One, called **Operation Smack** (25 January 1951), was a demonstration of close air support by fighter-bombers for an infantry attack on **T-Bone Hill**. Little was proved by this unfortunate effort and the controversy remained throughout the war.

ARMY, DEMOCRATIC PEOPLE'S REPUBLIC OF KOREA (NORTH KOREAN PEOPLE'S ARMY, NKPA). The NKPA was at full strength when it attacked the **Republic of Korea**, consisting of about 135,000 men in a border constabulary, seven infantry divisions (active) and three divisions in reserve, a tank brigade, a motorcycle regiment, and an independent infantry regiment. The NKPA operated as a triangle organization with three regiments in each division, three battalions in each regiment. Many of the men were combat trained, having fought against the Japanese and with the **Communist Chinese Forces** in their civil war. While a tough-fighting force, they did, nevertheless, suffer terribly in the long fight to **Pusan** and repeated attacks against the perimeter. The NKPA was reconstituted after the Chinese entered the war and eventually reached 211,100 troops in seven corps and 23 divisions. **Kim Il-Sung**, premier of North Korea and marshal, took command during the war. In theory Kim would have been "legal" command of the Chinese volunteers. The relationship with Chinese Marshal **Peng The-huai**, commander of the Chinese forces, was not well defined but more than likely his primary orders were coming from China.

ARMY, PEOPLE'S REPUBLIC OF CHINA (COMMUNIST CHINESE FORCES, CCF). Elements of the Chinese People's Liberation Army, identified as the **Chinese People's Volunteers**, totaling about 380,000 men crossed into Korea, composed of the 9th and 13th army groups. Thirteenth Army Group was divided into nine field armies (about the size of the United States corps). Each consisted of three 10,000-man infantry divisions, a cavalry regiment, and assorted artillery units. Ninth Army Group crossed into Korea under General Song Shi-lun. Before the cease-fire the Chinese Communist Forces consisted of 14 field armies organized into 40 divisions. Casualty figures are unavailable but estimates are that the CCF and **Democratic People's Republic of Korea** lost 500,000 killed and one million wounded.

ARMY, REPUBLIC OF KOREA (ROK). Officially created on 15 December 1948 and based on the eight Constabulary Regiments formed in 1946, the Republic of Korea Army (ROKA) was poorly equipped and badly trained. In June 1950 it included 115,000 men divided into eight divisions: Capital Division, First, Second, Third, Fifth, Sixth, Seventh, and Eighth. The force of the invasion drove ROK units south, and it was not until they had time to regroup that they began to fight back effectively. By the end of the war the ROK had 590,911 men in three corps. These corps consisted of 16 combat-hardened divisions. Primarily equipped and trained by the United States, they fought both independently and as a part of United Nations units.

ARMY, UNITED STATES. During the Korean War United States forces, primarily under **United Nations Command**, consisted of **Eighth United States Army** divided into three corps: **I Corps, IX Corps**, and **X Corps** divided into divisions and regimental combat teams. The United States divisions were the **1st Cavalry**, the **2nd, 3rd, 7th, 24th, 25th, 40th, and 45th Infantry Divisions**, the **1st Marine Division**, the **5th Regimental Combat Team**, and the 187th Airborne Regimental Combat Team. During the **Naktong Perimeter** period a provisional marine brigade was organized later to be folded into the 1st

Marine Division. The 40th and 45th Infantry Divisions did not arrive until 1952.

ARTILLERY. While both the technology of artillery and the methods for its use have altered considerably over the past ten decades, its role remains basically the same. Artillery is used primarily to provide close support for the infantry. During the Korean War all the belligerents took full advantage of artillery. Most of the field pieces were those perfected and used during World War II. *See also* ARTILLERY, COMMUNIST; ARTILLERY, UNITED NATIONS.

ARTILLERY, COMMUNIST (DEMOCRATIC PEOPLE'S REPUBLIC OF KOREA AND PEOPLE'S REPUBLIC OF CHINA). The **People's Republic of China** and the **Democratic People's Republic of Korea** forces employed 122mm howitzers, 76mm field guns, Su-76 self-propelled guns on T-34 chassis, and 45mm antitank guns. With the exception of a few captured Japanese pieces, most CCF and NK artillery was provided by the **Soviet Union**. The Soviet 152mm howitzers were only available on rare occasions. The **North Korean People's Army** lost much of its artillery during the United Nations counterattack. When the People's Republic of China entered the war, it sent eight artillery divisions to Korea.

ARTILLERY, UNITED NATIONS. The primary artillery weapons in Korea were the 105mm, 155mm, and the 8-inch howitzer. The **United Nations** employed 54 battalions of field artillery in Korea, 27 of the light-towed 105mm, two of the self-propelled 105mm, eight 155mm towed howitzers, 22 tractor-drawn and self-propelled 155mm guns, and three heavy tractor-drawn 8-inch howitzers. As the war progressed more reliance was placed on the larger weapons, and by late 1952 **Eighth United States Army** had available 45 8-inch and 36 155mm guns. As an illustration of the massive use of artillery the **United Nations Command**, on 22 May 1951, fired 49,986 rounds. *See* ANTI-AIRCRAFT ARTILLERY; MORTARS.

ATOMIC BOMB. *See* NUCLEAR WEAPONS.

ATROCITIES. The determination of atrocities is somewhat dependent on who is making the determination. Certainly extremes of warfare were suffered throughout the Korean War, and some actions seemed far beyond the heat of battle. The **North Korean People's Army** murdered American **prisoners of war**, shooting them in the back of the head after tying their hands. The North Koreans were also very harsh with prisoners for the **Republic of Korea**. The **Republic of China** forces were less inclined to such behavior and the **United Nations** official policy was to avoid such behavior. But isolated events occurred throughout the war for which all parties must take some blame.

ATTLEE, CLEMENT R. (1883–1967). Prime minister of **Great Britain** at the outbreak of war, Atlee was very supportive of the **United Nations**. He committed British troops and agreed to a strong response to the **North Korean People's Army**. However, he was concerned that the **United States** not expand the war to include a conflict with the **People's Republic of China**. When China entered the war, and President **Harry Truman** hinted at the use of **nuclear weapons** (November 1950), Attlee was disturbed and arranged a hasty trip to Washington for consultation.

Great Britain urged a negotiated settlement and suggested political considerations be granted to the communists in return for cooperation. He also expressed concern over General **Douglas MacArthur**'s seeming autonomous behavior. Attlee got little of what he came for; the United States was not willing to make political concessions nor did it react well over concerns expressed about General MacArthur. President Truman was unwilling to give Attlee anything more than a promise to consult with him before using atomic weapons. When Attlee returned to London he may have exaggerated his success, which in time caused difficulty in his Labour Party.

AUSTIN, WARREN R. (1877–1962). The **United States** representative to the United Nations from 1946 until 1953, he was a defender of United States policy. He saw the war in Korea, and the UN's involvement in it, as a moral crusade and was a spokesperson for pushing the military effort to unite all of Korea. He worked to bring about the **United Nations Resolution of 1 February 1951** that identified the **Communist Chinese Forces** as the aggressors. He supported **Harry Truman**'s decision to recall General **Douglas MacArthur** and eventually to limit the war. Austin moved from the center of activity with the increased involvement of **Secretary of State Dean Acheson**.

AUSTRALIA. Australia was quick to respond to the **United Nations**

request for aid in Korea. By 28 November 1950 it had provided an air force squadron, three naval vessels, ground forces, foodstuffs, medicine, and laundry soap. The naval support included the **HMAS** *Bataan* and the frigate **HMAS** *Shoalhaven*. These were joined by **HMAS** *Warramunga* and four frigates. In the air the Royal Australian Air Force's 77th Squadron was made available and operated with the **Fifth United States Air Force**. On the ground the Third Battalion, **Royal Australian Regiment**, linked up with the 27th **British Commonwealth Brigade**. Several other units came in and out of Korea during the fighting. The peak of Australian forces was 2,282 soldiers. *See also* HER MAJESTY'S AUSTRALIAN SHIPS.

AUSTRALIA–NEW ZEALAND–UNITED STATES SECURITY TREATY (ANZUS TREATY). The war in Korea moved up the American timetable for the revival of **Japan**. Yet there was enough concern among those nations that had taken the brunt of the Japanese aggression that the **United States** found it necessary to offer a guarantee against future Japanese aggression. While most of the signers of the treaty were involved in the Korean War the treaty organization itself had little effect on the outcome of the war, other than to increase Japanese effectiveness as a supplier. *See also* JAPANESE PEACE AGREEMENT; MAKIN, NORMAN.

–B–

B-26 INVADER (A-26) . The invaders that flew in Korea were a version of the A-26. A two-engine plane, it could reach the speed of 322 miles per hour with a range of 2,850 miles. It was designed for, and primarily used as, a night intruder.

B-26 MARAUDER BOMBER. This **United States** twin-engine attack **bomber** had a speed of 283 miles per hour, was armed with 11 machine guns, and carried a maximum bomb-load of 4,000 pounds.

B-29A SUPERFORTRESS. This was a **United States** four-engine bomber built during World War II and used against both static and moving targets. Manufactured by Boeing Aircraft and operated by a crew of 10, it was the largest aircraft used during the Korean War. It was capable of flying 358 miles per hour with a ceiling of 31,850 feet and a range of 4,100 miles. It was armed with a 20mm cannon and 10

.50 caliber machine guns. It could carry up to 20,000 pounds of bombs.

BABBLER, ALES (1907–1981). Babbler was **Yugoslavia**'s delegate to the **United Nations** who worked to secure aid for Yugoslavia. With the outbreak of the war in Korea Yugoslavia made every effort to maintain neutrality without aggravating the **United States**. With this neutrality he abstained when it came to voting on the resolution of 25 June 1950 and was the only vote against the 27 June resolution. Yugoslavia's Premier Tito, however, declared the vote was unauthorized and that Yugoslavia would not oppose UN involvement in Korea. During his tenure as president of the UN Security Council he made numerous efforts to initiate discussion between the warring parties but was never able to accomplish this mission.

BACTERIOLOGICAL WARFARE. *See* BIOLOGICAL WARFARE CONTROVERSY.

BAILLE, HUGH (1890–1966). A journalist who gained a sound reputation for "on site" reporting, his fame increased as he was often the person through which General **Douglas MacArthur** released his pronouncements. He went on to become president of United Press after the war.

BAJPAI, GIRJA S. (1891–1954). The conservative minister of external affairs for **India**, he worked as a moderate in Indian Prime Minister Nehru's government. While he was loyal to the prime minister and sympathetic to his anti-colonial positions, Bajpai supported both **Great Britain** and the **United States**. And, with **K. M. Panikkar**, he played a significant role in transmitting messages back and forth to Peking, London, and Washington. While he was respected by both **Dean Acheson** and President **Harry Truman**, the U.S. administration's reluctance to show any weakness meant it was unwilling to follow up on many of Bajpai's peace efforts.

BALDWIN, HANSON W. (1903–1990). An ex-navy man who became a journalist, he was the author of numerous articles on the Korean War. Generally supportive of America's intentions, he was nevertheless very critical of the manner in which the war was being fought. Baldwin did not believe that General **Douglas MacArthur** was insubordinate but was highly critical of his arrogance and limited intelligence capacity.

He disagreed with **Harry Truman**'s policies and urged support of the **Republic of China**. He urged a greater economic effort, rather than military adventurism, to prevent communist expansion. He wrote in favor of the **cease-fire** that was, he concluded, the only way out of Korea.

BAR. *See* BROWNING AUTOMATIC RIFLE.

BARR, DAVID G. (1895–1970). Major General David G. Barr was the commanding officer of the **Seventh Infantry Division** during the Korean War. He received his commission in 1917 in the army reserve, served in World War I, and rose to serve as chief of staff for 6th Army during World War II. He served for two years in pre-communist China as head of the Army Advisor Group. In 1949 he was in Japan as commander of the 7th Division. He left Korea in 1951 to become the commanding general at the Armored Center.

BATTALION. A tactical unit usually composed of two or more companies or batteries and a headquarters.

BATTERY. The term, during the Korean War, was used in one of three ways: a tactical or administrative unit that corresponds to a company; guns of a ship that operate as an entity; or a group of guns set up under a unified command.

BATTLE FATIGUE. The Korean War name for post-traumatic stress disorder. The pressure of combat sometimes drives people to the point where they need relief. Three actions taken during the Korean War cut down on the number of people with this problem: soldiers were removed only as far back as regimental aid stations; soldiers were in Korea for a set amount of time rather than "for the duration"; **Rest and Recuperation (R&R)** was initiated mid-tour.

BATTLESHIP. Developed by the U.S. Congress in 1890 for the defense of American coasts. Ten fast battleships were completed during World War II. All of the last four ships of the Iowa-class—*Iowa, Missouri, New Jersey, Wisconsin*—saw bombardment service during the Korean War where they fired many more rounds than had been fired during World War II.

BAYONET. A tapered-edged steel weapon designed to be fitted on the muzzle of a rifle. In Korea the bayonet was used more as a knife and had the distinctive blood groove.

BAZOOKA. The common name for the 2.36 or 3.5 rocket launcher. It was 54 inches long, breech-loading, and fired a **rocket** of about three pounds for 400 yards. The accepted source for its name is that it was named after a noise made by comedian Bob Burns.

BEDCHECK CHARLIE. The name given to the slow, low-flying planes launched by North Korea that showed up in the late evening to make a nuisance by dropping grenades or firing on compounds. In many cases the troops came to look forward to "Charlie's" arrival as a not-very-dangerous break in the monotony.

BELGIUM. This small nation responded to the United Nations call for aid and sent a voluntary infantry battalion, which included a 44-man detachment from Luxembourg. It also provided several DC-4 air transports and a large quantity of sugar. The Belgium battalion operated as an attached unit to either British Commonwealth or **United States** units. At the peak it had nearly 950 men in Korea. The battalion made a determined stand against the **Communist Chinese Forces** 63rd Field Army at the Battle of Imjin River.

BENDETSEN, KARL (1907–1989). When the Korean War broke out he had a long history of organization and management behind him, including the relocation of Japanese-Americans during World War II, the organization of the Provost Marshal Office, Army Military Police Corps, and as part of the general staff for the Normandy invasion. In 1950 he became assistant secretary of the army where he developed a five-year plan for expanding the United States Army Reserves. When President **Harry Truman** established federal control over United States railroads, he appointed Bendetsen as director. In May 1952 he became under secretary of the army. He left government service soon afterward but was a consultant to presidents, including the chair of Strategic Defense Institute under President Ronald Reagan.

BERENDSEN, SIR CARL A. (1890–1973). This strong anti-communist was **New Zealand**'s ambassador to the **United States** who believed that the United States and the **United Nations** had a strong moral authority to become involved in the war in Korea. He believed that the **Soviet**

Union was calling the shots in the **Democratic People's Republic of Korea** and urged that the Western nations make a strong stand of loyalty and allegiance. He considered the many efforts at a negotiated cease-fire as a form of appeasement, favored the bombing of the **People's Republic of China** north of the Yalu River, and opposed the eventual armistice negotiations.

BEVAN, ANEURIN (1897–1960). A strong anti-communist who served as British minister of labour at the start of the Korean War. He was supportive of the **United States** but leery of British involvement at the expense of domestic stability. He expressed British concern that the involvement of the **People's Republic of China** might lead to an expanded war. When **Great Britain** voted in support of the condemnation of the People's Republic of China, Bevan found his position untenable and resigned on 11 April 1951.

BEVIN, ERNEST (1881–1951). A determined anti-communist, Bevin served as British Foreign Secretary from 1945 until 1961. Frightened of an expanding war in Korea he strongly supported the **United States** but also made several attempts to bring the war to a close. He appealed to the **Soviet Union** to help in the cause, offered proposals of a buffer zone, suggested the United States trade concessions about **Taiwan** and the admission of the **People's Republic of China** to the United Nations. Admittedly his primary concern was with the possibility of war in Europe and fear that United States occupation with Korea would weaken its involvement in Europe. Despite his concerns and some rather undiplomatic rejections by **Dean Acheson**, Bevin led **Great Britain** in its strong support of the United States.

BIOLOGICAL WARFARE CONTROVERSY. The charge of using germ warfare was leveled at the **United States** and the **United Nations**. On 2 February 1952 Jacob Malik, the Soviet delegate to the UN accused the United States of using toxic gas. The **People's Republic of China** and the **Democratic People's Republic of Korea** joined in, expanding the charge to the dropping of bacterial agents—lice, ticks, etc.—to spread typhus and bubonic plague. The "confessions" of several airmen to this effect made the matter worse as did the United States delay in dealing with the charges. Little evidence has been available to support these claims, but some historians have not yet put the charges to rest.

BLACK SOLDIERS. Despite the desegregation order of 1948, when the war broke out in Korea most black service personnel served in segregated units commanded, at least at the field level, by white officers. The all-black 24th Infantry Regiment of the **25th Infantry Division**, with the all-black 129th Field Artillery Battalion and 77th Engineer Company, landed in Korea on 13 July 1950. They launched the first successful counterattack of the war. Black units continued to come into Korea and were placed into action immediately. During the Korean War the accepted term was either Colored or Negro with Black being less acceptable.

The segregation policy had pragmatic problems and humanitarian ones. Because of the policy, black replacements were unassigned while white units were in desperate need of replacements. Early in 1951 black soldiers began to be assigned to white units and General **Matthew B. Ridgway** ordered total integration of fighting units in Korea. Beginning in October 1951 black units were disbanded or integrated by assigning white soldiers. By July 1953, 90 percent of all blacks in Korea were in integrated units. Both the air force and the marines were integrated with only the navy holding out. Statistics show that 3,223 or 9 percent of those killed in action were black.

BLAIR HOUSE MEETING, FIRST. The first of several meetings held by President **Harry Truman** at the temporary White House. Meeting on 25 June 1950, Truman received the report of the **State Department** that supported evacuation of Americans and limited aid to the **Republic of Korea** but indicated little support for sending troops. The report recommended that General **Douglas MacArthur** do a review of the situation and suggest what aid was needed. **Dean Acheson** proposed the sending of the Seventh Fleet to the Taiwan Strait to prevent any aggression there. Other advisors urged the use of naval and air forces, if necessary, before committing ground troops. In a press release Truman suggested that they were acting to protect the citizens and would not become further involved unless the **Democratic People's Republic of Korea** Army ignored the United Nations request to withdraw.

BLAIR HOUSE MEETING, SECOND. On 26 June 1950 a second meeting was held following the North Korean failure to respond to the **United Nations** resolution. **Secretary of State Dean Acheson** recommended lifting restrictions on the use of naval and air power in Korea. President **Harry Truman** insisted that they operate only south of the

38th Parallel. The president also acted to provide for the neutralization of **Taiwan** by dispatching the Seventh Fleet to the strait. Secretary of Defense **Louis A. Johnson** disagreed with Acheson's desire to send troops. The gathered leaders discussed the fact that intervention would require mobilization and left the decision limited to naval and air responses. The report to the nation on this meeting suggested that there was still hope that the **Republic of Korea** could protect itself.

BLOCKADE. Throughout the Korean War the oceans around Korea were under the control of the United Nations. From the beginning it was understood that it was necessary to limit the movement of troops and supplies by sea, and the Naval Forces Far East were given the task of restricting this activity. Given the length of the Korean coastline and the thousands of inlets and bays, the blockade was surprisingly successful. *See* TASK FORCE 95, BLOCKADING AND ESCORT FORCE.

BLOCKADE AND ESCORT FORCE (TASK FORCE 95). This was a significant subordinate command composed of Task Group 95.1, West Coast Group; Task Group 95.2, East Coast Group; Task Group 95.6, the Minesweeping Group; and Task Group 95.7, the **Republic of Korea** Navy. Their assignments were the control of the seas surrounding Korea, the blockade of **Wonsan Harbor**, the interdiction of enemy strongholds and supplies via aerial attack and shore bombardment, and the launching of commando raids along the coasts to destroy prime targets. During the course of the war they fired over four million rounds, and destroyed hundreds of buildings, locomotives, trucks, tanks, bridges, and supply centers. The minesweeping element cleared over 1,500 mines. The cost to the United Nations was 82 ships damaged by enemy fire. Four ships and an ocean-going tug were sunk by mines.

BLOOD CHIT. This was usually a piece of cloth or paper on which was printed a U.S. flag and, in several languages (usually Korean, Chinese, Japanese, English, French), a promise to pay anyone who helped the bearer.

BLOODY RIDGE, BATTLE OF. Intense fighting occurred along three hills (983, 940, and 773) and the connecting ridges between them, from 18 August to 5 September 1951. Holding the ridges gave the occupying army better visibility and, as the negotiations continued, the ridges became the focus of discussion. When, on 17 August, the **Republic of**

Korea was ordered to take the ridges, a long bloody conflict began. After firing a record 451,979 rounds on the ridge and a series of frontal and flanking attacks supported by the **2nd Infantry Division**, the **North Korean People's Army** was driven from the ridge, retreating to nearby **Heartbreak Ridge**. The battle cost more than 3,000 UN casualties and an estimated 15,000 communist casualties.

BOATNER, HAYDON L. (1900–1977). Brigadier General Haydon L. Boatner was assigned as commandant of the **United Nations** prisoner-of-war camp at **Koje** following the breakdown and the capture of the camp commander. A long military career and service in pre-communist China led to his appointment at the outbreak of the war as deputy commanding general of the **2nd Infantry Division**. He had a reputation for being fair but tough, and he acted quickly and strongly to deal with the prisoner situation. He had the situation under control when, on 1 September 1952, he returned to the **United States** 4th Infantry Division, and later as provost marshal general in Washington, D.C. Upon his retirement he became very critical of the U.S. prisoner-of-war policy, feeling that it was ill-informed and unrealistic.

BOHLEN, CHARLES E. (1904–1974). Soviet expert Bohlen was involved in diplomatic and economic missions to the **Soviet Union** since its recognition in 1933. Unlike other Soviet experts Bohlen did not think that the Korean War was the outbreak of either World War III or a European attack. He supported President **Harry Truman**'s intervention but warned against entering the **Democratic People's Republic of Korea**. He visited Korea with General **Omar N. Bradley** in 1951and came away assured that a military solution was improbable. In April 1951 he became the ambassador to the Soviet Union, and it was he who proposed a direct approach to Soviet Foreign Secretary **Vyacheslav M. Molotov**. His message was delivered at the same time **John Foster Dulles** was delivering his atomic warning. It is hard to know which, if either, led to the final cease-fire.

BOLIVIA. Unable to supply troops to the war in Korea because of a lack of domestic support for involvement, the Bolivian government sent medical supplies.

BOLTE, CHARLES L. (1895–1989). He fought in France as a lieutenant with the 4th Infantry Division. After the war he joined the War Plans

Division, attended Command and General Staff School, and served with the 15th Infantry in Tientsin, China. In World War II he served as chief of staff for **United States** forces in Europe. In 1949 he was active in developing the plans for the United States military withdrawal from Korea. In the spring of 1950 he testified to Congress that the **Republic of Korea** could defend itself against invasion. When the **People's Republic of China** attacked, Bolte warned that the United States should prepare for global war. In the meantime, he advocated the evacuation of U.S. forces in Korea. Replaced in 1952, he assumed command of 7th Army in Germany and later served as vice chief of staff. He had two sons, both officers and both wounded in Korea.

BOMBER. An airplane primarily designed to drop bombs. Usually distinguished by range as light (under 1,000 nautical miles), medium (1,000 to 2,500 nautical miles), and heavy (over 2,500 nautical miles). During the Korean War both propeller-driven and jet-propelled planes were used. Several types of planes were used, the light **B-26 invader**, the propeller-driven **B-29 Superfortress**, and the much heavier **B-26 marauder bomber**. The **Communist Chinese Forces** had bombers in the field but never committed them to combat

BOMBER COMMAND. A specific headquarters established on 8 July 1950 for controlling strategic bombing in Korea. Located at Yokota Air Base in Japan, it was a significant subordinate command of Far East Air Forces (FEAF), **Bomber Command** (Provisional). The exact size depended on the mission, and at the end of the war it consisted of the 987th and 307th Bomber Wings and the 19th Bombardment Group, with an overall strength of 99 **B-29 Superfortress**.

BONNET, HENRI (1888–1978). France's ambassador to the **United States** until 1955, he was instrumental in assuring that France had a role in determining policy during the Korean War. He proposed postponing any discussion of political agenda until the military situation could be improved. He was active in the development of the Joint Policy **(Greater Sanctions)** Statement.

BORDER CLASHES. This term was used to describe two sets of events, the clashes between May 1949 and June 1950 prior to the outbreak of war and the clashes along the **Demilitarized Zone (DMZ)** since the signing of the **Armistice** in July 1953. The pre-war clashes were often of battalion size with one side or the other penetrating miles into enemy territory. The **Republic of Korea** was the primary motivator under **Syngman Rhee**'s "march to the north" policy and was probably more successful because the **Democratic People's Republic of Korea (DPRK)** used local troops to guard the border. However the DPRK took its share of responsibility and toward the end of 1949 brought regular troops to the area. The two sides often fought over advantageous terrain, always accompanying any victory with propaganda to match. The clashes may well have supported **Kim Il-Sung's** appeal for Soviet help and provided justification, if needed, for the later invasion.

Following the war, border clashes continued, though much more controlled and without any particular advantage to be gained. Over the years these have decreased but have not stopped. Today the DMZ is still a dangerous place to be stationed.

BOWLES, CHESTER (1901–1986). As American ambassador to **India**, he was an advocate of Indian efforts to mediate an end to the Korean War. He was deeply interested in the **United States** expanding role in Asia. He urged the United States to endorse the Menon resolution, which became the basis for a modified cease-fire.

BOWLING ALLEY. This term identified a stretch of road about 13 miles in length that ran northwest from the city of Taegu and was named for the sound of ricocheting shells from enemy tanks that rolled down the stretch. During August of 1950 the **United Nations** forces managed to inflict serious damage to the **North Korean People's Army** at this point.

BRADLEY, OMAR NELSON (1893–1981). A 1915 graduate of the United States Military Academy, he saw no service in World War I. He was commandant of the Infantry School when World War II broke out. He commanded the 82nd Infantry (later Airborne) Division. Sent to North Africa, he commanded II Corps and First Army for the invasion on D-day. He was appointed army chief of staff in February 1948 and was the first chair of the **Joint Chiefs of Staff** in January 1949. Receiving his fifth star in September 1950, he served as head of the Joint Chiefs during the Korean War. He left active service in 1953.

BRADLEY–BOHLEN VISIT TO KOREA. The suspension of the cease-fire negotiations on 23 August 1951 due to the **People's Repub-**

lic of China charging that the United States had bombed neutral areas around Kaesong, led General Matthew Ridgway to suggest bringing the talks to a close. Because of Ridgway's concern, the chair of the Joint Chiefs of Staff, General Omar N. Bradley and Charles E. Bohlen, an advisor to the State Department, went to Korea to discuss the problem. The outcome of the trip was a clarification of the United States position: to abandon any insistence on a military victory. The trip also defined Ridgway's role and supported his demand that the peace talks be moved from Kaesong. They were eventually moved to Panmunjom.

BRAINWASHING. A technique of interrogation and **prisoner-of-war** control called Xinao, it was labeled brainwashing by the **United States** as a means of explaining the behavior of captured **United Nations** and U.S. soldiers. The process was more indoctrination than brainwashing. It was the perceived inability to fight this sort of treatment that led many Americans to believe that their fighting men had gone soft. The myth, perpetuated by journalist Eugene Kincaid and W. L. White, was without evidence. The facts were effectively refuted by Albert Biderman in the 1960s but the myth continued, in part supported by such films as *The Manchurian Candidate*. Concern for this problem, however, led to United States military strengthening escape and evasion procedures.

BRAZIL. It considered sending troops but wanted significant military and economic aid in return. On 22 September 1950 the country provided 50,000,000 cruzeiro in aid.

BRIDGEFORD, SIR WILLIAM (1894–1971). A graduate of the Imperial Defence College, London, Lieutenant General Sir William Bridgeford served as the commander of the **British Commonwealth Division**. While in this command he dealt with a serious break in the Commonwealth command when **Canada** disagreed with the use of its troops, which were separated and sent as guards at **Koje-do prisoner-of-war camp**. He was able to maintain the Commonwealth Division and strong relations with the **United States** commands.

BRIGADE. A term more popular among British forces, it usually meant two or more battalions and a headquarters. It was used by the Canadians and Turks as well. During the early months of the war the still incomplete **First Marine Division** put the First Marine Provisional Brigade into the field near **Pusan**. The term was recalled and used during the Vietnam War as each United States Army division consisted of three brigades each of three infantry battalions.

BRIGGS, ELLIS O. (1899–1976). From November 1952 until April 1955 Briggs, a journalist, diplomat, and writer, served as the **United States** ambassador to the **Republic of Korea**. His job was to restore the United States relationship with **Syngman Rhee**, which had soured a bit under **John J. Muccio**. The difficulty was that Rhee's views on the war were often in opposition to those of the United States. Briggs, somewhat conservative and strongly anti-communist served well, continuing on under the new **Dwight D. Eisenhower** administration, until 1955.

BRISCOE, ROBERT PEARCE (1897–1968). Briscoe attended the Naval Academy in 1918. He served several hitches as an instructor at the academy and, as assistant director of the naval research facilities, was a pioneer in electronic development. During World War II he commanded Destroyer Squadron Five and later the cruiser USS *Denver*. In January 1952 he was named commander of the Seventh United States Fleet and in June of 1952 replaced Admiral **C. Turner Joy** as commander **Naval Forces Far East**. He retired in January 1959.

BRITAIN. *See* GREAT BRITAIN.

BRITISH COMMONWEALTH DIVISION. Composed of forces from **Australia**, **Great Britain**, **Canada**, and **New Zealand**, it consisted at its largest point of 24,015 troops. Because the British rotated units rather than people, the construction of the Commonwealth Division was always changing. In August 1950 it consisted of British 27th Brigade to be joined in September by 3rd Battalion, Royal Australian Regiment. At that time the unit was renamed the 27th Commonwealth Brigade. In January 1951 it was reinforced by 2nd Battalion of Princess Patricia's Canadian Light Infantry, the 16th New Zealand Field Artillery, and the King's Royal Irish Hussars (tanks).

BRITISH DMZ PROPOSAL. Fearing an expanded war the British foreign minister proposed the creation of a **Demilitarized Zone** on a line from Hungnam-Chongju to the **Yalu River**. The **North Korean People's Army** within the area would be asked to put down its guns and the area would be administered by the United Nations. Both **Canada**

and **India** supported the plan but Secretary of State **Dean Acheson** did not, urging that military operations not be suspended. On 23 November, while the **United States** was delaying, the British talked with the **People's Republic of China** but they also delayed and finally the United States said no as General **Douglas MacArthur** began his "home by Christmas" campaign. The Communist Chinese Forces attacked within a few days.

BRITISH PEACE EFFORTS. Great Britain, though supportive of the **United States** efforts in Korea, saw two dimensions to its role: first, to keep the Western powers focused on the economic and military needs in Europe and second, to prevent the outbreak of World War III by keeping the **Soviet Union** in a low profile and not pushing the **People's Republic of China** too far. This often led to disagreements with United States policy, especially in the case of the role of the **Republic of China** and the PRC membership in the **United Nations**.

In January 1951 Britain joined **Canada** and **India** to sponsor a five-point peace settlement in Korea. While the United States felt the need to support it, they were not discouraged when the Chinese turned it down. A second effort, the acceptance of Korea as a unified nation and the withdrawal of all foreign forces from Korea, also failed. A third major effort was to support the October 1952 plan proposed by **V. K. Krishna Menon**, the diplomat from India, dealing with a **prisoner-of-war** settlement proposal. Each of these proposals caused some rift with the Anglo-American relationship, but never to the point of a withdrawal of British support.

BRONZE STAR. This was awarded for heroic or meritorious service against an armed enemy and given for acts of a lesser degree than those required for the **Silver Star**. Additional awards were marked by an oak leaf cluster or, for navy and marines, a gold star. It was first authorized during World War II.

BROWNING AUTOMATIC RIFLE (BAR). This standard squad automatic weapon designed during World War I was used effectively in World War II and Korea. The BAR can fire about 550 rounds per minute at a range of 3,500 yards from a 20 round magazine of .30 caliber cartridges. It weighed about 16 pounds with tripod.

BUDDY SYSTEM. *See* KOREAN AUGMENTATION TO THE U.S.

ARMY.

BUFFER ZONE PROPOSAL. *See* BRITISH DMZ PROPOSAL.

BUG OUT FEVER. This was a popular term for troops that ran in the face of the enemy. This lack of "an aggressive fighting spirit" was particularly evident in the early days of the war when men and supplies were limited. The appointment of General **Matthew Ridgway** and the increase in the morale of **Eighth United States Army** eased the problem. But it reemerged after the intervention of the **People's Republic of China**. Ridgway dealt harshly with such situations and replaced officers he felt were not maintaining the fighting edge.

BULLETPROOF VEST. *See* ARMORED VESTS.

BURKE, ARLEIGH A. (1901–1998). A graduate of the United States Naval Academy in 1923, he saw combat in World War II where he gained the nickname "31 Knot Burke." He became an outspoken supporter of the navy from his position in the Organizational Research and Policy Division of the Office of the Chief of Naval Operations. His aggressiveness led, in 1949, to his name being removed from the promotion list to rear admiral but it was reinstated by President **Harry Truman**.

At the outbreak of the Korean War, Rear Admiral Burke was the navy representative to the Defense Research and Development Board. Transferred to **Japan** as a representative of the **Chief of Naval Operations**, he worked with Admiral **C. Turner Joy** on plans and operations as deputy chief of staff, commander, United States Naval Forces Far East. In May 1951 he took command of Cruiser Division Five located off the coast of Korea but was soon sent to participate on the negotiating team. He was frustrated by the negotiating sessions and voiced his concern that power was the only thing the **People's Republic of China** paid any attention to. He returned to Washington to serve on many planning groups and, from 1955 to 1961, as chief of naval operations.

BURP GUN. This term was often used to mean a submachine gun. In Korea it was the name given to the Soviet Pistolet-Pulemyot Shpagina obr 1941 (PPSh41) used by troops of the **North Korean People's Army**. The **People's Republic of China** also manufactured a version of this weapon. It fired a 7.62mm bullet, usually from a 75 round drum at about 900 rounds per minute. The name comes from the sound of its firing.

–C–

C-46 COMMANDO. During the Korean War these two-engine transports were used extensively to resupply combat forces in combat areas. Capable of a top speed of 245 miles per hour, it had a range of 1,200 miles.

C-47 SKYTRAIN. This United States two-engine transport could fly at 230 miles per hour, reach 24,000 feet, with a range of 1,600 miles. It could carry 27 troops.

C-54A SKYMASTER. This American-made four-engine transport, first introduced in 1943 by Douglas Aircraft, could travel 3,900 miles at a ceiling of 22,000 feet. Its top speed was 265 miles per hour. It was unarmed. Worked by a crew of six, it could carry as many as 50 passengers. A workhorse during the Korean War, this long-range heavy transport moved men and supplies to the field all over Korea.

C-119 FLYING BOXCAR. This heavy transport could carry 62 troops at 291 miles per hour. It had a range of 1,630 miles and was equipped with a twin-boom tail.

CAIRO DECLARATION (1 DECEMBER 1943). The meeting, in Cairo, brought Franklin D. Roosevelt, Winston Churchill, and Madame Chiang Kai-Shek together and was held to discuss the future of Korea once Japan was defeated. President Roosevelt believed that only the combined action of the Allies could steer the postwar development of Korea and lead to independence "in due course." He outlined a three- or four-power trusteeship, but increasing hostilities between the **United States** and the **Soviet Union** during the closing months of World War II prevented the development of a trustee plan, and it was necessary to settle for partition and occupation instead. Dividing Korea along the **38th Parallel**, the Soviet Union occupied the north and the United States the south.

CAMPAIGN MEDALS. *See* SERVICE MEDALS.

CAMPAIGNS. The American military identified 10 campaigns during the Korean War. A battle ribbon and/or star was awarded for each.

27 June–September 1950	UN Defensive
16 September–1 November 1950	UN Offensive
3 November 1950–24 January 1951	CCF Intervention
25 January–21 April 1951	First UN Counteroffensive
22 April–8 July 1951	CCF Spring Offensive
9 July–27 November 1951	UN Summer/Fall Offensive
28 November 1951–30 April 1952	Second Korean Winter
1 May–30 November 1952	Korean Summer/Fall
1 December 1952–30 April 1953	Third Korean Winter
1 May–31 July 1953	Korean Summer/Fall

CANADA. By 26 September 1950, Canada had offered three naval vessels, an air force transport squadron, use of the commercial facilities of the Canadian–Pacific Airlines, and ground forces. During the war this contribution expanded. The eventual contribution included the destroyers *Nootaka, Haida, Huron, Iroquois, Cayuga, Athabaskan, Sioux,* and *Crusader.* The **Canadian Air Transport Command** served in Korea delivering more than 13,000 passengers and nearly seven million pounds of freight. The **Royal Canadian Air Force**, attached to the United States **Fifth Air Force**, provided 20 pilots, and technical officers and men. *See also* HIS MAJESTY'S CANADIAN SHIPS.

CANADIAN AIR TRANSPORT COMMAND. The Royal Canadian Air Force provided the 426th Transport Squadron (Thunderbird) and pilots for the Pacific Ocean airlift.

CARRIER AIR GROUP, TASK FORCE 77. Eleven attack carriers (CVA) were assigned to this group, several on more than one tour. These were USS *Antietam* (36), *Boxer* (21), *Bon Homme Richard* (31), *Essex* (9), *Kearsarge* (33), *Lake Champlain* (39), *Leyte* (32), *Oriskany* (34), *Philippine Sea* (47), *Princeton* (37), and *Valley Forge* (45). These carriers provided 24 Carrier Air Groups totaling 100 squadrons (22 reserve).

CASSELS, SIR ARCHIBALD JAMES H. (1907–1996). As the initial commander of the First Commonwealth Division Field Marshal Cassels had the job of trying to form a fighting unit from three brigades of different nationalities. He also had to deal with the fundamental differences between the methods of operation of **Great Britain** and the **United States**. Because of his unusual position, he had been given an unusual tool: a directive that authorized him to go over the head of his military commander in any case where his force was endangered to an unusual degree. He did not use this authority, but it gave him a great deal of strength and allowed the Commonwealth Division to operate pretty much as Cassels directed.

CASUALTIES. Exact casualty figures are difficult to obtain both because of the fluid nature of the war, and because many nations have never publicly acknowledged their casualties. The generally accepted numbers are as follows: **United States** 33,651 killed, 103,824 wounded, 8,184 missing, 7,140 taken prisoner (another 22,617 military personnel died during the Korean War period); **Republic of Korea** 47,000 killed, 183,000 wounded, 8,656 prisoners (and about 1 million civilians); **Democratic People's Republic of Korea** 520,000 killed or wounded, 110,723 prisoners (and about 1 million civilians); **People's Republic of China** 360,000 killed or wounded, 21,374 prisoners; other **United Nations** countries 3,194 killed, 11, 297 wounded, 2,769 missing in action.

CATES, CLIFTON BLEDSOE (1893–1970). Having been appointed commandant of the United States Marine Corps in 1948, General Clifton Cates was responsible for the rebuilding and expansion of the Corps during the early years of the Korean War. In 1952, at the completion of his tour as commandant, he reverted to the rank of lieutenant general and became the head of the Marine Corps Schools.

CAVALRY, UNITED STATES. The regiments of the **First Cavalry**, the Fifth, Seventh, and Eighth, had been converted to infantry during World War II and fought as infantry during the Korean War. The traditional role of the horse cavalry was performed, primarily by regimental intelligence and **reconnaissance platoons**. There were cavalry units in Korea, however, as the **Republic of Korea** Capital Division still had a mounted cavalry unit. The **People's Republic of China**, when they invaded, had some active cavalry division.

CEASE-FIRE. The cease-fire was a military agreement among military commanders. It became effective on 2201 hours 27 July 1953. It was signed by **Marshal Peng The-huai** of the **Communist Chinese Forces**, General **Mark Clark**, the United Nations Command and senior delegate General **William K. Harrison**, Marshal **Kim Il-Sung** and General **Nam Il** of the North Korean People's Army. It was not signed by any representative of the **Republic of Korea**.

CENSORSHIP. Press censorship was imposed on 20 December 1951 and administered first by **Eighth United States Army** and then by Far East Command on 15 June 1951. This censorship was approved by the press and lasted until the end of the Korean War. *See also* CORRESPONDENTS; MEDIA.

CENTRAL INTELLIGENCE AGENCY (CIA). Created in 1951 by the **National Security Act** of 1947, it was the successor to the Office of Strategic Services (OSS). Its first director, Admiral Roscoe H. Hillenkoetter, was replaced by Army General **Walter Bedell Smith**.

    Central Intelligence Agency, Capabilities of the Democratic People's Republic Of Korea Government. This 19 June 1959 report suggested that the primary objective of the **Soviet Union** and the **Democratic People's Republic of Korea** was the unification of Korea under communism. It also suggested that while the **North Korean People's Army (NKPA)** had so far failed to invade, they were capable of doing so. The report assumed that the NKPA was controlled by the Soviet Union.

    Central Intelligence Agency, Failure to warn of Invasion by Democratic People's Republic of Korea. Only shortly in business, and with no field offices in Japan until May of 1950, the **Central Intelligence Agency** was unable to provide any advanced warning. The failure cost director Admiral Roscoe H. Hillenkoetter his job.

    Central Intelligence Agency, Failure to Warn of People's Republic of China Intervention. Despite its efforts to establish an intelligence network in Korea and Japan, the **Central Intelligence Agency** had failed to give the United States any warning of the **People's Republic of China** intervention in 1950.

    Central Intelligence Agency, Report on Factors Relating to a United Nations Military Conquest of All of Korea. In July the **State Department**'s Policy Planning Staff favored a restoration of the status quo rather than a military advance into the **Democratic People's Republic of Korea**. The **Central Intelligence Agency** agreed with the State Department that the risk of crossing over into the DPRK greatly outweighed the advantages. Not only might the **People's Republic of**

China become involved, but the **Soviet Union** would probably become involved to some degree. They also noted that **Syngman Rhee** lacked support in the **Republic of Korea** and had none at all in the DPRK.

Central Intelligence Agency, Report, Soviet Union Intentions in the Current Situation (2–5 December 1950). The analysis of the **People's Republic of China (PRC)** intervention led the **Central Intelligence Agency (CIA)** to believe that it was prepared for a general war with the **United States**. They concluded the PRC would put itself in that risk without Soviet support. The report concluded that while the **Soviet Union** might well come into the conflict if the United States entered the PRC, the report did not suggest the Soviet Union would enter the war if it remained in Korea. They believed that Soviet aggression would continue regardless of the outcome of the efforts in Korea. While they admitted that the Soviet Union might well have begun steps leading to global war, they had no intelligence that would support such a thesis.

Central Intelligence Agency, Report, The Position of the United States with Respect to People's Republic of China. Reporting on 11 January 1951, the **Central Intelligence Agency** warned that the **United States** could not solve the problem on mainland China, and that the People's Republic of China would have control of the mainland in the foreseeable future. They warned that any attempt at an economic assault would be unworkable and a naval or aerial attack would not be sufficient to bring down the existing government.

Central Intelligence Agency, Report, Threat of Intervention by the People's Republic of China. In a 12 October 1950 report, the **Central Intelligence Agency** concluded that while the **People's Republic of China (PRC)** might be able to enter the war with some effect, their lack of air and naval forces meant that they could not be decisive. It was the CIA's best understanding that the PRC would not invade in any major way. The People's Republic of China was so weak economically that any outright confrontation with the **United States** would ruin them economically. Only with a **Soviet Union** decision to engage in global war was it probable that the PRC would become involved.

CENTURION III. This heavy-armored, heavy-armed British tank was used in Korea. During the course of its use, it went through 13 different models. The M-13 weighed 52 tons, had a speed of 23 miles per hour, had one 105mm gun, and one .50 caliber machine gun.

CHAFFEE TANK (M24). Developed in 1943 this light **United States**

tank weighed about 20 tons and was armed with a 75mm cannon.

CHANG, JOHN M. [CHANG MYON] (1899–1966). As the South Korean ambassador to Washington, it was Chang's job to seek aid from the **United States** following the invasion by the **Democratic People's Republic of Korea**. Earlier, when **Dean Acheson** delivered his 15 January 1950 speech to the National Press Club in which he identified Korea as being outside the area of American concern, Chang went to President **Harry Truman** and asked for military assistance so the country could defend itself. He was ignored. He returned to the Republic of Korea in 1951 to become prime minister but soon broke with **Syngman Rhee** and participated in the organization of a new party that, in 1960, briefly brought him to power.

CHANGJIN RESERVOIR. *See* CHOSIN RESERVOIR CAMPAIGN.

CHAPLAINS. Sixteen hundred United States chaplains, and chaplains from 15 **United Nations (UN)** countries, served in Korea. Major General Ivan Bennett was the UN command chaplain, and Major General Roy H. Parker served as Far East chief of chaplains. Chaplains assumed responsibility for the troops in their area without regard to denomination. Thirteen chaplains were killed and 26 were wounded. Twenty-two were awarded the **Silver Star**. Four American chaplains died in captivity.

CHEJU-DO PRISONER-OF-WAR UPRISING (1 OCTOBER 1952). Chinese **prisoners** were instructed, in June 1952, to disobey the camp regulations and to plan an uprising in which they determined to kill the camp commander. When the plot was discovered and an effort made to separate the leadership in the camp, open rebellion broke out on 1 October 1952. The prisoners were armed with spears, stones, and clubs, and the violence resulted in 51 prisoners killed and 90 wounded. Several prison guards were wounded.

CHEJU-DO REBELLION (1948–1949). An unexpected attack by communist-led guerrilla bands on the island led to an uprising that eventually claimed nearly 60,000 citizens or 20 percent of the island population. The **United States** military governor, General **William F. Dean,** ordered it suppressed, but he was unable to stop it spreading to the mainland. The rebellion resulted from failures in the United States occupation policy and the defection of **Republic of Korea** soldiers to the guerrillas. It was finally suppressed, but not until the ROK was further weakened by this confrontation between the left and the right.

CHEMICAL MORTAR. Designed and used to fire chemical projectiles using 4.2-inch heavy mortars, these were maintained to give the military a toxic gas capability if the decision was made to use chemicals. During the Korean War the battalions were used primarily as artillery or, in some cases, as infantry. The Second Chemical Mortar Battalion in Korea consisted of three mortar companies and a headquarters. They were equipped with 12 4.2 (M-2) mortars. In October 1952 the chemical mortar battalions were transferred to the infantry.

CHEN YI (CHEN L) (1901–1972). Leader of the communist 3rd Field Army that, at the Battle of Huaihai in 1946, scattered Chiang's troops and marked the beginning of the end of the Kuomintang (KMT) in China. After the **People's Republic of China** (PRC) was proclaimed, Chen was planning on seizing **Taiwan** as the final battle in the civil war. His plans were changed when **Harry Truman** sent the Seventh Fleet to guard the Taiwan Strait. He encouraged the PRC to enter the war against the **United States** and began moving his 3rd Field Army into Korea in October 1950. He was responsible for the orderly withdrawal of the **Chinese People's Volunteers Army** after the **Armistice**. In 1958 he was promoted to marshal and became the foreign minister of the PRC.

CHIANG KAI-SHEK (JIANG JIESHI) (1887–1975). After the death of the Chinese revolutionary Sun Yat-sen, Chiang assumed the leadership of the **Kuomintang** Party in China. He launched a war against the warlords and managed to secure some unity in China prior to the Japanese invasion. During World War II he was China's generalissimo but after the war lost out to the communist forces and retreated with his countrymen to **Taiwan** in 1949. President **Harry Truman** promised support, and when war broke out in Korea he sent the Seventh Fleet to prevent an invasion by either the communists or the Kuomintang. Chiang offered troops to fight with the United Nations in Korea and he and General **Douglas MacArthur** communicated about their mutual interests. He became president of the increasingly democratic **Republic of China** and served until his death.

CHIEF, JOINT CHIEFS OF STAFF. As of 1949 the **Joint Chiefs of**

Staff was presided over by a chair chosen from the various services on rotating basis. The chief served for four years. General of the Army **Omar N. Bradley** was the first chief of the Joint Chiefs of Staff and held the position during the entire Korean War.

CHIEF OF NAVAL OPERATIONS. This was the senior officer of the United States Navy and a member of the **Joint Chiefs of Staff**. Unlike either the army or air force, he also exercised command over the navy's operating forces. Admiral **Forrest P. Sherman** held this position when the Korean War broke out. He was replaced by Admiral **William M. Fechteler** who served for the rest of the war.

CHIEF OF STAFF, UNITED STATES AIR FORCE. The senior officer in the air force and member of the **Joint Chiefs of Staff**. At the outbreak of the Korean War General **Hoyt S. Vandenberg**, appointed in 1948, served in this role. He was replaced 30 June 1953 by General **Nathan F. Twining**.

CHIEF OF STAFF, UNITED STATES ARMY. This was the senior officer in the United States Army and a member of the **Joint Chiefs of Staff**. General **J. Lawton Collins** was appointed to this position 16 August 1949 and served in this capacity until the end of the Korean War. He was succeeded by General **Matthew B. Ridgway**.

CHILE. Chile refused to send troops in support of the **United Nations** action because there was a lack of domestic support, but during the course of the war this Latin American nation supplied support in terms of strategic materials.

CHINA LOBBY. Those who supported the government of the **Kuomintang** Chinese leader **Chiang Kai-shek**. This was a powerful group who blamed **Harry Truman** for the loss of China to the communists. The pressure they exercised was partly responsible for Truman's decision to enter the Korean War. Later the lobby, primarily composed of Senator Robert Taft of Ohio, William Knowland of California, Styles Bridges of New Hampshire, industrialist Alfred Kohlbert, and publisher William Randolph Hearst, sided with General **Douglas MacArthur** in his disagreement with President **Harry S. Truman**.

CHINA, PEOPLE'S REPUBLIC OF (PRC). On 21 September 1949

the PRC was proclaimed with Beijing (previously Peking) as the capital. Following 22 years of fighting the **Chinese Communist Party** (CCP) had won its civil war, pushing the **Kuomintang** onto the island of **Taiwan** (previously Formosa). Heading this new nation were Premier **Chou En-Lai** and Chairman **Mao Tse-tung**. At first the PRC was not involved in the activities in Korea but after the **United Nations Command** crossed the **38th Parallel** the Politburo decided, on 4 October 1950, to enter the war. Chinese troops crossed the **Yalu River** on the night of 13–14 October and conducted a series of skirmishes. During the war it is estimated that the **Communist Chinese Forces** and the **North Korean People's Army** together lost about one million men including the son of Mao Tse-tung. The **People's Republic of China** was one of the signers of the **Armistice** and withdrew most of its troops shortly after that. Listing the action in Korea as **China's Resist America and Aid Korea** movement, Mao used this as a cover for cleaning up a significant amount of opposition at home.

CHINA, REPUBLIC OF (ROC). Reestablished on the island of **Taiwan** the Kuomintang government declared itself the only legal government of China. Led by **Chiang Kai-shek**, the government claimed it would return to the mainland. President **Harry Truman** had little interest in the **Republic of China** until the invasion of Korea. Then Truman acted to neutralize Taiwan by stationing the Seventh Fleet in the Taiwan Strait. Chiang Kai-shek offered troops to aid in the war in Korea, but they were refused. There was concern that such an action would further upset the **People's Republic of China**. The potential of an attack on the mainland was always a possibility and prevented the transfer of some **Communist Chinese Forces** from possible attack zones. After assuming the presidency, Dwight Eisenhower released the Kuomintang Chinese but no action was taken.

  China, Republic of, Offers Troops. The **Republic of China** offered to provide three infantry divisions, 20 C-47 transports, coal, rice, salt, and DDT. All of the offers were refused by President **Harry Truman** for political reasons.

CH'IN CHI-WEI (QIN JIWEN) (1911–1997). He gained a reputation for bravery and loyalty during the Chinese Civil War and when the **People's Republic of China** was established, he was named commander of the **Chinese People's Volunteers** 15th Army. His experience and tactics were not sufficient to meet the power of a modern army, and he suffered several defeats. After a brief period for retraining he returned to command the 15th against **United States Seventh Infantry Division** and the **Republic of Korea** 3rd and 7th Divisions. He held the line and was promoted to lieutenant general at the end of the Korean War to serve as vice-commander of the Kunming Force.

CHINESE MILITARY DISENGAGEMENT. *See* UNSAN, BATTLE OF.

CHINESE MILITARY INTERVENTION. When General **Douglas MacArthur** took **United States** troops across the **38th Parallel**, he convinced **Mao Tse-tung** that the **People's Republic of China (PRC)** was in danger. While many communist leaders opposed the intervention, Mao won them over, and the decision was made to send "volunteers." In a last effort to avoid war, Premier **Chou En-Lai** warned the ambassador from India, **K. M. Panikkar**, that the PRC would enter the war if the **United States** continued. **Dean Acheson**, and many of President **Harry Truman**'s advisors, believed the PRC was bluffing. On 8 October 1950 the order was sent to begin the **Communist Chinese Forces** movement. The order was canceled and movement stopped when **Joseph Stalin** indicated that he was not ready to send air support. Then, on 13 October, the PRC decided to go it alone.

CHINESE PEOPLE'S VOLUNTEERS ARMY. The **People's Republic of China** decided on the term "volunteers" to suggest that the troops did not represent an official decision, thus making it harder for the **United States** to expand the conflict into a war against the PRC. The command was composed, primarily, of the Northeastern Border Forces. Originally unwilling to support the **Communist Chinese Forces** with air power, **Joseph Stalin** was so pleased with the Chinese victories that by late 1950 the **Soviet Union** sent two air divisions to **Manchuria**. During the war the PRC deployed more than 2.3 million soldiers (25 Field Corps) and at times had as many as 66 percent of its forces fighting in Korea.

CHINESE SPRING OFFENSIVE (1951). Launched on 22 April 1951 after an essential buildup, nearly half-a-million troops of the **People's Republic of China** drove against the defenses at **Seoul**. Secondary drives were launched against Kap'yong and against the eastern end of the line. The **United Nations (UN)** forces fell back and moved into defenses at **No Name Line**. There the line held. In early May 21 divisions of the **Communist Chinese Forces (CCF)** and nine **North Korean** divisions struck at the UN line, which held. A minor breakthrough against **Republic of Korea** forces was stopped by swift counteroffensives. The failure of this offensive effort seemed to prove to the CCF that it was unable to obtain a victory in this manner. Fearing that the increasingly strong UN would attempt another drive into the **Democratic People's Republic of Korea**, the CCF opted for the beginning of negotiations.

CHINESE SUMMER OFFENSIVE (1953). On 10 June, while the negotiation teams were completing agreement on **Agenda Item IV** (POWs), the **People's Republic of China** attacked several **Republic of Korea (ROC)** positions and moved into an extended campaign. The negotiations came to an abrupt halt on 18 June when ROK President **Syngman Rhee** ordered the release of several thousand **North Korean People's Army** prisoners of war in an effort to break off armistice talks. In early July the **Communist Chinese Forces** pushed its offensive against ROK units and caused high casualties. The effort appears to have been designed to show the ROK that it could not go it alone without **United States** support. Finally **United Nations** commander General **Maxwell D. Taylor** sent divisions to support the ROK and launched a counteroffensive on 17 July that advanced UN forces back to within six miles of the original line. Maxwell did not want to begin another major campaign so he stopped his forces at the Kumsong River. **Dean Acheson** was concerned that the war might end on a CCF victory, but the military argued that a stable line was more significant than a victory. Both sides returned to the table and by 19 July the CCF accepted the United States assurance that it would maintain the truce even if Syngman Rhee broke it. The drive to move the line slightly south cost the Chinese 28,000 **casualties**.

CHINNAMPO. This port city was at the mouth of the Taedong River about 30 miles south of Pyongyang. During the retreat of December 1950, ships from **Australia**, **Canada**, and the **United States** used Chinnampo to evacuate **United Nations** and **Republic of Korea** troops. The city is known today as Nampo.

CHIPYONG-NI, BATTLE OF. This small northwestern village was the location of one of the most significant battles of the Korean War. Here elements of the **2nd Infantry Division**, the French battalion, the First

Ranger Company, three artillery units, and a tank unit found themselves facing the left flank of the advance of the **Communist Chinese Forces (CCF)**. The battle ranged from 13 to 15 February 1951. Surrounded by elements of six CCF divisions the **United Nations** forces managed to hold and, on 15 February, were relieved when the Fifth Cavalry Regiment supported with tanks broke though and the siege was ended. Despite heavy casualties–259 wounded, 52 killed, and 42 missing—the action halted the CCF drive into South Korea.

CHO PYONG-OK [CHOUGH PYUNG] (1894–1960). When Korea was liberated at the end of World War II, he was one of the founding members of the highly conservative Korean Democratic Party. He was appointed by **Syngman Rhee** as the representative to the **United Nations**. As minister of home affairs, he reorganized the police force that fought against the **Democratic People's Republic of Korea** after the invasion. In 1951, due to a disagreement with Syngman Rhee, he became his sharpest critic.

CHOI DUK SHIN [CHOE TOK-SIN] (1914–1989). General Choi Duk Shin was the **Republic of Korea** representative to the armistice talks. He served as commander of the ROK 3rd and 8th divisions. Appointed to the cease-fire talks, he promised **Syngman Rhee** he would not release non-repatriated **North Korean People's Army prisoners of war** and when the commission agreed to that as a part of the cease-fire, he boycotted the remaining negotiations. He supported Rhee in his unilateral release of nearly 27,000 NKPA POWs. After the war he became a fighter for unification and in 1987 moved to the **Democratic People's Republic of Korea** where he was vice-chair of the Committee for the Peaceful Reunification of the Fatherland.

CHOI YONG-KON (1900–1972). He was defense minister of the **Democratic People's Republic of Korea (DPRK)** and commander of the **North Korean People's Army (NKPA)** at the outbreak of the Korean War. For more than 20 years he occupied the position as second in the political hierarchy of the DPRK. In 1962 he was elected to chair of the Presidium of the Supreme People's Congress. He was a close supporter of **Kim Il-Sung** and a major force in the creation of the **Democratic People's Republic of Korea**. When the war broke out, he was commander of the **North Korean People's Army**.

CHONGCHON RIVER, BATTLE OF. The Chongchon River was the last major water barrier between **Pyongyang** and the **Yalu River**. When the **People's Republic of China** first entered the war, in late October 1950, **Eighth United States Army** troops were pushed back across the Chongchon River. When the Chinese seemed to disappear, Eighth moved north again. On the evening of 25 November **Communist Chinese Forces** crossed the river, overwhelming the unprepared troops, capturing artillery positions, and driving the troops south. Unable to stop the CCF advance, portions of Eighth United States Army retreated. The CCF recaptured Pyongyang and drove the UN back across the **38th Parallel**. This retreat took a heavy toll in terms of casualties, and to a very large degree, demoralized the United Nations troops. Rather than be home for Christmas as **Douglas MacArthur** had promised, they were facing a whole new war.

CHOSIN (CHANGJIN) RESERVOIR CAMPAIGN. In late October 1950, **X Corps** landed at Wonsan and began to move overland to the Chosin Reservoir. On the west **Eighth United States Army** was moving north. Unknown to the **United Nations Command** the **Chinese Communist Forces (CCF)** 42nd Army was moving from **Manchuria** into the Chosin area. From 8 to 17 November the **First Marine Division**, fighting the CCF and the cold, managed to make it up the road from **Hungnam** on the coast to the Chosin Reservoir. The **7th Infantry Division** moved into Magaru-ri. On 27 November the CCF 27th Army, supported by several divisions from the 20th, attacked the **United States** forces. The U.S. forces held the perimeter supplied by air, but by the end of December the CCF controlled the land between the Chosin Reservoir and Hungnam.

CHOU EN-LAI [ZHOU ENLAI] (1898–1976). Chou En-Lai was responsible, in 1936, for the diplomacy that established a pause in the civil war in China and united the Kuomintang and the communists against the Japanese. When the **People's Republic of China (PRC)** was established he became premier and foreign minister and was serving in those capacities when war broke out. He was against a war between the **United States** and the PRC and made a diplomatic effort to keep the United States from crossing the **38th Parallel**. He urged restraint. In 1952 he issued a statement that suggested that the only way peace could be established was if the United States withdrew from Korea and **Taiwan**. Chou was the PRC representative at the funeral of **Jo**

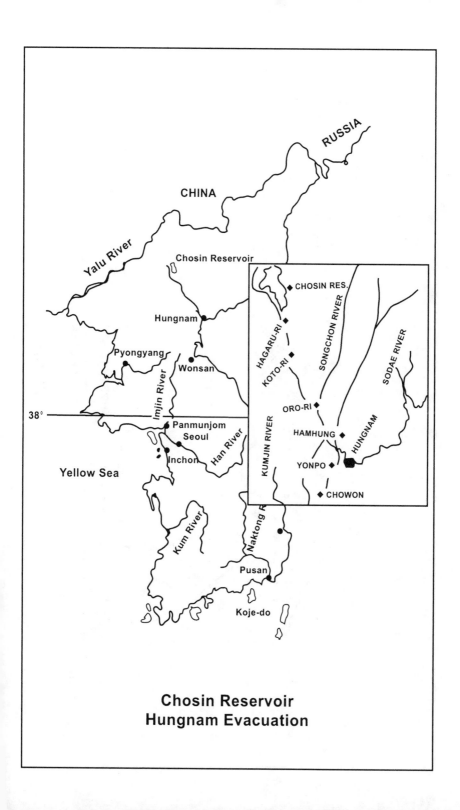

**Chosin Reservoir
Hungnam Evacuation**

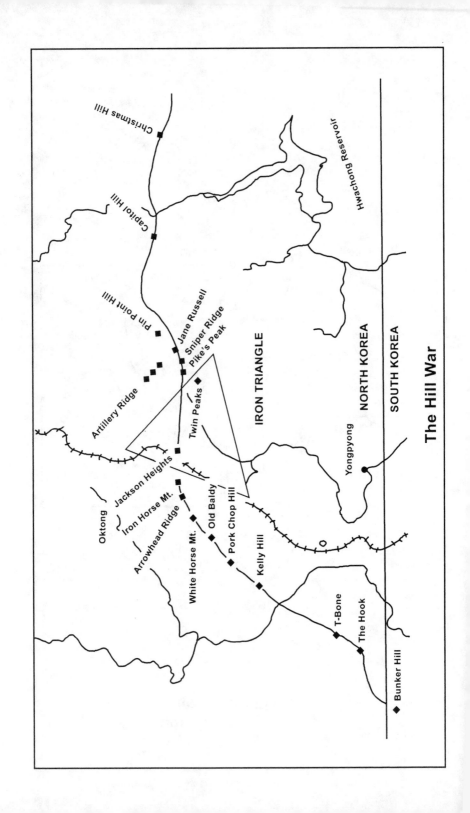

The Hill War

seph Stalin, and on his return voiced a willingness to come to some agreement with the **United Nations Command** on **Agenda Item IV** (POWs). After the war he became well accepted as a skilled diplomat.

CHOU EN-LAI POW SETTLEMENT PROPOSAL. Shortly after his return from **Joseph Stalin**'s funeral, Chou En-Lai proposed that **prisoners of war** who wished to be exchanged should be returned to their home, and that a neutral nation would assume responsibility for the rest. The neutral state would then be responsible for a just solution. This plan received the endorsement of the **Soviet Union** and on 9 April 1953 was formally presented at **Panmunjom**. The proposal led to the resumption of talks on 26 April 1953. While it did not solve all the questions on the table it did show a serious interest in arriving at a cease-fire. The negotiations concluded in July 1953 and the POW exchange operated much as Chou En-Lai recommended.

CHOUGH PYUNG OK. *See* CHO PYONG-OK.

CHUNCHON. Located on the east coast of Korea, it was the last holdout before the **Republic of Korea Army** 6th Infantry Division, pressured and cut off, began their retreat on 28 June 1950.

CHURCH, JOHN H. (1892–1953). Major General Church led the 24th Infantry Division through some of the toughest fighting of the Korean War. He replaced **General William Dean**, who was captured. He was the man General **Douglas MacArthur** sent to Korea on 27 June 1950 to determine what was needed if the **United States** was to save the **Republic of Korea**. At the end of his survey he recommended that extreme measures were essential if the situation was to be stabilized and Korea held. He was relieved by General **Matthew Ridgway** early in 1951 and returned to command the Army Infantry School at Fort Benning, Georgia. *See also* ADVANCE COMMAND AND LIAISON GROUP IN KOREA (ADCOM).

CHURCHILL, WINSTON (1874–1965). Sir Winston Churchill was prime minister of **Great Britain** during most of the Korean War. He had been prime minister during World War II but had lost power in 1945. He returned to power in October 1951 on the wave of economic dissatisfaction with the Labour Party government. Primarily concerned with maintaining Great Britain's role in world affairs, he nevertheless supported **Harry Truman**'s effort to stand up to the **Soviet Union**. Churchill made every effort, though not very successfully, to maintain the appearance of the Anglo–American solidarity that existed during World War II.

CHURCHILL'S VISIT TO WASHINGTON. Prime Minister **Winston Churchill** visited Washington from 5 to 15 January 1952. Churchill sought a powerful alliance between the **United States** and **Great Britain** as a response to the **Soviet Union** and provided a masterful endorsement of **Harry Truman**'s actions in Korea. Churchill's strong American ties must have softened the British Foreign Office's effort to run their own Asia policy. But privately there was considerable disagreement between the two nations concerning the approach to both the **Republic of China** and the **People's Republic of China**. Churchill was concerned with the United States suggestion that it might use **nuclear weapons** and accepted **Dean Acheson**'s promise that no such action would be taken without talking with the British.

CIVILIAN CONTROL OF OCCUPIED COUNTRY. Because of **Syngman Rhee**'s dictatorial and uncooperative attitude, the **Joint Chiefs of Staff (JCS)** were reluctant to see the **Republic of Korea (ROK)** assume responsibility for the occupied areas of the **Democratic People's Republic of Korea (DPRK)**. The General Assembly of the **United Nations (UN)** created the UN Commission for the Unification and Rehabilitation of Korea (UNCURK) to assume that responsibility. Despite this, however, Rhee set out to take control. In response the JCS told General **Douglas MacArthur** that he was not to recognize the ROK government, and the **UN Interim Committee** resolved that no specific government would have control over the occupied area. The **United Nations Command (UNC)** was to exercise control in the name of the United Nations. The argument became irrelevant when, with the intervention of the **People's Republic of China**, the UNC retreated from all occupied territory by late December 1950.

The DPRK only occupied the ROK for two months during 1950, but during that time it made the effort to reconstitute the people's committees as a means of local control. Many of those in the ROK rallied behind the DPRK and in July 1950 more than half of the ROK National Assembly gave allegiance. During the short period of occupation, the DPRK made a considerable effort to win the hearts of the citizens, distributing food and material stuffs, but offsetting were harsh reprisals and large-scale vandalism and looting.

CLARK, EUGENE FRANKLIN. Lieutenant Clark had been a yeoman during World War II, had commanded an LST and later the USS *Errol*, and served as chief translator during the war crimes trial on Guam. Transferred to intelligence he was on **Douglas MacArthur**'s staff when war broke out. Assigned to the **Inchon Landing**, he headed a group of "line-crossers," who were located at Yonghung-do, a small island near the Inchon invasion site, from which he provided last-minute information on enemy activities and tide tables. Discovering a workable lighthouse on nearby Palmi-do, he lit the light during the early morning of 14 September 1950 as naval vessels headed into **Flying Fish Channel** to begin the bombardment of Inchon.

CLARK, MARK WAYNE (1896–1984). He was a graduate of the United States Military Academy (1917) and saw action during World War I. Given command of the Army Ground Forces in June 1942 he took command of Fifth Army in Italy in 1943 and 15th Army Group. In May 1952 he replaced General **Matthew B. Ridgway** as commander in chief, Far East Command and commander United Nations Command. It was General Clark who finally signed the Korean War cease-fire. He retired from active duty in October 1953 and was president of the Citadel for the next eleven years.

CLUBB, O. EDMUND (1901–1989). A China expert with the **State Department**, Clubb offered advice on the essential nature of the **People's Republic of China**. He was one of the few who took **Chou En-Lai**'s statements seriously and warned that the People's Republic of China would enter the war. He also feared that this might activate the Sino–Soviet Treaty of Friendship and Alliance and bring the **Soviet Union** into the war. Running into charges from the House Committee on Un-American Activities, in December 1951 a Loyalty Review Board labeled him a poor risk. He was suspended from the State Department.

COAST GUARD, REPUBLIC OF KOREA. The Korean Coast Guard consisted of lightly armed junks and sampans. They played a small but significant role in watching and protecting inland waters.

COAST GUARD, UNITED STATES. In theory, because the events in Korea were not a declared war, the United States Coast Guard was not integrated with the other military units. However, Coast Guard cutters served in several areas of operation as air rescue, communication support platforms, troop and supply ship control, and on meteorological duty at two ocean stations, Sugar and Victor. The Coast Guard cutters eligible for the **Korean Service Medal** were: *Bering Strait, Chautauqua, Durant, Escanaba, Falgout, Finch, Foster, Gresham, Ironwood, Iroquois, Klamath, Koiner, Kukui, Lowe, Minnetonka, Newell, Planetree, Pontchartrain, Ramsden, Richey, Taney, Wachusett, Winnebago,* and *Winona.*

COLLINS, JOSEPH LAWTON (1896–1987). He attended the United States Military Academy, commanded a battalion during World War I, served in the army of occupation in Germany with the Philippine Scouts and on the faculty of the Army War College. During World War II he commanded the 25th Infantry Division and in February 1944 was given command of VII Corps in Europe, taking the corps ashore on D-Day. Appointed army chief of staff 16 August 1949, he held that role during the Korean War. He was reassigned on 14 August 1953 to become President **Dwight D. Eisenhower**'s representative to Vietnam with the rank of ambassador.

COLLINS–SHERMAN VISIT TO TOKY0 (19–25 AUGUST 1950). Only General **Douglas MacArthur** seemed to be convinced that he could pull off the **Inchon Landing**. The dangers involved were significant and several efforts were made to talk him out of it. In August the army and navy chiefs of staff went to talk with him about it. While that part of the mission was countered by MacArthur's masterful defense of his plan, they did reach consensus on another topic. They agreed that if the war could be turned around it would be necessary to cross the **38th Parallel** and destroy the **North Korean People's Army** or in time they would have to face another attack. On their way home they stopped by Korea and, after appraising the situation, decided there was no need to relieve General **Walton Walker** who had been under attack from some quarters.

COLLINS–VANDENBERG VISIT TO TOKYO (13–14 JULY 1950). General **Douglas MacArthur** had by 7 July 1950 more than doubled his assessment of manpower needs. President **Harry Truman** sent Army Chief of Staff General **J. Lawton Collins** and Air Force Chief of Staff General **Hoyt S. Vandenberg** to Tokyo to make their own report.

MacArthur was sure that he could stop the advancing **North Korean People's Army**, but that more troops were needed for a counterattack and the unification of Korea. After an assessment of air interdiction against possible supply routes, the generals returned with a report recommending reinforcements.

COLLINS–VANDENBERG VISIT TO TOKYO (15 JANUARY 1951). General **Douglas MacArthur** was pressuring the **Joint Chiefs of Staff** for more troops saying that it might be necessary to withdraw completely from Korea. President **Harry Truman** wanted it clearly explained to MacArthur that **United States** policy was to hold Korea if at all possible without weakening commitments elsewhere. United States Army and Air Force chiefs of staff General **J. Lawton Collins** and **Hoyt S. Vandenberg** went to Tokyo to confer with MacArthur. After a visit to Korea and talks with General **Matthew Ridgway**, the two leaders returned with reports that the situation was much more positive than described by MacArthur and that no plans for a withdrawal should be executed.

COLOMBIA. In addition to economic assistance, Colombia provided a frigate *Almirante Padilla* in 1950 and the 1st Colombian Battalion, the only Latin American ground unit to fight in Asia. The 1,060-man force even brought its own band. The battalion joined with the American 24th Infantry Division and later with the Seventh Infantry Division. They suffered 134 casualties.

COLSON, CHARLES F. On 7 May 1952, **Koje-do prisoner-of-war camp** commander Brigadier General Francis T. Dodd was lured into the camp and taken prisoner by the communists. In order to gain Dodd's release, Brigadier General Charles F. Colson, the next in command, signed a statement confessing to the mistreatment of prisoners. Following Dodd's release, both Dodd and Colson were found blameless by a board of investigation. General **Mark Clark**, however, insisted on a second board that reversed the decision and both generals were reduced to the rank of colonel. *See also* KOJE-DO PRISONER-OF-WAR UPRISING.

COMBAT CARGO COMMAND. The command, created on 25 January 1951, consisted of the 315th Air Wing and flew **C–46s, C–47s, C–54s, C–119 Flying Boxcars**, and C–124 Globemasters. It was organized under the command of Major General William H. Turner who was responsible for both the "hump" and the Berlin airlifts. During the war the command moved significant numbers of personnel and equipment, from blood plasma to mail.

COMBAT CARGO OPERATIONS. From the very beginning of the Korean War the movement of cargo and personnel was essential. The 374th Troop Carrier Wing (C–54) was available at first. Soon the First Troop Carrier, 21st Troop Carrier, and 314th Troop Carrier Wing were formed into the 315th Air Wing. During the war the command averaged 140 combat-ready aircraft, flew 210,343 **sorties**, and evacuated 307,804 medical cases, 15,836,400 tons, and flew 126,336,700 passengers.

COMBAT INFANTRY BADGE (CIB). First authorized in World War II, it was awarded to people who had served 30 or more days in combat and were recommended by the commanding officer. The CIB is highly regarded as it identifies those who actually fought in the ground war. The award was available only to army personnel.

COMBAT MEDICAL BADGE. Authorized during World War II, it was awarded to distinguished army **Medical Department** personnel, and navy and marine personnel attached to an army unit who offered medical support for an infantry unit engaged in combat for a period of 30 days or more. The navy provided no such award for their corpsmen who served with marines.

COMBAT MEDICAL PERSONNEL. Often called aid men these combat medics (corpsmen in the marines) were attached to rifle companies via regimental medical teams. Those assigned to marine rifle companies were attached from the naval medical units. Their difficult job in Korea was complicated by almost impossible terrain and weather conditions.

COMMANDANT, UNITED STATES MARINE CORPS. This was the senior officer of the U.S. Marine Corps. It was not until 1952 that the marine commandant began to sit with the **Joint Chiefs of Staff**. General **Clifton B. Cates** was the commandant when the war began and served until 1 January 1952, the end of his four-year term. At that time General **Lemuel C. Shepherd Jr.** was named commandant, and he served for the remainder of the war.

COMMONWEALTH DIVISION. *See* BRITISH COMMONWEALTH DIVISION.

COMMUNIST CHINESE FORCES (CCF). The military arm of the **People's Republic of China (PRC)**, it was also called the **Chinese People's Volunteers Army** for political reasons. These forces as they fought in Korea were generally identified as Chinese Communist Forces (CCF). Under the command of General **Peng The-huai**, the force was composed of 380,000 men in the IX and XIII Army Groups. Each army group was divided into nine armies about the size of a United States corps. The field armies were further divided into some 30 infantry divisions. At the time the truce talks began in July 1951, the CCF consisted of 248,000 with 14 field armies organized into 40 divisions. **Casualty** figures for either the CCF or the People's Republic of Korea are very difficult to establish but conservative estimates are that together they had more than half-a-million deaths and one million wounded. Interestingly Marshal Lin Piao and Marshal Peng The-huai survived the war but were eventually executed by the PRC during political upheaval.

COMMUNIST PRISONER-OF-WAR SETTLEMENT PROPOSAL (7 MAY 1953). Communists proposed sending non-repatriated prisoners of war to a neutral state where, after interviews with their own army, they could make their decision. The **United Nations** objected because it did not make clear how long POWs could be held. Lieutenant General **Nam Il**, the chief delegate from the **People's Republic of China**, suggested that repatriated prisoners be released within two months, that four months be given for those who chose after discussions with their nation's representatives, and that a conference be held within three months after the cease-fire to determine the disposition of all others. This proposal was accepted by the **United Nations Command** and eventually led to the **Armistice**.

COMPANY. The basic organization unit commanded by a captain, it consists of two or more platoons. During the Korean War a rifle company was composed of six officers and 195 enlisted men. A tank or artillery unit was usually about half this size. **United States** companies were usually identified by letters (Able Company, Charlie Company) but some single units and British units were numbered (First Company). *See also* BATTERY.

CONGRESS AND THE KOREAN WAR. Congress did not play its usual role in this event since President **Harry Truman** avoided congressional commitment to war by calling the events in Korea a police action. He used the **United Nations** resolution as the authority for his intervention. Congress, however, did support the effort with a continuation of the Selective Service laws, voted the money necessary, and one or two members of Congress joined the services. *See also* GREAT DEBATE.

Congressional Meeting with President Truman (June 1950). On 27 June 1950 at the Blair House, President **Harry Truman** discussed his actions in Korea with the leadership of **Congress**. Two reasons were given for the immediate action: that the **Republic of Korea** could not hold out on its own, and that the nations of Western Europe were waiting to see what the **United States** would do. In Truman's statement he affirmed that the United States could not let this go unchallenged or the **Soviet Union** would take one country after another (later called the "domino theory"). On 30 June Harry Truman met again to discuss the placement of troops. Senator Kenneth S. Wherry objected to the fact that Congress had not been consulted but that was not the general feeling expressed. It did lead, however, to the identification of the conflict as "Mr. Truman's War."

CONNALLY, TOM (1877–1963). A strong supporter of the **United Nations** and chair of the Senate Foreign Relations Committee, Democratic senator from Texas, Connally nevertheless came out in May 1950 in favor of the **United States** withdrawing from Korea. When war broke out, he supported the efforts of President **Harry Truman**, was one of those who suggested **Congress** not be asked for a declaration of war, and urged Truman to relieve **Douglas MacArthur** after he had gone beyond his authority.

CORDIER, ANDREW W. (1901–1975). Advisor to the **United Nations (UN)**, he served in a variety of political positions. He served as executive assistant to the UN secretary general from 1946 to 1961. He was instrumental in a variety of efforts to establish a **cease-fire**.

CORPS. The term is used in the military in two different ways: (1) a body of men and women who share a similar function as in the Marine Corps or the Signal Corps; (2) an army unit subordinate to a field army and usually composed of two or more divisions. It may have artillery units attached but generally does not have support or logistic services. Commanded by a lieutenant general, a corps usually was formed for a specific combat operation. In Korea four corps were assigned: the I, II, X, and XVI, but the XVI never saw action in Korea.

The Chinese Communist Forces called their corps-sized units armies. Twenty CCF armies served in Korea: 1st, 12th, 15th, 20th, 23rd, 24th, 26th, 27th, 28th, 39th, 40th, 42nd, 46th, 47th, 60th, 63rd, 64th, 65th, 67th, and 68th.

CORPS OF ENGINEERS. From the beginning the Corps of Engineers was involved in the action in Korea fulfilling the three roles of their mission: build, destroy, fight. The building part of the mission was immediately necessary, as they had to work out ways to move people and supplies in Korea. This effort consisted of cutting roads into the land, building bridges, building airfields, constructing bunkers, maintaining railways, and just about any job related to the fighting efficiency of the troops. Called on to slow the enemy the engineers destroyed supplies and roads, broke rail lines, and provided support when called on. The engineers also fought when they were needed, and in Korea they did a great deal of fighting. Even after the truce the engineers were involved in developing the **Demilitarized Zone** and in the location and burial of the dead. *See also* OPERATION GLORY.

CORPSMEN. *See* COMBAT MEDICAL PERSONNEL.

CORRESPONDENTS, WAR. There were about 350 war correspondents accredited by the **United Nations Command**. Eighteen combat journalists were killed. The media did not have the freedom they enjoyed during World War II, and much of the news released was provided in the form of briefings. Television was new and not well used but photojournalism played a significant part in reporting the war. *See also* MEDIA.

CORSAIR. *See* F4U.

CORY, THOMAS J. (1914–1965). A career diplomat with ties to the **People's Republic of China**, he was the advisor to the **United States** delegation to the **United Nations** in May 1951. It was Cory who arranged the meeting between **George F. Kennan** and Soviet Ambassador **Jacob A. Malik** that led eventually to talks concerning a **cease-fire**. Earlier he had aided in the evacuation of Americans from Korea.

COSTA RICA. Unable to supply troops to the Korean War effort, Costa Rica provided the use of air and sea bases for the **United Nations Command.**

COULTER, JOHN B. (1891–1983). He assumed command of IX Corps before its 18 August 1950 arrival in Korea. Lieutenant General Coulter had been in Korea during the occupation and briefly commanded the U.S. **Army Forces in Korea** (USAFIK). Once back in Korea he was shifted to IX Corps, and in February 1951 he received his third star. After a brief period as deputy commander **Eighth United States Army** he was appointed as director of the **United Nations Korean Reconstruction Agency (UNKRA).**

COUNTERINSURGENTS. *See* PARTISANS.

CRUISER. Designed for screening and scouting missions, these vessels had enough speed, armament, and protection to travel alone. Very active during World War II, this type of warship was engaged in a variety of roles and suffered considerable damage. Following World War II most of the cruisers were put in mothballs, though some remained on active duty to provide flag duty or operational support for amphibious actions. Cruisers saw some service during the Korean War.

CUBA. Cuba, which voted for the United Nations Resolution of 27 July 1950, was unable to provide troops but did contribute 2,000 tons of sugar.

–D–

DAM RAIDS OF 1953. Having bombed nearly everything they could find, **Far East Air Force** planners took note of the importance of rice and recommended attacks on the dams that fed the irrigation system. A series of raids followed first on the Toksan dam on the Podong River on 13 May 1953 and then against the Chasan dam on the Taedong River on 15 and 16 May. While the results are not easily evaluated, a temporary replacement dam had been erected at Toksan within two weeks. The air force argued the raids had created enough pressure that it eventually brought the **People's Republic of China** to the negotiation table and to agreement on the **prisoner-of-war** question.

DATES (KOREAN WAR). The hostilities are dated 25 June 1950 to 27 July 1953. The official **Korean War Era** is recognized as 25 June 1950 to 31 January 1955 in order to define a period of eligibility that included the harsh uneasy peace following open hostilities.

DAVIES, JOHN PATON (1908–1999). This **State Department** expert on the **People's Republic of China (PRC)** warned that the PRC might well attack if pushed. He recommended an early strategy of threats and warnings suggesting what the **United States** would do if the PRC entered the war. Once the People's Republic of China had entered the war John Davies urged acceptance of an early peace agreement. At one point he was accused of treasonous behavior because of his respect for the communist government in the PRC and because he supposedly had a hand in the success of **Mao Tse-tung** during the civil war. He was identified by Senator Joseph McCarthy as a member of the "crimson crowd." Under pressure he was transferred to a minor post in Peru and, in 1954 when he refused to retire, he was dismissed.

DEAN, ARTHUR (1898–1987). Arthur Dean served as the military governor of **Seoul** in 1947. He was given ambassadorial rank to head the delegation that was supposed to reach a peace agreement and decide on the future of Korea after the **cease-fire** went into effect. Neither side wanted any agreement that failed to unify Korea under their own government, however, and in December 1953 the talks ended.

DEAN, WILLIAM F. (1899–1981). General Dean failed admission to West Point but was commissioned into the regular army in 1923 from the University of California. During World War II he rose to the rank of major general and was appointed as commander of the 44th Infantry Division. After World War II he was assigned as military governor to Korea. He briefly commanded the **Seventh Infantry Division**, then served as **Eighth United States Army** chief of staff until October 1949 when he was given command of the **24th Infantry Division**.

The first troops into Korea after war began were elements of Dean's command. Taking command in Korea, Dean slowed the enemy with a fighting retreat that finally reached **Taejon**. When the **Democratic People's Republic of Korea** took the city, Dean became separated from his unit. He managed to avoid the **North Korean People's Army (NKPA)** for 36 days, but he was finally captured on 25 August 1950. He was the highest-ranking military prisoner held by the NKPA. He was released

released on 4 September 1953, four weeks after the **Armistice**, and was received as a hero. He was awarded the Congressional **Medal of Honor** for his part in the defense of Taejon. He retired in 1955.

DECLARATION OF WAR. The Constitution of the **United States** provides that **Congress** shall declare war (Section 8, Article I) and identifies the president as the commander in chief with authority over the armed forces (Section 2, Article II). Throughout the history of the nation, presidents have committed military forces on a temporary basis in times of crisis. President **Harry Truman**, rather than declaring war on 25 June 1950, issued a "war message" during which he identified his actions as a response to the **United Nations** call to provide aid. Avoiding the term war, he accepted the term "**police action**" that caught on with the press, but that did not limit the criticism leveled against his decision. *See also* CONGRESS.

DEFECTORS. This name was used to describe the 349 Korean and Allied soldiers who refused repatriation at the end of the war. The largest numbers were from the **Republic of Korea**, but there was one soldier from **Great Britain** and 23 from the **United States**. On further questioning two additional Americans agreed to return and, since the war's end, more than half of the original number have quietly returned to the United States. These defections shocked the United States, and resulted in numerous accusations that American soldiers were soft. In 1955 a new Code of Conduct for United States prisoners of war was implemented. The pressure on the individual soldier was immense and the treatment harsh. Thirty-eight percent of those captured died in captivity. Of the prisoners held, 14,702 from the **People's Republic of China**, and 7,900 from the **Democratic People's Republic of Korea**, also refused repatriation.

DEFENSE APPROPRIATIONS ACT. On 6 September 1950 **Congress** approved the budget for fiscal year 1951 that included more than $13.2 billion for defense. Following President **Harry Truman**'s request, Congress approved another $11.7 billion. On 6 January 1951 yet another supplementary appropriation provided $16.7 billion in additional funds. Congress passed a final supplement on 31 May 1951 for $6.3 billion. These figures, of course, were not totally for Korea as the **United States** maintained forces in a variety of areas. Defense spending for 1952 reached $60.4 billion. In 1953, as the nation grew tired of the expense, Congress approved $44.3 billion for 1953. However, after the Korean War defense spending increased and continued to do so as the Cold War continued.

DEFENSE DEPARTMENT. The Defense Department was created in 1947 by the **National Security Act**. It was reorganized in 1949 in accordance with the Defense Reorganization Act. The National Security Act of 1947 created a **Central Intelligence Agency (CIA)**, a **National Security Council (NSC)**, a new Department of the Air Force (previously the army air corps), and a National Military Establishment headed by the secretary of defense. In an effort to consolidate more power with the secretary of defense, **Congress** amended the National Security Act eliminating the National Military Establishment and creating the Department of Defense. The service secretaries (Department of the Army, Department of the Air Force, Department of the Navy) were removed from the cabinet and made subordinate to the Defense Department. Budget responsibility fell to the secretary of defense. During the Korean War, however, operational decisions were made primarily by the **Joint Chiefs of Staff**.

DEFENSE PRODUCTION ACT. Passed by **Congress** on 8 September 1950 it provided President **Harry Truman** with the authority to produce what was needed to maintain the war effort. The measure allowed him to waive anti-trust laws when it was in the national interest. Failing to get the voluntary effort he called for, Truman used the sweeping power provided and declared a state of **national emergency**. The Act proved to be successful both in providing the military production needed and in retaining some control over inflation.

DEFENSIVE PERIMETER. *See* ACHESON, DEAN NATIONAL PRESS CLUB SPEECH.

DEFICIENCY APPROPRIATIONS ACT, 29 JUNE 1950. Congress passed the **Far Eastern Economic Assistance Act** 1950 before the outbreak of the Korean War. When the **Democratic People's Republic of Korea** attacked the **Republic of Korea**, Congress—in what appeared to be unity with President **Harry Truman**'s decision to counter the expansion of communism—provided an additional piece of legislation appropriating another $50 million aid. This brought the total to $110 million.

DEMARCATION LINE. This line was designed to separate the two political and military forces. During the negotiation process both sides agreed that the identification of a demarcation line and a demilitarized zone was essential to cease hostilities. Several attempts were made to identify such a line, primarily a line parallel with the **38th Parallel** or the front between the warring forces current at the time of the cease-fire. The final line was determined militarily and reflected the front line as it was on 27 July 1953. The line ran just south of the 38th Parallel on the west coast, through **Panmunjom** and the **Iron Triangle** until it reached the east coast just north of the 38th Parallel.

DEMILITARIZED ZONE (DMZ). Both sides in the conflict wanted a **military demarcation line** (MDL) and a demilitarized zone (DMZ) to separate the two political entities and their forces. When talks began, the Soviet ambassador to the **United Nations, Jacob Malik**, suggested the **38th Parallel**, and the Allies suggested a zone 50 miles wide. The MDL became a major issue in the negotiation but by 5 November 1951 both sides agreed to a line four kilometers wide centered on the line of contact. Thus the DMZ decision, when it came, was a military decision rather than a geographical one. It was based on the military contact line 27 July 1953. The DMZ is administered by the **Military Armistice Commission**. Thousand of incidents between the **Democratic People's Republic of Korea** and the **United Nations Command** have been registered and more than 50 Allied soldiers have died along the zone since the **Armistice** was signed. *See also* AGENDA ITEM II.

DEMOCRATIC FATHERLAND FRONT (DFF). This communist organization in the **Democratic People's Republic of Korea** was designed to push for the unification of Korea without military action. Less than a month before the invasion it proposed unification by peaceful means. The conditions proposed were difficult and the **Republic of Korea** rejected them. On 10 June members of the front met with the **United Nations Commission on Korea** to discuss a plan of unification. This meeting failed and a few days later three men entered the Republic of Korea with a peace manifesto. When this failed, the Democratic Fatherland Front proposed a meeting of the two legislatures for the purpose of developing a new constitution and calling for new elections. The failure of these unification efforts may been a cause for the later invasion, or simply propaganda in preparation for it.

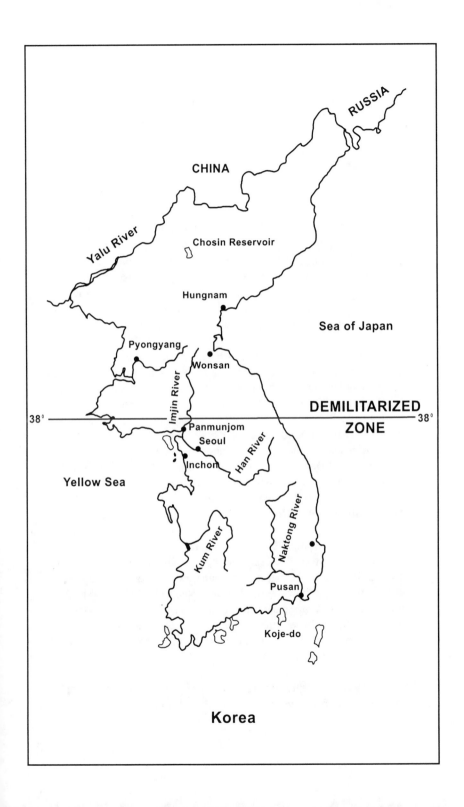

Korea

DEMOCRATIC FRONT FOR THE UNIFICATION OF THE FATHERLAND (DFUF). Originally the Democratic National United Front, it was renamed on 25 June 1949 and was dominated by the leadership of the **Korean Workers' Party**. A rather extraordinary degree of authority was given to this body including some responsibility for execution of the war plans.

DEMOCRATIC PEOPLE'S REPUBLIC OF KOREA (DPRK). Shortly after the **United Nations** elections in the **Republic of Korea** on 9 September 1948, **Kim Il-Sung** announced the creation of the Democratic People's Republic of Korea (DPRK). Kim was dedicated to the unification of Korea and pursued a strong military front in order to accomplish this by force if necessary. While premier of the DPRK he was also chair of the **Korean Workers' Party** and thus maintained communist control. Kim shared his power with **Kim Tu-bong**, chair of the Supreme People's Council, and Pak Hon-yong, the foreign minister and vice-president of the Korean Workers' Party. After the **People's Republic of China** entered the war, Kim Il-Sung began eliminating his political rivals and executed Pak Hon-yong for misleading the party about the potential of communist uprisings in the Republic of Korea. Toward the end of the war Kim had emerged as the "Great Leader" and launched a cult of personality as credible as **Joseph Stalin** or Chairman **Mao Tse-tung**. Kim Il-Sung's dream, however, was a dream of independence and self-reliance for the People's Republic.

Release of Democratic People's Republic of Korea Prisoners of War. As negotiations were reaching a successful completion President **Syngman Rhee**, on 18 June 1953, released 27,000 prisoners from the **Democratic People's Republic of Korea**. The gates were opened, the prisoners left, and most of them merged into the civilian population. Rhee's intentions were to stop the **Armistice** agreement. President **Dwight Eisenhower** was afraid the negotiations would fail and that the **United States** would either have to withdraw or let the war drag on for years. By this time, however, the **People's Republic of China** wanted the armistice and so allowed the action to disturb the talks only temporarily. The policy that followed, one of coercion and concession, was able to get Rhee's promise of no more disruptions and the agreement was signed. *See also* ROBINSON, WALTER.

DENMARK. By 26 September 1950 Denmark had offered medical supplies, the hospital ship *Jutlandia*, the motorship *Bella Dan,* and quantities of sugar.

DEPARTURE DATES. The close of the combat phase of the Korean War on 27 July 1953 meant the fighting stopped. The Korean War continued. **United States** units were withdrawn (from first tours) as follows: **Third Infantry Division** 10 January 1954; the **40th Infantry Division** in March 1954; the **45th Infantry Division** in May 1954; the **Second Infantry Division** in September 1954; the **25th Infantry Division** in October 1954; the **First Marine Division** in March 1954; the **First Marine Air Wing** in January 1965; the **24th Infantry Division** in March 1954; the **First Cavalry Division** in October 1957 and July 1965; and the **Seventh Infantry Division** in September 1960.

DESTROYER. Often referred to by the nicknames "tin can" or "greyhound of the seas," the destroyer was designed to destroy torpedo boats attacking capital ships. During the Korean War those ships were primarily aircraft carriers, but they also screened battleships and cruisers. The destroyer was small and fast and was used for a wide variety of missions. Identified by class (Fletcher, Geering, Summer), the destroyer's size and armament grew during the years.

DISTINGUISHED FLYING CROSS (DFC). This was given for an extraordinary achievement or heroism while participating in aerial flight. Subsequent awards were marked by an **oak leaf cluster** worn on the ribbon for the army and air force and a star by the navy and marines.

DISTINGUISHED SERVICE CROSS (DSC). The DSC, along with the U.S. Navy Cross and U.S. Air Force Cross, is America's second highest award for bravery. The act identified had to be so extraordinary that it set the individual apart from all others. Subsequent awards were marked by an **oak leaf cluster** worn on the ribbon.

DISTINGUISHED SERVICE MEDAL. A bronze medal awarded for exceptionally meritorious service in a duty of prime responsibility. The **United States** medal was established in 1917.

DIVISION, NORTH KOREAN PEOPLE'S ARMY. The army of the **Democratic People's Republic of Korea** consisted of the First, Second, Third, Fifth, Sixth, Seventh, Eighth, Ninth, 11th, 12th, 15th, 18th, 19th, 23rd, 24th, 27th, 32nd, 37th, 45th, 46th, 47th infantry divisions; the Fourth, Fifth, and 105th armored divisions; and the Ninth and 17th mechanized divisions. There were approximately 12,000 soldiers in a division of the **North Korean People's Army**.

DIVISION, PEOPLE'S REPUBLIC OF CHINA.   The basic combined arms organization, the division consisted of approximately 10,000 people, organized into three infantry regiments and three battalion artillery regiments. During the Korean War the **People's Liberation Army (Chinese People's Volunteers Army)** had 54 divisions that saw action: 7th, 29th, 31st, 33rd, 34th, 35th, 44th, 45th, 58th, 59th, 60th, 67th, 69th, 70th, 72nd, 73rd, 74th, 76th, 77th, 78th, 79th, 80th, 81st, 112th, 113th, 114th, 115th, 116th, 117th, 118th, 119th, 120th, 124th, 125th, 126th, 140th, 141st, 148th, 149th, 150th, 179th, 180th, 181st, 187th, 188th, 189th, 190th, 191st, 192nd, 193rd, 194th, 195th, 203rd, and 204th Infantry Divisions.

DIVISION, UNITED STATES AIR FORCE. This term is used to designate a unit smaller than a numbered air force but larger than an air wing. It was usually commanded by a major general. During the Korean War two air divisions were organized: 314th Air Division in **Japan** and the 315th Air Division, which provided tactical airlift and combat cargo service.

DIVISION, UNITED STATES ARMY. During the Korean War the division in the United States Army consisted of three **regiments** of infantry, four battalions of artillery (three 105mm howitzer, one 155mm howitzer), an anti-artillery **battalion**, a tank battalion, a reconnaissance company, an engineer battalion, a medical battalion, supporting ordnance, and supply companies. It consisted of approximately 20,000 soldiers depending on attachments. The **United States** had nine divisions in Korea: the **First Cavalry, Second, Third, Seventh, 24th, 25th, 40th, and 45th Infantry, and the First Marine Division**. A division is usually commanded by a major general.

DODD–COLSON PRISONER-OF-WAR CONFRONTATION. Brigadier General Francis Dodd was commander of the **Koje-do prisoner-of-war camp**. On 7 May 1952 he was lured into the camp and taken prisoner. In order to gain his release, Brigadier General **Charles F. Colson**, the next in command, signed a statement confessing to the mistreatment of prisoners. After Dodd was released, and the outbreak of the riot settled, both Dodd and Colson were found blameless by a board of investigation. General **Mark Clark**, however, insisted on a second board that reversed the decision and reduced both Dodd and Colson to the rank of colonel.

DRAFT. Involuntary conscription was legislated during the **United States** Civil War and used in World Wars I and II. President **Harry Truman**, seeking an extension to the draft, signed a continuation of the **Selective Service Act** on 24 June 1948. The draft was suspended in January 1949. After war began, **Congress** passed a two-year extension on 9 July 1950 and by September 50,000 men were drafted each month.

DRUMRIGHT, EVERETT F. (1906–   ). This counselor with the **United States** embassy located in **Seoul** received the initial word of the invasion of the **Republic of Korea**. He had been working in Korea in an effort to strengthen the Republic of Korea economically and militarily and believed that only reunification would solve the primary political problems. He had considerable difficulty, however, working with **Syngman Rhee**. In 1951 he transferred to New Delhi.

DULLES, JOHN FOSTER (1888–1959). He came into politics from a long line of distinguished diplomats and was appointed by President **Harry Truman**, despite the fact he was an articulate Republican, as the representative to work out a peace treaty with Japan. Dulles also visited Korea at this time to convince **Syngman Rhee** that the outcome of the treaty with Japan would not weaken Korea. On 19 June 1950 he delivered a talk to the **Republic of Korea** National Assembly promising that Korea was on the "front line of freedom." He had only just returned from his Asian trip when he had to face the **Democratic People's Republic of Korea**'s invasion of the Republic of Korea. He supported Truman's decision to go to war in Korea. He was President **Dwight D. Eisenhower**'s choice as secretary of state, a role that he executed with a skill often defined as "brinkmanship." He maintained a strong anti-communist stance and was involved to some degree in ending the war by displaying a willingness to expand the war. Serving as secretary of state under President Eisenhower, John Foster Dulles visited New Delhi, India, in May 1953. During this time he warned the Indian leaders, aware they would pass it on to the **People's Republic of China**, that if armistice negotiations failed, the United States would use stronger rather than weaker methods, including unrestricted weapons.

–E–

ECUADOR. The nation of Ecuador, in response to the **United Nations** request for help, offered medicinal substances and 500 tons of rice.

EDEN, ANTHONY (1897–1977). A strong supporter of the intervention in Korea he was, unlike many of his colleagues, less committed to preserving good relations with the **People's Republic of China (PRC)**. As foreign minister in the government of **Winston Churchill** he agreed with the idea of making a joint policy statement threatening the People's Republic of China if the peace talks did not progress. He was nevertheless unwilling to endorse the idea of forcible repatriation and felt the **United States** was taking far too rigid a stand on that aspect in order to embarrass the PRC. He was openly critical of President **Dwight D. Eisenhower**'s "release of National China" and insisted on consultation prior to an expansion of the war. Even after the **Armistice**, Eden felt the United States was being too soft on **Syngman Rhee**.

EIGHTH UNITED STATES ARMY (EUSA). Constituted in 1944, Eighth United States Army was in Japan when the Korean War broke out. On 9 July 1950 it established a headquarters in Taegu. On 13 July 1950 the commanding general of Eighth United States Army assumed command of all United States Army forces in Korea. On 17 July 1950 Eighth United States Army assumed command of all **Republic of Korea** troops through the ROK Army chief of staff. Participant nations also placed commands under Eighth United States Army. For a brief period from August to December 1950, **X Corps** operated as a separate command.

EISENHOWER, DWIGHT DAVID (1890–1969). Born in Texas he graduated from the Military Academy in 1915. He saw no combat during World War I but after the war served in a variety of staff functions. He was ordered to England in May 1942 to take command of the United States Army European Theater of Operations. He commanded the North African invasion in November 1942 and commanded Allied forces for the invasion of Europe. After the war he retired, served as president of Columbia University, but returned to assume the duties of supreme commander of the **North Atlantic Treaty Organization**. In November 1952 he was elected president of the United States and served two terms. He is often credited with bringing the Korean War to an end.

    Eisenhower's Trip to Korea. While campaigning for the presidency in 1952 **Dwight D. Eisenhower** promised, if elected, he would go to Korea to bring the conflict to an end. He fulfilled his promise to go with a five-day visit during December 1952. He would later threaten to use nuclear weapons unless serious negotiations were resumed. This decision is considered to be instrumental in the **Armistice** agreement.

EL SALVADOR. During 1950, in response to the **United Nations** call for member support, El Salvador offered financial aid and volunteers.

EMMONS, ARTHUR B. III (1910–1962). This Harvard-trained diplomat was appointed, shortly after the invasion by the **Democratic People's Republic of Korea**, as officer in charge of Korean affairs for the **State Department**. While one of the few in the administration who had spent any time in Korea, he played a relatively minor role. In 1952 he was sent to Paris with the delegation to the General Assembly.

END OF WAR OFFENSIVE. *See* HOME BY CHRISTMAS OFFENSIVE.

ENGINEERS. *See* COMBAT ENGINEERS.

ENLISTED RANKS. Rank during the Korean War was different for enlisted men than it was in World War II. The pay numbering system was reversed so that E-1 (recruit) was the lowest and E-7 (master/first sergeant) was the highest. The technical ratings T/3, T/4, and T/5 were eliminated and the half-sized color stripes distinguished between combatants (blue strips on gold) and non-combatants (gold stripes on blue).

ENTEZAM, NASROLLAH (1900–1981). Iranian foreign minister, ambassador to the **United States**, and permanent delegate to the **United Nations (UN)**, he was often in the position to play a significant role during the Korean War. Entezam was involved in several efforts by Arab and Asian nations to bring about a **cease-fire**. Though these efforts failed his quiet negotiation kept the peace issues at the forefront of UN considerations. On 1 February 1951 he became chair of the **United Nations Good Offices Committee**.

ETHIOPIAN BATTALION. The Ethiopian Battalion arrived on 7 May 1951 and was assigned to the United States **Seventh Infantry Division**. They fought most aggressively at the battles of **Old Baldy** and **Pork Chop Hill** and were considered by many as one of the strongest units in Korea. Emperor Haile Salassie rotated the unit in March 1952 and replaced it in March 1953. Of the 3,518 Ethiopian soldiers who fought in Korea, there were 657 casualties.

EXECUTIVE AGENT. The executive agent system was unique in the Korean War. In effect it allowed for one entity to serve as the agent for the many that were involved. The agent was usually the one with the largest commitment. At the **United Nations (UN)** request, the **United States** served as the executive agent for the UN, and President **Harry Truman** in turn named General **Douglas MacArthur** to serve as the executive agent of the **United Nations Commission**. Direction was given through the army chief of staff acting as executive agent for the **Joint Chiefs of Staff** and coordinated action by the navy and air force.

–F–

F2H BANSHEE. A United States jet built by McDonnell, it was a single-seat twin-engine plane developed for the **United States Navy** and first flown in 1947. It went through several versions. Those in Korea had a speed of about 600 miles per hour.

F4 PHANTOM II. Built by McDonnell, the Phantom was a single-seat jet interceptor designed for the **United States Navy**. It flew at speeds up to 487 miles per hour and was armed with four .50 caliber machine guns.

F4U CORSAIR. United States single-pilot piston fighter, flown by the **United States Navy** and the **United States Marines** throughout the course of the war. Manufactured in 1943 by the United Aircraft Corporation, it had a speed of 425 miles per hour with a ceiling of 37,000 feet and a range of 1,015 miles. They carried six .50 caliber machine guns and could carry 2,000 pounds of bombs.

F7F TIGERCAT. Built by Grumman, the Tigercat was a piston twin-engine, two-seat night fighter (single-seat day fighter) developed for the **United States Marines** shore operations. It flew at a maximum speed of 435 miles per hour and was armed with four 20mm cannons and four .50 caliber machine guns.

F9F-2 PANTHER. This United States carrier-based jet fighter was developed by Grumman for the **United States Navy** in the late 1940s and was one of the few planes available for service when the Korean War broke out. The swept version was called the Cougar. It had a speed of 712 miles per hour and was armed with four 20mm cannons and racks for four 1,000-pound bombs.

F-51 MUSTANG. Built by North American as a single-seat, single-engine, long-range fighter, it was introduced in October 1940 and produced in numerous varieties during World War II. It flew at 437 miles per hour and was armed with six .50 caliber machine guns and could carry one 1,000-pound bomb or two 500-pound bombs or six 5-inch rockets. The fighter was recalled for use in Korea.

F-80C (P-80) SHOOTING STAR. This United States jet fighter single-seat fighter developed by Lockheed was the first operational jet. It had speeds of up to 580 miles per hour, was armed with two .50 caliber machine guns or eight 5-inch rockets, and could carry two 500-pound bombs. The Shooting Star was one of the few planes available for service when the Korean War broke out. This was the first United States fighter to exceed speeds of 500 miles per hour on level flight and was the first United States jet in combat.

F-82 TWIN MUSTANG. This all-weather plane was in reality two mustangs connected. It had a range of 2,200 miles. It was armed with six .50 caliber machine guns or two 5-inch rockets. It was the last propeller-driven plane produced in quantity.

F-84 THUNDERJET. A **United States** single-engine jet fighter, it was one of the few planes available for service when the war broke out. The jet arrived in Korea on 6 December 1950. It had a speed of up to 622 miles per hour, a range of 6,000 miles, and was armed with six .50 caliber machine guns or eight 5-inch rockets or 2,000 pounds of bombs. The Thunderjet gained considerable fame during the Korean War.

F-86A SABRE. A **United States** single-pilot plane manufactured by North American Aviation, it became the standard **United Nations** aircraft during the Korean War. It arrived in Korea on 15 December 1950. It had a speed of 675 miles per hour, a ceiling of 48,000 feet, with a range of 655 miles. The first swept-wing jet, it was armed with six .50 caliber machine guns. It was stable in flight but the **MiG** could climb faster and had more armament. The later model (F86) was vastly improved and appeared later in the war. Made by North American it was a single-engine, single-seat swept-wing fighter developed in 1947. It has a speed of 687 miles per hour, a range of about 1,000 miles, and carried six .50 caliber machine guns and two Sidewinder missiles or two 1,000-pound bombs. There were several modifications made during the 1950s.

F94 STARFIRE. Lockheed produced this fighter that was a two-place single-engine plane developed for the **United States Air Force**. First available in 1949, it carried 48 2.75-inch rockets and could fly at a speed of 646 miles per hour.

FAIREY FIREFLY. Created in 1939 for the Royal Navy, it was a single-seat piston aircraft. The Firefly had a speed of 340 miles per hour and a range of 660 miles. It carried four 20mm guns and two 1,000-pound bombs.

FAR EAST AIR FORCE (FEAF). Part of the occupation force in Japan, the Far East Air Force was reorganized when the Korean War broke out. It consisted of the 13th and 20th Air Forces, which stayed in Japan to provide air defense, and the Fifth Air Force that took tactical responsibility in Japan. Three new elements were created: **Bomber Command** (long-range B-29s); **Combat Cargo Command** (later 315th Air Division); and the Japan Air Defense Force (later 314th Air Division). Originally commanded by Lieutenant General **George E. Stratemeyer** (USAF), command changed in May 1951 to Lieutenant General **Otto P. Weyland** (USAF), who held command the remainder of the war. Far East Air Force not only served as the air advisor Far East Command/United Nations Command, but also coordinated the **Military Air Transport Service**, the inter-theater air lift, and the naval and marine corps air assets of the **Naval Forces Far East** (NAVFE).

FAR EAST COMMAND (FECOM). Created as a geographical command by the **Joint Chiefs of Staff**, it contained most of the elements of its predecessor, General **Douglas MacArthur**'s World War II Southwest Pacific Command. At first it did not meet the intentions of the joint chiefs that there would be a coequal command of army, navy, and air force officers. Many felt that it was strictly an army command. In late June 1950 **Syngman Rhee** placed the **Republic of Korea** (ROK) armed forces under this command and in early July 1950 FECOM took command over all Allied personnel. President **Harry Truman** appointed MacArthur as commander in chief, **United Nations Command (CINCUNC)**. Both General MacArthur and General **Matthew Ridgway** continued to maintain the predominately army nature of this command. In May 1952, when General **Mark Clark** took over, he made United Nations Command a more orthodox headquarters, and it ended the war as a legitimate joint command. After Korea the headquarters was moved to Honolulu, renamed

United States Pacific Command, placed under an admiral, and eventually was given responsibility for the conduct of the war in Vietnam.

FAR EASTERN ECONOMIC ASSISTANCE ACT OF 1950. On 14 February 1950 the **United States** authorized aid to the **Republic of China** and the **Republic of Korea**. Just a month before, **Congress** had rejected a bill that gave aid to Korea alone. **Dean Acheson** moved quickly to reconsideration and extended the bill to cover the Republic of China in hope of gaining approval from those Republicans reflected in the China lobby. *See also* KOREAN AID BILL.

FATHERLAND FRONT UNIFICATION PROPOSAL. On 7 June 1950 the **Democratic Front for the Unification of the Fatherland** (DFUF) proposed a meeting to discuss unification of Korea by peaceful means. They called for the formation of a committee that could conduct an election in August to select delegates to a national assembly. South Korea's President **Syngman Rhee** would be excluded from the proposed meeting, and he rejected it. A. B. Jamieson, the **Australian** acting chair of the **United Nations Commission on Korea** (UNCOK), supported the idea. Members of the United Nations Commission on Korea and representatives of the **Democratic People's Republic of Korea (DPRK)** met on 10 June 1950. There was considerable confusion over the meeting, including some unidentified gunfire, and the DPRK refused to allow the **United Nations** any further part in the discussions. Three days later three men who entered the **Republic of Korea (ROK)** with a peace proposal were arrested. The DFUF made another effort and recommended the two legislatures merge for the purpose of electing a national government. The ROK wanted nothing to do with it. Within a few weeks the DPRK sought unification by other means and attacked.

FECHTELER, WILLIAM MORROW (1896–1967). Born in San Rafael, California, on 6 March 1896 he graduated from the Naval Academy in 1916. He served aboard the USS *Pennsylvania* and the USS *Indiana* and was commander, Amphibious Group Eight, Seventh Fleet, when World War II ended. He was commander of the Atlantic Fleet when the Korean War began. He was appointed by President **Harry Truman** as **chief of naval operations** on 16 August 1951 and served in that capacity during the Korean War. After the Korean War he served as commander of Allied Forces in Southern Europe and retired in July of 1956.

FIELD ARTILLERY. The war in Korea made full use of field artillery. The **United Nations** forces deployed 54 **battalions**. The table of organization and equipment prescribed that each infantry **division** have a battalion of medium 155mm howitzers and three light 105mm howitzers. The **Regimental Combat Teams** had one light 105mm battalion. There were also four field artillery battalions from the 11th Marine Regiment available. The rest of the artillery units were assigned to the **corps** and were shifted to meet the tactical situation. By the fall of 1952 **Eighth United States Army** had 45 heavy 8-inch howitzers and 36 155mm howitzers available and two 240mm howitzers. The amount of firepower that could be unleashed became a logistics problem. On one day alone, 22 May 1951, X Corps artillery fired nearly 50,000 rounds of ammunition.

The **Republic of Korea Army** (ROKA) had only a single 105mm battalion per division available in the early months, but May 1952 the artillery available had increased to three 105mm and one 155mm battalion per division. Other nations provided artillery: **Great Britain** fielded the 45th Royal Artillery, **New Zealand** 16th Field Artillery Battalion, **Canada** First Canadian Horse Artillery, and the assigned artillery of the **Turkish Brigade**.

The forces of the **People's Republic of China** deployed little field artillery when it first entered the war, but eventually the artillery available expanded to a total of eight artillery divisions in Korea. These pieces were either 75mm or 76mm guns with a few 105mm, 122mm, and 155mm howitzers.

The **North Korean People's Army** was equipped with Soviet-made field artillery, each division assigned 12 122mm howitzer, 24 75mm guns, and 12 SU-76 self-propelled guns. In addition each regiment deployed four 76mm howitzers.

FIFTH REGIMENTAL COMBAT TEAM. This unit was composed of the Fifth Infantry Regiment, the 555th Field Artillery Battalion, and a regimental tank company supplied with M-4A3E8 **Sherman** medium tanks. Deactivated following World War II, it was recalled on 15 January 1949 and in June 1949 was stationed at Schofield Barracks in Hawaii. On 25 July 1950 it was ordered to Korea arriving on 31 July 1950. First operating independently within **Eighth United States Army**, the Fifth Regimental Combat Team was assigned to the **24th Division** on 26 August 1950. From January 1952 until the end of the war it was deployed as an independent unit under **IX Corps** and then **X Corps**. During the war the **Fifth Regimental Combat Team** suffered 4,222 **casualties**. Segments of the RCT won the **Presidential Unit Citation** from both the **United States** and the **Republic of Korea**.

FIFTH UNITED STATES AIR FORCE. During World War II the Fifth fought in the Pacific as a tactical element of the United States **Far East Air Force (FEAF)**. It was stationed in **Japan** after the war, flying **F-51** and **F-82 Mustangs** (propeller) and **F-80** (jets). President **Harry Truman** authorized the use of air power on 27 June 1950 and the Fifth, which had provided air support for the evacuation, began operation. It was a Fifth Air Force F-82 that shot down the first enemy plane, a **North Korean Air Force YAK** fighter. During the war the Fifth flew 66,997 counter air **sorties** and was credited with 950 enemy losses, 192,581 air interdiction sorties, and 57,665 close air support sorties. It was also involved in flying reconnaissance and air control missions. It dropped 386,037 tons of bombs, thousands of rockets, and rounds. Fifth Air Force was the command for the squadrons of the Royal Australian Air Force, the South African Air Force and the **First Marine Aircraft Wing**. The initial commander was Lieutenant General **Earle E. Partridge** who was replaced 21 May 1951 by Lieutenant General **Frank E. Everest**, on 20 May 1952 by Lieutenant General Glenn O. Barcus, and on 31 May 1953, for the rest of the war, by Lieutenant General Samuel E. Anderson.

FIGHTER AIRCRAFT. The **United States** (and many of the allies) had propeller-driven **F-51 Mustangs** and **F-82 Twin Mustangs**, the **F-80 Shooting Star** (jet), **F-86 Sabrejets**, **F-84 Thunderjets**, and **Meteor-8** jets. The navy and marine pilots used the propeller-driven **AD Skyraider**, the **F7F Tigercat**, and the **F4U Corsairs**, as well as the jet **F2H Banshees**, **F9F Panthers**. **Great Britain** flew propeller-driven Hawk **Fairey Fireflies**, **Seafires**, and the **Supermarine Seafuries**. The **Democratic People's Republic of Korea** began with propeller-driven **YAK-3**, **YAK-7**, and **YAK-9**; **Il-2** and Il-10; LA-5, LA-7, LA-10, and **LA-11** fighters. The **People's Republic of China** flew the Mikoyan and Guerevich (**MiG**) 15 Fagot jet fighter. *See also* DESIGNATION FOR AIRCRAFT.

FILM. There were surprisingly few films about the Korean War produced either during or after the war. Less than 120 films were produced about the war in comparison to the more than 1,700 with World War II as the theme. Most were "B" films with unknown casts and simple plots. A few, however, recorded the war significantly, especially the air war. Certainly *The Steel Helmet* (1951) and *Pork Chop Hill* (1972) would be among the best.

A negative image was created for the public by the production of several unflattering portrayals of Korean veterans in films. Films like *Niagara* (1953), *A Hatful of Rain* (1955), *The Manchurian Candidate* (1959), *Five against the House* (1955), *Shock Corridor* (1963), and *Lilith* (1964) and even *M*A*S*H* (1970) are examples of this trend.

FINLETTER, THOMAS K. (1891–1980). He was secretary of the air force in 1950 at a time when severe budget cuts were being felt. The outbreak of the war allowed him to move into a period of organizational and tactical expansion. In attendance at the first **Blair House meeting**, he spoke against the use of ground troops. Once war was declared, he worked with Secretary of the Army **Frank Pace** in working out an agreement called "organic aviation" that would permit the army to maintain **helicopters**. He retired to private life in 1953.

FIREFLY. The name used during the Korean War for the **United States Air Force C-47** transport aircraft that had been modified to drop flares. It was also called "Lighting Bug" and the "Old Lamplighter of the Korean Hills." *See also* C-47.

FIRST CAVALRY DIVISION. An infantry **division** in everything but name, it had a long history as a cavalry unit, then as the first in Manila. The **First Cavalry Division** was stationed in **Japan** when the war broke out. It was composed of the Fifth, Seventh, and Eighth Cavalry Regiments; the 61st, 77th, and 99th field artillery battalions (105mm); the 82nd Field Artillery Battalion (155mm); the 70th Medium Tank Battalion; the 8th Engineer Battalion; the 16th **Reconnaissance Company**; and the 92nd Antiaircraft Artillery Battalion. The division landed at Pohang-dong on 18 to 20 July 1950 and was engaged at the **Naktong Perimeter**, fought the **People's Republic of China** at **Kunsan**, and was replaced in December 1951 by the **45th Infantry Division**. The unit received the **Presidential Unit Citation** (ROK). It suffered 16,498 **casualties**.

FIRST CORPS (I CORPS). Always referred to as "I" **Corps**, it was reactivated on 2 August 1950 to serve as one of **Eighth United States Army**'s battlefield control headquarters. The make-up of the corps was determined by its particular assignment. Commanded originally by Lieutenant General **John R. Coulter** then by Lieutenant General **Frank W. Milburn**, who commanded during the breakout from the **Naktong Pe-**

rimeter, the advance into the **Democratic People's Republic of Korea**, and the retreat following the Chinese involvement. In the fall of 1951 he was replaced by Lieutenant General **John W. O'Daniel** who commanded until 29 June 1952 when replaced by Lieutenant General **Paul W. Kendall**. Finally on 10 April 1953 Lieutenant General Bruce C. Clarke assumed command and led through the rest of the war.

FIRST KOREAN WAR. In 1871 a **United States** military survey team tried to chart the Salee River (connecting channel of the **Han River** leading to **Seoul**) as the prelude to a trading treaty. At noon on 1 June 1871 the survey party was fired on and two casualties inflicted. After waiting nine days for an apology, a punitive expedition set out that eventually did battle with the defenders. Approximately 243 Koreans were killed with the United States losses at 20 before the Americans withdrew, sailing for home. Nine men were awarded the **Medal of Honor**. A treaty with Korea was finally signed in 1882.

FIRST MARINE AIRCRAFT WING (1st MAW). From October 1950 until the end of the war, the First Marine Aircraft Wing was under the operational command of the **Fifth Air Force**, a departure in the usual way in which the U.S. Marines were used. The wing consisted of two Marine Aircraft Groups (MAG): 12 and 33. At the peak, in 1953, the wing consisted of six attack squadrons (VMA 121, 212, 251, 312, 323, and 332), two fighter squadrons (VMF 115 and 311), a night-fighter squadron (VMF[N] 513), a photographic squadron (VMJ 1), a helicopter transport squadron (HMR 161), an observation squadron (VMO 6), and the First 90mm Antiaircraft Artillery Gun Battalion and its support units. Flying from both shore establishments and light and escort carriers, the marines flew **F4U Corsairs**, **AD-4 Skyraiders**, **F7F Tigercats** and jets, the **F3D-2 Skyknights**, **F9F Panthers**, and the **F2H-2 Banshees**. They also operated **HO3S-1** observation helicopters and HRS 1 cargo helicopters. The unit was awarded two **Republic of Korea Presidential Unit Citations** and the United States Army **Presidential Unit Citation**.

FIRST MARINE DIVISION. Activated in February 1941, it saw action in the Pacific during World War II. Primarily deactivated after the war only the 5th Marine Regiment and the 11th Marine Regiment artillery units were on active duty. Recalled reservists and new recruits brought the **division** up to strength. It ultimately included the First, Fifth, and

Seventh Marine **regiments**, a **battalion** of the First **Republic of Korea Marine Regiment**, four artillery battalions of the 11th Marine Regiment, First Tank Battalion, First Amphibious Tractor Battalion, First Armored Amphibious Battalion, First Engineer Battalion, and a variety of service and supply units.

The marines landed at Inchon (minus the Seventh Regiment that was still en route) on 15 September 1950, suffered at **Chosin Reservoir**, and spent most of the rest of the war along the eastern defensive line. They returned to Camp Pendleton in April 1955. The First Marine Division received three United States **Presidential Unit Citations**, a **Navy Unit Citation**, and the **ROK Presidential Unit Citation**. It suffered 30,112 **casualties** (excluding the ROK regiment or Marine Air Wing). *See also* FIRST PROVISIONAL MARINE BRIGADE.

FIRST PROVISIONAL MARINE BRIGADE. When General **Douglas MacArthur** asked for the **First Marine Division**, it was suffering from years of near deactivation. They began to rebuild the **division**. In the meantime a First Provisional Marine Brigade was established and sent to support the defense at **Pusan**.

FLAMETHROWER, UNITED STATES. The primary weapon issued was the M2A1 operated by one man who carried two tanks of fuel and one of compressed air. Having been perfected during World War II, it found considerable use in Korea against bunkers and entrenched positions. The gun was held in the hand. The range for liquid fuel was 20 yards and, with thickened fuel, 45 yards.

FLYING FISH CHANNEL. The approach channel to Inchon was narrow, winding, and affected by the Inchon tides of some 33 feet. It was a difficult passage even in daylight. The channel was so narrow that if a ship floundered, the vessels ahead would be trapped. It was up this channel that in mid-September 1950 ships of the invasion force moved toward the island of Wolmi-do and the port of Inchon. *See also* INCHON LANDING.

FOOTWEAR, PEOPLE'S REPUBLIC OF CHINA. These troops often wore traditional Asian boots and shoes, sometimes with rope soles. In the winter they often added spiral puttees or heavy felt leggings that were worn over boots or shoes. The varieties were Manchurian leather shoes, the cloth and leather shoes of the **Democratic People's Repub-**

lic of Korea, and the soft slipper called the Yenan.

FOOTWEAR, UNITED STATES. The model 1943 two-buckle boot was still being used as the war in Korea expanded. It was replaced by the M-1943 boot (parachute boot) and eventually the much warmer model 1944 Shoepac with a rubber sole. Care for the feet is one of the most important things a soldier does. Thousands of United States soldiers suffered from frostbite of the toes.

FORMOSA. *See* NEUTRALIZATION OF THE REPUBLIC OF CHINA; REPUBLIC OF CHINA; TAIWAN.

40TH INFANTRY DIVISION. This California National Guard **division** was called up during World War I, saw action in World War II, and was moved to Korea in September 1945 as part of the occupation. Released in 1946 they returned to California only to be recalled 1 September 1950. At that time it consisted of the 160th, 223rd, and 224th Infantry Regiments; the 143rd, 625th, 980th, and 981st Field Artillery; the 40th Reconnaissance Company; and the 578th Engineer Battalion. The "Sunshine Division" participated in four **campaigns** and won the **Presidential Unit Citation**. It suffered 1,848 **casualties**, 10 MIA, and 15 POWs.

45TH INFANTRY DIVISION. An Oklahoma National Guard **division** was called up for World War II and served in the European Theater. In 1946 it returned to Oklahoma only to be recalled on 1 September 1950. At that time it consisted of the 179th, 180th, and 279th Infantry Regiments; the 158th, 160th, 171st Field Artillery (105mm); the 189th Field Artillery Battalion; the 14th Anti-Aircraft Artillery; the 245th Medium Tank Battalion; the 45th Reconnaissance Company; and the 120th Engineer Battalion. The 45th replaced the **First Cavalry Division** and went on to participate in four campaigns. It was awarded the **ROK Presidential Unit Citation**. During the war the "**Thunderbird Division**" suffered 4,038 **casualties**, 1 MIA, and 33 POWs.

FORWARD AIR CONTROLLERS (FAC). Close air support for ground troops engaged in combat was essential. During the Korean War, trying to avoid the rather difficult process used in World War II, a new and somewhat *ad hoc* method was developed. Forward Air Controllers in **T-6 Texan** propeller-driven trainers, called Mosquitos, were used to relay requests for air support directly to the Tactical Air Control Center.

With this effort, supported in October 1950 with the 502nd Tactical Control Group and the 20th Signal Company Air–Ground Liaison, the support grew even better. In combination with other **United Nations** air groups, the air force flew more than 62,000 close air support sorties. The **First Marine Aircraft Wing** flying gull-wing **Corsairs** were the favorite of ground troops and often had aircraft in the area on "air alert" waiting to be called. While there was disagreement between the two services, the air force would later adopt the marine system. *See also* FIRST MARINE AIRCRAFT WING.

FOURTH MEETING OF CONSULTATION OF MINISTER OF FOREIGN AFFAIRS OF AMERICAN STATES. *See* WASHINGTON CONFERENCE.

FRANCE. France was deeply involved in the war in Indochina in the early 1950s and President **Harry Truman** was already sending assistance teams. Nevertheless, France responded to the request for help and sent the **frigate** RFS *La Grendière* and the *Battalion de Corée*, an infantry **battalion** led by legendary French foreign legionnaire Ralph Monclar. The battalion received three **United States Presidential Unit Citations**. Figures for French casualties were not recorded separately, but 13 prisoners of war were repatriated. The battalion left Korea in July 1953 and was transferred to Indochina.

FRANKS, SIR OLIVER (1905–1997). Franks was British ambassador to the **United States** from 1948 to 1952 and a good friend of Secretary of State **Dean Acheson**. Franks was a strong supporter of the United States and a major factor in **Great Britain**'s decision to send ground troops. But he differed with the United States on the question of the **People's Republic of China**. He diplomatically carried the burden of Anglo–American disagreement on such things as President **Harry Truman**'s atomic bomb press conference and the frequent criticism of Great Britain's continued trade with the People's Republic of China.

FRIGATE. Sized between a corvette and a destroyer, it was designed to operate independently or with a strike force, particularly against **submarines**. Normal armament consisted of 3- and 5-inch guns and antisubmarine equipment.

–G–

GENERAL HEADQUARTERS (GHQ). *See* FAR EAST COMMAND.

GENEVA CONFERENCE OF 1954. As required by the **prisoner-of-war** item on the **Armistice** agreement, a meeting of all interested parties was held to discuss the unification of Korea. It began on 26 April, but it was not long before the agenda of the various nations became increasingly clear. The unification of Korea was not a highly significant issue for any of the major powers. Besides, most nations were already involved in the next step in this long struggle, the war in Indochina. On 15 June 1954 the **United States** and supportive **United Nations** members withdrew from the conference on the grounds there was no longer any possibility of a settlement.

GENEVA CONVENTION OF 1949. The **People's Republic of China (PRC)** viewed the **United Nations** demand for **voluntary repatriation** as a violation of the Geneva Convention of 1949. The **United States** had signed but not ratified the convention, but when the Korean War broke out General **Douglas MacArthur** announced that the **United Nations Command** would accept the humanitarian provisions of the agreement. The People's Republic of China that had not signed the agreement indicated they would adhere to its general principles. During the course of the war there were violations of the convention by both sides. Throughout the discussions, the PRC maintained a legal interpretation assuming the terms of the convention that said "prisoners shall be released and repatriated without delay" (Article 118) meant return was automatic.

GERM WARFARE. The germ warfare charge appeared several times during the Korean War. On 2 February 1952 **Jacob Malik**, **Soviet Union** ambassador to the **United Nations**, accused the **United States** of using bullets filled with toxic gas. The **People's Republic of China** and **Democratic People's Republic of Korea** expanded this to charge the United States with bacterial bombs and shells carrying ticks, beetles, lice, and fleas, designed to spread bubonic plague and other diseases. The charges were expanded by "confessions" provided by American **prisoners of war** who were forced to broadcast verifications of the charges. Despite the questionable validity of the charges, the late and low-key response by the United States intensified the emotion and the charges actually caused considerable public relations damage among nonaligned nations.

GLOSTER METEOR 8 JET. The British Gloster Meteor was the only Allied jet to see service during World War II. A single-seat plane, powered by two turbojet engines, it could reach a speed of 493 miles per hour. The Meteor carried four 29mm Hispano cannons. It was flown in Korea by the Royal Australian Air Force.

GLOUCESTER HILL, BATTLE OF. Hill 235 was a part of the defensive line developed by **Eighth United States Army** and held by elements of the 29th British Brigade. The Gloucestershire (Glosters) Regiment held the left, a **Belgium** battalion the right, and the Royal Northumberland Fusiliers the center. On 22 April 1951 a Communist Chinese Force (CCF) of nearly a quarter million attacked along a 40-mile front and the British found themselves facing three CCF divisions. The CCF immediately cut off the Belgium battalion and drove a wedge between the Fusiliers and the Glosters. The Fusiliers, Belgian survivors, and the Royal Ulster Rifles that had been in reserve began to withdraw three days later but the Glosters were cut off. The soldiers established themselves on the hill and attempts were made, unsuccessfully, to re-supply them by air. Finally on 25 April 1952 the Glosters were ordered to abandon the hill and move toward their own lines. Of the 850 men of the First Battalion Glosters, 681 were either killed, wounded, or captured. The unit was awarded the **U.S. Presidential Unit Citation**.

GOLD STAR. This term is used in two primary ways: first, a small flag with a gold emblem in the center granted to families of servicemen who were killed during the war. The second use was to describe the metallic star given to indicate subsequent awards in the marine corps and **coast guard**. It served the same role as the **oak leaf cluster** used by the army and the air force.

GRAFSTROM, SVEN (1902–1955). A representative of the Swedish Foreign Service, he was a member of the **United Nations Good Offices Committee** and later the **Neutral Nations Supervisory Commission**. He supported the **United Nations** decision to enter the war in Korea but did not feel the **Soviet Union** should be blamed for the attack. In 1961 when **India** voted not to serve on the Good Offices Committee, Grafstrom was appointed. However, after several months of trying and the lack of success experienced, he resigned and accepted the position as Swedish minister to **Mexico**.

GREASE GUN. Common term for the **United States** .45 caliber submachine gun M3 and M3A1 that were used late in World War II and in the Korean War.

GREAT BRITAIN. The quickest response to the **United Nations** call for member nations to commit to the effort in Korea came from Great Britain. Following the **Republic of Korea** and the **United States** involvement, that of Great Britain was the largest. The relations between Great Britain and the United States had been strained somewhat by the British recognition of the **People's Republic of China**. Britain's contribution to the war in Korea was based on its defense of the United Nations' goals rather than either becoming involved in a civil war or giving into pressure from the United States. The Labour Party government of Prime Minister **Clement Attlee** faced a challenge from the left wing that drew up a motion calling for immediate mediation, the withdrawal of United States forces, and the admission of the People's Republic of China to the United Nations. The bill was tabled, but Attlee expressed concern over the fact that General **Douglas MacArthur** was pushing the war to the **Yalu River**, and the fact that President **Harry Truman** had considered the use of nuclear weapons. The emergence of **Winston Churchill** as prime minister eased the situation, as did the recall of General MacArthur. But the strain on Anglo–American relations again grew with the bombing of hydroelectric plants just south of the Yalu River. The British government considered this an expansion of the war. On 6 February 1952 King George VI died, marking an end to the long years of trial and the beginning of more prosperous years under the new young Queen Elizabeth II. *See also* HIS MAJESTY'S SHIPS.

Great Britain, Ground Forces. British ground forces arrived on 29 August 1950 as members of the First Battalion Middlesex Regiment and the First Battalion of the **Argyll and Sutherland Highlanders Regiment**. They had come from Hong Kong and disembarked at **Pusan**. During the course of the war the number of British troops increased and at its peak totaled 14,198. The British, unlike the **United States**, rotated entire units so during the length of the war units from several **regiments** served in Korea: The Gloucestershire, Argyll and Sutherland Light Infantry, Royal Ulster Rifles, the Northumberland Fusiliers, the King's Royal Irish Hussars, the Kings Own Scottish Borderers, the Middlesex, the Black Watch, the King's Liverpool, and the Royal Norfolk. *See also* BRITISH COMMONWEALTH DIVISION.

Great Britain, Navy. Rear-Admiral Sir **W. G. Andrewes's** contingent arrived almost immediately with the carrier **HMS *Triumph*,** the cruisers **HMS *Belfast*** and ***Jamaica*,** the destroyers **HMS *Consort*** and ***Cossack*,** and the **frigates HMS *Alacrity, Black Swan,*** and *Heart.* During the war the United Kingdom provided three aircraft carriers (**HMS *Glory, Ocean,*** and *Theseus*), three cruisers (**HMS *Birmingham, Kenya,*** and *New Castle*), three destroyers (**HMS *Cockade, Comus,*** and *Charity*), three frigates (**HMS *Morecombe Bay, Mounts Bay,*** and *Whitesands Bay*), and the hospital ship **HMS *Maine.***

GREAT DEBATE. Following the April 1951 release of Far East Commander General **Douglas MacArthur,** the **Senate Armed Services Committee,** in conjunction with the Foreign Relations Committee, inquired into the administration's conduct of the war. These meetings began in May 1951, sometimes called the MacArthur Hearings, and turned out to be a debate on the conduct of the Korean War. Despite the emotions concerning MacArthur's release and the presence of critics of the **Harry Truman** administration, the committee soon lost the public interest and in the end generally accepted the administration's management of the war and the release of MacArthur. *See also* CONGRESS; HOOVER'S GIBRALTAR AMERICAN ADDRESS.

GREATER SANCTIONS STATEMENT. *See* JOINT POLICY STATEMENT.

GREECE. In October 1950, at the outset of the war, **Greece** provided an infantry battalion, which was assigned (19 December 1950) to the Seventh Cavalry Regiment, **First Cavalry Division** with which they served most of the war. In addition Greece provided Flight 13, **Royal Hellenic Air Force** that arrived on 26 November 1950. It, with the C-47 Skytrain planes, was assigned to the 21st Troop Carrier Squadron (USAF). The 21st received a United States **Presidential Unit Citation** for their work at **Chosin.** At the height of the war 1,263 Greek soldiers and airmen were in Korea.

GRENADES, NORTH KOREAN PEOPLE'S ARMY AND PEOPLE'S REPUBLIC OF CHINA. Stick grenades were of the same type as the **United Nations**: fragment, chemical, concussion, but they were filled in metal heads and mounted on a wooden stick. This made them harder to carry but they could be thrown much farther. The concussion grenades were thin explosive canisters; the fragmentation came in the pineapple style not unlike the **United States** weapon and a smooth iron head like the **Soviet Union**-made RGD-33. Chemical grenades included smoke and incendiary. They also made good use of satchel charges, canvas bags filled with explosives that could be thrown into bunkers or under tank tracks.

GRENADES, UNITED NATIONS. Most of the grenades used by the **United Nations** in Korea were manufactured by the **United States**. Grenades, regardless of type, consist of a hollow body filled with an explosive or chemical agent that can be thrown by a single soldier or modified to be fired from the end of a rifle. The basic grenades available were M-1 and M-3A1 concussion grenades, M-2A1 fragmentation grenades, M-15 white phosphorous grenades, and M-14 thermite grenades. Bangalore torpedoes, explosives used for blowing holes in obstacles, were made of lengths of pipe (about three feet).

GROMYKO, ANDREI A. (1909–1989). This Soviet leader held just about every significant post in the government: minister of foreign affairs, member of the Politburo, president and chair of the Presidium of the Supreme Soviet. He was foreign minister during the period of the Korean War and was instrumental in getting the early **Armistice** talks started. He backed up **Jacob A. Malik**'s radio message by suggesting to the **United States** ambassador in Moscow that it reflected the **Soviet Union**'s desire for peace. He suggested the Armistice talks be limited to military considerations, a decision that opened the way for serious discussion.

GROSS, ERNEST R. (1906–1999). In his position as deputy representative to the **United Nations (UN)**, it was Gross who was available to contact delegates and prepare them for the **United States** resolutions that called upon the United Nations to condemn the **Democratic People's Republic of Korea** as invaders. Because of the **Soviet Union** boycott of the United Nations, he was able to secure the votes needed and the resolution passed. When his superior, **Warren R. Austin**, returned to the UN, Gross stepped aside though he continued, until his retirement in 1953, to be a tireless diplomat in support of the United States.

GROUP. A command structure that was usually a unit commanded by a colonel and composed of several **battalion**-sized elements but subordinate to a **brigade**. Groups were usually used to define artillery, engineering, or quartermaster units, and any unit that might have several battalions under it. In the navy a group was a control headquarters, under a navy captain or marine colonel and subordinate to a wing.

GUERRILLAS. This term was used to indicate anti-government forces. Bands of guerrillas were frequent in the **Republic of Korea (ROK)** even before the Korean War broke out. When the fighting started, they emerged full bloom and were, after the September **United Nations** breakout, reinforced by soldiers of the **North Korean People's Army** who had been cut off. In response, the ROK on 1 December 1951 declared martial law and launched **Operation Ratkiller**, led by Task Force Paik (Lieutenant General **Paik Son-Yup**). The combined forces of the ROK Eighth and Capital divisions and segments of the National Police moved through the area and killed 1,612 guerrillas and captured 1,842. Moving north the last of December, they captured or killed another 8,000, and by the end of the campaign (15 March 1951) had eliminated more than 19,000 guerrillas, far more than had been estimated.

–H–

HAMMARSKJÖLD, DAG H. A. C. (1905–1961). Dag Hammarskjöld, Swedish-born diplomat, became secretary-general of the **United Nations** in April 1953 just before the end of the Korean War. While he supported the **Armistice**, he played only a small role in the Korean War period.

HAN PYO-WOOK (1916–1983). He was first secretary of the Korean embassy when the Korean War broke out and served as the **Republic of Korea** delegate to the **United Nations** Security Council. He remained in Washington to coordinate between **Seoul** and the **Department of State**.

HAN RIVER. This central river flows 278 miles north to south through the Republic of Korea capital of **Seoul** and then west. It was an early location of defense.

HAN RIVER OPERATIONS. General **Douglas MacArthur**'s first response to the advance of the **North Korean People's Army (NKPA)** was to establish a defense along the **Han River**. Starting on 29 June 1950 **United States** planes from Suwon Airfield—the last airfield in Allied hands—flew a series of **sorties** in support of **Republic of Korea** troops digging in. On 30 June the airfield was lost. As the main force of the NKPA units hit the industrial center of Yongdung-p'o and other units began crossing the Han River, the defensive line cracked, and in two days the main line of resistance collapsed. The rapid advance of the NKPA and the limited defense possible by the Republic of Korea Army (ROKA) forced General MacArthur to reconsider his earlier request for troops, increasing from two **United States divisions** to four.

HANGUL. The Korean language is one of the oldest in the world and belongs to the Ural–Altaic family that includes Finnish and Hungarian, rather than the assumed tonal family such as Mandarin and Vietnamese. It was originally written in Chinese ideographs but in 1446 King Sejong devised a phonetic alphabet made up of 28 characters, later reduced to 24.

HARRIMAN, W. AVERELL (1891–1986). At the outbreak of the Korean War, Harriman was President **Harry Truman**'s special assistant for national security. Following a trip to Korea in 1946 he suggested a policy of fairness toward the **Soviet Union** and supported the occupational policy of Lieutenant General **John R. Hodge**, the Korean commander. He was a significant player in the early days of the war and served as a mediator between the **Joint Chiefs of Staff** and General **Douglas MacArthur** over such things as the **Inchon Landing**. In August 1950 he was sent to Tokyo to persuade General MacArthur to cooperate more fully with the Truman administration policy on the **Republic of China**. He tried, and failed, to get the Democratic presidential nomination in 1952 and later served as governor of New York.

HARRISON, WILLIAM K., JR. (1895–1987). When Vice-Admiral **C. Turner Joy** stepped down as the chief **United Nations** delegate at **Panmunjom**, Major General **William K. Harrison Jr.** replaced him. Harrison had gone to Korea in 1951 as deputy commander of **Eighth United States Army** and joined the Armistice group in January 1952. He was a strong anti-communist and hard negotiator and, when it became evident the talks were not going anywhere, he recommended a recess. The discussions were recessed by the **United States** on 8 October 1952. In March 1953, when the **People's Republic of China** softened its position, Harrison led the United Nations delegation through the details of the final arrangements. He remained with Eighth United States Army until 1954.

HAWKER SEA FURY. This single-seat piston fighter was perhaps the best to enter service with the **Royal Air Force**. It had a speed of 405 miles per hour and a range, at 30,000 feet, of 700 miles. It was armed with four 20mm guns and could carry two 1,000-pound bombs.

HEADGEAR, COMMUNIST NATIONS. The primary headgear was the Manchurian-style cap with a flap. The **Chinese People's Volunteers Army** often wore the standard Soviet-style cap with artificial fur, some of which also had flaps. The troops of the **North Korean People's Army** usually wore an insulated field cap or on occasion the lined winter cap with flaps.

HEADGEAR, UNITED NATIONS. The vast majority of the **United Nations** fighting men in Korea wore the M1951 Pile Field Cap with flaps or the Model 1943 field cap. The **Australians** wore the "digger hat," the **British** the "Comforter" or in summer the "Bush Jungle" hat, while the **Canadians** had a fur-lined Field Cap. Most **French** forces wore a beret.

HEARTBREAK RIDGE, BATTLE OF. In some ways this was a continuation of the **Battle of Bloody Ridge**. After being driven from Bloody Ridge, elements of the **North Korean People's Army (NKPA)** withdrew to **Heartbreak Ridge**, consisting of the ridge between three hills (851, 931, and 894), where the battle continued from 13 September to 15 October 1951.The attack involved battalions from the 23rd Regiment of the 2nd Division that faced a previously concealed regiment of the NKPA 6th Division. After two weeks of assault and counterattack, the attack was reorganized into a broadened offensive that would attack adjoining hills. On 5 October, joined by M-4 tanks, the assault against Hill 931 resumed by the 23rd and resulted in the hill being cleared. Two days later elements of the 23rd, supported by the French Battalion, took Hill 851 and two days later occupied Hill 1220. An extremely costly battle, losses to the 2nd Infantry Division amounted to more than 3,700. The NKPA and **Communist Chinese Forces** involved lost an estimated

25,000 men. *See also* OPERATION TOUCHDOWN.

HELICOPTERS. Certainly one of the major innovations of the Korean War, the conditions and terrain of Korea meant the helicopter was well suited. They were used for observation, evacuation, rescue, transport, and minesweeping. It was the United States **Marine Corps** that most quickly understood the value of helicopters and put them into use. The Marine Observation Squadron Six included four Sikorsky HO3S-1, which had the distinction of being the first unit in overseas service. The Chickasaw was used effectively for troop movement in Korea, especially rescue and medical evacuation. A light fast copter, it could reach 112 miles per hour with a range of 330 miles. In the air force the H-5 light observation helicopter and the H-19 and H-21 medium cargo helicopters were put into use primarily for the evacuation of the wounded and the delivery of medical supplies. The army used several Bell Sioux H-13 and Hiller H-23 Raven light helicopters that were organized into mobile ambulances and gradually relieved the air force from the role of battlefield evacuation. By June 1953 H-19 helicopters of the Sixth and Seventh Transportation Companies delivered supplies to the front line for the first time.

HELMETS, UNITED NATIONS. The majority of **United States** and **United Nations** troops were issued the basic M1 helmet adopted in 1941, but with an improved helmet liner. They had a strap to be slung under the chin but the strap was usually worn up over the helmet. The United States Marines usually wore some sort of camouflage cover over their helmets.

HEMORRHAGIC FEVER. This was a viral disease whose cause and carrier remained unknown throughout the war. It rose to epidemic proportions along the defensive line near **Seoul** in 1951 where mortality reached 20 percent. After defined treatment, the mortality rate was reduced to 5 percent.

HENDERSON, LOY W. (1892–1986). Because the **United States** did not have diplomatic relations with the **People's Republic of China**, the state of **India** became the line through which communications could be achieved. Loy Henderson was the American ambassador to India. As a neutral nation, India feared an expansion of the war, and Henderson capitalized on this to push India into a variety of **cease-fire** proposals.

Yet Henderson was also successful in delaying such proposals when the United States did not feel the timing was in its best interests. When he learned that the **People's Republic of China** had warned that they would enter the war if the United States pushed north toward the **Yalu River**, he urged that the warning be taken seriously These warnings were discounted. Henderson was transferred to Iran after which he had little involvement with the Korean War.

HER NETHERLANDS MAJESTY'S SHIPS (HNMS). The Netherlands responded to the **United Nations** call by sending ships that took part in the blockade, bombardment, landings, and sieges. The ships included HNMS *Dubois* that served in Korea from May 1953 to October 1954; the HNMS *Eversten* that served in Korea from 19 July 1950 assigned to a British bombardment group that took part in the preinvasion shelling of Inchon; the HNMS *Johnan Mauris Van Nassau* that served in Korea from January 1953 to May 1953; the HNMS *Piet Hem* that served in Korea from January 1952 to January 1953 and was assigned to the **United States** Fleet, **Task Force 95**, and had the distinction of destroying an enemy train by gunfire from sea; the HNMS *Van Galen*, a destroyer that served in Korea from April 1951 to January 1952; and the HNMS *Van Zilil* that served in Korea from October 1954 to January 1955.

HICKERSON, JOHN D. (1898–1989). A key figure in the creation of the **North Atlantic Treaty Organization**, John Hickerson was responsible for **United Nations** affairs for the **State Department**. In attendance at that first **Blair House meeting**, he was responsible for arranging the emergency meeting of the United Nations and preparing a draft resolution for its consideration. He continued to play a vital role in coordination between the State Department, the United Nations, and other nations involved in the effort in Korea. In 1953 he joined the faculty of the National War College.

HICKEY, DOYLE O. (1892–1961). Deputy chief of staff under General **Douglas MacArthur** and chief of staff under General **Matthew Ridgway**, Major General Doyle was acting chief of staff when MacArthur appointed Major General **Edward Almond** to be the commander of **X Corps**. As a lieutenant general, Hickey was *de facto* commander in chief **United Nations Command** after Douglas MacArthur's recall and until Matthew Ridgway's arrival. He retired in 1953.

HIGGINS, MARGUERITE "MAGGIE" (1920–1966). This colorful reporter for the *New York Herald Tribune* was the first woman **correspondent** in Korea. She went to Korea shortly after the outbreak of war and retreated with the **Republic of Korea** and **United Nations** forces. She was aggressive, feisty, and managed to get places where many were restricted. She was outspoken, challenging President **Harry Truman** and the poorly equipped American army. She was there during the early part of the **Hungnam evacuation**. As the war became more difficult and most correspondents were forced out, she headed to Tokyo. She later wrote of her adventures in *War in Korea: The Report of a Woman Combat Correspondent* (1951).

HIS MAJESTY'S AUSTRALIAN SHIPS (HMAS). At the beginning of the war **Australia** sent destroyers and **frigates** that were generally assigned to bombardment duty. The majority, but not all, of the ships are listed under their own name. *See also* HMAS.

HIS MAJESTY'S CANADIAN SHIPS (HMCS). When the call went out for help, **Canada** sent naval vessels. Many of the most active ships are described under their names. *See also* HMCS.

HIS MAJESTY'S NEW ZEALAND SHIPS (HMNZS). During the Korean War **New Zealand** placed seven ships in service. The HMNZS *Hawae*, HMNZS *Kaniere*, HMNZS *Rotoiti*, HMNZS *Taupo*, **HMNZS *Pukaki*,** and **HMNZS *Tutira*.**

HIS MAJESTY'S SHIPS (HMS). Great Britain's response was immediate and consistent throughout the war. The British generally assumed responsibility for blockade and bombardment service on the southern and western coasts of Korea. Most, but not all, of the British ships in service in Korea are listed under their names. *See also* HMS.

HIS THAI MAJESTY'S SHIPS. Thailand sent several ships to join the United Nations effort in Korea: HMRTN *Bangpakon*, HMRTN *Prasae*, and HMRTN *Sichang*.

HISTORIOGRAPHY OF THE KOREAN WAR. The best source of information on this critical aspect of Korean War history is either Allan R. Millett or Philip West (both listed in bibliography). Generally efforts to record the political and military aspects of the war are divided into one of several sub-themes. The narrative histories, of which there are many, are generally written from a bias. For indictments of the **United States**, see the early account by I. F. Stone or the later works by Jon Halliday or Bruce Cumings (*The Unknown War*) who are inclined to see the communist effort as more legitimate and humanitarian than were those of the United States. Popular histories, of course, run the gamut from excellent to poor but John Toland (*In Mortal Combat*) offers some insight from sources in the **People's Republic of China**, and Clay Blair (*The Forgotten War*) provides a good look at the nature of the fighting. The works of two British authors, Peter Lowe (*The Origins of the Korean War*) and Max Hastings (*The Korean War*), are better books that provide a somewhat less emotional perspective but still tend to avoid discussions of political justification for the United States involvement. T. R. Fehrenbach (*This Kind of War*) provides a military view that criticizes the United States for lack of preparedness and a variety of political mistakes. Generally works on the Korean War are directed toward causes, United States political direction, Korean views of the war, the history of branches of the armed forces (with the marines running ahead in number and the navy poorly covered), the contribution of allies, special operations, China's involvement, prisoners of war, and the aftermath. Lester Brune (*The Korean War*) and Paul M. Edwards (*The Korean War*) provide the most useful bibliographies.

HMAS *ANZAC*. Australian **destroyer** under the orders of Commander Plunket-Cole, Captain G. G. O. Gatacre, and Captain J. S. Mesley served as a bombardment vessel at Pyong-do and Songjin and as a screening destroyer for a series of British aircraft carriers, primarily HMS *Ocean* and *Glory* at Pyong-do to silence guns along the west shore.

HMAS *BATAAN*. This Australian **destroyer** took part in the troop landing at Pohang. Under the command of Commander W. B. M. Marks and Commander W. S. Bracegirdle, she was an element of the first offensive bombardment group near Kunsan and aided in the evacuation of troops and civilians from Daido-Ko. In December 1950 she moved with **HMCS *Athabaskan*** and **HMCS *Sioux*** up the Taedong River to rescue trapped **United Nations** troops near Chinnampo. Later she participated in the **Hungnam evacuation**. The **USS *Bataan*** and the **HMAS *Bataan*** served together from 13 to 15 March 1951.

HMAS *CONDAMINE.* This Australian **frigate** under the command of Lieutenant Commander R. C. Savage was generally assigned to west coast operations. The *Condamine* was called on occasion to operate near Songjin and the north. On one occasion she used her guns to prevent the capture of Tok Som on the Haeju estuary. She later served as a screen for the British aircraft carriers HMS *Ocean* and HMS *Glory.*

HMAS *MURCHISON.* This Australian **frigate**, under Lieutenant Commander A. N. Dollard, was assigned to blockade duty. On one occasion she engaged in an elongated firefight with a shore battery near Yesung from 28 to 29 September, her 4-inch guns winning the day. When the negotiations at **Panmunjom** required a show of force, all **Republic of Korea** vessels and other **frigates** were ordered to the **Han River** estuary where they conducted a heavy bombardment near the northeast point of the island of Kyodong-do.

HMAS *SHOALHAVEN.* This Australian **frigate** arrived in Korea on 29 June 1950. Under Lieutenant Commander I. H. McDonald, she was assigned to **Task Force 96.6** that bombarded the southern coast of Korea. On 4 July 1950 a complete blockade was put in force and the *Shoalhaven* was one of the Australian ships assigned. Under operational order 7-50 the *Shoalhaven* ferried **24th Infantry Division** troops from Japan to Pusan.

HMAS *WARRAMUNGA.* This Australian **destroyer**, under Commander (later Captain) O. H. Becher and Commander J. M. Ramsey, served in the escort and bombardment group and screened for the USS *Iowa* in an attack on the industrial city of Chongjin. In December 1950 she moved with the **HMCS** *Athabaskan* and **HMCS** *Sioux* up the Taedong River to rescue trapped **United Nations** troops near Chinnampo. The *Warramunga* was involved in the attack, by **Task Force 95.2**, on industrial targets near Chongjin and scored 10 direct hits on factory targets.

HMCS *ATHABASKAN.* A **Canadian** 2,745-ton **destroyer** commissioned in 1948 at Halifax, she was armed with six 40mm guns, six squid mortars, depth charges, and torpedoes. She received battle honors in Korea for three tours from 1950 to 1953 during which time she was under the command of Commanders R. P. Welland, D. G. King, and J. C. Red. In December 1950 she moved with **HMCS** *Sioux* and **HMCS** *Cayuga* up the Taedong River to rescue trapped **United Nations** troops near Chinnampo. After the intervention of the **People's Republic of China (PRC)**, the *Athabaskan* became part of a British unit and took part in the **Hungnam evacuation**. **Great Britain** recognized the PRC and felt that any accidental violation of Chinese territory would lead to the conference table not an expansion of the war. The group would move in as close as navigation would allow and then fire at significant targets on-shore and wait for the PRC to fire its batteries. Then the ship would engage, and hopefully, destroy the enemy battery. The *Athabaskan* was involved in the attack, by **Task Force 95.2**, on industrial targets near Chongjin.

HMCS *CAYUGA*. A **Canadian destroyer** commissioned in 1947 at Halifax, she was armed with six 40mm guns, six squid mortars, depth charges, and torpedoes. She received battle honors in Korea from 1950 to 1953 during which time she served four tours of duty. During this period she was under the command of Captain J. V. Brock and Commanders J. Plomer and W. P. Hayes. In December 1950 she moved with the HMCS *Athabaskan* and HMCS *Sioux* up the Taedong River to rescue trapped **United Nations** troops near Chinnampo. She also took part in the **Hungnam evacuation**. After the intervention of the **People's Republic of China (PRC)**, the *Cayuga* became part of a British unit. The group would move in as close as navigation allowed then fire at significant targets on-shore and wait for the PRC to fire its batteries. Then the ship would engage the batteries in hope they could be destroyed.

HMCS *CRUSADER*. A **Canadian destroyer**, commissioned in 1945 at John Brown Limited, Scotland, she was armed with four 40mm guns, depth charges, hedgehog, and torpedoes. She received battle honors in Korea for three tours of duty from 1952 to 1953, during which time she was under the command of Lieutenant Commander J. H. Bovey and Commander W. H. Wilson.

HMCS *HAIDA*. A **Canadian destroyer** commissioned in 1943 at Vickers and armed with six 40mm guns, six squid mortars, depth charges, and torpedoes. She served two tours and received battle honors in Korea from 1952 to 1953 during which time she was under the command of Commander Dunn Lantier and Captain J. A. Charles.

HMCS *HURON*. A **Canadian** 2,745-ton **destroyer** commissioned in

1943 at Vickers and armed with six 40mm guns, six squid mortars, depth charges, and torpedoes. She received battle honors in Korea from 1951 to 1953 during two tours under the command of Commanders E. T. G. Madgwick, R. C. Chenweth, T. C. Pullen, and J. C. Pratt.

HMCS *IROQUOIS*. A **Canadian destroyer**, commissioned in 1942 at Vickers, she was armed with six 40mm guns, six squid mortars, depth charges, and torpedoes. She received battle honors in Korea during four tours from 1952 to 1953, during which time she was under the command of Commander W. M. Landymore, Captain W. M. Landymore, Lieutenant Commander S. G. Moore, and Commander M. F. Oliver.

HMCS *NOOTKA*. This **Canadian destroyer** commissioned in 1946 at Halifax arrived in Korea the first time in September 1951. Armed with six 40mm guns, depth charges, six squid mortars, and torpedoes, she received battle honors for three tours in Korea from 1951 to 1952 during which time she was under the command of Commanders A. B. F. Fraser-Harris and R. M. Steele. The *Nootka* executed the only capture at sea when she took a **North Korean People's Navy** minesweeper near Chinnampo harbor. The ship provided support for the flank of the United Nations Command, fought it out with a battery on Wolmi-do, served as screen with *Theseus*, and served with the deep penetration command that bombarded north of Songjin during 1952. From March to November 1952 she served with the screen for the *Ocean.*

HMCS *SIOUX*. A **Canadian destroyer**, commissioned in 1944 at J. Samuel White, Isle of Wight, she was armed with four 40mm guns and two 20mm guns, six squid mortars, depth charges, and torpedoes. She received battle honors in Korea for three tours from 1950 to 1952, during which time she was under the command of Commanders P. D. Taylor and A. H. Rankin. In December 1950 she moved with the **HMCS Athabaskan** and **HMCS *Cayuga*** up the Taedong River to rescue trapped **United Nations** troops near Chinnampo. She also took part in the **Hungnam evacuation.** After the intervention of the **People's Republic of China (PRC)**, the *Sioux* became part of a British unit. Because **Great Britain** recognized the PRC, it was felt that any accidental violation of Chinese territory would lead to the conference table not expand the war. The group would move in as close as navigation allowed the, fire at significant targets on-shore, and wait for the PRC to fire its batteries. Then the ship would engage, and hopefully, destroy the enemy battery.

HMNZS *PUKAKI*. This Loch class, **New Zealand frigate** arrived in Korea in July 1950 and was part of the **Wonsan** blockade and the Inchon invasion force. Under the command of Lieutenant Commander Herrick, she served as a screening ship for the troops moved from Japan to Inchon. After the intervention of the **People's Republic of China (PRC)**, the *Pukaki* became part of a British unit. Because **Great Britain** recognized the PRC, it was felt that any accidental violation of Chinese territory would lead to the conference table not expand the war. The group would move in as close as navigation allowed. They would then fire at whatever targets were exposed and try to lure the PRC to return the fire. Once located the ship would engage in hope of destroying the enemy battery.

HMNZS *TUTIRA*. A Loch class, **New Zealand frigate** that arrived in July 1950 was commanded by Lieutenant Commander Hoare and took part in the battle of the buzz saw. After the intervention of the **People's Republic of China (PRC)**, the *Tutira* became part of a British unit. Because **Great Britain** recognized the PRC, it was felt that any accidental violation of Chinese territory would lead to the conference table not expand the war. The group would move in as close as navigation allowed then fire at significant targets on-shore and wait for the PRC to fire its batteries. Once they had located the enemy batteries, the ship would open fire in hopes of silencing the shore battery.

HMS *ALACRITY*. This was a **British frigate** that served three tours of duty in Korea under Commander H. S. Barber, Lieutenant Commander N. R. Taylor, and Commander H. A. I. Luard. On 4 July 1950 a complete blockade was established, and the *Alacrity* was one of the ships assigned.

HMS *ALERT*. A **British frigate** that served one tour of duty in Korea under the command of Commanders R. D. L. Brooke and J. R. I. Moore, she served as a screen with the British **aircraft carrier HMAS *Sydney*.**

HMS *AMETHYST*. A **British** sloop, she was crippled near Nanking on 20 April 1949 and grounded by communist shore batteries along the Yangtze River. Despite efforts to rescue those aboard, more than 44

British sailors lost their lives in the fighting, serving under Commanders P. E. Fanshawe and A. R. L. Butler. She appeared on mine "check sweeping" in Korea in May 1952 where she provided protection for the United States **minesweepers** *Curlew, Gull, Swallow*, and *Mocking Bird.*

HMS *BELFAST*. This **British cruiser** served two tours in Korea from June to August 1950 and January to September 1952. On 4 July 1950 a complete **blockade** was put in force. Of the few dozen ships available the *Belfast* was one of the ships assigned. She also served with the **Pusan** fire support group.

HMS *BIRMINGHAM*. This **British cruiser** served two tours in the summers of 1950 and 1953. Assigned to the role of protection of the west coast islands against any threat of invasion, the *Birmingham* relieved the *HMS Belfast* as the leader of **Task Force 95**.12. In that capacity the *Birmingham* was involved in the evacuation of prisoners from the island to take part in **Operation Little Switch**.

HMS *BLACK SWAN*. This **British frigate** served three tours of duty in Korea. A complete blockade was imposed on all ports and the *Black Swan* was one of the ships assigned as a part of the blockade group. She served with the **USS *Juneau*** and took part in the only naval battle, the sinking of four **Democratic People's Republic of Korea** motor torpedo boats.

HMS *CEYLON*. A **British cruiser**, she was in **Pusan** and unloaded elements of the Argyll and Sutherland Highlanders. Involved in the attack, by **Task Force 95**.2, on industrial targets near Chongjin, the *Ceylon* under Captain C. F. J. L. Davis, scored a series of hits on industrial targets when her guns were directed by air observers. She served in Korea from August 1950 to July 1952. She took part in the pre-invasion shelling of Inchon.

HMS *CHARITY*. This **British destroyer** served six tours of duty in Korea. Under Lieutenant Commander P. R. G. Worth, she was a part of the pre-invasion shelling of Inchon and was the ship that deposited Lieutenant **Eugene F. Clark**, who was assigned to pre-invasion reconnaissance on the harbor islands.

HMS *COCKADE*. This **British destroyer** served four tours of duty in

Korea. Her first assignment was with Admiral **William Andrewes** at sea southwest of Japan as she waited to see what the **Soviet Union**'s intentions were. Later the *Cockade* was involved in the attack, by **Task Force 95**.2, on industrial targets near Chongjin.

HMS *COMUS*. This **British destroyer** served five tours of duty in Korea. Her first assignment was with Admiral **William Andrewes** at sea southwest of Japan as she waited to see what the **Soviet Union**'s intentions were. She was an element of the **Hungnam evacuation**.

HMS *CONCORD*. This **British destroyer** served six tours of duty in Korea. Her first assignment was with Admiral **William Andrewes** at sea southwest of Japan as she waited to see what the **Soviet Union**'s intentions were.

HMS *CONSORT*. This **British destroyer** served five tours of duty in Korea. On 4 July 1950 a complete **blockade** was called for and the *Consort* was one of the ships assigned and became a part of the original blockade group and **Pusan** fire-support group.

HMS *COSSACK*. **British destroyer** under Captain R. T. White and Commander V. C. Begg, she took part in the pre-invasion shelling of Inchon and served in the **blockade** ordered on 4 July 1950.

HMS *GLORY*. **British aircraft carrier** with squadrons 804 and 812 on board, it served a tour from April to September 1951. It then served from January to May 1952, and November 1952 to May 1953, with the 801 and 821 squadrons aboard. It was an element of the **Hungnam evacuation**.

HMS *HART*. This **British frigate**, under command of Commander N. H. H. Mulleneux, was part of the first contingency to arrive and on arrival joined the **escort and blocking force**. On 4 July 1950 a complete **blockade** was put in force and the *Hart* was one of the ships assigned.

HMS *JAMAICA*. This **British cruiser** served a tour from June to October 1958. The *Jamaica* was one of the ships assigned to enforce the 4 July 1950 order for a complete **blockade**. The ship was a part of the group that took Lieutenant **Eugene F. Clark** to Tokehok from which he began pre-invasion reconnaissance of Inchon.

HMS *KENYA*. This **British cruiser** served a tour from July 1950 to August 1951, in Korea. She was an element in the **Pusan** fire-support group and took part in the pre-invasion shelling of Inchon.

HMS *MAINE*. This **British hospital ship** served in Korea from June 1950 to July 1953 under the command of Captain S. G. Kent and Captain W. W. Peddle.

HMS *MOUNTS BAY*. A **British frigate** that served six Korean duty tours, under Captains J. H. Unwin, J. B. Frewen, and A. F. P. Lewis, it took part in the **Inchon landing**. After the intervention of the **People's Republic of China (PRC)**, the *Mounts Bay* became part of a British unit. Because **Great Britain** recognized the PRC, it was felt that any accidental violation of Chinese territory would lead to the conference table not expand the war. The bombardment group sailed as close as was possible to engage shore targets. The hope was that the PRC would return fire and thus expose their batteries. Then the ship would engage, and hopefully, destroy the enemy battery.

HMS *OCEAN*. This **British aircraft carrier** served two tours from March to October 1952 with 802 and 825 squadrons, and from March to July 1953 with squadrons 807 and 810.

HMS *THESEUS*. This **British aircraft carrier** served two tours between 29 September 1950 and 23 April 1951 with two air squadrons, the 807 and 810.

HMS *TRIUMPH*. This **British aircraft carrier**, on tour from July 1950 to September 1950 with squadrons 800 and 827, took part in the **Inchon landing**. The *Triumph* was with Admiral Charles Turner Joy and his bombardment group that blockaded the southern coast of Korea. On 4 July 1950 she conducted a bombardment of **Pyongyang**.

HMS *UNICORN*. This **British aircraft carrier**, on Korean duty tour from July 1950 to July 1953 under the command of Captains H. S. Hopkins, J. Y. Thompson, and R. R. S. Pennefather, ferried elements of the **Argyll and Sutherland Highlanders**.

HMS *WHITESANDS BAY*. Under command of Lieutenant Commander J. V. Brothers, Commander A. N. Roswell, and Commander M. W. B.

Craig, the *Whitesands Bay* was involved in three tours. She took part in the **Inchon Landing**. After the intervention of the **People's Republic of China (PRC)**, the *Whitesands Bay* became part of a British unit. Because **Great Britain** recognized the PRC, it was felt that any accidental violation of Chinese territory would lead to the conference table, not expand the war. This group went seeking enemy batteries and tried to lure them into a response by firing on inland targets. If the PRC returned fire then the guns were directed toward silencing the battery. The ship took part in the hit-and-run amphibious raid on Kusan.

HODGE, JOHN R. (1893–1963). In August 1945 the War Department withdrew Lieutenant General John Hodge and his XXIV Corps from 10th Army and ordered him to occupy the southern end of Korea, south of the **38th Parallel**. While he had a fine reputation as a "soldier's soldier," he lacked diplomatic skills and was unschooled in Korean culture or history. Because of this he made some serous mistakes including a harsh interpretation of the preservation of law and order and a reliance on wealthy and conservative leaders, many of who had collaborated with the Japanese. While assisting **Syngman Rhee** during the president's return from exile, the two men soon disagreed because the general tried to foster a moderate political agenda and refused to call for elections or a separate government in his area. Rhee's opposition soon led to Hodge's recall. He retired in 1953.

HODGE, JOHN R. (1894–1979). When Major General Bryant E. Moor died in February 1951, Lieutenant General **Matthew Ridgway** named Major General John R. Hodge commander of IX Corps. He held this commission until November 1951. A brilliant, hard-driving, aggressive leader, he led his troops in a series of actions in central Korea that stabilized the defensive lines near the **38th Parallel**. He was critical of the military leadership of the **Republic of Korea** and was instrumental in preventing the development of 10 additional divisions that **Syngman Rhee** had requested. He retired in 1955 as a four-star general.

HOME BY CHRISTMAS OFFENSIVE. This name was given to General **Douglas MacArthur**'s offensive drive toward the **Yalu River** and his efforts to bring the **Democratic People's Republic of Korea** to capitulation. Unwilling to believe that the **People's Republic of China (PRC)** would enter the war, and later identifying this campaign as a "reconnaissance in force," MacArthur launched his campaign on 24

November 1950. During the first phase there was little resistance but shortly the PRC entered the war and immediately drove a wedge between **Eighth United States Army** and **X Corps**. The **United Nations** retreat opened up a whole new phase to the war.

HOME FRONT. Unlike World War II, very little of the disastrous character of the Korean War affected those resting comfortably at home. Only those men and women who had been called up, or recalled, were really aware of it, and the generous draft deferment provided an easy escape for many. The domestic charges of **Joseph McCarthy** made a big slash but did not disturb the way of life for most Americans. There was no rationing of goods and/or services and what little tax increase was felt was generally offset by an increase in wages. The adults of that age had already passed through the Depression and one or two world wars and did not scare easily by attacks on the American way of life. The young people were often described as "other directed" or even conformists.

HOOK, BATTLE OF THE. The Hook was a four-mile ridge northwest of the crossing of the Imjin and the Samichon River. It was an area in which five major actions took place. The first **People's Republic of China** attack was on 26–27 October 1952 and was resisted by members of the United States 7th Marine Regiment. A second attack came on 18–19 November that resulted in 106 United Nations troops killed, lost, or wounded. The third came on 21 March 1953 when the Hook was successfully defended by the United States **2nd Infantry Division**. On 28–29 May 1953 in the shadow of the armistice, the **Communist Chinese Forces** attacked the Duke of Wellington's Regiment, but the regiment held at the cost of nearly 150 killed, wounded, or missing. The last attack, on 24–25 July 1953, was against the 2nd Battalion of the Royal Australian Regiment supported by United States and Commonwealth artillery. The attack was turned back at the cost of nearly 4,000 communist troops.

HOOVER'S GIBRALTAR AMERICAN ADDRESS. On 20 December 1951 former president Herbert Hoover opened the **Great Debate** over foreign policy that occupied the government during 1951. Hoover stated that the **United States** could not police the world and that primary responsibility for controlling communism had to rest with other nations. He questioned the policies of President **Harry Truman** at a time when **United Nations** forces were reeling under communist attack. Quoting a figure that suggested the communist nations had 800 million people and 300 combat divisions, he argued that the **United States** could not possibly stop communism everywhere. Rather, he recommended, the United States should prepare the Western hemisphere and a few island strongholds—the **United Kingdom, Japan, Philippines**, and **Taiwan**—and not try to maintain armies all over the world. In fact he implied that Asia and Europe could well end up under the influence of the **Soviet Union** without seriously harming the United States.

HOSPITAL SHIPS. When the Korean War broke out there were no hospital ships available. The first to arrive was the British **HMS** *Maine*. Three **United States** ships were recommissioned and by 16 August 1950 the USS *Consolation* (AH 15) arrived. By October 1950 the USS *Response* and *Haven* had joined her. First the *Consolation*, and then all hospital ships, were fitted with **helicopter** pads so they could receive casualties directly from the line. Unlike those used in World War II, hospital ships in Korea served as base hospitals. The Dutch hospital ship *Jutlandia* was also in service in Korea.

HOSPITALS. *See* MEDICAL SERVICES.

HULL, JOHN E. (1895–1975). On 7 October 1953, after the **Armistice** had been signed, Lieutenant General **Mark Clark** was recalled and replaced as Commander in Chief **United Nations Command** by Lieutenant General John E. Hull. Known as "the general nobody knows" because of his years of behind-the-scenes staff work, Hull was responsible for carrying out the conditions of the **cease-fire**. He took a firm position with the **Neutral Nations Repatriation Commission** and oversaw the release of **prisoners of war** resisting repatriation by 22 January 1954. He completed the established schedule and was replaced in 1955 by Lieutenant General **Maxwell D. Taylor**.

HUMAN WAVE (ATTACKS). There are some accounts of both the **Democratic People's Republic of Korea** and the **People's Republic of China** attacking with massive waves of humans against a defensive position. The term "human wave" is often used to describe any massive attacks, usually by the communists. This was not a common tactic.

HUNGNAM. A highly significant port city on the east coast of the Korean peninsula that became the site of the greatest military evacuation in United States history. After the evacuation the city was primarily destroyed.

Hungnam Evacuation. On November 30, having been warned of the impending disaster at the **Chosin Reservoir**, Vice-Admiral **C. Turner Joy**, commander of **Naval Forces Far East**, moved **Task Force 90** into Korean waters. The evacuation began on 10 December 1950 as elements of the **First Marine Division** loaded and on 15 December sailed for **Pusan**. The **Republic of Korea Army** followed on 17 December, **Seventh Infantry Division** on 21 December, and **Third Infantry Division**, which served so well as the rear guard, pulled out on 24 December 1950.

Air cover for the evacuation and interdiction raids was provided by seven **carriers** from **Task Force 77**—USS *Philippine Sea, Leyte, Princeton,* and *Valley Forge*—and **Task Force 95**—USS *Sicily, Baedong Strait,* and *Bataan*. The USS *Missouri* provided heavy bombardment as did the **cruisers** USS *St. Paul* and *Rochester*, and the **destroyers** *Forrest, Royal, Norris, Borie, English, Lind, Hank,* and *Massey*. In addition rocket ships LSMR 401, 403, and 404 were involved.

Evacuation by air was conducted by the 112 **C-119 Flying Boxcars** of the **Far East Air Force** and 10 marine transports and a variety of other transports found to be available. These efforts evacuated 3,600 men, 196 vehicles, and 1,300 tons of cargo from Yonpo Airfield at Hungnam.

The success of the evacuation is shown in the fact that 105,000 **United States** and **Republic of Korea** troops were taken away, along with 91,000 civilian refugees, some 175,000 vehicles and 35,000 tons of cargo. When the evacuation was complete the harbor was blown, and on 26 April 1950 a siege of the port began that lasted until the **Armistice**.

Hungnam Landing. The responsibility for evacuation of the divisions of X Corps was given to **Naval Forces Far East, Task Force 90**, the Amphibious Force Far East. The fleet, supported by ships of the **Seventh Fleet Striking Force**, began evacuations on 10 December 1950, and they were completed on 24 December 1950. The term Hungnam landing refers to the forces involved in embarking more than 105,000 military personnel, 91,000 civilians, and more than 17,500 vehicles.

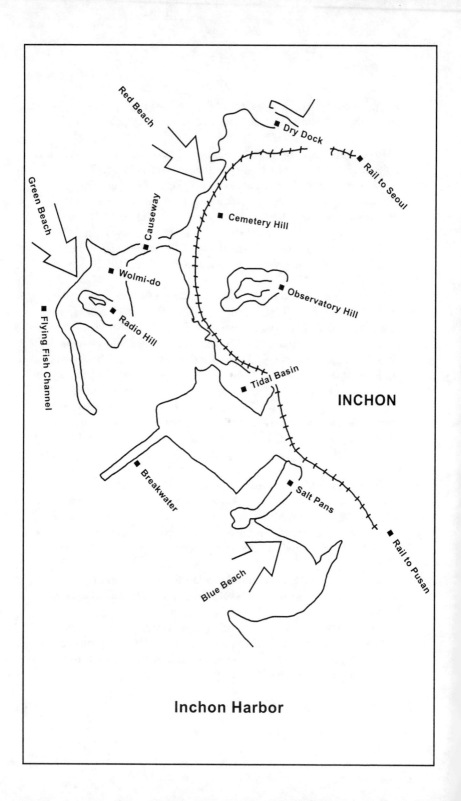

Inchon Harbor

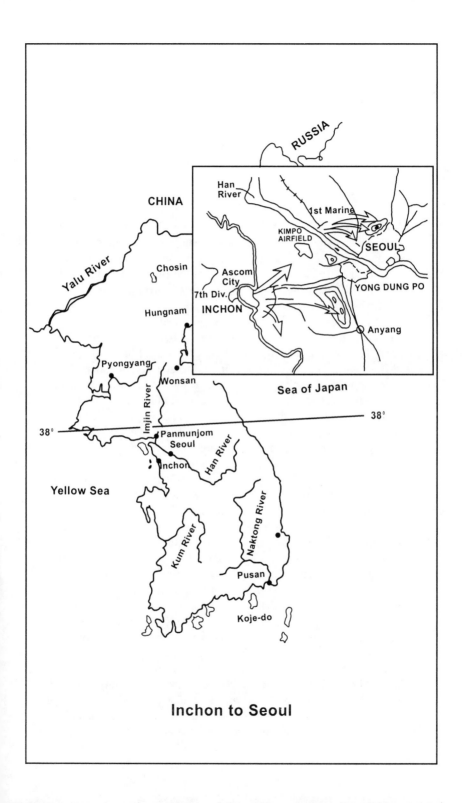

Inchon to Seoul

–I–

ICELAND. Provided 125 tons of cod liver oil by September 1950 in response to the **United Nations** call for help.

I CORPS. *See* FIRST CORPS.

IMJIN RIVER. The river runs for 157 miles from just north of **Wonsan** to where it empties into the **Han River** estuary on the **Yellow Sea**. The final 30 miles of the river lies just south of the main line of resistance held 1951 to 1953 and became a part of the **Demilitarized Zone** between the **Democratic People's Republic of Korea** and the **Republic of Korea**.

    Imjin River, Battle of. The **Imjin River** runs southwest from **Wonsan** on the east coast of Korea to the Han River Estuary on the west. The most western 30 miles became the **Main Line of Resistance** (MLR) during later 1951 to 1953. It was the later base of **Kansas Line**. Because of the location it was often the site of serious conflict. The most significant occurred during the Chinese Fifth Phase offensive from 22–25 April 1951. Defended by the 29th British Infantry Brigade where the crossing of the river made the most natural approach to Seoul, it was the logical point to break **Eighth United States Army** line. While they managed to hold the **Communist Chinese Forces** for several days the battle was very costly, especially to the Gloucestershire. *See also* GLOUCESTER HILL, BATTLE OF; OPERATION KILLER.

    Imjin River Line. At the point where the river crossed the **38th Parallel**, **Eighth United States Army** made its first stand after withdrawing from the **Democratic People's Republic of Korea**. Also called "Line B," it later was a part of the **Kansas Line**. This river area was the scene of some desperate fighting throughout the war.

INCHON LANDING. The landing of **X Corps** at Inchon on 15 September 1950 was one of the boldest moves of the Korean War and the turning point of the first phase of the war. The location, though obvious in military terms, was a hard decision because of the high tides (as much as 35 feet) and the vast mud flats when the tide was out. Combining the **First Marine Division** and the **7th Infantry Division** (about 70,000 men), General **Douglas MacArthur** formed X Corps and placed Major General **Edward M. Almond** in command. Supported by significant naval bombardment and air strikes, the first wave of marines hit the beach of **Wolmi-do** (a harbor island) at 0633 hours. By 18 September 1950 X Corps was at **Kimpo Airfield** and the capital city of **Seoul** was recaptured by 28 October 1950. Eighth United States Army units, having broken from the **Naktong Perimeter**, united with X Corps on 7 October 1950. The invasion strike, called **Operation Chromite**, cost approximately 3,000 **casualties**.

The invasion operation was extensive and consisted of the Advanced Group under Admiral J. M. Higgins that conducted reconnaissance in force, the Attack Force under Rear Admiral J. H. Doyle that made the assault landing, the Landing Force (X Corps) under Major General **Edward A. Almond**, the Blockade and Covering Force under British Admiral **William G. Andrewes**, the Fast Carrier Group under Admiral E. C. Ewen to conduct air operations, and the Logistic Support under Captain B. L. Austin. *See also* OPERATION CHROMITE.

INDIA. India supported the **United Nations** resolutions calling for nations to aid the **Republic of Korea** but it was only willing to send medical units to Korea. Prime Minister Jawaharlal Nehru felt the conflict was between the two superpowers and kept India in a position of neutrality. Still he was willing to provide some support to the **United Nations** and sent the Indian 60th Parachute Field Ambulance and Surgical Unit, a uniformed contingent that served with the **Commonwealth Division**. The Indian medical personnel provided significant service and performed an estimated 2,234 surgical operations. The Indian government, in August 1953, provided the Indian Custodial Force that oversaw the screening of **Democratic People's Republic of Korea** and **People's Republic of China** soldiers who expressed an unwillingness to return to their home countries.

INDIA PEACE INITIATIVES. Indian Prime Minister Jawaharlal Nehru was supportive of the **United Nations (UN)** decision to resist the invasion of the **Republic of Korea**, but he was never at ease with the continued military activity there. During the course of the war he and his government promoted several attempts at peace plans. The first, launched shortly after the fighting began, called for the **United States** to recognize the **People's Republic of China**, end the **Soviet Union** boycott of the United Nations, and support the political reunification of Korea. While neither the **Soviet Union** nor the People's Republic of China was happy with the suggestions, the United States was very upset. They refused to accept "Red China's" entry into the UN as a part of any plan. In mid-August 1950 India tried again, this time in an effort to prevent the People's Republic of China's entry into the war. This effort received no support. In December, India met with a 13-member Asian–Arab block calling for a three-person committee to seek a cease-fire and then work out the details after an armistice was signed. The Soviets refused to consider such an agreement until UN troops were pulled out of Korea.

INDOCHINA AND KOREA. Though the war in Korea and Vietnam are linked as efforts designed to "contain communism," attempts to compare the two are generally speculative. It is often pointed out that both were essential moments in the long and eventual victory in the Cold War. Certainly the war in Vietnam can be partly traced to the **United States** intensification of the effort to control communist expansion and the manner in which the war was fought reflects the continued fear that the **People's Republic of China** would lend its support to the national forces in Vietnam.

INFANTRY. No matter how sophisticated a war becomes it is eventually the infantry that takes and occupies enemy territory. Considered the "queen of battle," the infantry supplies the majority of the fighting forces. In Korea it was even more an infantry war because of the nature of the country: mountain ranges, monsoons, and desperate cold. During the war infantry units were awarded dozens of unit citations, and the vast majority of those receiving the **Medal of Honor** were infantrymen. *See also* ARMY, UNITED STATES.

INFILTRATION. A major problem during the Korean War was the movement of soldiers of the **Democratic People's Republic of Korea** and the **People's Republic of China** passing through the **United Nations (UN)** lines posing as refugees. **North Korean People's Army** soldiers wearing traditional clothing blended in with the millions of citizens of the **Republic of Korea** who were fleeing from the devastation of war. Once the enemy had moved through the line, the infiltrators would organize and attack the UN positions from the rear. The problem eased off somewhat as the line became stabilized.

INMUN GUN. *See* NORTH KOREAN PEOPLE'S ARMY.

INTELLIGENCE. *See* MILITARY INTELLIGENCE.

INTELLIGENCE AND RECONNAISSANCE (I&R) PLATOONS. A good portion of battlefield intelligence was gained by reconnaissance troops on the front line that were routinely sent out in small patrols to determine the location and strength of the enemy. Each **infantry regiment** was aided by an I&R platoon, and each **division** had a reconnaissance company. The **U.S. Air Force** provided aerial reconnaissance but because of military cutbacks between the wars, it was January 1951 until the 67th Tactical Reconnaissance Wing was available. First Marine Aircraft Wing's Photographic Squadron provided much essential reconnaissance, and that supplied by flying boats, British Air Force Sunderland, proved useful.

INVOLUNTARY REPATRIATIONS. *See* PRISONERS-OF-WAR REPATRIATION.

IRON TRIANGLE. A triangular-shaped semi-plains located in the mountain area 30 miles north of the **38th Parallel**. The triangle was formed between Chorwon on the west, Kumhwa on the eastern base, and Pyonggang (not the capital **Pyongyang**) at the northern apex. Because of its location it was an important rail and road center and thus considered significant by both sides. It was a part of Line Wyoming and changed hands several times only to be divided eventually by the **Demilitarized Zone**.

ISRAEL. Newly recognized as an independent nation and involved in both domestic and regional crisis, Israel did not send troops but provided some medical supplies in August 1950.

ITALY. The Italian government sent 77 **Red Cross** medical personnel into Korea in early November 1951. They considered themselves as neutrals in the struggle but provided highly valuable medical help. They operated a hospital, primarily for civilians, in Seoul until it burned to the ground in February 1953. The Italian government rebuilt the hospital and continued to operate until January 1955.

IX CORPS. *See* NINTH CORPS.

–J–

JACKSON, CHARLES DOUGLAS (1902–1964). President **Dwight D.**

Eisenhower's special assistant for Cold War planning, he believed that a propaganda war could bring an end to both communist aggression in Korea and the communist threat worldwide. He developed a plan for preventing the demoralization of the **Republic of Korea** and a public relations plan for "directing" the **Geneva Conference of 1954**. He left the Eisenhower administration in 1954.

JAMESTOWN LINE. A multinational offensive operation called Commando was launched in April 1951 to secure the **Wyoming Line** and control the **Iron Triangle** by the establishment of the Jamestown Line. *See also* OPERATION PILEDRIVER.

JAMISON, ARTHUR (1910–). Jamison was the **Australian** delegate to the **United Nations Commission on Korea**. He was often critical of **Republic of Korea** leader **Syngman Rhee**, whom he considered brutal, vicious, and reactionary. As a delegate he represented the Australian position that the **United Nations**, rather than Rhee, should be responsible for maintaining collective security.

JAPAN (JAPANESE). In June 1950 Japan was still an occupied country governed by the commander in chief **Far East Command** as the Supreme Commander Allied Powers (SCAP). The **United States** used Japanese bases without permission until 28 April 1952 when the **Japanese Peace Treaty** went into effect. After that bases were used by provisions of the Japan Mutual Security Treaty. Concern that Japan might be attacked led to the formation of **XVI Corps** in May 1951. Japan served as a highly significant base for pursuing the war in Korea, especially the port city of Sasebo that was just 165 miles from **Pusan**. Not only did Japan serve as a logistic headquarters, but Japanese industry produced many of the products needed to continue the war.

JAPANESE LOGISTICS COMMAND (JLC). Established on 24 August 1950 to supply **Eighth United States Army (EUSA)** in Korea, maintain stock, and operate ports, depots, and other installations in **Japan**, it also served to administer EUSA's responsibility for occupation duties. On 10 July 1952 a **Korean Communication Zone** was established to assume some of the logistic demands, and on 1 October 1952 a new unit, **United States Army Forces, Far East** became the primary administrative headquarters in Japan. The JLC was discontinued.

JAPANESE PEACE AGREEMENT. During the early phases of the Korean War, the **Joint Chiefs of Staff** did not want a Japanese treaty to take place until the conflict in Korea was settled. But concern over the lack of occupation troops, and the validity of Japanese help, led to a change of position. Finally **George C. Marshall**, who had become secretary of defense, over-ruled the military, and a peace treaty was concluded on 8 September 1951. In the treaty **Japan** renounced any claim to Korea and recognized the independence of Korea.

JEBB, SIR GLADWYN H. M. (1900–1996). The permanent **United Nations** representative from **Great Britain**, he served as president of the **United Nations Security Council** in September. In this position he worked for the recognition of the **Republic of Korea** and negotiations with the **People's Republic of China**. His primary concern reflected his government's fear that expanded efforts in Asia would weaken the security of Europe.

JESSUP, PHILIP C. (1897–1986). This **United States** representative to the **United Nations (UN)** was influential in implementing U.S. policy during the Korean War. He persuaded the UN to set up the **United Nations Temporary Commission on Korea** to observe the vote on 10 May 1948. An enemy of the **China Lobby**, he was put in the same category as those who were responsible for the loss of China and was on the receiving end of sustained attacks on his loyalty from Senator **Joseph R. McCarthy**. When the Senate Foreign Relations Committee voted against his nomination for a sixth term as UN representative, he resigned.

JOHNSON, LOUIS A. (1891–1966). After a stint with the American Expeditionary Force in France during World War I, he became active in Democratic politics, serving from 1937 to 1940 as assistant secretary of war. In March 1949 he was appointed **secretary of defense** under **Harry S. Truman**. He was a strong proponent of cutting the armed forces. He visited Tokyo from 18 to 23 June 1950, at which time he met with **Douglas MacArthur** and discussed the general's views on the strategic significance of the **Republic of China**. He was in a great part responsible for the Truman administration increase in military and economic aid to the Kuomintang Chinese. Under considerable pressure for failures experienced in the mobilization for the Korean War, he resigned on 19 September 1950 to be replaced by **George C. Marshall**.

JOHNSON, U. ALEXIS (1908–   ). An expert on Korea, he served briefly with General **John R. Hodge** during the occupation. When war broke out he returned to Washington where he served as advisor to Assistant Secretary of State **Dean Rusk**. He took the threats of the **People's Republic of China** seriously and urged that only **Republic of Korea** troops should be used north of the **38th Parallel**. He spoke against **Douglas MacArthur** being retained as supreme commander in **Japan** and prepared **Dean Acheson**'s material for the **MacArthur hearings**. He recommended that **Harry Truman** accept the **unilateral release proposal**. He was responsible for coordinating the **Geneva Conference of 1954**.

JOINT CHIEFS OF STAFF (JCS). Formalized by the **National Security Act of 1947**, it consisted of the **chief of staff** of the army and air force and the **chief of naval operations**. In 1949 a chair was selected by rotation from the various services. In 1952 the commandant of the **U.S. Marine Corps** was added to sit in on discussions dealing with the marines. Strictly an advisory body with no command authority, it issued its directives to the president and the **secretary of defense** who, during the Korean War, passed them on to the **commander in chief, Far East Command**. During the Korean War the chiefs were General **J. Lawton Collins** (army), General **Hoyt S. Vandenberg** (air force) who was replaced on 1 July 1953 by General **Nathan F. Twining** (air force), Admiral **Forrest P. Sherman** (navy) who was replaced in August 1951 by Admiral **William Fechteler** (navy), and General **Lemuel C. Shepherd** (marines) on 1 January 1952 who was the first marine representative to be a part of the making of discussions.

JOINT CHIEFS OF STAFF DIRECTIVE, 6 DECEMBER 1950. On 6 December 1950 the Joint Chiefs of Staff directed General **Douglas MacArthur** to exercise extreme caution in public statements and not to speak to the press on military matters. This directive was in response to the fact that MacArthur had spoken out suggesting he was prevented from victory by limitations imposed by the **Harry Truman** administration. Two months later MacArthur issued his **"pronunciamento"** in direct violation of his orders. This violation, and MacArthur's letter to **Joseph Martin**, led to his dismissal.

JOINT CHIEFS OF STAFF DIRECTIVE, 12 JANUARY 1951. This instructed General **Douglas MacArthur** to maintain the situation for a protracted time to give the **United States** and the **United Nations** time to explore all possible diplomatic solutions. The **Joint Chiefs of Staff** refused to implement MacArthur's 9 January 1951 plan for victory.

JOINT CHIEFS OF STAFF DIRECTIVE, 31 MAY 1951. The purpose of this directive was to instruct General **Matthew B. Ridgway** that all previous directives were rescinded, and it outlined the future conduct of the war. Basically it denied Ridgway's request to launch retaliatory air strikes on the **People's Republic of China**. He was to keep the **United Nations** Forces on the defensive, inflict maximum damage to enemy personnel and equipment within the existing geographical boundaries, and maintain conditions that would be favorable to the end of the Korean conflict.

JOINT CHIEFS OF STAFF REPORT ON KOREA'S STRATEGIC SIGNIFICANCE. In effect the significant aspect of this 29 September 1947 report was that, as far as the military was concerned, there was little strategic interest in maintaining troops in Korea. Being forced to withdraw, as against withdrawing, would be humiliating, thus it recommended early withdrawal. President **Harry Truman**, however, did not like the idea of abandoning the area to communist control and waited until June 1949 to remove **United States** troops..

JOINT POLICY (GREATER SANCTIONS) STATEMENT. The 16 **United Nations** members which had military forces in Korea signed this statement on 27 July 1953. It warned that if the **People's Republic of China (PRC)** attacked Korea after the signing of the **Armistice**, it might not be possible to limit the war within the boundaries of Korea. When **Syngman Rhee** released **prisoners of war** under his control, Secretary of State **John Foster Dulles** was concerned with the effect of the statement. Therefore it was released by the United Nations in its report of 7 August 1953 without any fanfare. What effect it had upon the PRC is unknown, but it did work to strengthen Syngman Rhee's commitment to abide by the Armistice.

JOY, CHARLES TURNER (1895–1956). He graduated from the United States Naval Academy in 1916 and served on the USS *Pennsylvania* during World War I. Prior to World War II he commanded the USS *Litchfield* on the Yangtze, served at the Academy, and was with the Pacific Fleet when World War II began. His World War II service included captain of the cruiser USS *Louisville* and commander of the Cruiser Division. On 26 August 1949 he was assigned commander **Naval Forces Far East**, a position he held from 26 August 1949 until 23 May 1951. Admiral Joy served as senior delegate for the **United Nations** at the Armistice conferences. He returned to the **United States** in 1952 as superintendent of the Naval Academy and retired in July of 1954. The destroyer USS *Turner Joy* (DD-951) was commissioned in his honor.

JUTLANDIA. The Danish hospital ship, she was a converted passenger and cargo ship staffed with volunteers. She made two trips from the Pacific to Europe to return wounded **United Nations** troops to their home nations. When General **Matthew B. Ridgway** suggested a meeting between the Commander in Chief of Communist Forces in Korea and the **United Nations Command**, he proposed meeting aboard the *Jutlandia*. The ship was neutral and provided adequate facilities. However, **Kim Il-Sung** rejected the location, pushing instead for **Kaesong** on the **38th Parallel**.

–K–

K1C2 (KOREAN 1, COMMUNISM, CORRUPTION). This political phrase was used by Republican Senator Karl Mundt of South Dakota who supported Richard Nixon's vice-presidential bid. It reflected the growing frustration with which the American people looked at the war in Korea. Candidate **Dwight D. Eisenhower** promised to go to Korea and find a way to end the war.

KAESONG. The ancient capital of Korea located just below the **38th Parallel** and about 35 miles northwest of **Seoul**, it was the site of the first **cease-fire** discussions.

    Kaesong Bombing Proposal. Colonel Charles W. McCarthy, a senior member of the **United Nations Command** liaison, proposed the **Joint Chiefs of Staff** authorize the bombing of the 28 square mile sanctuary granted to **Kaesong** because of the truce talks. General **Mark W. Clark** also felt the area was being used to move equipment and troops and asked that the sanctuary status be removed. The president considered authorizing an end to the sanctuary status but it was not executed because the charges of abuse in the area turned out to be false. In February a temporary abrogation of the immunity was considered for as long as the communists were in recess. However, a return to the talks meant that the proposal was never acted upon.

Kaesong Neutral Zone Controversy. The site for the first **cease-fire** talks was selected despite the objections of General **Matthew Ridgway**. It was located in communist-held territory and considered unsatisfactory to the **United Nations** delegates. An agreement was reached with the **Communist Chinese Forces** that provided unrestricted travel to the site. A circular five-mile security zone was established. Despite communist agreement, the situation was tense. There were numerous violations and charges of violation. After the talks were suspended on 23 August 1951, the **United Nations Command** agreed to resume discussion only if a more neutral site was found. When the talks resumed on 25 October 1951, they were held at **Panmunjom**.

Kaesong Truce Talks. The **cease-fire** talks that began at **Kaesong** on 10 July 1951 were conducted between the **North Korean People's Army**, the **Chinese People's Volunteers Army**, and the **United Nations Command**. The goals of the negotiations were to end the fighting, establish a demilitarized zone near the **38th Parallel**, and to establish a neutral body to enforce the cease-fire. The Republic of Korea announced its opposition even before the talks began. The discussion almost immediately became bogged down over the agenda.

KANG KŎN (1918–1950). Lieutenant General **Kang Kŏn** was the chief of staff of the **Democratic People's Republic of Korea** forces. He died in September 1950 shortly after the war had begun. Known to the Americans as "King Kong," he was instrumental in the creation of the **North Korean People's Army** established on 8 February 1948. He was killed by a land-mine explosion and was succeeded by Lieutenant General **Nam Il**.

KANSAS LINE. As the result of **Operation Rugged**, in early April 1951, a defensive line was created north of the **38th Parallel**. It ran northeastward from the junction of the **Han River** and the **Imjin River** to the west of Yang-yang in the east.

KANSAS–WYOMING LINE. As **Eighth United States Army** returned to the vicinity of the **38th Parallel**, Lieutenant General **Matthew Ridgway** established a defensive line that started at the junction of the **Han** and **Imjin Rivers** and ran northeastward to Yang-yang. He identified this line as the Kansas Line. He then pushed his forces another 20 miles

miles north and established the **Wyoming Line**. Here he intended to keep contact with the enemy and hold the line against attack. Ridgway's undertaking was a significant one, for he was aware that there would be no massive reinforcement, and that the **Armistice** talks would need to establish a demilitarized line at some point. The Kansas–Wyoming line became the primary line of resistance for the **United Nations** forces.

KAO KANG (1902–1954). One of the six vice-chairs of the **Chinese Communist Party** (CCP), he initially opposed China's entry into the war. A man of considerable influence in the **People's Republic of China**, he seemed to have some desire to establish an independent kingdom in **Manchuria**. He later quarreled with **Mao Tse-tung** and was eventually purged in 1950. At that time he was reported to have committed suicide.

KAPYONG, BATTLE OF. This battle was actually a series of limited actions in which the **Communist Chinese Forces (CCF)** attempted to break through the line held by the 27th Commonwealth Brigade. The assaults began 23 April 1951 and continued until 25 April 1951. Finally the CCF determined it could not break the defense and withdrew. A single brigade had managed to hold a CCF division for a significant period of time. The battle was also significant in that the Commonwealth Brigade took many Chinese prisoners for the first time, leading to the belief that the CCF was exhausted and out of supplies.

KATUSA. *See* KOREAN AUGMENTATION TO THE U.S. ARMY.

KEISER, LAURENCE B. "Dutch" (1895–1969). A graduate of West Point, he served with distinction in World War I and in January 1949 was promoted to major general and given command of the **Second Infantry Division** at Fort Lewis, Washington. The division was dispatched to Korea in September 1950. The Second Division was basically destroyed as an effective force when the army of the **People's Republic of China** attacked and it was forced to retreat along a stretch of road from **Kunu-ri** to Sunchon. The attackers held the high ground and in the resulting battle Keiser's group suffered nearly 3,000 **casualties**. General **Walton Walker** blamed Keiser for the defeat, and he was relieved in December 1950. He assumed command of the 5th Division and retired in 1953.

KENNAN, GEORGE F. (1904–). As the **State Department's** Soviet expert, George Kennan played an important role during the war even though he was not always in a position of authority. Initially he favored the **United States** resisting the **North Korean** invasion, but he cautioned that it was an expansion of Soviet influence, not a part of the European situation. Kennan left the State Department after voicing his disagreement with the decision to move north of the **38th Parallel**. In 1951 he was asked to informally contact **Jacob A. Malik**, the **Soviet Union**'s ambassador to the **United Nations** to see if the conflict could be settled. His talks led to Malik's radio address of 23 June 1951 in which he suggested Soviet willingness to support a resolution of the war. Kennan was temporary ambassador to the Soviet Union, but in October 1952 the Soviets declared him *persona non grata* because of a derogatory comment he made. He wrote about American–Soviet relations, often signing his work Mr. "X."

KENNAN–MALIK CONVERSATIONS. There were two secret conversations between **State Department** representative **George Kennan** and the **Soviet Union** ambassador to the **United Nations Jacob Malik**. The first on 31 May 1951 took place at the Soviet retreat at Glen Cove on Long Island. Kennan stated that a **cease-fire** could not be attached to any alteration in Chinese–American relations. The meeting broke without either indicating any real basis for a cease-fire. When they met a second time, on 5 June 1951, Malik had apparently received some further instructions and suggested the Soviet Union desired that a peaceful settlement be reached. He advised that the **United States** contact the **People's Republic of China** and the **Democratic People's Republic of Korea**. It was seen as a positive sign and the first step in the beginning of negotiations.

KILLED IN ACTION (KIA). This distinction was for those people who died while involved in combat. It is a more precise distinction than the word **casualties**, which means both killed and wounded.

KIM CH'AEK (1903–1951). General Ch'aek was the **North Korean People's Army** front-line commander beginning in September 1950. Trained by the Russians during the war with Japan, he returned to Korea with the **Soviet Union** in 1945. He was appointed vice-premier along with **Pak Hon-yong** and **Hong Myong-hui**. He was a major leader in the **Democratic Front for the Unification of the Fatherland**

when, in June 1950, it was given responsibility for prosecuting the war. He was killed in a bombing raid in January 1951.

KIM CHONG WŎM (1922–1964). Known as "Tiger," he was a tough **commander** in the **Republic of Korea Army** and a representative of **Syngman Rhee**. Those who believe that the **Republic of Korea** started the war make reference to his unit, 17th Regiment, claiming that he attacked the **Democratic People's Republic of Korea (DPRK)** early in the morning of 25 June 1950. At one point he ordered 50 DPRK prisoners beheaded. He was given command of the military police during the time the **United Nations** occupied the DPRK capital at **Pyongyang**. He was imprisoned in 1951 because of a massacre of several hundred villagers on the charge they collaborated with the communists. Rhee later pardoned him.

KIM IL-SUNG (1912–1994). He was born near **Pyongyang**. He came to the forefront as a guerrilla leader in **Manchuria** in 1931 when the Japanese invaded. He was listed as the commander of the Sixth Division, Chinese Communist First Route Army, one of the Korean units that fought at Stalingrad. When the **Soviet Union** occupied Korea at the close of World War II, it brought Kim to administer the country. He changed his name from Kim Song Ju to honor an uncle, a martyr of the cause. In 1946, with Soviet backing, he was unanimously elected chair of the Provisional People's Committee for North Korea and head of the **Korean Workers' Party**. He was appointed premier of the **Democratic People's Republic of Korea** and, after the war began, served as marshal and supreme military commander of the DPRK army. He was proclaimed the "Great Leader."

There is considerable disagreement about the facts behind Kim Il-Sung's rise to power, but little disagreement about his involvement in the decision to launch an attack on the **Republic of Korea**. When the **United States**, with the **United Nations**, entered the war, he sought help. The **People's Republic of China (PRC)** entered the war, for reasons related to national interests, in October 1950. Following that PRC Marshal **Peng The-huai**, the **Communist Chinese Forces** leader, would be the primary commander in Korea.

KIM SŎK WŎN (1893–1978). When war broke out, he was a retired brigadier general in the **Republic of Korea Army**. He retired because his outspoken desire to invade the **Democratic People's Republic of**

Korea was used as evidence that the Republic of Korea had been the invader. In August 1950 he was recalled and commanded the 3rd Division, then became the head of the Taegu Defense Command, and later had command of the Capital Division. Nevertheless his failure to prevent the advance of the **North Korean People's Army** meant that while promoted to major general he never commanded more than a **division**. He retired in 1956.

KIM TU-BONG (1889–1961). One of the leaders of the **Democratic Front for the Unification of the Fatherland**, established in 1949, he was chair of the presidium of the **Supreme People's Assembly** of the **Democratic People's Republic of Korea** and member of the Politburo of the ruling **Korean Workers' Party**. After the war he was expelled from the party on charges he was working against **Kim Il-Sung** and reportedly died as a farm laborer.

KIM UNG (1928–). The commander of the **North Korean People's Army** I Corps, he had been a division commander with the 8th Route Army during the civil war. In September 1950 he was named chief of staff for General **Kim Ch'aek** and then became a front-line commander. General Ung was purged by **Kim Il-Sung** in 1958 but reappeared in 1973 as ambassador to South Yemen.

KIMPO AIRFIELD. The first action of the war took place at this base located on the perimeter of **Seoul**. On 27 June 1950 F-82 Twin Mustangs shot down three **North Korean Air Force YAK** fighters that were interfering with the evacuation of **United States** citizens. Later, the same day, four **F-80 Shooting Stars** destroyed four NKAF Il-10 Stormovik fighters. The airfield was taken early in the war but was recaptured in September 1950 as part of the push from Inchon to Seoul. By 19 September 1950 the field was in operation and the Marine Aircraft Group landed VMF 212s there. Recaptured by the **Democratic People's Republic of Korea** on 5 January 1951, it was taken again by **Eighth United States Army** in April 1951 and held throughout the war. Kimpo was designated as airfield K-14. Today it is a significant air hub in support of Seoul.

KING KONG. *See* KANG KŎN.

KIRK, ALAN G. (1888–1963). The **United States** ambassador to the

Soviet Union, he served in the navy in a variety of assignments including executive officer on the presidential yacht. He commanded **U.S. Navy** forces in 1944. He retired in 1946 to become a diplomat and served as the ambassador to Belgium, Luxembourg, and the Balkans. When war broke out Kirk, ambassador in Russia, was an advocate of American intervention. He left Moscow in 1951 and went on to head a variety of anti-communist groups.

KIRK–VYSHINSKY DISCUSSION OF 5 OCTOBER 1951. This meeting was considered the key to getting Korean armistice negotiations started after the initial break, and in switching the site from **Kaesong** to **Panmunjom**. The discussions between the **United States** ambassador in Moscow and the **Soviet Union** foreign minister considered both **United Nations** and communist reasons for halting the meetings. Vyshinsky promised to convey Kirk's concerns to **Joseph Stalin**. The negotiations resumed on 25 October 1951.

KNOWLAND, WILLIAM F. (1908–1974). United States Republican senator from California and staunch critic of the **Harry Truman** administration, Knowland advocated the bombing of the **People's Republic of China**, a **blockade**, and the support of the **Republic of China** in an invasion of the mainland. A supporter of Senator **Joseph R. McCarthy**, he condemned the release of General **Douglas MacArthur**. He lost a bid for governor of California in 1958.

KOJE-DO. An island off the south coast of Korea, some 146 miles square and the second largest island in Korea. It is about 30 sea miles from Pusan. It was the location of the **United Nations prisoner-of-war** camps.

    Koje-Do Prisoner-of-War Camp. The primary prisoner-of-war camp was located on the 146-square-mile island of Koje-do, off the southern coast of Korea. By November 1950, following the successful landing at Inchon, the **United Nations** forces had more than 130,000 prisoners. At the end of January 1951, nearly 50,000 prisoners of war had been located there. The camps were hard to control and riots broke out on several occasions, leading to the loss of life. On 7 May 1952 the camp commander was captured, and as a result an expanded force was sent to control the camp. In the difficulty that followed 31 prisoners and one soldier were killed; 13 others were wounded. *See also* DODD–COLSON PRISONER-OF-WAR CONFRONTATION.

Koje-Do Prisoner-of-War Uprising. This was an uprising by communist prisoners of war in Compound 76 located on **Koje-do** island. The **People's Republic of China** sent men into battle with the express purpose of being captured so they could take command in prison camps. In a well-organized effort they captured the camp commander on 7 May 1951 and demanded their terms be met. The release of General **Francis T. Dodd** was negotiated by Brigadier General **Charles F. Colson** in a manner that was unfavorable to the **United States** and to the **United Nations**. Continuing disturbances led to harsher measures and a bloody clash on 10 June 1951. After that, incidents were much less common.

KOREA. *See* DEMOCRATIC PEOPLE'S REPUBLIC OF KOREA; REPUBLIC OF KOREA.

KOREAN AID BILL OF 1947. Recommended by the **State Department**, the bill was designed to accomplish two purposes: the building of Korean fertilizer plants to expand rice production, and export of rice to Japan to ease the food shortage suffered there. It ran into political difficulties and, on 4 August 1947, the Departments of State, War, and Navy proposed a policy (**SWNCC 176/30**) that would minimize the commitment of money and personnel in Korea. The Korean Aid Bill was withdrawn.

KOREAN AID BILL OF 1949–1950. Despite the earlier decision to end **United States** support of personnel and money to Korea, the **State Department** developed an economic plan that it hoped would make Korea self-sufficient and thus avoid a collapse when American troops left. On 19 January 1950 the bill was defeated. **Dean Acheson** and **Harry Truman** began to lobby **Congress** while reducing the cost of the plan. They also added limited assistance to the **Republic of China** to encourage Republican support. The revised bill, the **Far Eastern Economic Assistance Act of 1950**, had hardly started implementation when war broke out.

KOREAN–AMERICAN TREATY OF 1882. *See* FIRST KOREAN WAR.

KOREAN AUGMENTATION TO THE U.S. ARMY (KATUSA). In an effort to strengthen the reduced **United States Army** units the **United Nations Command** on 15 August 1950 ordered each company size unit of **Eighth United States Army** to expand by 100 **Republic of Korea (ROK)** soldiers. The ROK, in agreement with this plan, administered and paid these troops, but they were fed and equipped by the units to which they were attached. The idea was that a buddy system would be created with the United States soldier serving as mentor to the ROK, but this was not usually the case. The ROK often served as separate units. By June 1951 there were 12,718 KATUSAs. The program was deemed successful and the number increased to 27,000 by the end of the war. The same sort of arrangement was made with the **British Commonwealth Division**.

KOREAN COMMUNICATIONS ZONE. The concept had its origins with the establishment of the Pusan Base Command on 4 July 1950. The idea was to designate an area where ports and supply could be established, and where a command responsible for logistics and refugees could relieve the front line commander. *See also* PUSAN LOGISTICAL COMMAND.

KOREAN MILITARY ADVISORY GROUP (KMAG). The **United States** had been providing military direction and training to the **Republic of Korea (ROK)** since January 1946. The first role was the establishment of the Korean Constabulary Regiments as police reserves. By 1948 this group consisted of more than 50,000 men. On 15 December 1948 shortly after the Republic of Korea became independent, the Constabulary formed the basis of the **Republic of Korea Army**. Under the direction of KMAG, the ROKA grew to eight **divisions**.

The **United States Coast Guard** had been sent to Korea to form the basis of a navy and remained until August 1948 when they were replaced by civilian technicians. On 4 August 1950 the **Republic of Korea Coast Guard** was placed under the command of the United States **Naval Forces Far East**. On 14 October 1949 the ROK, despite objections from the **United States**, organized an air force. While there had been some limited training, it was not until after the war began that 10 **F-51 Mustang** fighters were given to them.

When the fighting began, KMAG became a subordinate of **Eighth United States Army**. As the war progressed, members of KMAG served as unit advisors but the demand outgrew those available. The rapid movement of the **North Korean People's Army** led many to be critical of KMAG, renaming it "Kiss My Ass Goodbye," but throughout the war KMAG played an important role in the success of the Republic of Korea soldiers. When the war ended the ROK had 590,911 soldiers under arms.

KOREAN PEOPLE'S AIR FORCE (KPAF). The KPAF began as the Korean Aviation Society, organized in 1945 using the model of the **Soviet Union** flying clubs. In 1946 the Society assumed military status as the aviation division of the **Korean People's Army**. In November 1948 the aviation section became the Korean Air Regiment and then the Korean People's Air Force, with status equal to that of the army and navy under the minister of national defense. In January 1950 it was expanded into a fighter **regiment** with three **battalions**. By April 1950 the air **division** was made up of about 1,675 officers and enlisted men including 76 pilots with approximately 178 planes including 63 Soviet planes that were provided by 15 April 1950. After the war began, the KPAF harassed troops, engaged in minor air battles, and occasionally hit at United States aircraft over targets in the **Democratic People's Republic of Korea**. After mid-July, however, there was little evidence of any serious involvement. Some evidence indicated that **United Nations** bombing destroyed more than 150 KPAF planes on the ground. When the **People's Republic of China** entered the war, most airfield facilities were made available to them.

KOREAN PEOPLE'S NAVY (KPN). Formed from a Soviet-sponsored coastal defense force, it was set up shortly after World War II. In 1946 it was reorganized as the Korean Coast Guard, then in 1948 as the Korean People's Navy. On 25 June 1950 the KPN had three squadrons: the 1st at Chogjin, the 2nd at **Wonsan**, and the 3rd at **Chinnampo**. The fleet consisted primarily of P-4 Soviet-designed motor torpedo boats, Japanese crewed, and a **United States minesweeper**. The only naval battle took place on 2 July 1950 when United States naval ships ran into four P-5 torpedo boats and destroyed them with gunfire. Other than landing small amphibious groups along both coasts and planting minefields near major ports, the navy was not significantly involved. The majority of vessels were withdrawn to the waters of either **People's Republic of China** or the **Soviet Union** and did not return until after the **Armistice**.

KOREAN SERVICE CORPS (KSC). Commonly known as the "mule team," the KSC was a unit of civilian porters that carried vast amounts of materials (50 pounds up to 10 miles a day) across impossible terrain usually on **A-frames**. Mules were sometimes available, and **helicopters** began to be used late in the war, but the majority of items were carried by humans. In mid-1950 the civilian and ad hoc nature of this group was replaced with the **ROK Civil Transport Corps**, controlled by **Eighth United States Army** transportation officers. Eventually the porters received military training and served as "regular" soldiers. By 4 November 1951, the KSC reached 60,000 in numbers and 100,000 by the end of the war.

KOREAN SERVICE MEDAL. *See* SERVICE MEDALS.

KOREAN WAR BRIEFING MEETINGS. The first of these meetings, arranged by the **United States**, was held in **Canada** on 30 November 1950. Designed for discussion between **United Nations** member nations that were contributing to the war in Korea, representatives from the principal countries met to discuss the progress of the war. The idea was to meet monthly, but meetings began to occur more often. The United States used the meetings to work out political unity for the conduct of the war.

KOREAN WAR VETERANS MEMORIAL. The U.S. memorial to those who fought in the Korean War is located in Washington, D.C., and was dedicated 27 July 1995, 45 years after the beginning of the conflict. Located on the mall adjacent to the Lincoln Memorial, it cost $18.1 million, which was raised from veterans, business, and industry including several Korean establishments. The sculptor was Frank C. Gaylord. On the monument is recorded a paraphrase of remarks made by **Secretary of Defense** Frank Carlucci:

> Our Nation Honors
> Her Sons and Daughters
> Who Answered the Call
> To Defend a Country
> They Never Knew
> And a People
> They Never Met.

KOREAN WORKERS' PARTY. The ruling party of the **Democratic People's Republic of Korea**, it was headed by **Kim Il-Sung** as chair.

KUM RIVER. A principal river of the **Republic of Korea**, it runs 216 miles.

Kum River, Battle of. In an effort to stop the advance of North Korean forces, Lieutenant General **Walton Walker** ordered **Eighth United States Army** into a defensive line along the Kum River just north of Taejon. Prior to the assault, army engineers destroyed the bridges across the Kum and the 21st Regiment was placed in reserve. The 24th and 34th Infantry Divisions were placed along the high ground. On 14 July elements of the **North Korean People's Army (NKPA)** 4th Division crossed the river in barges and attacked. On 16 July the North Korean 3rd Division crossed the Kum and faced the United States **24th Division**. The 24th was forced to withdraw, leaving behind its commander Major General **William Dean**. While not stopping the NKPA, the effort did delay them long enough for General Walker to establish the **Naktong Perimeter** along the Naktong River.

KUNU-RI, BATTLE OF. Kunu-ri was a small village in the **Democratic People's Republic of Korea** at the junction of the north-south road from Sunchon and a primarily east-west road. Defense of this area was vital to the withdrawal of **Eighth United States Army** in late November 1950, as it was the obvious location for a Communist Chinese Forces (CCF) flanking attack. Combined United States, Republic of Korea, and Turkish troops, supported by artillery were set up to protect the flanks. As the retreat continued, a six-mile gauntlet through mountain passes separated the defensive units and provided the advantage to the CCF. The Ninth and 38th Infantry Regiments of the Second Infantry Division were decimated. By the time the survivors made it to the British lines on 1 December 1950 the division had lost nearly a third of its strength.

KUO MO-JO (1892–1978). He became chair of the national committee of the **China's Resist America and Aid Korea Movement** in 1952. He was also the **People's Republic of China**'s spokesperson in the World Peace Council. A scholar and intellectual, he launched constant attacks on the **United States** in defense of Chinese policies.

KUOMINTANG. The political party of Chiang Kai-shek and the government behind the Nationalist Army. On 1 August 1927 the newly organized Communist Party of China launched its attack against Chiang Kai-shek's forces. The battle continued until 1934 when Chiang Kai-shek's forces had the Communist Chinese Forces surrounded. The communist forces escaped nearly 6,000 miles, during what is called the Long March to regroup in Yenan. After the Japanese were defeated, the civil war broke out again, leading to the defeat of the Kuomintang Party, and its retreat to **Taiwan**.

–L–

LANDING SHIP MEDIUM ROCKETS (LSMR). A **United States Navy** medium landing ship designed as a base for firing rockets.

LANDING SHIP, TANK (LST). With a standard displacement of 1,653 tons, it was 31 feet long with a speed of 11 knots and a complement of 211 men. It was armed with seven 40mm guns and two 20mm antiaircraft guns, with a cargo capacity of 2,100 tons. Because of limited speed, it was nicknamed "Large Slow Targets."

LATIN AMERICA. Cuban and Ecuadorian votes were necessary in passing the **United States**-backed resolutions condemning the **Democratic People's Republic of Korea** as the aggressor and calling on **United Nations** members for help. Collectively Latin American nations followed the lead of the United States in the United Nations. On several occasions the United States asked Latin American countries for aid but only **Colombia**, which sent a battalion, responded. Most Latin American nations favored economic pressures rather than military ones. **Mexico**'s **Luis Padilla Nervo**, while not wanting to send troops, was deeply involved in seeking some basis for a negotiated settlement.

LAY, JAMES S. (1911–1987). During the Korean War period Lay was the executive secretary of the **National Security Council**. It was his job to brief President **Harry Truman** on intelligence information and, while he did not formulate policy himself, he was influential in the drafting of National Security Council documents. He retired in 1971.

LEBANON. On 26 July 1950 Lebanon provided $50,000 in aid.

LEE HYUNG KEUN [YI HYONG-GUN] (1920–   ). A graduate of the **United States** Infantry School at Fort Benning, Georgia, he was commander of the 2nd Division, **Republic of Korea Army**, at the outbreak of the war. His insubordination in failing to locate his command east of Uijongbu allowed the **North Korean People's Army** to advance quickly on 28 June 1950 and shattered the ROK 7th Division.

LEVIERO, ANTHONY H. (1905–1956). He was a Pulitzer Prize winner for his coverage of the agenda and the events of the meetings between **Harry S. Truman** and General **Douglas MacArthur** on Wake Island. Assigned to cover the president, he served with intelligence during World War II and rose to the rank of lieutenant colonel. He released information from the conference that suggested MacArthur had erred in his estimation of the behavior of the **People's Republic of China**, a position that led to charges he was being manipulated by the Truman administration. During the Korean War, Leviero was bureau chief for the *New York Times* in Washington. He died while covering the 1956 presidential election.

LI K'E-NUNG (1889–1962). Primary delegate to the **cease-fire** talks, Li K'e-nung had been the deputy chief of staff in the **Chinese People's Liberation Army**. Following the war, he was promoted to full general in 1956 and became a member of the Chinese Communist Party Central Committee. While the **Democratic People's Republic of Korea** delegate was to take the lead, Li K'e-nung was the leader of the Negotiations Delegation Party Committee. While he generally was quiet and stayed out of the limelight, he was a primary designer of the cease-fire agreement.

LIBERIA. In July 1950 Liberia sent 22,400 pounds of natural rubber to the **United Nations** cause.

LIE, TRYGVE (1896–1968). First secretary-general of the **United Nations (UN)**, he managed to lead the organization with great care during this period, avoiding the appearance of siding with either of the major factions. But with the invasion of the **Republic of Korea**, he took an aggressive role in addressing the attack. He was a significant force in the calling of an emergency meeting and in the passage of both the 25 June and the 27 June American-backed resolutions. He favored UN control of the **United Nations Command** but once it was determined the **United States** would act as executive agent, he supported the plan. His position in support of the Republic of Korea brought serious reaction from the **Soviet Union**. During the war Lie made several efforts to come to a peaceful solution, and disagreed with, but lost to, the United States-backed decision to cross the **38th Parallel**. He encouraged secret talks between the UN and both the **Democratic People's Republic of Korea** and the **People's Republic of China**. The Soviet Union refused to recognize his extended term as secretary-general and he resigned in November 1952 to be replaced by **Dag Hammarskjöld**.

LIGHTNER, LYMAN L. (1899–1988). A highly successful diplomat and a major general in the **United States Army**, Lightner was instrumental in the development of the **North Atlantic Treaty Organization** and was director of the Office of Foreign Military Assistance in 1949. Lightner commanded the 11th Airborne Division and then the **Seventh Infantry Division** from 1951 to 1952. In 1952 he became deputy chief of staff for planning, as commander in chief of the **Far East Command** (including the **United Nations Command**) from 1955 to 1957. He also served as chair of the **Joint Chiefs of Staff** and Supreme Allied Commander, Europe.

LIMB, BEN C. (1893–1976). Limb, a long-time friend and supporter of **Syngman Rhee**, was minister of foreign affairs from 1949 to 1951. His prime assignment was to obtain military and economic assistance for the **Republic of Korea**. He tried to warn both Brigadier General **William L. Roberts** and Ambassador **John J. Muccio** that the **Democratic People's Republic of Korea** was expanding its military force. He would later report that no one was listening. After war broke out, he was sent to the **United Nations** as the permanent delegate and later, in 1967, became ambassador to India. He was a spokesperson for the concept of the economic, rather than a military, reunification of Korea.

LIN BIAO [LIN YU YUNG] (1907–1971). He was a member of the Chinese Communist Party in 1926 and commanded a unit of the Long March. In 1936 he was named president of the Worker–Peasant Red Army University (later known as the Anti-Japanese Military and Political University). During the civil war he commanded the Shantung Military Region. When the Korean War began he was first secretary of the Chinese Communist Party's Central–South Bureau. Information about his service in the Korean War is confusing. Official **United States** histories say he was the early commander of all the forces of the **People's Republic of China** that inflicted much damage on **Eighth United States Army** late in 1950. He became China's minister of defense in

1959. He was seen as the heir to **Mao Tse-tung** but they had a serious disagreement and after an assassination plot against Mao, Lin Biao died in a plane crash on his way to the **Soviet Union**. Other reports say that he never directed troops during the Korean War and was killed in 1971 by guards of Mao Tse-tung.

LINE. The term line was used in Korea to mean several things: the main line of resistance that separated friend from foe, the bomb line as the line beyond which bombs could be dropped without endangering allied troops, and battlefield control measures to mark the limit of an advance or the location of a defensive position. *See also* JAMESTOWN LINE; NO NAME LINE; UTAH LINE; WYOMING LINE.

LITTLE SWITCH. During the period of 20 to 26 April 1953, **United Nations** and Chinese/North Korean forces exchanged sick and wounded **prisoners**. The exchange that occurred at **Panmunjom** resulted in 6,670 communist prisoners and 684 Allied prisoners being exchanged. This number included 149 from the **United States**, 471 from the **Republic of Korea**, and 32 from **Great Britain**. Other returned prisoners were from **Australia, Canada, Colombia, Greece, Philippines, The Netherlands, Turkey**, and the **Union of South Africa**.

LLOYD, SELWYN (1904–1978). From 1952 to 1953 he was minister of state for foreign affairs for **Great Britain**. A member of the Conservative Government, he served in a variety of ministerial appointments. He was a firm opponent of the **Soviet Union** and the **People's Republic of China** and the aggression in Asia. He felt that it was necessary for the **United States** to consult with **Great Britain** on the conduct of the Korean War, and he visited Tokyo in June 1952 with Lord Alexander of the ministry of defense to discuss the war with General **Mark W. Clark**. He used his good offices to encourage President **Harry Truman** to accept the **V. K. Krishna Menon** POW settlement proposal.

LODGE, HENRY CABOT, JR. (1902–1985). Senator Lodge, who served in the Senate until 1953, and who lost his seat to John F. Kennedy, was President **Dwight Eisenhower**'s selection to be the **United States** permanent delegate to the **United Nations**. He knew Eisenhower, having worked as an interpreter with the general during World War II. Lodge was in favor of the Korean War and praised the quick action taken. His view during the final years of the Korean War is hard to define because he was against any form of appeasement, yet he worked to persuade **Syngman Rhee** to accept the terms of a **cease-fire**. In 1960 he was Richard Nixon's running mate and later John F. Kennedy named him ambassador to Vietnam.

LOGISTICAL REIMBURSEMENT ISSUE. The **United States** provided the vast majority of supplies needed for the military requirements of all the **United Nations** member nations. The expectation was that there would be payment in terms of United States dollars. The amount of money was not highly significant but the political implications were important. While the member nations supplied only about 7 percent of the ground forces and 2 percent of the air force, the bill still reached about $200 million. By December 1952 about $40 million had been paid. **Canada** and **Denmark** paid on delivery. Only **India** did not make any effort to pay for supplies extended.

LOGISTICS. The ability to collect supplies and deliver them to the forces that need them is one of the most significant jobs in the military. From the beginning of the Korean War, logistics was a constant problem. On 29 June 1950 President **Harry Truman** authorized the use of **United States** essential logistic services. Within 24 hours supplies were being collected and delivered. Orders were placed, materials collected, transportation provided, and eventually supplies were moved across the ocean to **Japan** and redistributed to Korea. At first the limitation of supplies, and the facilities to move and distribute them, made the defense of **Pusan** very difficult. As it was, the logistic system worked well, followed **Eighth United States Army** north, supported **X Corps** in the invasion of **Inchon**, supplied the forces as they moved toward the **Yalu River**, and evacuated men and supplies from **Hungnam** when necessary. The total tonnage sent from the **United States** to Korea was 31.5 million tons at an estimated cost of $17.2 billion. Of that $2,192,461,000 was paid as wages to the soldiers.

LOVETT, ROBERT A. (1895–1986). He was secretary of defense under President **Harry Truman**. During World War I, he organized and commanded a United States Naval Air Squadron. A proponent of aircraft production, he was called to serve as assistant secretary of war during World War II. After leaving office he continued to be an "advisor" to several presidents. He replaced **George C. Marshall** in September 1951. As secretary he was more interested in **logistical** and administrative matters and **Omar Bradley**, chair of the **Joint Chiefs of Staff**, served as the president's military advisor.

LOWE, FRANK C. (1885–1968). Major General Frank Lowe was President **Harry Truman**'s emissary to Korea to evaluate the performance of **National Guard** and reserve forces. During World War II he had been chief of the United States Army Reserves and was national vice-commander of the American Legion. A confirmed Republican, he was also a supporter of **Douglas MacArthur**. Part of his mission was to determine MacArthur's physical health. He found the general healthy and came to agree with the general's assessment of the **People's Republic of China (PRC)**. After the involvement of the PRC, Lowe became increasingly concerned and supported MacArthur, hoping that the **United Nations** would withdraw its restraints and allow him to take the war to the PRC. He was very critical of both the **Korean Military Advisory Group** and the **Republic of Korea**. His reports were varied and often handwritten comments and, in the main, lacked any overall evaluation of the total situation. He was ordered home in April 1951 and retired in May. He believed that forces close to the president had not reported on MacArthur as he had written, and that the president's recall of MacArthur was a mistake.

–M–

M-1 RIFLE (THE GARAND). Adopted by the **United States Army** in 1932, the .30 caliber (garand after its designer John C. Garand) was the standard issue in World War II and in Korea. The rifle weighed nine pounds, eight ounces; had an eight-round clip; was gas operated; and fired semi-automatically. It could be fitted with a 9.75-inch knife-blade bayonet. A strong and very accurate weapon, it had a good reputation with most troops.

M-4 TANK. *See* SHERMAN.

M-24 TANK. *See* CHAFFEE.

M-26 TANK. *See* PERSHING.

M-34. The Russian-built tank, first introduced in 1944 and considered the best tank during World War II, was the primary armor of the **North Korean People's Army**. The **Soviet Union** had a newer and far superior tank, the Joseph Stalin III, but it was not made available to it allies.

MACARTHUR, DOUGLAS (1880–1964). He was one of the United States' greatest generals, the son of **Medal of Honor** winner Arthur MacArthur, and a distinguished military leader. A graduate of the Military Academy, he served in World War I as a division commander, was twice wounded, and heavily decorated for bravery. After the war he served as superintendent of the U.S. Military Academy and army chief of staff. He retired in 1937 to become field marshal of the Philippine Army. Recalled to active duty in 1941 and appointed commanding general **U.S. Forces Far East**, his policy of strategic envelopment proved successful and in January 1945 he returned to free the Philippines as he promised. He accepted the surrender of **Japan** and went on to serve as commander in chief, **Far East Command** and military governor of Japan. When the Korean War broke out he was designated as chief of the **United Nations Command** (8 July 1950). He reversed the series of defeats suffered by the United Nations Command with his **Inchon landing** on 15 September 1950, and by 1 October 1950 his command had completed the **United Nations (UN)** assigned mission.

When the decision was made to move north to the **Yalu River** MacArthur made the questionable decision to divide his forces. The intervention of the **People's Republic of China** proved a disaster. The general was caught off guard and his forces suffered a major defeat. UN troops pulled back, abandoned **Seoul**, and soon found themselves barely hanging on to the peninsula. When General **Walton Walker** died in an accident and General **Matthew Ridgway** replaced him, **Eighth United States Army** began the push back toward the **38th Parallel**. At this point political goals, and thus military strategy, changed as the **United States** decided it was not necessary to free all of Korea but simply to contain communist expansion. Disagreement over the policy, and some apparent—if not in fact actual—insubordination, led to a disagreement between MacArthur and President **Harry Truman**.

MacArthur pushed the limit of obedience and raised questions of military–civilian control when he injected partisan politics into the discussion by addressing a letter to **Joseph Martin**, Republican Representative of Massachusetts. The letter, read on the floor of Congress on 5 April 1951, was followed by MacArthur's release on 11 April 1951.

Following a tremendous welcome by the American people, he addressed Congress on 19 April 1951. His case was investigated by a congressional hearing in what is known as the "**Great Debate**," but little came of the inquiry. Like his father he won the **Medal of Honor** and was one of very few to be promoted to the rank of General of the Army (five stars). *See also* TRUMAN FIRES DOUGLAS MACARTHUR.

MACARTHUR HEARINGS. On 25 April 1951 the Foreign Relations Committee and the Armed Services Committee of **Congress** voted to conduct a joint inquiry primarily to investigate the firing of General Douglas MacArthur and to evaluate the Far East policies of President **Harry Truman**. Beginning on 3 May 1951 the interrogation began with General MacArthur, Secretary of Defense **George C. Marshall**, Secretary of State **Dean G. Acheson**, and others in attendance. As the hearing wore on it became increasingly apparent that most Americans agreed with the policies of General Marshall and, before long, the majority ceased to be interested one way or the other. Little came of the inquiry.

MACARTHUR'S "DIE FOR TIE" STATEMENT. During a press statement in March 1951 MacArthur criticized **Harry Truman**'s handling of the war and indicated that he was restricted by abnormal limitations on the military. While MacArthur used phrases like "military stalemate" and "limitations on our freedom to encounter" it was the press that came up with the "die for tie" statement. Whether he said it or not the indiscreet public statement, along with his later "**pronunciamento**," would eventually lead to his dismissal.

MACARTHUR'S MEMORANDUM ON TAIWAN'S STRATEGIC SIGNIFICANCE. General **Douglas MacArthur** was deeply committed to the idea that **Taiwan** was not only essential to **United States** security, but that the United States had a moral obligation to support the political independence of the **Republic of China** against the communists. In a memorandum dated 14 June 1951 he advised the **Joint Chiefs of Staff** to direct a survey about what was necessary to protect Taiwan from communist domination. General MacArthur made a visit to Taiwan shortly after the Korean War broke out, and in doing so, publicized the difference between his point of view and that of the **Harry Truman** administration.

MACARTHUR'S MESSAGE TO THE VFW. Responding to their request, General MacArthur sent a message to be read at the annual Veterans of Foreign Wars (VFW) convention on 20 August 1950. It was openly critical of President **Harry Truman**'s policies, especially concerning the **Republic of China**. He portrayed the Republic of China as a powerful ally and called on the **United States** to take action against the **People's Republic of China**. The Truman administration was upset by this challenge and feared it would provoke the People's Republic of China into action. Truman ordered MacArthur to withdraw the message. General MacArthur did so, but defended his view and his right to say it.

MACARTHUR'S PERIODIC REPORTS SENT TO THE UNITED NATIONS SECURITY COUNCIL. *See* UNITED NATIONS CONTROL OF UNITED NATIONS COMMAND.

MACARTHUR'S "PRONUNCIAMENTO." *See* PRONUNCIAMENTO.

MACARTHUR'S "RECONNAISSANCE IN FORCE." This term was used by **Douglas MacArthur**, and quickly picked up by his supporters, for his decision to divide his command and send **X Corps** up the eastern sector toward the **Chosin Reservoir**. The "Reconnaissance in Force" was to determine where the **North Korean People's Army** was making a stand and what the **Republic of China** was doing.

MACARTHUR'S SPEECH TO CONGRESS. On 19 April 1951, shortly after General **Douglas MacArthur** was relieved of duty, Representative Joseph Martin arranged for him to speak to a joint session of the United States **Congress**. While he delivered an emotional statement of his convictions and actions, his speech is primarily remembered for the statement "old soldiers never die."

MACARTHUR'S SURRENDER ULTIMATUM SENT TO THE DEMOCRATIC PEOPLE'S REPUBLIC OF KOREA. General **Douglas MacArthur** had made several requests to the **Joint Chiefs of Staff** for authorization to issue an emphatic demand for surrender. Following the success at **Inchon** and the movement north, MacArthur wanted to warn the **Democratic People's Republic of Korea** that he would destroy their country if they did not agree to a **cease-fire**. On 9

October 1950, two days after the **United Nations** voted to continue the war, he issued an ultimatum demanding the **Chinese Communist Forces** surrender in order that the United Nations resolution might be carried out. Democratic People's Republic of Korea leader **Kim Il-Sung**, both premier and commander of DPRK armed forces, rejected the ultimatum on 10 October 1950. This rejection was used by some as justification for the fact that **United Nations Command** forces were pushing toward the **Yalu River**.

MACARTHUR'S VICTORY PROPOSAL. After telling an audience he had a recommendation on how to end the Korean War, General **Douglas MacArthur** met with President **Dwight Eisenhower** and outlined a 14-point proposal. The proposal would require Eisenhower to demand the unification of Korea. And if this was not done the **United States** should clear the **Democratic People's Republic of Korea** by means of **nuclear bombs** designed to create an area of radioactive waste. While the president was not willing to entertain such a proposal, he would later use the threat of nuclear weapons to pressure the **People's Republic of China** back to the **Armistice** talks.

MACARTHUR'S VISIT TO KOREA, 29 JUNE 1950. Following the outbreak of war, General **Douglas MacArthur** made the first of 17 trips to Korea. His mission was to identify what was happening and to make decisions about the next move. The visit was successful in several ways; it gave a psychological boost to the **Republic of Korea**, it provided a firsthand look, and offered the chance to make plans for the deployment of **United States** troops. He landed at Suwon, met with Brigadier General **John H. Church** and with **John J. Muccio**, the American ambassador, and Republic of Korea President **Syngman Rhee**, and was briefed on the situation. He took a personal inspection trip to the **Han River** where he witnessed the massive evacuation of troops. He informed Washington that without United States armed forces it would be impossible to hold the line or, perhaps, to recapture lost territory. Based on this report President **Harry Truman** committed the use of United States armed forces.

MACARTHUR'S VISIT TO TAIWAN. Douglas MacArthur believed that the **Republic of China** was a potential source of military power and support against the **People's Republic of China**. Without authorization he sent weapons and "advisors" to aid in the defense of **Taiwan**.

On 31 July 1950 MacArthur and some staff met with **Chiang Kai-shek** and announced they had agreed on some ways to support each other in actions against the Chinese communists. The action cut into the **United States** plan to control Chiang Kai-shek's actions and was made more difficult when MacArthur suggested sending jets to Taiwan for possible attacks on the Chinese mainland. President **Harry Truman** vetoed the idea and informed MacArthur that only the president could make such decisions and commitments. When the **Kuomintang** on Taiwan offered to provide troops for the fight in Korea, they were refused.

MACHINE GUN. A rapid-fire weapon that fires automatically and with sustained fire, it fires small-arms ammunition. A machine gun can be belt or link fed, air- or water-cooled and either recoil or gas operated. It is usually fired from a mount. At the squad level **United States** troops were equipped with the **Browning Automatic Rifle** (M–1918A2) in place of a machine gun. The primary machine guns used by the **United Nations Command** include the Browning air-cooled, belt-fed .30 caliber (M–1919A6) machine gun. They also had available the Browning water-cooled, belt-fed .30 caliber (M1917.A1) machine gun and the heavy machine gun, the Browning .50 caliber. The British used the .303 caliber Mark 1 Bren Gun with a 30-round magazine. The standard British machine gun was the belt-fed .33 caliber, water-cooled Mark 1 Vickers.

Both the **North Korean People's Army** and the **Communist Chinese Forces** used the Soviet 7.62 air-cooled DP (Degtyaryova Pakhotnyi) 1928. It was mounted and carried a 47-round drum. The water-cooled gun was the belt-fed 7.62mm PM (Pulemyot Maxima)1910 mounted on a wheeled carriage. The heavy machine gun was the Soviet belt-fed, air-cooled, 12.7mm DshKM (Degtraryova–Shpagina–Krupnokalibernyi model) 1938/1946.

MAIN LINE OF RESISTANCE (MLR). The line that, at least in theory, divides friendly from enemy forces. In the very maneuverable war of 1950/1951, it was sometimes hard to identify just where such a line existed. Later, when battle positions became more fixed, the MLR was stabilized and fortified.

MAIN SUPPLY ROUTE (MSR). The limited network of roads in Korea made it particularly important to identify and control the primary supply route. The main route from the source of supplies to the line where the supplies were being used often consisted of nothing more than a single narrow road.

MAKIN, NORMAN J. O. (1889–1982). Using **Australia**'s support of the **United States** as evidence of a strong friendship, Australian ambassador to the United States Makins pushed for a treaty. He was instrumental in the final **Australia–New Zealand–United States (ANZUS) Treaty**. He expressed concern over the United States seeking retaliation against the **People's Republic of China** and voiced his government's view that **nuclear weapons** should not be used. After he voiced opposition to the United States decision to cross the **38th Parallel**, he was replaced in May 1952. He retired in 1963. *See also* AUSTRALIA–NEW ZEALAND–UNITED STATES TREATY.

MAKINS, ROGER M. (1906–1996). Makins was deputy under secretary of state for **Great Britain** when war began in Korea. He was a strong supporter for an active role for Britain in the Commonwealth and, in conjunction with the **United States**, in world affairs. This required that the United States keep its eye on Europe and not over-react to the events in Asia. He retired in 1964 and was created Lord Sherfield having served as Great Britain's ambassador to the United States from 1953–1956.

MALENKOV, GEORGI (1902–1988). A top leader of the **Soviet Union**, he came to power after the death of **Joseph Stalin** in March 1953. It was his "peace offensive" that would lead to a final **Armistice** agreement in the Korean War. He believed Stalin had brought economic ruin to the Soviet Union and nearly got it into a war with the **United States**. He "softened" the harshness of Stalin's positions. In 1945 Nikita Khrushchev accused him of being soft on capitalism and allowing for increasing industrial weakness in return for consumer goods. Under pressure Malenkov resigned and was assigned to a plant in Kazakhstan, primarily an exile, where he remained until he died.

MALIK, JACOB A. (1906–1980). The powerful and outspoken Soviet representative to the **United Nations** during the Korea War. Despite his strict and often dramatic public posturing, he was the key to **United States–Soviet Union** relations, particularly as it concerned Korea. He held private conversations with several **United States** representatives including **George Kennan**, which eventually led to Malik's public address that suggested the possibility of negotiations. *See also* MALIK'S RADIO ADDRESS OF 23 JUNE 1951.

MALIK'S RADIO ADDRESS OF 23 JUNE 1951. Jacob A. Malik, the **Soviet Union** ambassador to the **United Nations**, had been asked to deliver a speech as part of a series called "The Price of Peace." In the closing portion of his comments he suggested the difficulty in Korea could be settled if the parties would begin negotiations. The comment was the result of talks between Malik and **George F. Kennan** of the **State Department**. Later **Andrei A. Gromyko** confirmed the point of view and suggested the parties begin meeting to discuss the military issues of the war, not the political agendas of the nations involved. Acknowledging that the Soviet Union could not speak for either the **People's Republic of China** or the **Democratic People's Republic of Korea**, the suggestions nevertheless opened the way for the **Armistice** talks.

MANCHURIA. Originally a separate nation of several million people speaking Tungusic rather than Chinese, it was ruled by the Manchu Dynasty. It was invaded by the Japanese in 1931 as a part of its attack on **China** and made a puppet state. Because of its significance as an invasion route to China, the approach of troops, particularly American, was considered to be unacceptable. It was the planning site for the **People's Republic of China** prior to the invasion and a refuge for retreating members of the **North Korean People's Army**. Chinese airbases were located primarily in Manchuria. *See also* MANCHURIAN SANCTUARY.

MANCHURIAN SANCTUARY. Most of the planes of the **Communist China Air Force** were based in **Manchuria**, primarily at Changchun, Mukden, and Antung. For political reasons, however, the policy of the **United Nations Command** did not allow **United Nations** pilots to follow planes across the border into Manchuria or to attack the enemy fields. Because the pilots of both the **People's Republic of China** and the **Soviet Union** could escape by crossing the border, Manchuria was considered a sanctuary.

MAO TSE-TUNG [MAO ZEDONG] (1893–1976). The leader of the **People's Republic of China** (PRC) founded in 1949, he was one of the creators of the **Chinese Communist Party** in 1921. When the communist–nationalist coalition against Chinese warlords formed in 1924, he was recognized as an able leader and rose in the ranks. When the group split in 1927 he launched the Autumn Harvest Uprising. In 1934 his Red Army was forced to move north in what is identified as the Long March. In Shensi province he consolidated and expanded his leadership. He again allied with the Kuomintang Party of Chiang Kai-shek to defeat the Japanese but when that was accomplished he led his people in a civil war to clear mainland China. He entered the Korean War in 1950 aware that a victory would bring his new nation international recognition and, if he should lose, he could fight a protracted war by deserting the coastal provinces. He was a powerful and clever leader, and many of his theories on warfare were tried out in Korea, including the belief that if a fast victory was impossible, try for a slow one.

MARINE CORPS, UNITED STATES. When General **Douglas MacArthur** determined he would need to send troops into Korea , he called for the **First Marine Division**. At the time of the outbreak of war the division was basically disorganized. By calling upon fleet marines, and recalling significant numbers of reservists, the division was rebuilt and the first contingency, the **First Provisional Marine Brigade**, was involved in the defense of **Pusan**. The division, still minus the seventh regiment, landed at Inchon. With the third regiment finally attached, it aided in the capture of **Seoul** and, as a part of **X Corps**, moved into the **Chosin Reservoir** area in November and December of 1950. Following the retreat from Chosin and regrouping, they were assigned the eastern sector of **Eighth United States Army**'s line of defense near the **Punchbowl** area guarding the western sector and the approach to the capital of Seoul.

The **First Marine Air Wing** operated throughout the war. The marine strategy for air–ground support was very successful. They provided escort service to long-range bombing and were pioneers in the use of **helicopters,** not only for medical evacuation and supply, but as an advanced combat weapon. Official numbers place 424,000 marines in Korea during the war, with a total of 4,262 killed in action and 26,038 wounded.

MARINES, REPUBLIC OF KOREA (ROKM). The First Korean Marine Corps Regiment was organized in 1949 and had about 3,000 men. At the outbreak of the Korean War it was attached to the 5th Marines Regiment (United States) and took part in the **Inchon Landing**. Later it was permanently attached to the First Marine Division and became, in fact, the fourth **regiment**. The 2nd Korean Marine Corps Regiment protected islands along both coasts.

MARSHALL, GEORGE C. (1880–1959). Army chief of staff during World War II, General Marshall served in World War I and with the 15th Infantry in Tientsin, China. He served as senior military advisor to Presidents Franklin D. Roosevelt and **Harry Truman** and visited China in an effort to mediate the civil war there. He became secretary of state under President Truman and is perhaps best known for the European Recovery Act that bears his name: the Marshall Plan. When the Korean War broke out, he was asked to return to service as secretary of defense. He supported President Truman's decision to release General **Douglas MacArthur**. He retired on 12 September 1951.

MARSHALL PLAN. Named after Secretary of State **George Marshall**, it provided needed economic aid to Europe following World War II. The plan evolved from the belief that nations that were failing economically were inclined to embrace communism. It was design to extend American support to **Greece** and **Turkey**, and to mark the free world borders from the eastern Mediterranean to Asia Minor.

MARSHALL, SAMUEL LYMAN ATWOOD (1900–1977). Known generally as SLAM for his initials, he was a qualified and respected commentator on military affairs. A self-defined publicist for the army, he was basically a valid critic. While his stay in Korea was limited, he used his time there to illuminate the events he discovered and to witness the basic success of American forces. His books *Pork Chop Hill* and *The River and the Gauntlet* deal with the heroic deeds of the American infantryman. He was outspoken in defense of the American **prisoner of war** who had not, as many believed, shown weakness or betrayal. His battlefield study, reported as "Commentary on Infantry Operations and Weapons Usage in Korea, Winter of 1950–51," suggested that the Korean War soldier was much more likely to fire his weapon, and on occasion use his bayonet, than had soldiers of World War II. He continually sought to place a good face on the American fighting of the Korean War. He did have a tendency toward exaggeration and often created expanded explanations that went beyond his first-hand knowledge. Nevertheless, he played a significant role as a publicist of the American forces in Korea.

MARTIN, JOSEPH W., JR. (1884–1968). After serving in both the house and senate of his home state of Massachusetts, he was elected to the United States House of Representatives in 1924. He served long periods as House minority leader and speaker of the House. Martin favored supporting the **Republic of China** in an attack on the **People's Republic of China**. He wrote to General **Douglas MacArthur** about his criticism of President **Harry Truman**'s policies for he was especially concerned that the buildup of the **North Atlantic Treaty Organization** forces was at the expense of victory in Korea. General MacArthur replied, supporting the representative. Joseph Martin read the general's letter on the floor of the House. The letter voiced considerable criticism of Truman's policies and was an important link in the final decision to fire MacArthur. After MacArthur was released, Martin arranged for him to address a joint session of Congress and tried to push for MacArthur's nomination for president, but was unable to accomplish that. In 1959 he lost his own bid for reelection after 42 years and retired. *See also* MACARTHUR'S SPEECH TO CONGRESS.

MASH. *See* MOBILE ARMY SURGICAL HOSPITAL.

M*A*S*H. A film by 20th Century–Fox, produced by Ingo Preminger and directed by Robert Altman. The movie, written by Ring Lardner Jr. and starring Elliot Gould, Donald Sutherland, and Sally Kellerman, takes place in Korea, but it was written as a protest against the anti-cultural wars that the **United States** was fighting on the Asian mainland. Filmed as a comedy, and later as a television series, it nevertheless has become an unintended image for the Korean War.

MATTHEWS, FRANCIS P. (1887–1952). Secretary of the navy, he was known as the "rowboat secretary," because that was the only craft he ever commanded. While he led the effort to cut naval funds during the early years of President **Harry Truman**'s austerity program, he presided over a rapidly expanding navy once the Korean War broke out. On 25 August 1950 he disturbed Truman and the **State Department** by suggesting in a speech that the **United States** launch a preventive war. In 1951 he was released as secretary of the navy and appointed as ambassador to Ireland.

MATTHEWS, H. FREEMAN (1899–1986). A career diplomat, he was appointed as **Dean Acheson**'s deputy under secretary of state. It was his suggestion that led to the informal approach between **George F. Kennan** and **Jacob A. Malik** and Malik's eventual radio address on 23 June 1951 proposing both sides pursue a **cease-fire** and **armistice**.

MCCARTHY, JOSEPH RAYMOND (1909–1957). Elected to the United States Senate in 1946 from Wisconsin on the Republican ticket, McCarthy rose to considerable prominence by proclaiming that the government, particularly the **State Department**, was infiltrated by communists. He supported the war in Korea as a war against communism but was very critical of President **Harry Truman** for his restrictive policies and for allowing **Great Britain** so much influence. McCarthy demanded Truman's impeachment over the firing of General **Douglas MacArthur**. His unfounded and undocumented accusations ran rampant causing a great deal of fear and led to the departure of many of those with long service and expertise on Chinese affairs. His efforts fed the "Red Scare," and his attacks resulted in an over-reaction by the American people. When he attacked the army in 1954, Secretary of the Army Robert Stevens turned on him and used legal counsel to uncover distortions and lies. McCarthy's power began to diminish and he was censured by the Senate in 1954.

MCCLURE, ROBERT A. (1897–1957). During World War II, Major General Robert A. McClure served as chief of intelligence and chief of the Psychological Warfare Division. During the Korean War, he was chief of the United States Army Psychological Warfare Division. He voiced concern over soldiers from the **Republic of China** who were **prisoners of war** and felt that providing for the voluntary repatriation of POWs would encourage Chinese soldiers to surrender. His concern was expressed in the **Panmunjom** meetings and rejected by the Chinese. He then suggested that a political conference, convened after the end of the war, be called to deal with POW asylum. The POW issue continued to be a critical item on the **cease-fire** agenda.

"MEAT GRINDER" STRATEGY. This was the term given to Lieutenant General **Matthew Ridgway**'s plan to inflict maximum casualties on the **Communist Chinese Forces (CCF)** while allowing the smallest amount of **United Nations Command casualties** possible. It consisted of well-defended probes, territorial advances, and concentrated **artillery** attacks. His hope was that the policy would make it too costly for the CCF to continue. Only marginally effective, the policy did not force the

CCF into a withdrawal or to express more flexibility at the negotiation table, and it drew considerable criticism for its "brutality."

MEDAL OF HONOR. This great honor has been awarded since the United States Civil War and is given by the president in the name of the **Congress** to members of the Armed Forces who show conspicuous gallantry and bravery involving the risk of life. It is the highest decoration given by the **United States**. During the Korean War 131 Medals of Honor were awarded: army 78, marines 42, navy 7, and air force 4 (93 of these were awarded posthumously).

MEDIA. By 5 July 1950, when American troops began service in Korea, more than 70 reporters were there. The number rose to 238 by 1 September 1950 and at one time was as high as 270. The television industry was just beginning, so the coverage of the war was primarily print journalism with some "bites" of coverage thrown in. Press **censorship** was imposed (urged as much by the press as by the military) on 20 December 1950 and remained in effect until the war ended. The Korean War received "bad press" in terms of exaggerations, moody reporting, and a sense of apathy. Nevertheless 10 American **correspondents** died during the fighting. Perhaps the best-known correspondent, because she was breaking new ground, was *New York Herald Tribune* correspondent **Marguerite Higgins**. Perhaps the most infamous in the United States was the fact that Australian correspondent Wilfred Burchett and British correspondent Alan Winnington reported the war from the enemy strongholds.

MEDICAL EVACUATION. The percentage of wounds that proved fatal was reduced from 28 percent in World War II to 22 percent during the Korean War. This was due in large measure to improved methods of evacuation. Studies in both World Wars I and II proved that the time lag between being wounded and being treated was directly related to the number who died. The greatest innovation was the use of the **helicopter**. Immediate evacuation was still by litter but increasingly extended evacuation was done by helicopter. The medial evacuation was almost totally by air force and marine corps helicopters until in January 1951 an agreement was worked out so the army could provided aeromedical evacuation forward of its **Mobile Army Surgical Hospitals**, while air force transports provided medical air evacuation to hospitals at sea, in **Japan** and in the **United States**. The 801st Medical Air Evacuation

Squadron, and its successor (the 6481st Medical Air Evacuation Group), transported 311,673 sick and wounded to area hospitals and 43,196 to the United States.

MEDICAL INNOVATIONS. The percentage of wounded who died in hospitals dropped from 4.5 in World War II to 2.5 in Korea. This was due in part to improved **medical evacuation** methods and in part to medical innovations. Pioneering work in vascular surgery reduced the amputation rate for brachial wounds from 35 percent to zero, for femoral wounds from 61 to 4.8, and for popliteal wounds from 73 to 18. Other innovations included the use of plastic bags and bottles for intravenous solutions and blood. Another innovation was the treatment of battle fatigue in a manner that no longer considered it a psychological problem and treated it with rest, diet, and care at regimental stations. The recovery rate was far greater than in World Wars I and II.

MEMORIAL, KOREAN WAR VETERANS. *See* KOREAN WAR VETERANS MEMORIAL.

MENON, K. P. S. (1898–1982). India's member and chair of **United Nations Temporary Commission on Korea** (UNTCOK), he shared the assignment with representatives from **Australia, Canada**, the **Republic of China, El Salvador, France**, the **Philippines**, and Syria. Its mission was to prepare for the withdrawal of foreign troops, the supervision of elections, and the creation of a unified government in Korea. Without the cooperation of the **Soviet Union** there was little chance of success, and Menon was convinced that **Syngman Rhee**'s election would further aggravate the division or perhaps lead to a civil war. After submitting their report, the Koreans were pressed by the **United States** and **Great Britain** to accept elections in the south and eventually Menon supported separate elections. He resigned from the chair prior to the May 1948 election.

MENON, POW SETTLEMENT PROPOSAL. *See* MENON, V. K. KRISHNA.

MENON, V. K. KRISHNA (1896–1974). A friend of **India**'s Prime Minister Jawaharlal Nehru, he was appointed as the high commissioner in London. He was known for his fierce nationalism and for his efforts to keep India nonaligned in foreign policy. During the Korean War, he worked to keep the conflict confined while attempting to bring the nations to the bargaining table. Late in 1952 he presented a settlement proposal that, after some modifications, provided the foundation for the 8 June 1953 **prisoner-of-war** repatriation agreement. He was responsible, once the proposed Korean political conference failed to materialize, for the suggestion that non-repatriated prisoners be returned to their original custodians and released.

MENZIES, ROBERT G. (1894–1978). He, and his Australian government, considered the Korean War as a significant part of the struggle against international communism. As prime minister of **Australia** as of 1947 he committed Australian air and naval forces. At first Australia, like **Great Britain**, was reluctant to commit ground forces but did so realizing that the Australian commitment was closely related to the completion of the 1951 **Australia–New Zealand–United States Treaty**. He reflected concern over an expansion of the war but was a strong ally to the United States and the **United Nations** effort.

MERITORIOUS UNIT COMMENDATIONS. This award was given to a unit and worn by members of the unit for outstanding service. Each service awarded commendations, and each had distinct emblems and requirements. For the navy, it was awarded to combat or non-combat units with the same requirements as the Bronze Star for individuals. It consisted of a green ribbon with blue, gold, and red stripes. The army granted it for six months of outstanding service against an enemy with the requirements the same as for the Legion of Merit. The **Army Commendation** was first indicated by a cloth gold wreath worn on the sleeve but replaced with a red ribbon encased in a gold frame. The Air Force Unit Commendation consisted of a blue ribbon with white and red stripes and was awarded for combat or non-combat service.

MEXICAN POW SETTLEMENT PROPOSAL. While **Mexico** continued to avoid the involvement of troops, it did support the **United States** in the diplomatic arena. One of the most significant was Mexico's proposal for breaking the dispute over the repatriation of **prisoners of war**. It proposed a plan that recognized voluntary repatriation but those who refused would be given immigrant status. For those who changed their minds and wished to be returned to their country of origin, they could do so under the direction of the **United Nations**. While the plan never came to an official vote it did help to promote an eventual solution to the problem. *See also* PADILLA NERVO, LUIS.

MEXICO. It never signed a military assistance pact nor did it provide troops for **United Nations** operations in Korea. However, Mexico supported the **United States** on the three major resolutions relating to the war. In addition, Mexico was very active in efforts to achieve a negotiated settlement in Korea.

MiG-15. Russian-built swept-wing jet fighter that appeared in Korea in November 1950. It was sufficiently faster than American planes.

MiG ALLEY. A portion of northwest Korea, roughly between the **Yalu River** and Sinanju, it was given this name because it was where **Soviet Union** pilots gathered to attack **United States B-29 bombers** on the way to the **Yalu River** bridges. For a brief period around January 1951, the United States lost air superiority. The **MiG-15** was a very effective plane, and during the year January 1951/1952, the **United States** lost more than 600 bombers and fighter planes. The increasing allocation of **F-86 Sabre** jets eventually began to make a difference.

MILBURN, FRANK W. (1892–1962). A West Point graduate of 1914, he rose to the rank of major general and commander of XXI Corps in Europe. When war broke out in Korea, Milburn, who was deputy commander of American forces in Germany, was sent to Korea where he was given command of **I Corps**. He successfully pulled out of **Pusan** and moved north against the **Democratic People's Republic of Korea** until he reached the Chongchon River. There the **People's Republic of China** attacked and **Eighth United States Army** pulled back. Lieutenant General **Matthew Ridgway** promoted him to lieutenant general. Ridgway, apparently concerned about Milburn's aggressiveness, established his command post with I Corps. Milburn returned to the United States in 1951 and retired in May of 1952. Later he was instrumental in developing the code of conduct for American military personnel captured and held as **prisoners of war**.

MILITARY AIR TRANSPORT SERVICE (MATS). Created on 1 June 1948 by a merger of the Air Transport Command and the Naval Air Transport Service, MATS was under the command of the chief of staff of the **United States Air Force**. The command met the challenge of the

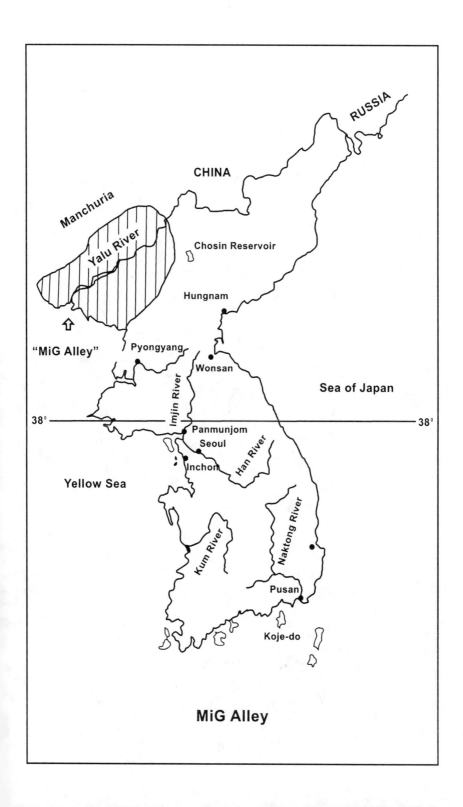

MiG Alley

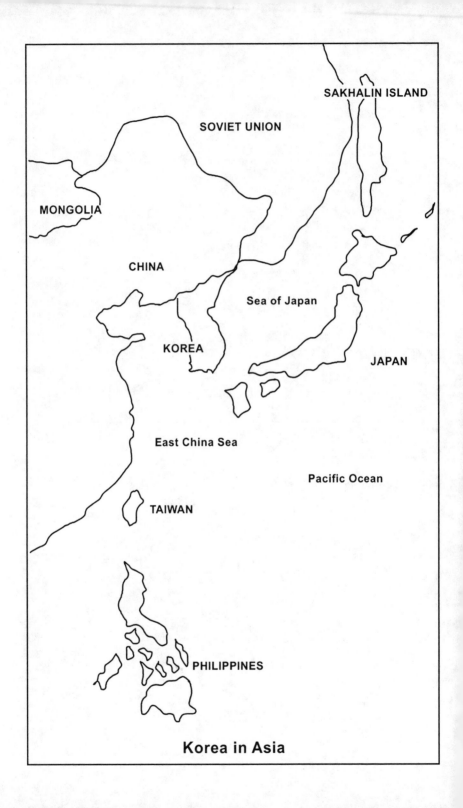

Korea in Asia

1948–1949 Berlin Air Lift during which more than 1.8 million tons of supplies were delivered by MATS. In Korea it provided supplies that traveled nearly 11,000 airline miles and in three years delivered 80,000 tons of cargo and 214,000 combat and support troops. Major General **William H. Turner** arrived to take command with 250 primarily **C-119 Flying Boxcars** and some **C-47**s taken out of storage. Among the first units airlifted were the **187th Airborne Regiment** and portions of the **First Marine Division**. In 1966 MATS was reorganized as the Military Airlift Command.

MILITARY ARMISTICE COMMISSION (MAC). This was the primary agency responsible for maintaining the **cease-fire**. The existence of such a commission was on the **United States** agenda from the beginning, feeling that it was necessary to preserve peace in Korea. The compromise agreement identified five officers from each side with instructions to be sure that neither side exploited the **Armistice** as a means to prepare for a resumption of the war. Despite the efforts, members were unable to either cooperate with each other or find a means to deal with the violations that were charged. Despite this, the commission has met on a regular basis since 28 July 1953 and other than exchanging insults and complaints has served as a means of communication between the two sides.

MILITARY INTELLIGENCE. There was no separate intelligence branch of the army until after the Korean War. Those servicing in intelligence positions (S-2 or G-2) were often untrained. In the field **prisoner-of-war** interrogation was a primary source of information and this source was considerably hampered by the limited number of Korean speakers available. Much intelligence was gathered by ground patrols or aerial overflights. The army used L-5 light planes for visual and photo reconnaissance. The **Army Security Agency** (ASA)—which became the **National Security Agency** in 1952—provided communication security and surveillance. The failure of intelligence during the Korean War was primarily at the national and international level, and most field units had a good reputation. During the war these units received 14 Meritorious Unit Citations and 14 **Presidential Unit Citations (ROK)**.

MILITARY POLICE (MP). Each division in the army had a military police company and several separate MP companies and battalions saw service in Korea. The primary roles were defined as traffic control, refugee control, **prisoner-of-war** control, and rear-area security. While all missions were important, the control of refugees turned out to be a significant difficulty. To deal with the expanding POW problem the 8137th MP Group was established in October 1951. The MP units provided both stationary and roving patrols.

MILITARY SEA TRANSPORT SERVICE (MSTS). During the Korean War the vast majority of troops and supplies were moved the 4,914 nautical miles from San Francisco to **Pusan** by ship. In October 1949 the Naval Transportation Service and the Army Transportation Corps were absorbed into the Military Sea Transport Service and established as a unified logistic organization by the **National Security Act of 1947**. The new unit was made up of civil service-staffed **United States** naval transport and cargo ships, commercially chartered vessels, and oil tankers from the **Defense Department**'s Military Petroleum Supply agency. The MSTS took control of Shipping Control Administration Japan (SCAJAP), which had a fleet of 12 freighters and 39 Landing Ship Tanks (LST). During the war the MSTS moved 52,111,299 measured tons of cargo; 21,828,879 long tons of petroleum; and 4,918,919 passengers.

MINES. This was an explosive encased in a plastic or metal container and designed to go off on contact or over the passage of time. Mines were made as anti-personnel, anti-vehicle, and anti-shipping devices. Sea mines played a significant part in the Korean War, preventing the **United States Navy** from moving where it wanted, when it wanted. *See also* MINESWEEPER.

MINES, BATTLE OF THE. The name given to the prolonged mine-sweeping activity in **Wonsan Harbor** during October 1950. Following the landing at **Inchon** and the relief of Seoul, General **Douglas MacArthur** planned to move **X Corps** to Wonsan. The advanced party found the harbor heavily mined. Mine Squadron, under Captain Richard T. Spofford, began a clearing operation. Hindered by shore batteries and facing an extremely large number of mines, the sweeping operation employed several new tactics including helicopter spotting and bombing. During the operation the sweepers *Pirate* and *Pledge* hit mines and sunk. The operation took until 25 October, by which time the **Republic of Korea** I Corps had captured the city.

MINESWEEPER. These were ships designed for the purpose of locating and exploding or removing **sea mines**. During the late 1940s most **United States** minesweepers were decommissioned. However, special ships, either metal or wood, designed for this task were in operation in Korea by September 1950. *See also* OPERATION YO–YO, WONSAN HARBOR.

MISSING IN ACTION (MIA). This term is used to define those who cannot be accounted for and, often, are later identified as **Killed in Action**. While the **United States** government has made a focused effort to identify all MIAs there are still, in 2001, more than 8,000 Korean War MIAs for which there is no accounting.

MOBILE ARMY SURGICAL HOSPITALS (MASH). The MASH system, a **medical evacuation** system developed during the Korean War, was responsible for saving many lives during the period. The MASH unit moved quickly, setting up and down like a circus outfit, and stayed as close to the frontline as possible. Patients received all the care they could and then were evacuated to hospital ships for further care and recovery. While the movie *M*A*S*H* (and the television series) was set in Korea and popularized the unit, the themes, problems, and responses of the characters in MASH were addressing the war in Vietnam, not Korea.

MOBILIZATION. The United States was not combat ready for the war in Korea. The military had been cut so deeply that the **divisions** given to **Douglas MacArthur** for the war in Korea had two, rather than three, units at each level. To meet the need, the general reserves had been cut drastically and so on 27 July 1950 **Congress** authorized the extension of enlistments by one year. The **Selective Service System** issued a call for 50,000 draftees. The **U.S. Marine Corps**, cut even more drastically, had only 74,279 men on active duty and marines were called up from reserve. Congress passed the Selective Service Extension Act of 1950 that allowed the president to call up Organized Reserve Corps and **National Guard** units into active service for 21 months. During the war more than 77 percent of the enlisted marine personnel, and 99 percent of the officers, were World War II veterans. The aviation units of the marines called up 6,341 from the reserves. The navy called the USS *Princeton, Bon Homme Richard, Essex,* and *Antietam* from mothballs and staffed them with largely reserve crews and sent them to Korea.

Twenty-two naval reserve fighter squadrons went with them. The air force recalled 145 **F-51 Mustang** fighters from the **Air National Guard** and more than 100,000 individual air force reservists. Beginning on 14 August 1950, eight army national guard divisions were called up—28th, 31st, 37th, 40th, 43rd, 44th, 45th, and 47th infantry—with three regimental combat teams, and 43 antiaircraft artillery battalions.

MOLOTOV, VYACHESLAV M. (1890–1986). He served as the **Soviet Union** foreign minister from 1939 to 1949 and then again after the death of **Joseph Stalin** in 1953. He held the office during the final stages of the **Armistice** negotiations. He was the Russian delegate to the **People's Republic of China** leaders meeting in August 1950 to discuss plans in case the **United States** crossed the **38th Parallel**.

"MORAL BREAKDOWN." A thesis established by psychiatrist William E. Mayer and journalist Eugene Kinkead that claimed American soldiers were weak and acted disloyally in allowing themselves to be captured. It received considerable attention in the popular press, staining the reputation of Korean veterans.

MORRISON, HERBERT (1888–1965). British foreign secretary from March to September 1951. He was generally unsuited to the job, and his lack of experience in foreign affairs was a source of some friction between the **United States** and **Great Britain**. While Morrison favored giving the **United Nations Command** the right to retaliate against Manchurian bases in case of a sudden or prolonged attack, he did so assuming consultation with the British.

MORTARS. A high-angle weapon carried by the **United States infantry**. A **company** was equipped with three 60mm mortars, a **battalion** with three 81mm mortars, and each **regiment** with six 4.2-inch (107mm) heavy mortars. **Commonwealth** troops carried a 3-inch mortar and the United States Second Chemical Mortar Battalion was equipped with three 4.2-inch mortars. The **North Korean People's Army** and the forces of the **People's Republic of China** were also well equipped with 61mm mortars at the company level, 8 mm mortars with the battalion, and 120mm mortars with a regiment. Because the communist weapons had slightly larger barrels, they could often fire captured United States shells.

MU CHONG (1905–1951). He was commanding officer of the **North Korean People's Army**'s Second Corps and a powerful influence in the development of the **Democratic People's Republic of Korea**. He was a member of the Central Committee of the **Korea Workers' Party**. It is hard to determine his total role during the Korean War, but on 4 December 1950, he was charged with the loss of **Pyongyang** and purged from the government.

MUCCIO, JOHN J. (1900–1989). A career diplomat, he served in the **State Department** beginning in November 1923. He held several posts in Asia (Hong Kong, Shanghai) and in **Latin America** during World War II. He was appointed to Korea in August 1948 as the personal representative of the president. When the new republic was recognized Muccio became the first ambassador and served there until November 1952. He was replaced by Ellis O. Briggs. He later served with the **United Nations Trusteeship Council** and as ambassador to Iceland and Guatemala. He retired in 1961.

MULE TRAIN. *See* KOREAN SERVICE CORPS (KSC).

MUNSAN. This was the site of the second jump by **United States** airborne forces. The **187th Airborne Regimental Combat Team** and the 2nd and 4th Ranger Infantry Companies (Airborne) parachuted into drop zones ahead of the armored advance toward Munsan. They managed to harass the enemy and then joined up with ground forces before nightfall. This March 1951 action was essential to the limited counteroffensive that **Eighth United States Army** was conducting.

MURPHY, CHARLES S. (1909–1983). A friend, confidant, and advisor to President **Harry S. Truman**, he was responsible for dealing with the legislators and was often the "backbone" of many Truman policies and affirmations.

MURPHY, ROBERT D. (1894–1978). A career diplomat, he served as ambassador to **Japan** from 1952 to 1953 and was instrumental in the **Armistice** agreement. He worked with General **Mark C. Clark**, Commander in Chief **United Nations Command (UNC)**, to provide the basis for an agreement. He believed that the **People's Republic of China** and the **Soviet Union** were using the **Democratic People's Republic of Korea** for their own purposes. He was in constant battle with the opposing tactics of President **Syngman Rhee**. Murphy believed the UNC should fight the war to its end and criticized the **United States** for not using its influence to make that happen. Nevertheless, he worked hard with General Mark Clark on the **Armistice**. While he was appointed as assistant secretary of state for **United Nations** affairs, he remained in Japan until the Armistice was signed.

MUSTANG. Primarily a naval term, but used in all the U.S. services to identify an officer who has come up from the enlisted ranks. *See also* F-51 MUSTANG.

–N–

NAKTONG BULGE, BATTLE OF. The **North Korean People's Army (NKPA)** attacked after the United Nations, failing to defend the Kum River, had retreated along the Naktong. If the UN could hold this line, the NKPA knew it would give the UN time to reinforce and eventually counterattack. The NKPA attack lasted from 5 to 9 August 1950 as it hit all along the line. In two places, however, soldiers forced a bulge. They crossed near Waegwan where they were met and stopped by the United States **First Cavalry** and the **Republic of Korea** 1st Divisions. In the south, along the Obong-ri Ridge, the NKPA 4th Division met the United States 24th and 25th Divisions. Fighting continued there through the last of September without any clear victory. On 17 September the NKPA launched an offensive that was stopped. At this point the UN forces held and all along the **Naktong Perimeter** UN forces were being strengthened. *See also* TAEGU, BATTLE OF.

NAKTONG DEFENSE PERIMETER, BATTLE OF. The more official name for the Pusan perimeter, it identified the **United Nation**'s initial effort to defend the **Republic of Korea**. It dates from 5 July 1950 when **Task Force Smith** made its appearance to the withdrawal into the Naktong Perimeter 1 to 4 August 1950. The battle was considered concluded 16 September 1950 when **Eighth United States Army** broke out and moved north following the **Inchon Landing**. The period included cost Eighth United States Army 19,165 **casualties**.

The perimeter ran from about 100 miles north to south and nearly 50 miles east to west encompassing the port city of **Pusan**. In defense were the United States **First Cavalry Division**, the **2nd Infantry Division**,

24th Infantry Division, and **25th Infantry Division**, the **First Provisional Marine Brigade**, the 27th British Brigade, and eight **divisions** of the **Republic of Korea Army** (ROKA). Air support was provided by marine and navy units flying off carriers and air force planes from **Japan**. The **North Korean People's Army** attacked with 13 divisions. As the fighting continued, United Nations personnel and supplies were coming into the port of Pusan at an increasing rate so that by the time of the **Inchon Landing** the NKPA were outnumbered. Eighth United States Army broke free and moved to Osan where it linked with **X Corps** on 26 September 1950. *See also* NAKTONG BULGE, BATTLE OF; TASK FORCE SMITH.

NAKTONG RIVER. In late summer 1950 the Naktong River formed the western edge of the **Naktong Perimeter**, running 281 miles from the Taebak Mountains and then flowing south until it entered the sea at the delta west of the city of **Pusan**. The longest river in the **Republic of Korea**, it and its tributaries comprise the primary river system in the nation.

NAM IL (1913–1976). This senior delegate to the **Armistice** discussions and lieutenant general was the chief of staff of the **North Korean People's Army**. Just before signing the Armistice document, he was promoted to general so he would outrank Lieutenant General **William K. Harrison**, senior delegate from the **United States**. After the war he avoided the purges **Kim Il-Sung** conducted and was named vice premier.

NAMSI, BATTLE OF. During the early months of the war, the UN maintained air superiority. This control was challenged with the arrival of Soviet-built MiG jets. Stationed in Manchuria and operating primarily in the northwest corner known as **MiG Alley** these planes began to attack bombers on the way to their targets. The MiGs badly damaged three **B-29** bombers in April 1951. On 24 October 1951, 150 MiGs broke through the defensive screen of 55 Thunderjets and destroyed four bombers and badly damaged three others, over the city of Namsi. By the end of that week another five B-29 bombers had been shot from the sky and eight others seriously damaged. Bombing raids over northwest Korea were suspended and additional Sabres were rushed to Korea to help reestablish air superiority.

NAPALM. A jellied gas named from its components naphthenic and palmitic acids and used in bombs and flamethrowers. The bombs were made of plastic and held about 100 gallons. The fire was very effective when used against tanks, bunkers, and massed personnel. During the war the air force dropped 32,357 tons of napalm.

NATIONAL DEFENSE SERVICE MEDAL (NDSM). Authorized as an award to those who served in the United States Armed Forces during the period 27 June 1950 to 27 July 1954. One did not have to have served in Korea to receive the NDSM.

NATIONAL GUARD. National Guard units can be called into national service in times of emergency. During the Korean War, the **40th Infantry Division** (California National Guard) and the **45th Infantry Division** (Oklahoma National Guard) saw service in Korea.

NATIONAL SECURITY ACT OF 1947. Passed on 26 July it provided for several governmental structures, the most significant being the **National Security Council** (NSC) consisting of the president, vice president, secretary of state, and the newly created secretary of defense and director of the **Central Intelligence Agency**. The **Department of Defense** including a statutory **Joint Chiefs of Staff** was also created, as was the **Central Intelligence Agency**. The act also recognized the independence of the **United States Air Force**. The agreement, which produced this act, provided that the **United States Navy** retrain it own aviation force and retained the **United States Marines** as a fighting force.

NATIONAL SECURITY COUNCIL (NSC). The NSC, at its creation in July 1947, consisted of the president and vice president, the secretaries of state and defense, and (acting as advisors) the chair of the **Joint Chiefs of Staff** and the director of the **Central Intelligence Agency**. At the time of the Korean War it served primarily as staff dealing with affairs of national security.

NATIONAL SECURITY COUNCIL DOCUMENT-8: POSITION OF THE UNITED STATES WITH RESPECT TO KOREA (2 April 1948). This **National Security Council** document emerged from the anticipation of the creation of the **Republic of Korea**. The army was anticipating a withdrawal, and President **Harry Truman** authorized disengagement from Korea before the end of 1948. It offered a means of withdrawal without abandoning the Republic of Korea in the process. It recommended a $185 million economic package and creation of a small constabulary army. The policy warned against too great a commitment to Korea, especially one that might draw the **United States** into conflict. Nevertheless, desire for as much security as possible delayed the United States withdrawal of its troops until June 1949.

NATIONAL SECURITY COUNCIL DOCUMENT-48/5: UNITED STATES OBJECTIVES, POLICIES, AND COURSES OF ACTION IN ASIA (17 May 1951). A significant hardening of **United States** policy toward the **People's Republic of China** had occurred. The United States approved resistance to the People's Republic of China through support of anti-communist activities, protection of the **Republic of China** on the island of **Taiwan**, and opposition to mainland China's membership in the **United Nations**. It acknowledged the intention to prevent an escalation of the Korean War and directed the support of Korean unification to economic and political efforts. It also called for assistance to the French efforts in Indochina. President **Harry Truman** approved this **National Security Council** document.

NATIONAL SECURITY COUNCIL DOCUMENT-68: UNITED STATES OBJECTIVES AND PROGRAMS FOR NATIONAL SECURITY (14 April 1950). Approved by President **Harry Truman** in September 1950, this document identified the **Soviet Union** and its mounting military strength as a great danger. In order to meet this global threat, NSC-68 recommended the rapid buildup of the free world's ability to meet the challenge, including a tripling of the defense budget. It was a turning point in **United States** thinking as it identified the Soviets as a major global threat. It also suggested the military response needed could be provided without upsetting the domestic economy and stressed the need to meet any threat, whatever it might be. Certainly the outbreak of war in Korea was a major factor in Truman's accepting this policy statement, and by the end of the war the United States had greatly expanded its commitments and appropriations. Whether NSC-68 could have been adopted without the outbreak of fighting during the Korean War is still debated.

NATIONAL SECURITY COUNCIL DOCUMENT-76: UNITED STATES COURSE OF ACTION IN THE EVENT SOVIET

FORCES ENTER KOREAN HOSTILITIES (21 July 1950). This **National Security Council** document resulted from a request by Secretary of Defense **Louis A. Johnson**, asking for a policy concerning the United States' response to potential Soviet interference in Korea. The **Joint Chiefs of Staff** suggested care in investing too many military resources in an area that was not primarily significant. If the **Soviet Union** entered Korea, it would most likely be part of a greater plan and thus the United States should exercise war plans that would include a full mobilization. It was referred to the National Security Council for additional consideration, including whether **Congress** would agree to such a war plan and to provide more detailed consideration of preparation needed. The plan was canceled after the adoption of NSC-81. *See* NSC-81.

NATIONAL SECURITY COUNCIL DOCUMENT-80: PEACE OFFENSIVE CONCERNING KOREA (1 September 1950). In early September 1950, prior to General **Douglas MacArthur**'s landing at Inchon, consideration was being given as to how the war should be won, and how a peace movement could be prevented at this time. The United States service secretaries proposed a strong counteroffensive. The memorandum was submitted to the **National Security Council** for consideration of a policy but on 12 October 1950 it was determined that the policy proposal was no longer needed.

NATIONAL SECURITY COUNCIL DOCUMENT-81: UNITED STATES COURSES OF ACTION WITH RESPECT TO KOREA (1 September 1950). This was an attempt to define a policy that advanced the interests of the **United States** in its relations with the **Republic of Korea** after either a victory or the voluntary withdrawal of the **North Korean People's Army**. It was in the United States' interest to move north of the **Yalu River** and unify Korea but not at the risk of a war with either the **Soviet Union** or the **People's Republic of China**. The United States, it held, should not allow itself under any circumstances to get into a war with either the Soviet Union or the People's Republic of China. **National Security Council** Document NSC 81-1 was submitted on 9 September and the conclusions approved by President **Harry Truman**.

NATIONAL SECURITY COUNCIL DOCUMENT-82: THE POSITION OF THE UNITED STATES REGARDING A BLOCKADE

OF TRADE WITH CHINA (4 December 1950). With the intervention of the **People's Republic of China**, it was necessary to establish a policy with regard to trade with that nation. The **State Department** recommended that a unilateral trade embargo, and the accompanying freezing of Chinese assets, would anger allies and do little to hurt China. On 16 December the **United States** put Chinese assets within the country under its control and prohibited United States vessels from entering the ports of the **People's Republic of China**. Exports would require a validated license. This decision was accompanied by efforts to assure allies that economic limitations would not draw the United States into a war with mainland China.

NATIONAL SECURITY COUNCIL DOCUMENT-95: UNITED STATES POSITION REGARDING A CEASE-FIRE RESOLUTION FOR THE KOREAN WAR (13 December 1950). This document was created in response to word of **cease-fire** efforts on the part of members of the **United Nations** General Assembly. It held that a cease-fire, if it was to be in the best interest of the **United States**, must be formed at some point along the **38th Parallel**. The cease-fire would be established across Korea and would prohibit new personnel from being introduced. Forces beyond the 38th Parallel would be withdrawn back through the **Demilitarized Zone**, and a commission that was to supervise the cease-fire would have access to all of Korea. While the **Joint Chiefs of Staff** was not recommending a continuation of the war, it did want to warn that the price of a cease-fire was the end of any hope of unifying Korea.

NATIONAL SECURITY COUNCIL DOCUMENT-101: UNITED STATES ACTION TO COUNTER CHINESE COMMUNIST AGGRESSION (15 January 1951). This document recommended a detailed military plan directed toward the **People's Republic of China**. The plan would include protection of **Japan** and the defense of the **Philippines**, the independence of **Taiwan**, the stabilization of the military in Korea, and to avoid war with the **Soviet Union**. It favored the strengthening of Japanese forces and their use in Korea, naval blockade of China, removal of all restrictions on the **Republic of China** in order to encourage aggression, and the use of air attacks against the mainland if necessary to retaliate for the People's Republic of China attacks in Korea. **National Security Council** Document-101.1 was given consideration and would have increased the pressure against China, but President **Harry Truman** decided the implications of 101.1 were too harsh.

NATIONAL SECURITY COUNCIL DOCUMENT-118: UNITED STATES COURSES OF ACTION IN KOREA (9 November 1951). Presented on 9 November 1951 this **National Security Council (NSC)** document considered **United States** policy if the Korean peace efforts failed. Because of the growing air power of the **People's Republic of China (PRC)**, the **Joint Chiefs of Staff** recommended that while the concept of "hot pursuit" should continue to be restricted, the select bombing of the PRC air bases would serve as a deterrent. The document acknowledged that this question had not been answered yet: Are the goals the United States seeks in Korea worth the cost of a greatly expanded commitment of personnel and equipment? In NSC 118.1 the concerns are addressed and in 118.2 the NSC position was identified. The primary object in Korea was the settlement of the conflict in a manner that would not jeopardize the United States in its relation with the **Soviet Union**, Taiwan, or the seating of the People's Republic of China. Should the cease-fire negotiations fail to produce an armistice, the United States should be prepared for a wider war, to increase military operations in Korea, to remove limits on advances into North Korea, to bomb targets on the Korean side of the **Yalu River**, and to bomb specific air base targets in **Manchuria** (with the permission of the president) when they threatened the security of the **United Nations** forces. The statement favored a naval **blockade** of mainland China. In case the Soviet Union entered the war, the United States should withdraw from Korea and prepare for general war.

NATIONAL SECURITY COUNCIL DOCUMENT-147: ANALYSIS OF POSSIBLE COURSES OF ACTION IN KOREA (2 April 1953). When this document was being prepared, the **Dwight Eisenhower** presidential administration was considering the use of nuclear weapons. Approaching the subject cautiously, the **Joint Chiefs of Staff** favored a combined air and naval operation against the **People's Republic of China**, feeling that the use of nuclear weapons was less efficient given the nature of the available targets. President Eisenhower finally agreed. While the president was, in part, trying to meet his campaign promise to end the war, he also let the discussions of NSC-147 leak out so that the **Democratic People's Republic of Korea** and the **People's Republic of China** were aware that nuclear weapons were still a consideration.

NATIONAL SECURITY COUNCIL DOCUMENT-148: UNITED STATES POLICY IN FAR EAST (6 April 1953). This document was an attempt to develop a general policy to cover the various individual policies concerning Asian countries. President **Dwight Eisenhower** thought the views were too broad and considered them only as recommendations. One aspect, the Far East Financial Summary, was used to estimate budget needs to be presented to **Congress**. Eisenhower was under a lot of pressure and did not think it was time to become involved in a policy change. NSC 148 was allowed to fade into non-existence.

NATIONAL SECURITY COUNCIL DOCUMENT-154.1: UNITED STATES TACTICS IMMEDIATELY FOLLOWING AN ARMISTICE IN KOREA (7 July 1953). This document was prepared while negotiations were still going on. It nevertheless was a warning that even if they agreed to an armistice the **People's Republic of China (PRC)** would continue their aggression in Southeast Asia. The paper suggested a trade embargo against the PRC and a multi-national statement that warned against further aggression in Asia. President **Dwight D. Eisenhower**, however, balked at a **blockade** and did not think he could get the allies to support such a warning. Instead he favored economic pressure and trade controls. NSC-154.1 also suggested that items in the security treaty with the **Republic of Korea** were far too broad and should not guarantee the political independence of Korea.

NATIONAL SECURITY COUNCIL DOCUMENT-156.1: STRENGTHENING THE KOREAN ECONOMY (17 July 1953). This statement resulted from a deal made with **Syngman Rhee**. The **Republic of Korea** president agreed to abide by the peace agreement in return for economic and military assistance. It was based on the theory that to prevent the growth of communism, the standard of living had to be raised and the **Republic of Korea** had to develop economic independence. More than one billion dollars was recommended. It was determined that this could be paid from funds saved by the conclusion of hostilities. Accepted by President **Harry Truman** on 7 July 1953, it became the economic lifeline for the Republic of Korea.

NATIONAL SECURITY COUNCIL DOCUMENT-157.1: UNITED STATES OBJECTIVES WITH RESPECT TO KOREA FOLLOWING AN ARMISTICE (7 July 1953). This document recommended that the **Soviet Union** might well sacrifice the **Democratic**

People's Republic of Korea in return for an agreement to remove all **United States** military forces and establish a neutralized Korea. The **Joint Chiefs of Staff** contended that a neutralized Korea would go the way of Czechoslovakia in 1948. But on advice from the **State Department**, and the suggestion that **United States** bases in Korea were not a military necessity, President **Dwight Eisenhower** favored an effort to neutralize Korea. This discussion was unrealistic in that it assumed the demise of both **Kim Il-Sung** and **Syngman Rhee** and the willingness of Moscow to give up its power in Korea. There were no reasons to believe any of the required agreements could be reached.

NATIONALIST CHINESE. *See* KUOMINTANG; REPUBLIC OF CHINA.

NATO. *See* NORTH ATLANTIC TREATY ORGANIZATION.

NAVAL FORCES FAR EAST (NAVFE). When hostilities broke out in Korea, Naval Forces Far East was the primary administrative unit and included **Task Force 90** (Amphibious) and **Task Force 96** (Naval Forces Japan), the **Seventh Fleet** (under CinCPAC), and British and Australian vessels in Far East waters. NAVFE was given command of the Seventh Fleet on 27 June 1950, and on 10 June 1950 the British naval forces were attached. When **United Nations Command** (UNC) was designated, NAVFE was its naval component. The **Republic of Korea Navy** was placed under NAVFE command on 14 July 1950. Naval operations were executed under four major command units: **Task Force 77** (Seventh Fleet Striking Force), **Task Force 95** (Blockading and Escort Force), Task Force 90 (Amphibious Force Far East), and Task Force 96 (Naval Forces Japan). *See also* NAVAL GUNFIRE; SORTIES; VICE ADMIRAL C. TURNER JOY; VICE ADMIRAL ROBERT P. BRISCOE.

NAVAL OPERATIONS. The assignment of the **United States Navy** was to seize control of the sea around the Korean peninsula. Once control was obtained, it could interrupt supplies and communications; provide gunfire support of inland troops; provide transportation; establish carriers for close support; control the air; support bombing runs; and land or pickup troops, partisans, or supplies at any point along either coast. On 25 June 1950 President **Harry S. Truman** ordered the United States **Seventh Fleet**, under the command of Vice Admiral **Arthur Struble**, in the **Taiwan Strait**. Four days later **Task Force 77**, a combined force of **Australia**, **Canada**, **New Zealand**, and the **United States** initiated the first shore bombardment firing on communist targets on the coast of Korea. At only one time was command of the seas in question, and that was during the assault on **Wonsan** when **mines** from the **Soviet Union** and the **Democratic People's Republic of Korea** so infested **Wonsan** Harbor that the assault was delayed for several days. Total **casualties** among the navy during the Korean War was 458 killed and 1,576 wounded. *See* WONSAN LANDING.

NAVY CROSS. The nation's second-highest award for bravery, it was awarded by the president to members of the **United States Navy** and **United States Marine Corps** for action against an enemy. The requirements were high and awarded for conditions of extraordinary courage.

NAVY, PEOPLE'S REPUBLIC OF CHINA. *See* CHINESE COMMUNIST NAVY.

NAVY, REPUBLIC OF KOREA (ROKN). At the outbreak of war the ROK Navy consisted of one **frigate**, *Bak Soo San*, that had been purchased from the **United States** by subscription among Korean naval officers. The complement was 6,000 men. The ROKN also maintained one LST (Landing Ship Tank) and 15 motor **minesweepers**. During the war additional frigates were added: *Kum Kang San, Apnok, Chi Ri San,* and *Sam Kak San.*

NAVY, UNITED STATES. During the Korean War, the United States employed four **battleships**, eight **cruisers**, 13 **aircraft carriers**, more than 80 destroyers, and hundreds of support ships. Unlike its role in other wars, the navy in Korea had to direct its operations almost exclusively to the support of ground troops. By September 1950 the navy had eliminated whatever forces the North Korean Navy could commit. The operations, from then on, included a variety of services: the assault on Inchon, minesweeping operations, the siege of **Wonsan** Harbor, rescue of downed pilots, bombardment of coastal areas, the evacuation of thousands at **Hungnam**, carrier support of major bombing raids, and the movement of personnel and supplies when needed. While the Korean War was primarily a ground war, it is hard to imagine that any sort of victory could have been won without the support of the navy.

NECK OF KOREA. *See* WAIST OF KOREA.

NEHRU, JAWAHARLAL (1889–1964). Mahatma Gandhi's primary lieutenant, he became **India**'s prime minister in 1947 and served until his death. He maintained a policy of Cold War nonalignment. While he finally supported the **United Nations** move in Korea, he was critical of the **United States** overreaction and attempts to put the blame on the **Soviet Union**. Despite several efforts to encourage peace efforts, Nehru never managed to get the trust of either the United States or the Soviet Union. He also allowed India to serve as a base of communications between the United States and the **People's Republic of China**.

NETHERLANDS, THE. The Netherlands provided one **battalion**, often called the "Dutch Battalion," and a Dutch **destroyer**, HNMS *Evertsen*. The Dutch were fighting a guerrilla insurgency in Indonesia but supported the **United Nations** action in Korea. The first soldiers of the Dutch Battalion arrived on 24 October 1950 and eventually included 636 men and three nurses. They first saw action with the United States **Second Infantry Division** near Wonju on 12 February 1951. The unit suffered more than 100 casualties, including its commander, Marinus P. A. den Ouden. A second commander, W. D. H. Eckhout, was also killed in action in May 1951. By the end of the war the Dutch Battalion had included 3,148, of which 120 were killed, 645 wounded, and three repatriated. The battalion received the **Presidential Unit Citation (United States)**.

NEUTRAL NATIONS REPATRIATION COMMISSION (NNRC). Created by the **United Nations** to oversee the processing of **POW repatriation**, the commission members were Sweden and Switzerland (friendly to the **United States**), Poland and Czechoslovakia (friendly to the **Soviet Union**), and was headed by **India**'s nonaligned General **K. S. Thimayya**. India provided more than 5,000 troops, whose job it was to keep order and provide security among the prisoners. After the screening process and the relocation of those requesting it, the remaining prisoners were released in January 1954. The commission voted itself out of existence on 1 February 1954.

NEUTRAL NATIONS SUPERVISORY COMMISSION (NNSC). Created by the **United Nations** as the result of considerable compromise, it was to supervise the terms of the **cease-fire** in Korea. The commission consisted of five nations. After Norway and the **Soviet Union** had been dropped from the list as a result of negotiation, Sweden, Switzerland, Poland, and Czechoslovakia were selected to join India. After the **Armistice** was signed, the commission began a series of inspections. The entire mission of the NNSC was buried in controversy. The **Democratic People's Republic of Korea** was accused of limiting its travel, the **United States** accused Poland and Czechoslovakia of conducting intelligence operations, and the United States, growing weary of the whole effort, tried to get Sweden and Switzerland to withdraw from the commission. The NNSC remained in limited operation until 1957 at which point the United States announced it would no longer recognize the commission's authority and began to rearm its troops.

NEUTRALIZATION OF THE REPUBLIC OF CHINA. This phrase was used to identify the **United States** effort to prevent a conflict in **Taiwan** by placing the **Seventh Fleet** in the **Taiwan Strait** to keep the **Republic of China** and the **People's Republic of China** apart. The **Harry Truman** administration made it clear that it did not want to be involved in the Chinese civil war, but on 27 June 1950 at the second **Blair House meeting**, the president agreed to the "neutralization," and the increase of military economic aid. It was a United States decision and was not related to the **United Nations** resolution. As the Korean War continued, President **Harry Truman** became more supportive of the **Republic of China** and it was, in part, confusion over what Truman wanted from the **Kuomintang** government on Taiwan that led to the split with **Douglas MacArthur**. **Mao Tse-tung**, of course, saw the actions of the **Seventh Fleet** as evidence of United States interference with, and threat to, China.

NEW ZEALAND. By 1 July 1950 New Zealand had provided sea and land forces and supplies of peas, milk, and soap. The naval contribution initially consisted of the frigates **HMNZS** *Pukaki* and *Tutira*. The land forces consisted of the 16th New Zealand Field Artillery. It was assigned to and fought with the **British Commonwealth Division**. *See also* HIS MAJESTY'S NEW ZEALAND SHIPS.

NICARAGUA. The government of Nicaragua, in response to the **United Nations** call, provided rice and medicinal alcohol in November and December of 1951.

NINTH (IX) CORPS. Having seen action in the Asia–Pacific theater, it was deactivated on 28 March 1950 only to be recalled on 10 August 1950. The corps became operational on 23 September 1950 at Miryang. It had no fixed organizational structure and would command a number of **corps** and **divisions**. Commanded first by Lieutenant General John R. Coulter, then by Major General Bryan E. Moore in January 1951 and, when Moore suffered a heart attack, Lieutenant General **William M. Hodge** took command. He was followed by Lieutenant General Willard G. Wyman and then in August 1952 by Major General Rugen E. Jenkins. The Corps received two **Presidential Unit Citations (ROK)**.

NITZE, PAUL H. (1907–). Highly influential with the **State Department** policy planning staff, he was the primary mover in **National Security Council Document 68** that urged the strengthening of the armed forces in light of the growing threat from the **Soviet Union**. Reinforced by the outbreak of the war in Korea, this view was behind the Cold War military buildup and arms race. Earlier he had helped draft the Marshall Plan. He left the government in 1953 only to return with the John F. Kennedy presidential administration. He was considered a hawk but played the role of a dove when he voiced disagreement with the Vietnam War, and he had a significant role during the Cuban Missile Crisis.

NO NAME LINE. The line ran from just north of **Seoul** through Sahaangu to Taep'op-ri on the coast just north of the **38th Parallel**. It was established by Lieutenant General **James A. Van Fleet** in response to the Chinese Fifth Offensive that began the night of 22 and 23 April 1951. Established quickly and without an operational name, it has retained the No Name identification. The line was penetrated during the advance of 15 May 1951 and on 20 May the counteroffensive began passing No Name Line, leaving it deserted.

NOBLE, HAROLD (1903–1953). One of the few to seriously predict the outbreak of war in Korea—in an article in the *Saturday Evening Post* in 1946—he was chief of the publications branch of the Civilian Intelligence Section of the **Far East Command**. During the Korean War, Noble, who was born in **Pyongyang** of missionary parents, was one of the most influential voices to be heard by **Republic of Korea** President **Syngman Rhee**. It was Noble who was selected to accompany Rhee when he retreated, with the government, following the invasion. He was a strong supporter of the Republic of Korea.

NOGUN-NI. In 1997 the **Republic of Korea Kuomintang** sought compensation from the **United States** for civilian deaths caused by troops firing on them near the railway bridge at Nogun-ni. Certainly civilians were killed in the fighting and this attack, alleged to have happened on 26 July 1950, had been reported as a significant illustration of deliberate killing. Many of the original charges have proven to be untrue, but there are many questions that remain. There is no doubt that the **North Korean People's Army** used refugees as a means of hiding troops or moving them through **United Nations** lines. Commanders sometimes issued orders freeing soldiers to fire into refugee groups when they felt they were in danger.

NORSTAD, LAURIS (1907–1988). He was an early force in the development of an independent air force and the youngest four-star general in United States history. General Norstad was deputy chief of staff for operations for the air force. Visiting Tokyo in August 1950, along with **W. Averell Harriman**, he recommended that General **Walton Walker** be replaced by General **Matthew B. Ridgway**. In 1951 Norstad became commander of Allied Air Forces in Europe.

NORTH ATLANTIC TREATY ORGANIZATION (NATO). This group of nations was created in 1949 by 12 Western countries as a military alliance to confront growing pressure. Considered by President **Harry S. Truman** to be a part of the "Truman Doctrine of 1947," it was seen as the initial defense against communist, primarily **Soviet Union**, aggression. Even during the Korean War personnel and materials were added to the growing strength in Europe.

NORTH KOREA. *See* DEMOCRATIC PEOPLE'S REPUBLIC OF KOREA.

NORTH KOREAN AIR FORCE (NKAF). Primarily a propeller-driven air force commanded by Major General Wang Yong who had been a bomber pilot in World War II, it was superior to that of the **Republic of**

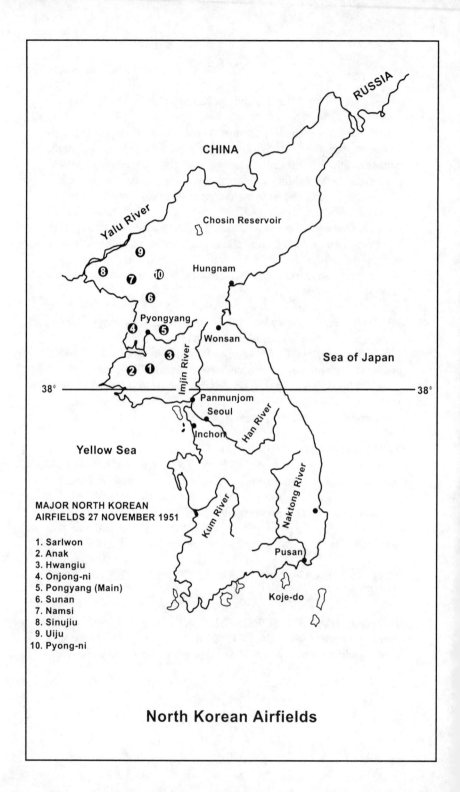

CHINA

RUSSIA

Yalu River

Chosin Reservoir

⑨

⑧ ⑦ ⑩ Hungnam

⑥

Pyongyang

④ ⑤ Wonsan

③

Sea of Japan

② ①

Imjin River

38° 38°

Panmunjom

Seoul

Inchon Han River

Yellow Sea

Kum River

Naktong River

MAJOR NORTH KOREAN
AIRFIELDS 27 NOVEMBER 1951

1. Sarlwon
2. Anak
3. Hwangiu
4. Onjong-ni
5. Pongyang (Main)
6. Sunan
7. Namsi
8. Sinujiu
9. Uiju
10. Pyong-ni

Pusan

Koje-do

North Korean Airfields

Korea (South). It had about 180 planes ranging in age and facilities from the Yakovlev (**YAK**) Soviet fighter, to the Plolikarpow PO-2 biplanes that were nearly a quarter-of-a-century old. Both bombers and fighters appeared early in the war but were quickly destroyed by **United Nations** fighter–interceptors. Other than brief appearances, the NKAF was not a viable enemy after the end of July 1950.

NORTH KOREAN COMMUNIST PARTY. *See* DEMOCRATIC PEOPLE'S REPUBLIC OF KOREA.

NORTH KOREAN PEOPLE'S ARMY (NKPA). *See* ARMY, DEMOCRATIC PEOPLE'S REPUBLIC OF KOREA.

NORTH KOREAN POLITICAL PRISONER EXCHANGE PROPOSAL OF 1950. The **Democratic Fatherland Front (DFF)** made a proposal on 7 June 1950 for an all-Korea election on 5 August 1950. The proposal was ignored by the **Republic of Korea (ROK)**. On 10 June **Pyongyang** suggested the exchange of Kim San-youn and Yi Chau-ha, two communist leaders imprisoned by the ROK, for **Kuomintang** leader Cho Man-sik. The ROK agreed on the condition that Cho, the former chairman of the Choson Democratic Party, was returned unharmed and that the **United Nations Commission** on Korea act in the exchange. The DFF rejected the offer, and the ROK upped their offer, but it was ignored. Apparently it was a ploy of some sort.

NORWAY. This country provided some 79 medical personnel by mid-1951, 109 by 1952, and 105 by July 1953. Norway also made available merchant ship tonnage by 18 July 1950.

NUCLEAR WEAPONS. At the outbreak of the Korean War there was some speculation that if this was the beginning of World War III the **United States** should take the war to the **Soviet Union** in the form of a nuclear attack. Secretary of Defense **Louis Johnston** discussed the idea informally and, at one point, Secretary of the Navy **Francis Matthews** took the idea into a public forum. After the **People's Republic of China** entered the war in late 1950, President **Harry S. Truman** raised the possibility of using nuclear weapons. He did so at a press conference but the discussion, which frightened **Great Britain** and some of the other allies, stopped there. In 1952 as the possibility of a **cease-fire** seemed to be diminishing, Truman considered giving the communists an ultimatum. When President **Dwight Eisenhower** took office, he too considered an ultimatum, but the nature of communist targets discouraged such an effort. General **Douglas MacArthur** met with President Eisenhower and proposed a 14-point victory proposal, which included the use of nuclear bombs to create a band of radioactive waste. Actually the fact that the United States possessed hundreds of bombs, and thousands of planes to drop them, made it possible for the nation to be a little more patient in the negotiations. The final push for communist discussions and agreement may well have been speeded up as word "leaked" out about discussion to use nuclear weapons. How much, and why, is yet to be fully understood.

NURSE CORPS, ARMY. During the Korean War approximately 550 nurses served with the **United States Army**. The majority were assigned to hospitals in Korea or Japan. However, a large numbers also served close to the front with **MASH** units.

–O–

OAK LEAF CLUSTER. Given by the **United States Army** and **Air Force** for subsequent awards of the same decoration. The **United States Navy** and **Marines** use a gold star for this purpose.

OCCUPATION OF DEMOCRATIC PEOPLE'S REPUBLIC OF KOREA. *See* CIVIL CONTROL OF OCCUPIED COUNTRY.

OCCUPATION OF REPUBLIC OF KOREA. *See* CIVIL CONTROL OF OCCUPIED COUNTRY.

O'DONNELL, EMMETT "ROSIE," JR. (1906–1971). Commander of the **Far East Air Force Bomber Command** in Korea from 1950 to 1951. After escaping from the Philippines in 1941, O'Donnell commanded the 10th Air Force in the India–Thailand–Burma theater. In November General O'Donnell led the first major B-29 raid against Tokyo. He would testify at the **Douglas MacArthur** hearings that he had destroyed everything there was to destroy in North Korea. He opposed MacArthur's plan for victory, believing the **Chinese Air Force** was getting too strong. He retired in 1963 and became president of the United Service Organization (USO).

OKINAWA. Part of the Japanese lands, it was occupied by the **United States** at the end of World War II. This 491-square-mile island was the home of the **29th Regimental Combat Team**, which was in support of the Strategic Air Command base at Kadena, and the **Far East Air Force** 20th U.S. Air Force at Naha Air Base. Okinawa served as the staging area for **B-29 Superfortress** raids on Korea.

OLD BALDY, BATTLE OF. The fight over this **United States** outpost was almost a siege as it continued from 26 June 1952 until 26 March 1953. Old Baldy (Hill 266) was one of a series of outposts on the front of the **45th Infantry Division**: Pork Chop Hill, Eerie Hills. During late June and early July of 1952 the **People's Republic of China** attacked, finally overrunning it on 17 July. On 1 August the 23rd Infantry Regiment took it back. It changed hands again in late September and finally on 23 March 1953 the Communist Chinese Forces gained control once again. Lieutenant General **Maxwell D. Taylor**, the new Eighth Army commander, decided that it was not worth the casualties involved in taking it again. *See also* PORK CHOP HILL, BATTLE OF.

187TH AIRBORNE REGIMENTAL COMBAT TEAM. Formed from the 187th Glider Infantry Regiment, it was a part of the 11th Airborne Division when war broke out. Supported by the 674th Field Artillery Battalion and other units, it formed the 187th Airborne Regimental Combat Team. On 20 October 1950, the team dropped at Sunchon–**Sukchon**, some 30 miles north of **Pyongyang**, in hope of rescuing captured Americans and capturing **North Korean** leaders. A second drop was at **Munsan** north of **Seoul** on 23 March 1951. The 187th served as regular infantry and spearheaded the **2nd Division** drive until it was recalled to **Japan**. The 187th was part of the force that reestablished control at **prisoner-of-war** camps at **Koje-do**. The 187th won two **Republic of Korea** Citations and a **United States Navy** and **United States Army Presidential Unit Citation**.

OPERATION ALBANY. As **Eighth United States Army** moved north of the **38th Parallel**, it discovered that more **prisoners** were being held than had been anticipated. There were few troops available to guard the scattered collections of prisoners, and there were limited facilities to provide for them. General **Matthew Ridgway** was concerned, as well, with the potential danger the prisoners presented. In the spring of 1951 Operation Albany was put into effect. It called for **prisoners of war** to be collected and relocated on the island of **Koje-do**, about 20 miles off the coast of **Pusan**. During the early stages as many as 1,000 prisoners were placed in the island camp every day. The massive grouping of prisoners would cause later difficulties.

OPERATION BIG SWITCH. The final **prisoner-of-war** exchange agreement was reached on 25 May 1953 and was worked out so that **India** served as the primary neutral nation to be responsible for repatriation. However, **Syngman Rhee** threatened that **Republic of Korea** soldiers would fire on Indians if they tried to enter the ROK. As a result the exchange point was created in the **Demilitarized Zone**, at a cost of nearly $8 million. The exchange of POWs began after the **Armistice** was signed. *See also* NEUTRAL NATIONS REPATRIATION COMMISSION.

OPERATION BLUEHEARTS. Following his visit to Korea General **Douglas MacArthur** envisioned a plan to deliver an amphibious group on the west side of Korea and cut off the **North Korea** lines of supply. He planned the invasion for 22 July 1950 but the troops he needed were tied up at **Pusan** holding off the push by the **North Korean People's Army**. MacArthur had to postpone his plan but was to recall it in September as **Operation Chromite**.

OPERATION CHEERFUL. In December 1951 the Canadians were given the responsibility for dislodging Communist Chinese Forces on the islands of Ung-do and Chongyong. Getting its name from the Christmas season, this operation was to be a combined Canadian naval and **United Nations** guerrilla attack, using the units known as Leopard and Salamander. Attacking in four junks, while the Canadians provided a heavy bombardment, the guerrillas were halted by fire and withdrew. The operation failed to accomplish its mission.

OPERATION CHOW CHOW (PLAN). Drawn up in July 1949 it called for General **Douglas MacArthur**'s **Far East Command** to evacuate all American civilian and military personnel from Korea in case trouble broke out between the **United States** and the **Soviet Union**. The plan did not consider that American ground troops would be called upon for action in Korea.

OPERATION CHROMITE. This was the name of the revised plan for the landing of **United Nations** troops at Inchon on 15 September 1950. Once proposed, **Douglas MacArthur**'s plan to formulate **X Corps** (**First Marine Division** and **7th Infantry Division**) and to land them in a highly risky venture at Inchon, came under considerable criticism. Despite concerns at several levels, MacArthur was able to sway army chief of staff General **J. Lawton Collins** and navy chief of staff Admiral **Forrest P. Sherman**. He was able to get **Joint Chiefs of Staff** approval on 30 August 1950. *See* INCHON LANDING; OPERATION BLUE-HEARTS.

OPERATION CLAM-UP. Launched between 10 and 15 February 1952, this operation was designed to capture a significant number of the enemy by convincing the communists that the **United Nations** had withdrawn from the line. All air strikes, artillery fire, and ground patrols were stopped. The Chinese either failed to notice or drew the wrong conclusions.

OPERATION COMMANDO. This operation was designed to strengthen the defensive position in front of **Jamestown Line**. Executed between 3 and 8 October 1952, Lieutenant General **J. W. O'Daniel** directed three **divisions** and advanced the line about 8,000 yards, including Maryang-san. Somewhat overextended, the line gave way to a heavy counterattack by the Chinese in November.

OPERATION COURAGEOUS. This operation was designed to carry on General **Matthew Ridgway**'s "**meat grinder**" **strategy** of killing as many of the enemy as possible. The first phase was called Operation **Killer**. The plan was to trap as many communists as possible and send the **187th RCT** to stage a drop behind the lines as **I Corps** launched a frontal attack. Ridgway was given instructions by **Douglas MacArthur** that the operations should continue across the 39th Parallel. As Courageous moved forward, the communists withdrew avoiding the trap. The operation was successful and opened the way for **Operation Rugged**.

OPERATION DAUNTLESS. Charged with creating an offensive bulge near the **Iron Triangle, I Corps** was then to advance to the **Kansas–Wyoming Line**. Beginning on 6 April 1951 the **corps** advanced to the Wyoming Line but, limited by logistic problems, they dug in at the Wyoming Line on 11 April and linked up with **IX Corps** and **X Corps** already at the **Kansas Line**.

OPERATION DECOY. It was believed that the threat of amphibious landings could be used to tie down communist troops. The operational order for Decoy called for a **Regimental Combat Team** to seize, occupy, and defend a beachhead in the Kojo area. The forces involved, from the **minesweepers** to the **aircraft carriers**, were unaware that it was a deception. Scheduled for 15 October 1952, it was under the command of Vice Admiral **Joseph J. Clark**. On the day of the attack, the boats pulled out and headed for shore. At a prearranged moment they were stopped, returned, and put back on the transports. Later intelligence would show that the threat had done little to alter the troop movement among the communists.

OPERATION EVERREADY. This was **Eighth United States Army** plan to take control of the government of the **Republic of Korea (ROK)** in case **Syngman Rhee** or ROK troops became hostile. The plan was to declare martial law and set up a cooperative government. When Rhee released **prisoners** from the **Democratic People's Republic of Korea** in an effort to stall the **Armistice** talks, the plan was considered but President **Dwight Eisenhower** preferred to negotiate. Under pressure Rhee finally agreed not to interfere with the armistice.

OPERATION GLORY. Part of the **Armistice** agreement was a plan to release the bodies of those who had fallen in enemy territory. Officially the **Korean Communications Zone** Op Plan 14–54, generally known as Operation Glory, was the program designed to locate and exchange the bodies of those who had died in the conflict. By 30 August 1953 the disinterments of deceased enemy military personnel was complete. The exchange of **United States** deceased continued until 21 September 1954 when the **Democratic People's Republic of Korea** turned over 123 remains, stating that was all. The final number was 4,023 turned over to the **United Nations** and 13,528 delivered to the DPRK and the **People's Republic of China**. Within the next three months an additional 144 bodies were returned making the total 4,167. Efforts continue to locate and return the bodies of United States servicemen from enemy territory.

OPERATION HOMECOMING. From July to August 1952, approximately 27,000 **prisoners of war** were released. These were people who had been identified as citizens of the **Republic of Korea** who, for one reason or another, had been imprisoned during the early days of the war, or who had been forced into service with the **North Korean People's Army**. The plan, originally suggested in November 1951, was delayed as long as some progress was being made at the truce talks. When the talks came to a halt in June 1952, and with President **Harry Truman**'s approval, the first group was released over the protests of the **People's Republic of China**. After additional screening another 11,000 prisoners were released in October and November.

OPERATION HUDSON HARBOR. This was a special operation set up to consider the potential use of **nuclear weapons** in Korea. Several commanders considered the use of nuclear bombs, and targets were identified with some practice runs executed. When **Dwight D. Eisenhower** became president, he approved a plan submitted in **National Security Council Document 147** that defined targets in the **People's Republic of China (PRC)** as means of getting the PRC back to the **Armistice** table. Negotiations continued and the use of force was unnecessary.

OPERATION INSOMNIA. Having observed that enemy supply trucks would leave an area of interdiction just as the raid was ending, pilots realized that the communist supply trucks were simply waiting for the attack to end before leaving. Beginning on 13 May 1952, the **United States Air Force** began to launch planes just after midnight for a night raid and then, a separate raid about 0200. The hope was that the second raid would get those trucks that were held back. The operation ended on 9 June 1952, as command acknowledged that the raids were accomplishing very little.

OPERATION KILLER. Operation Order 14, issued by General **Matthew Ridgway**, called for an advance of about 100,000 soldiers with the mission to inflict as much damage and kill as many of the enemy as possible. Heavy rains, deep mud, and an evasive enemy meant that the operation did not achieve all that was desired, but it did reaffirm the **United Nations** line and established Ridgway as an aggressive general. An interesting side effect, however, was that civilian authorities felt the names "Killer" and "Ripper" were too negative and suggested more acceptable names to his operations. The name given to this second phase of the sweep was **Operation Courage**.

OPERATION LEE. This operation, to be carried out by **Republic of**

Korea (ROK) naval patrol craft, was to capture and occupy the Tok-chok Islands for future **intelligence** efforts. With the aid of the **Canadian destroyer HMCS** *Athabaskan*, the ROK attacked and secured the island on 17 August 1950. They moved on to the island of Yonghung Do, and on 20 August destroyed radio equipment at the lighthouse on Palmi-do in Inchon Harbor. The operation, which continued until 2 October 1950, was successful in securing considerable intelligence and in holding troops of the **North Korean People's Army** in anticipation of further attacks.

OPERATION LITTLE SWITCH. Without solving the difficult question of the repatriation of **prisoners of war**, both sides at the **Armistice** table agreed on 11 April 1953, to the exchange of sick and wounded prisoners. This was accomplished with remarkable dispatch beginning on 20 April. By 3 May 1953, and under security of the nations involved, the **United Nations Command** turned over more than 6,600 prisoners, the communists released 684 prisoners, of which 149 were from the **United States**.

OPERATION MIG. On 9 July 1951 a pilot from the **People's Republic of China** ejected and his plane crashed onto a small sandbar off the coast of Korea. This operation was set up to recover the wreck. Despite enemy bombardment, the majority of the plane was recovered and its pieces sent back to the **United States**. *See also* OPERATION MOOLAH.

OPERATION MOOLAH. With the need to study a MiG-15, the **Joint Chiefs of Staff** offered $100,000 in cash and sanction to the first pilot to land a MiG-15 in **United Nations** territory. The **United States Air Force** set aside $250,000 for this purpose. An early effort to locate a downed plane—**OPERATION MIG**—had proven successful in 1951, but the offer was still available. It was not until after the **Armistice**, however, that **Democratic People's Republic of Korea** pilot Lieutenant No Kom-sok landed a MiG at **Kimpo**. The officer claimed he was unaware of the money offered.

OPERATION PILEDRIVER. In an effort to establish its position along the **Kansas–Wyoming Line**, **I Corps** was to advance into the triangle area. Starting on 1 June 1951, and continuing until 13 July, I Corps pushed the communists out of **Pyongyang**. Because the **Communist**

Chinese Forces held the high area overlooking the city, the **United Nations Command** withdrew. The operation was successful, however, because it established the line and left the Pyongyang area as part of the no-man's land that separated the two forces. This was the last large-scale effort before the Korean War settled down to fighting along given lines.

OPERATION POLECHARGE. On 15 October 1951 in an action called Polecharge, the 5th Cavalry Regiment and the Belgian battalion assigned to them, took Hill 346 and on 18 October were able to take Hill 230, all near the **Jamestown Line**.

OPERATION PRESSURE PUMP. A series of allied air raids on the city of **Pyongyang** from July to August 1952. The raids, directed at electrical power sources, went on 24 hours a day with planes from **Australia**, **South Africa**, **Republic of Korea**, and **United States** involved. The raids were in part an effort by General **Mark Clark** to bring pressure on the enemy delegates at **Panmunjom**. The raids accounted for a large number of **casualties** and the near demolition of the city.

OPERATION PUNCH. One part of the larger **Operation Thunderbolt**, it consisted of a task force made up of the **25th Division** supported by **artillery** and **armor**. Its job was to defeat the enemy forces that had established themselves on Hill 440 south of the city of **Seoul**. Beginning on 5 February and by 9 February 1951, they had cleared the **Communist Chinese Forces** from the hill and forced them north of the **Han River**. As planned, the success of Operation Punch cleared the way for the **I Corps** assault on Seoul.

OPERATION RATKILLER. Eighth United States Army was harassed by large groups of communist-equipped guerrilla units. A massive attack on those units, led by Major General **Paik Son-Yup** (Task Force Paik), managed to cut the communications of the guerrilla groups and destroyed many of them. Operation Ratkiller was established to operate as a pincer movement along a 163-mile perimeter. The operation was conducted in three phrases from 1 to 4 December 1952, 19 December to 4 January, and 6 to 31 January with the mop-up taking until 15 March 1953. The effort was highly successful, killing many of the guerrillas estimated by the **Republic of Korea** at 19,000 and by **General Matthew Ridgway** at 10,000.

OPERATION RIPPER. This was designed to create a bulge east of **Seoul** along the Idaho Line. I Corps was to hold the line at **Kimpo**, recently taken, and allow **X Corps** and **IX Corps** to advance westward until Seoul was surrounded. This would allow an easier recapture of the **Republic of Korea** capital. The move started on 7 March 1951 and had accomplished its purpose by taking the town of Ch'unch'on on 21 March.

OPERATION ROLLUP. Much of the material and equipment available to General **Walton Walker** at the outbreak of the war had been material collected in Operation Rollup. Initiated by the Far East command in 1948 military vehicles were collected from the numerous Pacific battlefields and returned to Tokyo for repair and availability. During July and August 1950 more than 4,000 such vehicles were repaired and made available.

OPERATION ROUNDUP. This was a plan (5 to 11 February 1951) to advance northward in preparation for an advance on **Seoul**. On 5 February Lieutenant General **Matthew Ridgway** moved the troops toward Hongch'on. The **Communist Chinese Forces** reacted quickly and staged a counterattack on the night of 11 February and pushed **Eighth United States Army** back to Wonju. The **Republic of Korea** 8th Infantry suffered near annihilation. From a new defensive position, Ridgway prepared for the **Battle of Chipyong-ni**.

OPERATION RUGGED. The name given **Eighth United States Army**'s advance to a line (later identified as the **Kansas–Wyoming Line**) north of the **38th Parallel**. Advancing from position between Ch'unch and Munsan, troops of the United States **187th Airborne RCT**; **1st Cavalry Division**; and the **3rd, 24th**, and **25th Infantry Divisions** began to advance on 3 April 1951 and within three days had crossed the **38th Parallel** and dug in along a defensive line (Kansas).

OPERATION SCATTER. This operation was to screen prisoners to determine the actual number who would be involved in a repatriation effort. The screening went well but was slowed by the fact that camps with strong communist units would not allow prisoners to be interviewed. Eventually it was determined that about 70,000 of the 170,000 POWs wanted to be returned to the communist side. The **People's Republic of China** was upset and eventually blocked any effort at neutral screening. Part of the result was the increase of disruptions at the POW camps, eventually leading to the revolt at **Koje-do**.

OPERATION SHOWDOWN. An offensive action conducted from 13 October to 8 November 1952 by units of the **IX Corps** and the 1st Republic of Korea Infantry Division; it was supported by more than 200 **sorties**. The mission was to capture the hills just northeast of Kumhwa in the area known as the **Iron Triangle**. The overlying purpose was to impress on the **People's Republic of China** that failure to reach an agreement on **prisoner-of-war** repatriation would cost them on the battlefield. A very costly battle with the **United Nations Command** suffering nearly 9,000 **casualties**, it provided evidence of the futility of such ground assaults and reaffirmed the use of air power to pressure the communists at the truce table.

OPERATION SMACK. In an effort to test a joint air–**armor–artillery–infantry** operation, ranking military officers and some press were invited to observe an attack on an enemy-held hill known as "Spud" hill. To inform those in attendance a brochure was produce that included the word "scenario," which became the focus of press reports. After a massive bombardment by air and artillery, the 31st Infantry Regiment, **Seventh Division**, started up the hill. Everything that could go wrong did so: equipment failed, the air attack hit the wrong hill, and confusion won the field. The troops were called back after the death of 73 soldiers. The press called it a Hollywood effort and blamed the military for "staging" such an event. A brief investigation showed that the effort was sincere and the target legitimate, but the experiment failed.

OPERATION SQUEEGEE. Just south of Sonjiin a bridge was named the "Rubber Bridge" because of the inability to knock it out. Finally a **Canadian destroyer**, the HMCS *Nootka*, was sent to support a mine sweep of the area. It, along with the USS *Stickle*, bombarded the bridge, shattered girders and supports, but the bridge still had not been destroyed when they were called to other targets.

OPERATION STRANGLE. This was an effort that continued from 5 June until 20 September 1951 in an attempt to restrict the flow of supplies to the **Communist Chinese Forces**. The plan consisted of dividing the territory of the **Democratic People's Republic of Korea** into areas and assigning them to various air units. An eight-group plan was devised that identified a one-degree strip across the neck of Korea.

Planes from the **First Marine Aircraft Wing**, the **Fifth Air Force**, and the planes of carrier **Task Force 77** were involved. Within the first two weeks it became apparent that the plan was not working as devised. Bomb craters did not prevent the use of crossroads, and the limited breaks created in the railway lines were usually repaired within a few hours.

OPERATION TAILBOARD. Following the success of the **Inchon Landing**, General **Douglas MacArthur** planned a two-pronged offensive with General **Walton Walker**'s **Eighth United States Army** moving northwest from **Seoul**, and General **Edward Almond**'s **X Corps** sailing to **Wonsan**, crossing the **waist of Korea** and joining Walker to envelop the capital city of **Pyongyang**. The first stage was the clearing of the harbor at Wonsan. Several sweepers hit **mines** and were lost and determined fire from coastal batteries made the sweep difficult. The delay meant that **X Corps** was not able to begin its move until 25 October by which time the **Republic of Korea Army** had taken the city of Wonsan. The significance of the mines at Wonsan was due not only to the delay, but to the fact that it represented a period during which the **United States Navy** had lost control of the sea lanes.

OPERATION THUNDERBOLT. Following up on information gained through **Operation Wolfhound**, General **Matthew Ridgway** organized a three-corps offensive against the front faced by **Eighth United States Army** and, on 25 January 1952, quickly retook **Wonju**. *See also* OPERATION PUNCH; TENTH CORPS; WONSAN LANDING.

OPERATION TOMAHAWK. Tomahawk was the second drop by the **187th Regimental Combat Team**, this time against Munsan-ni on 24 March 1951. Supported by the 2nd and 4th Ranger Companies, the drop involved 3,447 men in an effort to capture troops of the retreating **North Korean People's Army** I Corps, recapture American prisoners said to be with them, and hopefully capture some enemy leaders. The drop suffered some problems with navigational errors and unanticipated high winds, so while they did manage to drive I Corps farther north, they did not trap the enemy as expected.

OPERATION TOUCHDOWN. This was a second attempt to take **Heartbreak Ridge** by a plan to spread out the **North Korean People's Army** defenders by attacking several adjacent hills at the same time.

The attack, launched on 5 October 1951 by the 23rd Infantry supported by the French Battalion, was successful.

OPERATION WOLFHOUND. A limited reconnaissance offensive near the Suwon area, the operational unit consisted of the Wolfhound Regiment of the **24th Infantry Division** supported by armor. Its mission was to destroy as many of the enemy as possible and test the rumor that the **Communist Chinese Forces** were building up for an offensive. It started on 16 January 1951. By the end of the month the success of Operation Wolfhound led General **Matthew Ridgway** to order a three **corps** offensive.

OPERATION YO–YO. This was the GI name for **Operation Tailboard**. It was also called "Operation What-in-the-Hell." The plan was to move **X Corps** from Inchon to **Wonsan** for a second amphibious landing. The marines went by sea and the **Seventh Infantry Division** by rail to **Pusan** and then to Wonsan. The landing was scheduled for 20 October 1950, but when they arrived they found Wonsan Harbor heavily mined. **Minesweepers** finally cleared the harbor and the landing occurred on 25 and 26 October. By this time, however, troops of the **Republic of Korea** had driven north and taken Wonsan so the landing was administrative.

OSAN. The village where the **United Nations** troops first clashed with the **North Korean People's Army (NKPA)**. There on 5 July 1950 the 406 members of **Task Force Smith** were defeated by a significant force of NKPA troops supported by Russian tanks. It was also the location at which **X Corps** troops coming inland from the **Inchon Landing**, and **Eighth United States Army** coming north from **Pusan**, were to meet in September 1950.

    Osan, Battle of. On 5 July 1950 the first elements of the **United States** 24th Division (Task Force Smith) fought the first battle with the **North Korean People's Army (NKPA)** at the crossroad town of Osan. The fight was between 33 NKPA Soviet-made T-34 tanks leading the 4th Infantry Division and about 540 men of the United States 52nd Field Artillery and the **24th Infantry Division**. Smith, with only six high-explosive rounds and ineffective bazookas, was unable to stop the tanks. When the NKPA took the high ground, Smith ordered the withdrawal during which the unit suffered its highest casualty rate: 181 men killed, lost, or wounded. The NKPA stopped long enough to capture the

American equipment. This engagement was the first American trial and resulted in, if nothing else, a new respect for the troops and equipment they were facing. *See also* TASK FORCE SMITH.

OUTPOST LINE OF RESISTANCE (OPLR). In Korea a series of strong points were established in advance of the main line of resistance in order to warn of an enemy attack and, hopefully, delay the enemy long enough for the main line to prepare. The advanced line created by these outposts was the "Outpost Line of Resistance."

–P–

PACE, FRANK, JR. (1912–1988). Pace served as secretary of the **United States Army** from April 1950 to January 1953. He was one of those at the first **Blair House Meeting** who voiced opposition to sending troops to fight in Korea. He was with President **Harry Truman** at the **Wake Island Conference**. He dealt with the manpower problem at the beginning of the war and implemented a point rotation system for troops in Korea. He supported Truman's decision not to seek the unification of Korea after the **People's Republic of China** became involved. He resigned when **Dwight Eisenhower** became president in 1953.

PACKAGE PROPOSAL. On 28 April 1952 the **United Nations** delegates at the **Armistice** talks presented a proposal to solve all the remaining issues. In effect it called for an end to restrictions on airfield rehabilitation in the **Democratic People's Republic of Korea**, both sides to return only those prisoners of war who did not object to repatriation and agreed that the **Soviet Union** would not be a member of the neutral nations supervisory group. Instead the United Nations offered Switzerland, Sweden, Poland, and Czechoslovakia. General **Matthew Ridgway** wanted to deliver the proposal as an ultimatum but President **Harry S. Truman** did not want it presented in that manner. The communists rejected it. They could accept most of the proposal but continued to insist that all prisoners be returned without exception.

PADILLA NERVO, LUIS (1898–1985). **Mexico**'s representative to the **United Nations** and president of the General Assembly in late 1951, he had been Latin America's choice for secretary-general but the **United**

States wanted **Trygve Lie**. Padilla Nervo adopted a neutral position on the Korean War and served as a link between the United States and the Asian–Arab nations during the period when several peace proposals were submitted. He urged a compromise on the POW repatriation question, suggesting **prisoners** be given refuge in a neutral nation. Late in 1952 he was appointed Mexico's foreign minister.

PAEK SŎNG-UK (1897–1981). Minister of the interior of the **Republic of Korea**, he had been an early supporter of **Syngman Rhee** and served as an advisor and cabinet minister. He was a fatalist and military pessimist, and President Rhee called for his resignation in 1951 because of his defeatist attitude. He ran for vice-president unsuccessfully in 1952 and served for the next 10 years as president of Tong'guk University.

PAIK SON-YUP (1920–). Commander of the **Republic of Korea** 1st Division when war began, he fought a series of delaying actions in an effort to save **Seoul**. At the **Naktong Perimeter**, he fought bravely to hold the enemy. When the **United Nations** finally broke out of the perimeter he moved, in competition with the United States **1st Cavalry Division**, in a race to take **Pyongyang**. He entered the city on 19 October 1950 to win. From 1952 to 1954 he served as chief of staff for the **Republic of Korean Army**, and in 1953 became the first **Republic of Korea (ROK)** general of the army at the age of 33. He was the ROK representative at the **Armistice** talks.

PAIK TU CHIN (1908–1992). Republic of Korea prime minister and minister of finance during the Korean War, he was close to **Syngman Rhee** and played a significant role as mediator between Rhee and the **United States**. He urged the repayment of any money given to the **United Nations Command** to pay for maintenance, which would lead to the suspense account controversy and the eventual formation of the Combined Economic Board.

PAK HŎN-YŎNG (1900–1955). The minister of foreign affairs and vice-premier of the **Democratic People's Republic of Korea**. He claimed that if an invasion occurred more than 200,000 South Korean **(Republic of Korea)** communists would rise up and support the invasion. The fact that this did not happen led, in 1955, to his conviction and execution.

PAKISTAN. On 29 August 1950, Pakistan provided 5,000 tons of wheat to the Korean War effort.

PANAMA. Panama provided free use of training bases, highways, merchant marine space, and a consignment of volunteers by August 1950.

PANDIT, VIJAYA LAKSHMI (1900–1990). She was a sister of **India** Prime Minister **Jawaharlal Nehru**, India's ambassador to the **United States** and chief delegate to the **United Nations**. Friendlier with the **United States** than her brother, she nevertheless maintained **India**'s status as a neutral nation. Relations between India and the United States declined during her tenure, however, and she was not a part of the **V. K. Krishna Menon** peace proposal.

PANIKKAR, SARDAR K. M. (1893–1963). As **India**'s ambassador to the **People's Republic of China (PRC)**, he served as a significant conduit of communication between the **United States** and the PRC. The United States viewed the Indian government as pro-communist so it often gave India's reports on communist Chinese opinions little weight. It was through his offices that the two warnings came from the Chinese announcing they would enter the war if the United States crossed the **38th Parallel**. Secretary of State **Dean Acheson** did not believe it posed a real threat and was afraid any sign of reaction would be taken as a sign of weakness. Once the PRC entered the war Panikkar's influence was less significant.

PANMUNJOM. A village located on the main road five miles east of **Kaesong** and about 15 miles west of **Munsan**, where the **Armistice** talks were re-started on 25 October 1951. The site was considered to be easier to keep neutral. It continues today as the central point of the **Republic of Korea/United States** defense and as the site of meetings between the parties defending the Demilitarized Zone.

    Panmunjom Security Agreement. In order to avoid the difficulties they had encountered at **Kaesong**, liaisons met at **Panmunjom** to discuss security. Talks began on 10 July 1951 and by 22 October 1951 a mutual agreement was reached. Panmunjom was designated the center of a circular security zone with a 1,000-yard radius, a neutralized three-mile radius around **Munsan** and **Kaesong**, two military police and 15 military personnel with small arms were stationed there during the talks, and one officer and five armed personnel at other talks. They agreed to a no-fly zone but accepted the fact that planes might be forced over the area without intent, and finally the **People's Republic of China** agreed to build a tent and the **United States** agreed to provide flooring, lights, and heat. Four captive balloons would float at 1,000 feet above the site to mark the neutral zone. The agreement was signed on 24 October and the talks resumed the next day.

PARAGUAY. By November 1950 this country provided about $10,000 worth of medical supplies.

PARTISANS. When the **United Nations** was forced to retreat southward after the intervention of the **People's Republic of China**, thousands of people from the **Democratic People's Republic of Korea** were forced to flee to avoid punishment for helping the enemy. Largely for their own defense they organized into guerrilla bands that, in February 1951, the **United Nations Command** began to arm and equip. They were formed into **Eighth United States Army** G-3 Miscellaneous Group, 8086th Army Unit. In December 1951 they were incorporated into the **Far East Command** and predesignated as the United Nations Partisan Infantry Korea (UNPIK). They remained under **United States Army** command until the end of the war, at one time numbering about 22,000.

PARTRIDGE, EARLE E. (1900–1990). After service in France, he graduated from the Military Academy in 1924 as a second lieutenant in the air service. When World War II began, he was on the air staff, went on to be chief of staff of the 12th Bomber Command and deputy commander of the 15th Air Force. Later he served as deputy commander Eighth Air Force and commander Third Air Division. When the Korean War broke out, he was commander of the **Fifth Air Force** and took it to Korea where he commanded it until June 1951. He served with the Air Research and Development Command and returned to Japan in command of the United States **Far East Air Force**. In July 1955 he was named commander in chief of North American Air Defense Command (NORAD) and served there until retirement on 31 July 1959.

PATTON TANK. A full-track combat **tank** used by the army and marines, it had a crew of four with a 90mm gun and a speed of 30 miles per hour. Nearly 2,000 of the Patton M-48s in storage were given new transmissions and engines and sent to Korea as M-46s with a crew of five. In 1951 the four-man M-47 and in 1952 the M-48 with a one-piece hull and a four-man crew were used in the war.

PENG THE-HUAI (1898–1974). He was commander of the **Chinese People's Volunteers Army** and a ranking official of the **People's Republic of China** at the outbreak of the war. He attacked with the full force of 400,000 soldiers and drove the **United Nations** south of the **38th Parallel**. After the United Nations reorganized and pushed back to lines near the 38th Parallel, Peng concentrated on the construction of a system of tunnels and trenches that he identified as "an active defense in positional warfare." In July 1953 he signed the **Armistice** agreement that conceded some territory north of the 38th Parallel and accepted the voluntary repatriation of **prisoners of war**. His experience led him to believe that the **People's Liberation Army** needed reform, and he took on that job as minister of defense. He fell from power in 1959 at which time he was briefly imprisoned.

PEOPLE'S LIBERATION ARMY (PLA). The official title of the army of the **People's Republic of China** but a title the political officials chose not to use. They identified this force as the **Chinese People's Volunteers Army**.

PEOPLE'S REPUBLIC OF CHINA (PRC). After years of civil war, **Mao Tse-tung** was able to proclaim the beginning of the People's Republic of China on 1 October 1949. He considered it to be the only legitimate government in China and accepted no division of the nation. Thus, he felt that the presence of the **Seventh Fleet** in the Taiwan Strait was a violation of China's integrity. Despite his efforts, the PRC was unable to gain the Chinese seat in the **United Nations** because of the **United States** objection, although this was urged by the **Soviet Union.** While **Kim Il-Sung** must have had some discussion about the planned invasion, China was reluctant to become involved in the Korean War. It was the threat it perceived from the United States that led China to respond in defense of its territory. In fact the involvement in Korea, while an economic strain to the new nation, most certainly was instrumental in establishing the power of the new government.

    China's Campaign to Suppress Counterrevolutionaries. A radical effort to consolidate communist party control over the **People's Republic of China (PRC)** after the war in Korea reached a stalemate. This was a part of the larger strategy of **China's Resist America and Aid Korea Movement**. It is estimated that more than one million were executed and that hundreds of "intellectuals" and "liberals" were forced to flee the PRC. Later a movement, identified as a campaign to liquidate counter-revolutionaries, followed the same pattern in 1955 as the result of the frustrations of the Korean War. Information concerning the necessity of this postwar adjustment and the number involved in carrying it out are sketchy and open to serious question.

China's Resist America and Aid Korea Movement. A nationwide campaign in the **People's Republic of China** to enlist the support of the nation behind the war in Korea. It stressed the **United States** support for the independence of the **Republic of Korea**, the United States interference in the recently won civil war, and the pressure of the United States entering Korea and moving toward Chinese territory. Authorities question the long-term value of the movement, but a broad range of support among the Chinese people was identifiable. *See also* CHINA, PEOPLE'S REPUBLIC OF.

PEOPLE'S REPUBLIC VOLUNTEERS ARMY (PVA). This term was used to designate the armed forces of the **People's Republic of China** that were fighting in Korea. The Chinese did not want to encourage a full-front conflict with the **United States** or the **United Nations. Peng The-huai** was appointed commander of the PVA on 5 October 1950, and in two days the troops begun crossing the Yalu River. It consisted of two army groups: the 13th under Li T'ien-yu and the 9th under Sung Shih-lun with a total of nine armies. The size of the Chinese division at that time was about 9,000 or half the size of the United States division. Logistically the Chinese units were poorly equipped with no air cover, only two regiments (about 800 trucks) for transportation, and a large civilian transportation corps. Nevertheless they were tough, well trained, and most of them experienced. They used the tactics of the Chinese Civil War: concealed movement, surprise, cross-country movement, encirclement, and were very effective, especially at first, against advancing United Nations units. An estimated 2.5 million people rotated through Korea during the war. At the end of the war there were about one million men in Korea. Casualty figures are scarce but there is considerable agreement that they were very heavy. The last of the PVA departed Korea in 1958.

PERSHING TANK (M-26). Operated by a crew of five, this heavy **tank** was first completed in 1945. It could travel 25 miles per hour and was armed with a 90mm turret gun, .50 caliber machine gun on the turret, and a .30 caliber machine gun mounted on the hull.

PERU. This small nation supplied a million soles, at an estimated cost of $65,000, for boots for the troops.

PERUVIAN POW SETTLEMENT PROPOSAL. A proposal made on 3 November 1952 by Peru that was intended to break the deadlock over the repatriation of **prisoners of war**. The proposal itself was vague and seemed more intended to start discussion than it did to solve any existing problem. The **United States**, at this time, was not inclined to accept the suggestions of neutral nations, and the **Soviet Union** rejected it as totally unworkable. Discussion was soon forgotten after submission of the more pragmatic **V. K. Krishna Menon** proposal offered on 17 November 1952.

PHASES. *See* CAMPAIGNS.

PHILIPPINES. In 1950 the Philippines was fighting its own battle with the insurrection by Huk guerrillas. But in response to the **United Nations** request it had offered, by September 1950, 17 **Sherman tanks**, 1 tank destroyer, the **10th Battalion Combat Team** (nearly 1,500 men), and a battery of 105mm howitzers. In addition they supplied soap, vaccines, blood, and rice. The **battalion** was mistakenly attached to the 65th Puerto Rican Infantry Regiment in the belief the Filipinos spoke Spanish rather than Tagalog. At the end of the war 41 Filipinos were repatriated.

PHONETIC ALPHABET. The same alphabet was used for clarity in Korea as was used in World War II. Some of the phrases were used as titles, for example, white phosphorous (WP) became known as Willie Peter. The alphabet was Able, Baker, Charlie, Dog, Easy, Fox, George, How, Item, Jig, King, Love, Mike, Nan, Oboe, Peter, Queen, Roger, Sugar, Tare, Uncle, Victor, William, X-ray, Yoke, and Zebra.

POINT SYSTEM. Rotation during the Korean War was based on a point system. Those on the line received the highest number of points per month. Those in the rear areas received fewer points. A person was rotated as an individual on completion of 36 points. *See also* ROTATION OF TROOPS.

POLICE ACTION. This term was used by President **Harry Truman** as he tried to explain why the **United States** involvement in Korea was not a war. It was picked up by the media. Many who served in Korea consider it a misleading and unsympathetic term.

POLICY OF BOLDNESS. Presented as an alternative to the idea of containment, it was suggested by **John Foster Dulles**, a secretary of state advisor. Dulles, who would be **secretary of state** under **Dwight D. Eisenhower**, stressed two points that in the future might well prevent wars like Korea. The first point was a thesis of massive retaliation and use of deterrence. While he did not mention nuclear weapons, he implied the use of all weapons needed to strike back. Second, he favored what he called "liberation," which was a political offensive designed to challenge **Soviet Union** leadership and free captive nations of Europe. While cautious concerning the idea, Eisenhower used the concept of liberation as part of his presidential campaign.

PONGAM-DO POW UPRISINGS. After the **Koje-do uprising**, some 9,000 communist civilian internees were located at the detention camp on the island of Pongam near **Koje-do**. On 7 December 1952 prisoners defied authorities and conducted military drills. A few days later prisoners attacked a dispensary soldier. On 14 December the prisoners gathered in a mass formation and hurled rocks at the **Republic of Korea** guards. The guards opened fire killing 85 and wounding 113. As a result, the **Democratic People's Republic of Korea (DPRK)** accused the **United Nations** of brutality. Evidence shows that the outbreak was ordered by Lieutenant General **Nam Il**, chief delegate for the DPRK at the **Armistice** talks.

POPULATION OF KOREA. The peninsula of Korea was home for about 30 million people. In 1950 the population of the **Republic of Korea** was about 21 million. The population of the **Democratic People's Republic of Korea** was about 9 million. **Seoul**, the capital had an estimated 1,640,000. **Pyongyang**, the capital of North Korea, was estimated in 1952 at 500,000 people.

PORK CHOP HILL (RIDGE), BATTLE OF. Perhaps the best known of the hill battles, Pork Chop (Hill 234) was a part of the outpost connections near Old Baldy. The land was more significant as a political tool in the negotiations than it was as a military objective. The battle for the hill lasted from 23 March 1951 to 11 July 1953 during which time occupation changed hands numerous times. Late in March the **Communist Chinese Forces (CCF)** attacked but were stopped. The CCF hit again on 16 April and took the hill but could not occupy it. The battle lasted until 18 April. The CCF backed off but continued artillery onslaughts until 6 July 1953 when it launched a massive attack. For several days five United States battalions were committed against an estimated CCF division. As the armistice drew near, General **Maxwell D. Taylor** was reluctant to invest more troops and on 11 July America pulled off. *See also* OLD BALDY, BATTLE OF.

POTSDAM CONFERENCE (17 July–2 August 1945). The last of the inter-Allied conferences of World War II, it was code-named Terminal. Chief participants were President Roosevelt, Premier Stalin, Prime Minister Churchill, and Attlee, who was elected prime minister during the Conference. The **State Department** officials regarded the Korean Peninsula as too valuable to be abandoned to the **Soviet Union** and recommended a four-part trusteeship. The **United States** military establishment, however, did not consider Korea of strategic importance. It was finally the United States that suggested that a line be drawn at the **38th Parallel** and occupation responsibilities divided between the United States and the Soviet Union. This was quickly accepted by the Soviet Union.

POWER-PLANT BOMBING. *See* DAM RAIDS.

PRESIDENT OF THE UNITED STATES. In the **United States** the president is the elected head of the government and the commander in chief of the **United States Army**, **Navy**, and **Air Force**. **Harry S. Truman** was president when war broke out. He was succeeded in January 1953 by **Dwight D. Eisenhower**.

PRESIDENTIAL UNIT CITATIONS. These were awarded by the **president of the United States** to units that displayed the same heroic efforts as an individual who received the **Distinguished Service Cross** or **Navy Cross**. During the Korean War, the Presidential Unit Citation was offered to the navy. Those given to the air force and army were called Distinguished Unit Citations.

PRESS COVERAGE. When war broke out, reporters stationed either in

Seoul or **Japan** were the first involved, but by 5 July 1950 the pool had grown to 70. General **Douglas MacArthur** expected the press to act responsibly, and they were free to report much of what they saw. But the competition among correspondents led to some reporting the military considered harmful to carrying out the war. **United Nations** correspondents asked for censorship rules primarily to define what they were free to disclose, but the military was not willing to impose **censorship**. The maximum number of correspondents reached 270 and was divided among those who reported from the front line and those who responded to headquarters releases.

The number of articles critical of the military, the United Nations, and the **United States** grew and on 21 December 1950 MacArthur imposed full military censorship. During the war MacArthur expelled 17 reporters who questioned the policies and General **Matthew Ridgway** was no less strict. The tension came to a head during the **Armistice** talks as both access and restrictions were limited. Because of this some reporters, primarily Wilfred Burchett and Alan Winnington, who were attached to the communist delegation, relied on information from the **People's Republic of China**.

Ten American correspondents were killed during the war and one, Frank Noel, was captured and held prisoner until 1953. Noel worked for the Associated Press and won the 1943 Pulitzer Prize. Press coverage, during the Korean War was primarily print journalism, with radio, photojournalism, and occasional television supporting. Magazine coverage, often with combined text and photographs, was highly significant. *See also* MEDIA.

PREVENTIVE WAR CONSIDERATION. As in most Cold War conditions there were those who saw the Korean War as evidence that the **United States** should undertake an attack on the **Soviet Union**, while the United States still had nuclear superiority. During the Korean War several significant military officers made this suggestion. **Francis P. Matthews**, secretary of navy, advocated an initiative strike against the **Soviet Union** in a speech 25 August 1950. Shortly after, Major General Orvil Anderson, commander of the Air War College, suggested the appropriateness of an attack on the Soviet Union before it was too late. The **Harry Truman** administration took great pains to distance itself from any of the these proposals.

"PRICE OF PEACE." *See* MALIK'S RADIO ADDRESS OF 23 JUNE

1951.

PRISONERS OF WAR (POW). This term applied to people taken captive by the enemy and held in captivity, usually in camps. In the main, prisoners of war were those in the armed services but some civilians, primarily diplomatic staffs and business leaders, were also imprisoned for reasons of military security reasons. *See also* PRISONERS-OF-WAR CAMPS.

PRISONERS-OF-WAR CAMPS. When the number of prisoners of war proved to be much higher than expected, General **Matthew Ridgway** had camps located on two off-shore islands: Koje-do and Cheju-do. More than 50,000 POWs were transferred to Koje-do by the end of January 1951. The camp consisted of four areas, each divided into eight compounds. Control of the prisoners was difficult, and in September 1951 people's courts within the compound executed 15 prisoners considered to be disloyal. In February 1952 riots broke out at Koje-do and 55 were killed. On 7 May 1952 the prisoners captured the commandant and gained both actual and propaganda value before he was released. Cheju-do, a much smaller camp, fared better but attempted breakouts of both prisoners and civilian internees at Pongam-do, an island camp near Koje-do, resulted in the death of 85 prisoners.

On the other side the **People's Republic of China (PRC)** treated prisoners much better than did the army of the **Democratic People's Republic of Korea.** The DPRK maintained no camps but only collection points from which prisoners were marched to areas in the rear. These were especially brutal and in one march, in December 1950, only 75 of 400 prisoners captured at Kunu-ri survived. The PRC maintained several camps. The main one was War Camp Number 5 located near Pyoktong on the banks of the **Yalu River.** This was a model camp but others existed where prisoners were not so well treated. The People's Republic of China maintained a systematic program of indoctrination and several prisoners eventually made propaganda broadcasts accepting the blame for atrocities. *See also* CHEJU-DO POW UPRISING; KOJE-DO POW UPRISING; PONGAN-DO POW UPRISING.

PRISONERS-OF-WAR CODE OF CONDUCT REGULATIONS (POSTWAR). As a result of the "failure" of **United States** prisoners in the hands of communist captors, Executive Order 10631 (issued 17 August 1954 by President **Dwight D. Eisenhower**) required the training of all military personnel in how to resist any effort to gain information from the soldier other than name, rank, and serial number.

PRISONERS-OF-WAR MORALE. In September 1950 the **United States** took charge of all prisoners held by the **United Nations** or the **Republic of Korea**. Initially the prisoners were in areas around Pusan but by January 1951 they were moved to offshore camps on **Koje-do**. The United States was interested in winning the hearts of the prisoners it held and many were well treated, provided food, clothes, and even entertainment. Even under the best of circumstances, the life of the prisoner of war was not ideal, and by December 1951 an estimated 6,600 had died.

Mismanagement and ignorance in the administration of some camps made it harder for the guards to control camps. Political struggles within the camps, and organized resistance to camp control, led to a series of riots. The worst of these on Koje-do resulted in the capture of the American commander. In regaining control of the camps many prisoners and some **United Nations** soldiers were killed. Once these riots were under control, the United States began to separate prisoners on the basis of their political position and reduced fractional violence. *See also* PRISONERS-OF-WAR CAMPS.

PRISONERS-OF-WAR QUESTION. The primary issue during the extended peace talks had to do with the question of repatriation. The **United States** and **United Nations** held that prisoners should have the option to refuse repatriation. Many fighting with the **North Korean People's Army (NKPA)** were from the **Republic of China**, who had been captured in the Chinese Civil War, or captured **Republic of Korea** soldiers, who had been forced to serve in the NKPA. The communist position was that prisoners should be forced to return to the national army from which they were captured. In June 1953 the **People's Republic of China** and **Democratic People's Republic of Korea** finally agreed to a neutral nation taking custody of those refusing repatriation and determining if their choice was legitimate. President **Syngman Rhee** opposed this and on 18 June 1953 released some 25,000 NKPA prisoners who indicated their desire to remain in the Republic of Korea. On 23 September the **United Nations Command** turned over more than 22,000 non-repatriates to the **Neutral Nations Repatriation Commission (NNRC)** and the **Communist Chinese Forces** and **North Korean People's Army** released 359 non-repatriates the next day. The

NNRC kept the prisoners the required 120 days and released them in accordance with their choices. *See* PRISONERS-OF-WAR REPATRIATION.

PRISONERS-OF-WAR REPATRIATION. One of the most difficult questions of the **cease-fire** negotiations was the return of prisoners. The **People's Republic of China (PRC)** wanted prisoners to be returned to the army they were in at the time of their capture. The **United Nations (UN)** wanted prisoners to determine their own point of return. The argument between involuntary and voluntary repatriations continued for more than a year but in the end the UN got most of what it wanted, and a compromise was worked out where a commission of neutral nations would interview the prisoners of war and determine their return.

As agreed in the **Armistice** of 27 July 1953, more than 22,604 communist prisoners were turned over to the **Neutral Nations Repatriation Commission (NNRC)**. The communists released a little more than 13,000 prisoners of war to the NNRC, and the United Nations released nearly 23,000. Of those United Nations troops released by the communists, several chose not to return to the country of origin. Among there were 335 from the Republic of Korea, 23 from the United States, and one from Great Britain.

In **Operation Big Switch**, among those who were clear about their return, the communists released 13,444 prisoners: 8,321 Republic of Korea; 3,746 United States; 977 Great Britain; 243 **Turkey**; 41 **Philippines**; 32 **Canadian**; 28 **Colombians**; 26 **Australians**; 12 **French**; 9 South Africans; three **Greeks**; three Netherlanders; one **Belgium**; one **New Zealander**; and one from **Japan**. The United Nations released 82,493 prisoners, who included 75,823 from the **Democratic People's Republic of Korea** and 6, 670 from the People's Republic of China.

PRISONERS-OF-WAR RIOTS. *See also* CHEJU-DO POW UPRISING; KOJE-DO POW UPRISING; PONGNAM-DO POW UPRISING; PRISONERS-OF-WAR CAMPS.

PRISONERS-OF-WAR TREATMENT. The treatment of **prisoners of war** was more harsh under control of the **North Korean People's Army** than the **People's Republic of China (PRC)**. During the early months of the war, prisoners were forced to march to camps in the North, many dying along the route. On several documented occasions, the North Korean People's Army shot prisoners, sometimes after binding their hands with wire or, as in the case of the "October Killings," shooting 100 American prisoners while they disembarked from a train to pick up food. In the spring of 1951 the PRC took over control of the prisoners and treatment became increasingly humane. Life in the prison camp was harsh, nevertheless, with re-education and self-criticism classes, confined living conditions, and poor food. Unaccustomed to the limited food and its poor quality, and the disease and mistreatment in camps, thousands died in captivity. The best estimate is that 2,700 of the 7,140 United States prisoners died in captivity.

PRISONERS-OF-WAR UNILATERAL RELEASE PROPOSAL. The easiest way to solve the question of **prisoner-of-war** (POW) repatriation (**Agenda Item IV**) was to simply reclassify POWs who did not want to return to their home as political prisoners and release them. General **Matthew Ridgway** believed this would tarnish the **United Nations** and make them open to charges of treachery and deceit. In 1952 General **Mark Clark**, Ridgway's replacement, suggested taking all prisoners to the **Demilitarized Zone** and releasing them without further consideration. This plan, while it contained obvious difficulties, was seen as a possibility if the communists did not accept the **United Nations Command** final POW proposal of 25 May 1953. While this plan was dropped as progress was made at the **Armistice** talks, it was precisely the plan that **Syngman Rhee** implemented when he released POWs under his control.

PRONUNCIAMENTO. After **Eighth United States Army** had driven the **People's Republic of China** back across the **38th Parallel**, General **Douglas MacArthur** called upon the enemy commander, on 24 March 1951, to meet and agree to a cease-fire. In his statement he downplayed the **Communist Chinese Force**'s ability to continue the fight and threatened if they did not cease he might invade China itself. The effect was not to bring the People's Republic of China to the peace table but rather to bring a halt to the peace proposals upon which **Harry Truman** was working. In theory, a field commander can issue a surrender ultimatum but General MacArthur must have been aware that this appeared to violate the instructions of the commander in chief and was contrary to his wishes. Truman was furious but only reminded MacArthur of the restrictions requiring Washington's approval of public statements about the war. But while Truman considered it an act of insubordination, MacArthur continued on until 5 April 1951 his opinions were read on the floor of the House of Representatives. It was too much and Truman relieved him of duty. *See also* TRUMAN FIRES DOUGLAS MACARTHUR.

PROPAGANDA. The first psychological unit in Korea was the First Loudspeaker and Leaflet Company that arrived in Korea on 8 November 1950 and served as **Eighth United States Army** propaganda unit during the remainder of the war. In August 1951 the First Radio Broadcasting and Leaflet Group joined them. The leaflet war consisted of **Safe Conduct Passes**, warnings, suggestions of surrender, and suggestions the individual soldier was being misused. More than one billion leaflets were dropped over Korea during the war. While a number of the enemy turned themselves in carrying safe conduct passes, it is hard to know what the overall success was. Allied troops welcomed the passes, however, because they supplemented the meager toilet paper ration. *See also* PSYCHOLOGICAL WARFARE.

PSYCHOLOGICAL WARFARE. Like all strategies, psychological warfare was addressed at the tactical, operational, and strategic level. Tactically the **Chinese People's Volunteers Army** used bugles, whistles, and loudspeakers to confuse the **United Nations** troops; while the **United Nations** tended to paint their **tanks** as tigers or with other fierce signs. More important was the operational level at which both the United Nations and **Communist Chinese Forces** used a variety of **propaganda** techniques: leaflets, radio broadcasts, and air-delivered loudspeaker arguments. Radio Pyongyang broadcast the music and comments of **Seoul City Sue**. The Allies had the advantage because of control of the air and the ability to drop leaflets. At the national level the use of "**brainwashing**" and charges of **germ warfare** and mistreatment of prisoners were a part of the communist system.

PULLER, LEWIS B. "CHESTY" (1898–1971). Pulled back into the Korean War after a long illustrious career in the **United States Marines**, from the Caco rebels in Haiti to the "Horse Marines" in China, and the First Battalion, Seventh Marines Regiment during World War II, he was given command of the First Marine Regiment in Korea and landed with them at **Inchon**. Colonel Puller was awarded the **Distinguished Service Cross** and a fifth **Navy Cross** for his heroism and leadership in the break out of the Chosen encirclement. He was promoted to brigadier general in January 1951 and became assistant **divi-**

sion commander of the First Marine Division.

PUNCHBOWL, BATTLE OF THE. The area was named after an old volcanic crater about five miles in diameter, about 20 miles from the Hwach'on reservoir, which was rimmed with hills as high as 2,000 feet. Held by the **North Korean People's Army**, it provided an excellent position for directing fire on the Allies. In 18 August 1950 elements of the **Republic of Korea** I Corps and **Eighth United States Army** attacked from the northeast and finally took their objective 27 August 1951. The First Marines, including the ROK Marine Regiment, attacked again and captured the northern lip on 3 September 1951. It would remain in United Nations hands through the remainder of the war. The marines and their ROK unit took 1,503 casualties.

PURPLE HEART MEDAL. Authorized by General George Washington and revived in 1932 as an award given by the **president of the United States**, it is given for a wound received in action against an enemy of the United States. The wound must be treated by a medical officer and a record of the event thereafter maintained in the medical files.

PUSAN. Port city in southeastern Korea, it was the **Republic of Korea**'s second largest city and Korea's primary seaport. With a natural harbor and deep-water docks, the port could unload 30 ocean-going ships and discharged approximately 28,000 tons daily.

PUSAN LOGISTICAL COMMAND. *See* KOREAN COMMUNICATIONS ZONE.

PUSAN PERIMETER. *See* NAKTONG DEFENSE PERIMETER.

PYON YONG YANG (1892–1969). The **Republic of Korea** minister of foreign affairs and briefly prime minister, he was a strong advocate of **Syngman Rhee** and proponent of a "moral totalitarianism" to counter the power of communism.

PYONGYANG. Capital of the Koryo Dynasty (935–1392), and during the Korean War the capital of the **Democratic People's Republic of Korea**, it was North Korea's largest city and hub of the railway system. Located in north-central Korea along the Taedong River, it is about 50 miles from the port city of **Chinnampo** (Nampo) on the Yellow Sea. As an "objective" of the **United Nations Command** Pyongyang was bombed heavily. From 14 to 15 December 1950 the U.S. Air Force dropped 175 tons of bombs and napalm on this city. On 15 August 1951 the **United Nations** launched **Operation Strangle**, in an attempt to cut communication and supply, bombed Pyongyang again partially in an effort to "destroy" the civilian involvement in supply. In July through August 1952 **Operation Pressure Pump** consisted of 24-hour raids on the city and in one raid, on 26 August 1952, a reported 6,000 civilians were killed. By the end of the war the city was nearly flattened.

QIN JIWEN. *See* CH'IN CHI-WEI.

QUAD-FIFTIES. Actually designed as an anti-aircraft gun it was four .50 caliber machine guns mounted in a power-operated turret and carried on the back of a truck. It saw a great deal of use during the Korean War as support artillery and close-order fire.

QUARTERMASTER. A staff officer who has the responsibility for obtaining food, clothing, and certain supplies. During the Korean War the term was more unofficial than official.

QUESADA, ELWOOD R. (1904–1993). The **United States Air Force** general who was primarily responsible for developing the air–ground coordination techniques used during the latter part of World War II and in Korea. He had served as commander of the XII Fighter Command in Tunisia and southern Italy, and then as IX Tactical Air Command in England. During the Korean War, he headed special projects for the **Joint Chiefs of Staff**. He retired from the air force in 1951.

QUONSET HUT. These huts, a half-cylindrical prefabricated structure made of metal sheets, were developed by the United States Navy at Quonset, Rhode Island, and were based on the Nissen huts used by the British and reportedly named after their designer, Peter M. Nissen. They were used as barracks, warehouses, and offices.

–R–

RADFORD, ARTHUR W. (1896–1973). The leader of the "revolt of the admirals" in response to an undue emphasis on air power, Admiral Arthur Radford was commander in chief of the Pacific Fleet and commander in chief in the Pacific from 1949 through August 1953. A firm anti-communist, he believed the greatest threat to world peace lay in Asia not in Europe. He supported General **Douglas MacArthur**'s **Inchon Landing** plan, and was in favor of the military unification of Korea. He was frustrated by the limitations placed on the military in the fight against the **Communist Chinese Forces**. In 1952 he was with president-elect **Dwight D. Eisenhower**'s on his trip to the **Republic of Korea**, and it was Eisenhower who nominated Radford as head of the **Joint Chiefs of Staff**. After the war, Radford was a political advisor to Vice President Richard Nixon and Senator Barry Goldwater.

RADHAKRISHNAN, SARVEPALLI (1888–1975). India's ambassador to the **Soviet Union** tried to get **Joseph Stalin** to negotiate as early as July 1950. He urged the **United States** to agree to the seating of the **People's Republic of China** in the **United Nations** in return for a **cease-fire**, the withdrawal of foreign troops from the **Republic of Korea**, and an independent Korea. His proposal became the basis for the Indian peace initiatives of 1950. In 1952 he returned to New Delhi to serve as vice president and his influence over matters in Korea diminished.

RAKKASANS. *See* 187th AIRBORNE REGIMENTAL COMBAT TEAM.

RANGERS. Traditionally they played the role of spearhead, scout, and quick-response team. Six airborne ranger units operated in Korea during the war. The First Ranger Company arrived in Korea on 17 December 1950 and the Second, Third, Fourth, Fifth, and Eighth followed soon after. The 117-man teams provided a great service and suffered heavy casualties during their operations. Many commanders, however, considered the Ranger companies unnecessary and by October 1951 the **Far East Command** dissolved all ranger units. Most of the rangers were reassigned to the **187th Airborne Regimental Combat Team**.

RASHIN. This North Korean east coast port city was less than 20 miles from the Soviet frontier. Use of the base was leased by the **Soviet Union** and there may have been one or two submarines using the port. Because of its location and the fact that both rail and road transportation were available from the Soviet port of Vladivostok, it was a prime target for the **B-29s**. However, because of the possibility of mistakenly bombing the Soviet Union, there were several decisions not to bomb the area. Finally in August 1951 bombing runs were established and, in a first, the **United States bombers** were escorted by Navy **F9F Panther** and **F2H2 Banshee** fighters from the **carrier USS *Essex*.** The naval bombardment and **blockade** assignments excluded Rashin.

RAU, SIR BENEGAL NARSING (1887–1953). Representing **India** at the **United Nations**, he was the rotating president of the Security Council. He supported the resolution of 25 June 1950 but abstained in the vote because of lack of instructions from New Delhi. He tried to slow the movement of United Nations troops across the **38th Parallel** and was instrumental in establishing the **United Nations Cease-Fire Group**. When the **Communist Chinese Forces** crossed the **Yalu River**, he delayed passage of the condemnation proposal until conditions improved. Because India refused to serve on the **United Nations Good Offices Committee**, his influence diminished.

RECAPTURE OF SEOUL. *See* SEOUL.

RECOILLESS RIFLE. Designed as an infantry anti-tank weapon, these rifles were authorized for use by weapons platoons. **Eighth United States Army**, however, had only been issued 21 of their scheduled weapons. When **Task Force Smith** arrived in July 1950, they discovered that both the .57mm and .75mm recoilless rifles were primarily ineffective against the Soviet **T-34** tanks. They did find considerable use, however, as an anti-personnel weapon and artillery for the small unit.

RECONNAISSANCE. This defines the systematic search for information about enemy positions and dispositions conducted in the field by battlefield participants. *See also* RECONNAISSANCE COMPANIES; RECONNAISSANCE PATROLS.

Reconnaissance, Aerial. The **reconnaissance** role had been neglected after World War II, and it was not until January 1951 that the 67th Tactical Reconnaissance Wing was put together to work with **Fifth**

Air Force and the **First Marine Aircraft Wing**'s photographic squadron. Once started, aerial reconnaissance was increasingly effective, averaging about 1,700 photograph **sorties** per month with nearly three-quarters of a million negatives. Maritime reconnaissance was conducted by amphibious aircraft of both the **United States** and **Great Britain** operating along the coasts in search of **mines**.

Reconnaissance Companies. In the **United States Army** there were several specialized reconnaissance units. Each **infantry regiment** supported an **Intelligence and Reconnaissance platoon (I&R)** and each infantry **division** a reconnaissance company.

Reconnaissance Patrols. During the Korean War the **United Nations Command** and forces of the **People's Republic of China** and the **North Korean People's Army** all sent out patrols for the purpose of collecting information about the location and disposition of the enemy. In the majority of cases these were ad hoc units composed and selected for a specific assignment.

RED BALL EXPRESS. Named after the World War II truck supply train and attributed to the condition of the drivers after 24 hours on the road, the Red Ball Express served to supply the ground forces in Korea. The name was given to several efforts that brought supplies from the principal port **Pusan** to the advancing troops. At one time in November 1950 army trucks operated on a 24-hour basis. In order to supply **I Corps** north of the **38th Parallel**, **Second Infantry Division** ran 320 trucks on a 24-hour basis. Each unit had its own trucks, but on many occasions they were commandeered to meet particular needs to move people or supplies. In ordinary circumstances drivers worked 12 to 18 hours a day, road maintenance units accompanied the trucks, and planes were used to spot disabled vehicles. Trucks supplied the troops throughout the war but as the lines stabilized and rail routes were established, the demand became less taxing.

RED CROSS. The International Committee of the Red Cross (ICRC), a Swiss organization, included among its tasks the monitoring of a series of Geneva Conventions relating to war, the first having been adopted in 1864. The ICRC carried out this activity during the Korean War as well, also helping to provide relief supplies and track prisoners of war. National Red Cross societies, including in the **Republic of Korea**, acted more directly in helping to improve the health and sanitation situation. Other Red Cross societies from **United Nations** members also played a role.

REFERRAL OF POLITICAL QUESTION. *See* AGENDA ITEM V.

REFUGEES. There were literally millions of Korean men, women, and children who hit the road fleeing from the war. Many were citizens of the **Republic of Korea** trying to avoid the war; many were members of the **North Korean People's Army** infiltrating the allied lines. The transition from soldier to refugee was simple because of the traditional white robes worn by the refugee. Sometimes the lines of refugees contained both people fleeing the havoc of war and soldiers using the lines to get behind the allied forces. On numerous occasions the **United Nations** felt it had to fire on refugees in order to prevent the infiltration. When the **People's Republic of China** entered the war and allied forces were retreating, an estimated one million North Korean citizens fled the advancing Chinese. At **Hungnam**, as **X Corps** was withdrawn, more than 90,000 refugees were evacuated with them. Once the lines stabilized in the spring of 1951 the problem of refugees lessened.

REGIMENTAL COMBAT TEAM (RCT). This was essentially an **infantry regiment** with a **battalion** of **artillery** and often a unit of **armor** and engineer elements attached. Often they were created for limited and special operations. There were two particularly active units that served in Korea. The **Fifth RCT** from Hawaii (Fifth Infantry Regiment, 555th Artillery Battalion and a Heavy Tank Company) was in Korea by 31 July 1950. The second was the **187th Airborne Infantry Regimental Combat Team** (187th Airborne Infantry, the 674th Airborne Field Artillery) that made two drops during the war.

REGIMENT. This was the basic unit of combat organization for the **United States Army** and **United States Marines**, commanded by a colonel with three **infantry battalions**, each with three **companies**. Each battalion had 40 officers and 935 enlisted personnel, a 4.2 heavy mortar company, an **intelligence** and **reconnaissance** platoon, and often a **tank company**. In addition there would be a medical company and headquarters company with transportation and communication assignments. Regiments serving in Korea were the Fifth, Seventh, and Eighth Cavalry; Fifth, Seventh, Ninth, 14th, 15th, 17th, 19th, 21st, 23rd, 24th, 27th, 29th, 31st, 32nd, 34th, 35th, 38th, 65th, 160th, 179th, 180th, 223rd, 224th, 279th army; and the First, Fifth, Seventh Marine, and

11th Artillery Marine regiments.

REPATRIATION OF PRISONERS OF WAR. *See* PRISONERS-OF-WAR REPATRIATION.

REPLACEMENT DEPOTS. During the Korean War replacements were provided on an individual basis rather than by the unit, as was the case in World War II. Replacement depots in the **Zone of Interior** were located at Camp Stoneman at Pittsburgh, California, and Fort Lawton in Seattle, Washington. At these depots individuals were collected, housed, fed, and occupied while a shipment, by sea, was put together. There were 49,918,919 troops shipped by the Navy's **Military Sea Transportation Service** to and from the **United States** and Korea. At Camp Drake and Camp Zama near the Japanese port of Yokohama, and at Sasebo, Japan, troops were gathered for shipment to Korea. In Korea, troops were dispersed and returned from camps at **Pusan** and **Inchon**. A great many soldier-man-hours were wasted while troops waited in a "Repo Depot" for shipment.

REPUBLIC OF KOREA ARMY. *See* ARMY, REPUBLIC OF KOREA.

REPUBLIC OF KOREA CIVIL TRANSPORT CORPS. The successor to the **Mule Trains** and a lose organization of civilian porters carrying loads of up to 50 pounds on **A-Frames**. In 1951 it was finally replaced by the **Korean Service Corps**.

REPUBLIC OF KOREA COAST GUARD. *See* COAST GUARD, REPUBLIC OF KOREA.

REPUBLIC OF KOREA MARINES. *See* MARINES, REPUBLIC OF KOREA.

REPUBLIC OF KOREA PRESIDENTIAL UNIT CITATION. This was awarded by the president of the **Republic of Korea** to units that distinguished themselves on the battlefield. A red and blue yin–yang symbol on a streamer was added to the unit colors and, an individual award (a red, green, and white-striped ribbon in gold frame) was presented.

REPUBLIC OF KOREA (SOUTH KOREAN) NATIONAL GUARD SCANDAL. The National Guard Act of 1950 called for the training of guardsmen and activation in time of emergency. **Syngman Rhee** reorganized his private army, the Taehan Youth Corps, as the National Guard. While the **United Nations** forces were in retreat these forces headed out for training areas. The leaders took the opportunity to embezzle huge amounts of funds that led to the death, in January 1951, of nearly 1,000 enlisted men. On news of the event, the National Assembly dissolved the National Guard. Minister of Defense Shin Sung-mo was removed on 7 May 1951 and Commander Kim Yun-gun arrested. Five officers were accused, found guilty, and executed on 13 August 1951.

REPUBLIC OF KOREA (SOUTH KOREAN) POLITICAL CRISIS, 1952. Acknowledging his growing disagreement with the National Assembly, President **Syngman Rhee** tried to push through a bill that allowed the president and vice-president to be elected directly. When the 1952 Assembly defeated his bill, Rhee increased pressure on the assemblymen including charges of communism, recall elections, and personal pressure. **United States** officials suggested a **United Nations Command (UNC)** military takeover but General **Mark W. Clark** in Tokyo and General **James A. Van Fleet** in Korea feared that this would result in conflict between the UNC and the **Republic of Korean Army**. In July 1952 the assembly was held hostage by Rhee's security forces until it passed the bill and Rhee, in fact, became a virtual dictator. The Western nations—**Australia, Canada**, and **Great Britain**—tended to support U.S. President **Harry Truman**'s ineffective role.

REPUBLIC OF KOREA (SOUTH KOREAN) PRESIDENTIAL ELECTION 1952. Syngman Rhee's selection was a forgone conclusion and the **United Nations Commission on the Unification and Rehabilitation of Korea** indicated that the elections had proceeded with little interference. More important was the vice-president election and Rhee selected a man older than himself, Hahn Tae-yong. Hahn received nearly three million votes. It marked the end of **Yi Pom-sok** and his political followers.

REPUBLIC OF KOREA (TAEHAN–MINGUK). Inaugurated on the basis of the **United Nations (UN) resolution** of 14 November 1947, it was formally proclaimed on 15 August 1948 at the nation's capital, **Seoul**. It was the result of years of political struggle and an arbitrary division of the nation along the **38th Parallel**. When the UN efforts to create a united country failed, the **Republic of Korea** (often referred to as South Korea) was recognized. **Syngman Rhee**, long-time head of the March First Movement and the exiled Korean Provisional Government (KPG), became the first president.

RESERVE FORCES. When the Korean War broke out, the United States Reserves (Army, Navy, National Guard, and Air National Guard) were ill prepared, as were the active duty forces. Reserve units were called up, however, both to provide force structure and to provide individual replacements of men and equipment. President **Harry Truman** called up 135,000 reservists from the U.S. Army Reserves, 4 divisions from the U.S. Army National Guard, and more than 90 other specialized units, and the entire U.S. Marine Corps Reserves. By 1 September 1950 about 256,000 men had been called from the U.S. Army National Guard, U.S. Air National Guard, and the U.S. Air Force, U.S. Army, U.S. Navy, and U.S. Marine Corps Reserves for active duty.

REST AND RECUPERATION (R&R). Eighth United States Army established a relief system on 31 December 1950 that provided troops, usually after 180 days' active duty, a seven-day period of rest in **Japan**. At one of the three processing centers (Camp Kokura on Kyushu, Camp McNeely in the Tokyo–Yokohama area, or Osaka) the soldier was given a new uniform, money, free room at one of the military hotels, and left alone for seven days. R&R was provided through a variety of services including both air and sea transport to Japan. More than 800,000 individuals enjoyed this rest during the period of 1951 to 1953.

RETREADS. When the Korean War broke out, it was necessary to recall reserve and National Guard units, many of whose soldiers had served in World War II. These recalled men provided experience and stability, but many considered it too much to ask after their previous service.

REVOLT OF THE ADMIRALS. In April 1949 Secretary of Defense **Louis A. Johnson** canceled the construction of the new aircraft carrier, the USS *United States*. This action was a part of the defense cut mandated by President **Harry Truman** due to his belief in the superior role of the air force. It led to the resignation of Secretary of the Navy **John L. Sullivan** and the "revolt" of a number of high-ranking naval officers who believed the army and air force were out to weaken the navy and marines. After considerable unrest, and a series of congressional hearings in October 1949, a working agreement was established.

RHEE, SYNGMAN (1875–1965). This first president of the **Republic of Korea** (South) was born in what is now North Korea. Jailed for belonging to a student protest movement, he converted to Christianity, went to the **United States**, and received a PhD in theology from Princeton University in 1910. He briefly returned to Korea but was forced into exile again. In 1919 he was selected president of the Korean Provisional Government in exile. A stout nationalist and anti-communist, he was elected as president of the Republic of Korea (ROK) that was formalized on 15 August 1948. When war broke out he appealed to the United States and the **United Nations** for help and when the **United Nations Command** was established, Rhee placed his forces under its command.

A reasonably cooperative ally in war, he was determined that the war not end until Korea was united. In an effort to delay talks he released nearly 27,000 **North Korean People's Army prisoners**. The allied secret plan to overthrow Rhee, **Operation Everready**, was considered but not implemented. In early July the **Communist Chinese Forces** attacked ROK positions with 15 divisions and inflicted great damage. Rhee got the message and agreed to no longer fight the **cease-fire**. Nevertheless he never accepted nor signed it and continued to express his desire to march north and unify the nation. He was president until 27 April 1960 when a student coup forced his autocratic government into exile. Rhee died in Hawaii.

Rhee, Assassination Attempt. On 25 June 1952 a lone gunman raced to the podium, aimed a pistol at President **Syngman Rhee**, and in front of a crowd of nearly 50,000 people, pulled the trigger twice. The pistol failed to fire either time. The would-be assassin was caught and identified as Yu Sit'ae, a member of the Blood and Justice Association. Later two members of the Democratic Nationalist Party were arrested. The whole event seemed to be most opportune as Rhee was having considerable difficulty convincing either the **United States** or members of his own government that there was a plot against him. It created sympathy for Rhee who was in the midst of an effort to change the constitution in a manner that would ensure his re-election.

Rhee's Declaration of Martial Law. **Syngman Rhee** used martial law as a means of controlling the National Assembly and preventing popular opposition to rise against him. On 25 May 1952 he declared martial law in **Pusan** and in 22 counties, putting Major General **Won**

Yong-Duk in charge with orders to report directly to the president. So Min-ho, a critic of Rhee, and 45 members of the National Assembly were arrested. All but 12 were finally released, but the message was clear. While there was little doubt what he was doing was illegal, it was difficult to know how to stop him. Even after the National Assembly passed the amendments to the constitution on 3 July 1952 martial law was not lifted.

Rhee's Release of Prisoners of War. *See* DEMOCRATIC PEOPLE'S REPUBLIC OF KOREA.

RIDGWAY, MATTHEW B. (1895–1993). He graduated from West Point in 1917 and served as infantry officer, diplomat, and on staff assignments. He was a graduate of the Command and General Staff School and the Army War College. During World War II he commanded the 82nd Airborne and the XVIII Airborne Corps. In December 1950 Lieutenant General Ridgway assumed command of **Eighth United States Army** in Korea. Providing new strength and encouragement, he moved Eighth United States Army out of retreat and in a series of operations drove the Chinese back and established the main defensive line, **Kansas**, across Korea. In April 1951 he replaced General **Douglas MacArthur** as Commander United Nations Forces. Under directions from President **Harry Truman** he reluctantly started the peace negotiations that reached a **cease-fire** in 1953. Ridgway went on to replace **Dwight Eisenhower** as **NATO** commander, serve as chief of staff United States Army, act as one of the "wise men" under President Lyndon Johnson, and argue for the withdrawal from the war in Vietnam.

Ridgway's Armistice Broadcast. Following **Jacob A. Malik's radio address**, and on instructions from Washington, General **Matthew Ridgway** sent a message to the commanders of the **Communist Chinese Forces** and the **North Korean People's Army** on 30 June 1951. It asked that if they were in favor of a meeting to discuss a **cease-fire** and proposed a meeting on the Danish hospital ship in **Wonsan Harbor**. On 2 July Radio Peking responded saying that the meeting should take place between 10 and 15 July at the old capital at **Kaesong** at the **38th Parallel**. A liaison meeting took place on 8 July and talks began on 10 July 1951.

ROBERTS, WILLIAM I. (1891–1968). He was commander of the **Korean Military Advisory Group (KMAG)** established on 1 July 1949.

The unit consisted of about 500 men who aided in establishing the **Republic of Korea Army (ROKA)**. When North Korea attacked, KMAG retreated with the ROKA.

ROBERTSON, SIR HORACE C. H. (1894–1960). An Australian, he was commander in chief of the **British Commonwealth Forces** in Korea from 1950 to 1951. He was the most senior officer in the Far East under General **Douglas MacArthur**. While brilliant and efficient, he had a talent for upsetting people. Nevertheless he represented the Commonwealth in relations with MacArthur's headquarters. He returned to Australia in 1951.

ROBERTSON, WALTER S. (1893–1970). As assistant **secretary of state** for Far Eastern affairs, appointed in January 1953, he was the coordinator of Korean policy. When **Syngman Rhee** released **prisoners of war** in an effort to delay the **Armistice** negotiations, it was Robertson who was sent to Korea to persuade Rhee to abide by the decision. A friend of **Chiang Kai-shek** and a proponent of the **Republic of China** on **Taiwan**, he was an essential part of the China lobby, and an intense anti-communist. While he was sympathetic to Rhee's position, he delivered the administration's decision in a manner that assured Rhee would no longer interfere with the armistice negotiations.

ROCKET ARTILLERY. Generally rocket fire was difficult to pinpoint, but used as general **artillery** it proved to be very effective. Ship-to-shore, air-to-ground, and ground-to-ground rockets were used in Korea. The army maintained some multi-rocket launchers that fired 4.5-inch ground-to-ground rockets. The air force used 5-inch HVAR (high-velocity aircraft rockets) against ground targets. The navy maintained several of the **Landing Ship Medium Rockets (LSMR)** armed with 5-inch spin stabilized rockets. The communists had truck-mounted Katushka rocket launchers (Soviet-made) that fired four 82-mm rockets.

ROCKET LAUNCHERS. *See* BAZOOKA.

ROTATION OF TROOPS. About the time the **Armistice** talks began, the military began a system of rotation based on points. It assigned points based on combat involvement–four per month for those in combat–and rotated when the soldier earned 36 points. Under this system the average combat soldier would spend little more than one year in Korea. The advantages seemed obvious but the disadvantage came primarily from the fact that it rotated out experienced men and replaced them with inexperienced. It also created a class of "short-timers," who tended to grow more conservative as their points increased. *See also* POINT SYSTEM.

ROYAL AIR FORCE. *See* AIR FORCE, UNITED NATIONS.

ROYAL AUSTRALIAN AIR FORCE. *See* AIR FORCE, UNITED NATIONS.

ROYAL AUSTRALIAN REGIMENT (RAR). *See* AUSTRALIA.

ROYAL HELLENIC AIR FORCE. In early December 1950 **Greece** sent one air transport squadron to aid in Korea. The 13th Hellenic Air Force Squadron flew eight C-47 cargo planes. The group was involved in air lifting members of the United States **First Marine Division** from their retreat at the Chosin Reservoir.

ROYAL HELLENIC EXPEDITIONARY FORCE. A voluntary force of 850 men from the regular Greek army arrived in Korea in early December 1950. After receiving additional equipment they were attached to the 7th Cavalry Regiment (**First Cavalry Division**). A company from this **battalion** was sent to **Koje-do** to help after the riots there in May 1952. A second battalion arrived in Korea shortly after the war where they remained until 1955.

ROYAL NAVY. Great Britain responded quickly to the **United Nations** call for support. Ships in the area were assigned to the naval forces available and during the war they provided considerable significant service. The primary ships that saw service were carriers HMS *Theseus, Glory, Ocean,* and *Triumph;* cruisers HMS *Kenya, Ceylon, Belfast, Jamaica, Birmingham,* and *Newcastle*; destroyers HMS *Charity, Cossack, Consort, Cockade,* and *Comus*; and frigates *Black Swan, Alacrity, Hart, Morecombie Bay,* and *Whitesands,* and the hospital ship *Maine.*

RUSK, (DAVID) DEAN (1909–1994). He served in World War II in the China–Burma–India Theater. As a part of the Strategy and Planning Group, Operations Division, he helped select the **38th Parallel** as the diplomatic dividing line in Korea. In 1947 he was assigned as director of the **United States State Department**'s Office of Special Political Affairs and then assistant secretary of state for **United Nations** affairs. In March 1950 he became assistant secretary of state for Far Eastern Affairs. A strong supporter of **Chiang Kai-shek**, he nevertheless argued against expansion of the war in Korea. Rusk left public office in 1953 and then returned to serve as secretary of state under the John F. Kennedy and Lyndon B. Johnson presidential administrations.

–S–

SABRE JET. *See* F-86.

SAINT LAURENT, LOUIS S. (1882–1973). As **Canada**'s prime minister when the **Democratic People's Republic of Korea** invaded, he directed his delegates to support the **United Nations (UN)** for the defense of Korea. He authorized the sending of Canadian **destroyers** and a brigade of troops. He was not anxious to see the war with **People's Republic of China** expand and urged the **United States** and the UN to avoid condemning the People's Republic of China. A strong supporter of the United States he worked for compromise in Korea.

SALVATION ARMY. Organized by William Booth as the Christian Revival Association in London in 1865, this social-reform organization has been known as the Salvation Army since 1878. It provides military titles for its officers, the brass bands, Christmas collection, and weekly journal, the *War Cry*. Providing aid and comfort to the individual solider, the Salvation Army played a significant role in the morale of the **United Nations** troops by quietly caring for the needs of individuals through coffee houses, rest areas, books at the front, and in maintaining connections with folks at home.

SCORCHED EARTH POLICY. Realizing that he could not prevent the **People's Republic of China** advance, nor defend **Pyongyang**, General **Walton Walker** ordered the withdrawal south of the **38th Parallel**. To slow the communists, General Walker ordered the **United States** supply depot at Pyongyang burned, all highway and railroad bridges destroyed, all houses to be burned, livestock killed, and rice supplies destroyed. Everything that could not be taken was destroyed. On 4 January 1951, following the destruction of supplies at Inchon and **Kimpo**, the new **Eighth United States Army** commander General **Matthew Ridgway**

rescinded the order.

SCREENING POWS. *See* OPERATION SCATTER.

SEA FURY. *See* HAWKER SEA FURY.

SEA OF JAPAN. This body of deep water runs along the eastern coastline and produces a tidal range of no more than two feet. This calm made it easy for naval forces to get in close for land bombardment and to prevent coastal shipping by the enemy.

SEABEES. The U.S. Navy SEABEES (Amphibious Construction Battalions) were attached to **Task Force 90**. Primarily fighting engineers, they undertook hundreds of construction tasks under very difficult conditions. Perhaps the most noteworthy was a 2,400-foot runway on the island of Yo-Doin in **Wonsan** Harbor that was finished in 16 days rather than the anticipated 45.

SEARCH-AND-RESCUE OPERATIONS (SAR). Each branch of the service had methods for providing search-and-rescue operations. The **United States Air Force** had a formal organization and the **United States Navy** and **United States Marines** operated on a decentralized basis. The Third Air Rescue Squadron was a part of the **Military Air Transportation Service** and under the control of Far East Air Force. The rescue units used a SB-17, a modified World War II **bomber**, small two-seat **H-5A Sikorsky helicopters**, and a detachment of Grumman 5A-16 Albatross amphibian "flying boats." On 27 August 1950 the **Fifth Air Force** established a Rescue Liaison Office at the Joint Operation Center and on 4 September 1950 the first downed pilot was rescued from behind enemy lines. As the war progressed H-19 10-passenger helicopters arrived, and a full-scale SAR coordination center was established. On 1 March 1952 the Third Air Rescue Squadron was renamed the 2157th Air Rescue and assigned to operations in the **Democratic People's Republic of Korea**. Throughout the war 170 **United States** airmen were saved, as were 84 pilots from other nations.

SEARCHLIGHTS. The Allies used searchlights primarily to illuminate enemy positions by means of bouncing antiaircraft artillery lights off clouds. The communists used lights primarily as a defense measure. The lights could reach as high as 30,000 feet and were often radar directed.

The **United States** experimented with several 80 million candlepower lights attached to **B-26 bombers**.

SEBALD, WILLIAM J. (1901–1980). A specialist on the Orient, he served as a political advisor to General **Douglas MacArthur** during the period of the Korean War. He served as the primary channel between MacArthur and the **State Department**. The Joint Chiefs of Staff denied him permission to take part in the truce talks fearing he would emphasize the political implications of the talks. Upon MacArthur's release he remained in Japan until, in April 1952, he was named ambassador to Burma.

SECOND INFANTRY DIVISION. Nicknamed the "Indianhead Division," it was composed of the 9th, 23rd, and 38th **Infantry** Regiment; the 503rd Field Artillery Battalion (this African American outfit was deactivated in November 1950 and replaced by the 15th, 37th, and 38th Field Artillery), 72nd Medium Tank Battalion, the 82nd Antiaircraft Artillery Battalion, the 2nd Combat Engineers, and the Second Reconnaissance Company. The Second sent the first troops into Korea arriving on 8 July 1950. Nine days later the main body sailed. They were committed to the defense of **Pusan**, the **Battle of Chipyong-ni**, defended the Hwachon Reservoir, and fought at **Punchbowl**, **Iron Triangle** and the **Battle of Pork Chop Hill**. The **division** was awarded two **ROK Presidential Unit Citations**, the U.S. Navy Presidential Unit Citation and **United States Presidential Unit Citation**. The division suffered 25,093 **casualties**.

SECOND LOGISTICAL COMMAND. Also called the **Korean Communications Zone (KCOMZ)**, it identified a specified area behind the lines where ports and supply areas could be located. The KCOMZ began at the **Pusan** Base Command Zone on 4 July 1950. It was renamed the Pusan Logistical Command and in September identified as the Second Logistical Command. The responsibility of this command was to deal with **refugees**, **prisoners of war**, and logistical support for all **United Nations** forces in Korea. The Third Logistical Command was organized to supply **X Corps**. In June 1952 the Korean Communications Zone was created to relieve **Eighth United States Army** commander of territorial operations. Commanded by Major General **Thomas W. Herren**, it was designed to have 75,000 to 100,000 personnel and to support a force of 400,000. As it turned out they had about

30,000 troops and were supporting about 800,000 personnel and more than 100,000 POWs and civilian internees.

SECRET CEASE-FIRE NEGOTIATIONS. In January 1951 Pak Jin-mon, a member of the South Korean Workers Party, sought meetings that would encourage a peace movement to rise from the people of Korea. When the **Republic of Korea** learned of the effort Pak Jin-mon was labeled a communist. Nevertheless after the **Kaesong** truce talks began, the **United Nations** provided Pak a pass and he left on 28 July promising to return in 10 days. What resulted was a mass of confusion, accusation, and charges. Pak was later charged and found guilty.

SECRETARY OF DEFENSE. Under the president, the secretary of defense exercised authority over the army, navy, marines, and air force. While the secretary maintained actual control, the **Joint Chiefs of Staff** functioned with operational control. The secretary served in the president's cabinet. The chain of command during the Korean War was the president, secretary of defense, **Joint Chiefs of Staff**, to the commander in chief, **Far East Command**. **Louis A. Johnson** was secretary when the war began. He was replaced by former General of the Army **George C. Marshall** on 21 September 1950 who would serve until 12 September 1951. **Robert A. Lovett** served from 17 September 1951 until he was replaced, after **Dwight D. Eisenhower**'s election, by **Charles E. Wilson**.

SECRETARY OF STATE. Dean Acheson was secretary of state when the Korean War began and he served until **Dwight D. Eisenhower** replaced **Harry Truman** in January 1953. He was succeeded by **John Foster Dulles**. As a member of the cabinet he advised the president on matters of foreign policy and directed the **State Department**.

SEOUL. The capital (the name literally means capital) of the **Republic of Korea (ROK)** lies about 20 miles east of the port city of **Inchon** and on the north bank of the **Han River**. The capital was moved to Seoul in 1392 at the beginning of the Yi Dynasty. The pre-war population was estimated at 1.5 million. The capital of the ROK was occupied by forces of the **Democratic People's Republic of Korea** on 27 June 1950. While the invasion of the port city of **Inchon** was not strongly contested the **North Korean People's Army** fought hard to prevent the recapture of the capital city. The **First Marine Division** and the **Seventh Infan-**

try **Division** moved on the city. Despite being slowed by heavy resistance, **Tenth Corps**, under General **Edward M. Almond**, entered the city on 28 September 1950. After the intervention by Communist Chinese Forces, the city fell on 3 January 1951. It traded hands again on 15 March 1951 when **Eighth United States Army**, under General **Matthew B. Ridgway**, freed the city. During the war Seoul changed hands four times. In 1998 it was the home of the summer Olympics, and in 2001 was a city of more than 10 million people.

SEOUL CITY SUE. Anne Wallace Shur was the daughter of a Korean Methodist missionary who married a Korean nationalist with strong left-wing beliefs. She volunteered to broadcast to American soldiers appealing to them to surrender. While not much of a threat, she was often compared to Tokyo Rose of World War II.

SERVICE MEDALS. These were granted for service rendered during a particular period of time. In Korea the **National Defense Service Medal** was given for those on active duty from 27 June 1950 to 27 July 1951. Those who served in Korea or on adjacent waters, during this time frame, were awarded the Korean Service Medal and the United Nations Service Medal. Campaign stars were awarded for participation in any or all of the six official campaigns.

SEVENTH FLEET STRIKING FORCE. *See* TASK FORCE 77.

SEVENTH INFANTRY DIVISION. The "Bayonet" **Division** was composed of the 17th, 31st, and 32nd **Infantry Regiments**; the 31st, 49th, and 57th Field Artillery battalions; the 73rd Medium Tank Battalion; the 15th Antiaircraft Artillery Battalion; the 13th Combat Engineers; and the 7th **Reconnaissance** Company. When other divisions were first sent to Korea, the 7th was stripped for needed personnel, but when regrouped (basically through the addition of nearly 9,000 KATUSAs) it was selected to take part in the **Inchon Landing** as a part of **X Corps**. It took part in the liberation of **Seoul**, advanced with X Corps from **Wonsan** toward the **Chosin Reservoir**, and was caught there when the Chinese attacked. After evacuation from **Hungnam** on 19 December 1950, it was returned to **Eighth United States Army** and fought in the central front. It was involved in the **Battle of Pork Chop Hill** when the war ended. The division won three **ROK Presidential Unit Citations**, two army and two navy **Presidential Unit Citations**, and a Navy Unit

Commendation. The division suffered 15,126 **casualties**.

SHEPHERD, LEMUEL C., JR. (1896–1990). Major General Shepherd was the commander of the Sixth Marine Division throughout the Okinawa campaign, and when war broke out in Korea he was commanding general, Fleet Marine Force, Pacific. He participated in the **Inchon Landing** and in the retreat from **Chosin**. On 1 January 1952 he was named commandant of the marine corps and held that position during the war. He retired 15 September 1959.

SHERMAN, FORREST P. (1896–1951). Named as **chief of naval operations** on 2 November 1949, following the "**revolt of the admirals**," he was in that position when the war broke out. A strong supporter of **Douglas MacArthur** and of naval aviation, he was the leading force on the **Joint Chiefs of Staff** pressuring for the acceptance of the **Inchon Landing** plan. Nevertheless, in 1950, he sided with President **Harry Truman** on the need to dismiss MacArthur. He suffered a heart attack while in Italy and died on 22 July 1951.

SHERMAN TANK (M4A3E8). The Sherman was a **United States** medium **tank** developed in 1944 and assigned to armored divisions. It had a crew of five and was armed with one 76mm gun, one .50 caliber machine gun, and one .30 caliber machine gun. It weighed about 37 tons and traveled at 26 miles per hour. **Great Britain** also had a cruiser tank, the Sherman (VC) called "Firefly."

SHIN IK-HI (1894–1956). When forces critical of President **Syngman Rhee** took control of the National Assembly in 1950, they elected Shin speaker. Shin opposed Rhee politically. Despite his disagreement, he presided while Rhee pushed through a constitutional revision allowing the direct election of the president and vice president. Shin was the opposition candidate in 1956 and was expected to win over the aging and unpopular Rhee when he died of a stroke during the election. **John M. Chang**, his running mate, was elected president.

SHIN SUNG-MO (1891–1960). A friend of **Syngman Rhee**, he served as minister of the interior and commandant of the Taehan Youth Corps until being named minister of defense for the **Republic of Korea**. In early 1951 he was blamed for the **Korean National Guard** scandal and the Kochang incident, and Rhee was forced to release him. Shin had warned the **United States** that the **Democratic People's Republic of Korea** was building roads and preparing for war but was considered unreliable. He served briefly as ambassador to Japan.

SHIN TAI-YONG (1891–1959). A major general in the **Republic of Korea Army** (ROKA), he was fired in November 1949 because of conflicts within the ministry of defense, reinstated, then promoted to lieutenant general. He served as minister of defense until he replaced **Shin Sung-Mo**. He held the position until June 1952. He was later commander of the militia.

SHIP DESIGNATION, UNITED STATES NAVY. Naval ships in the **United States Navy** are designated by a first letter that indicates the general category, and with one or two descriptive modifiers. The general categories are as follows: A–auxiliary, C–**cruiser**, D–**destroyer**, L–landing, and P–patrol. The modifiers are C–command or craft, D–destroyer or dock, E–explosive or escort, H–hospital or **helicopter**, O–oiler or ocean, P–transports (personnel), T–tracked, tank, or torpedo, and V–aviation. *For designations referred to in this work see Abbreviations.*

SHON WON-IL (1908–1980). Acknowledged as the founder of the **Republic of Korea Navy** and its first chief of staff, Admiral Shon was named minister of defense in June 1952. He later served as the **Republic of Korea** ambassador to Germany.

SHORT, JOSEPH H., JR. (1904–1952). The first professional journalist to hold the position of press secretary, he was named by President **Harry Truman** in December 1950. Popular with the press, he was responsible for explaining many of the controversial issues raised by the war. He was best known for his 11 April 1950 press conference that released the information about Harry Truman's decision to fire General **Douglas MacArthur**.

SHTYKOV, TERENTY F. (1907–1964). A colonel-general in the **Soviet Union** army, he served as head of the Soviet delegation to the Joint Soviet–American Commission that was attempting the unification of Korea. He had served as Moscow's political advisor in **Pyongyang** during the Soviet occupation. When the **Democratic People's Republic of Korea** was recognized, **Joseph Stalin** appointed him ambassador.

SICK AND WOUNDED PRISONER-OF-WAR EXCHANGE. *See* OPERATION LITTLE SWITCH.

SIGNAL CORPS. The need to build up the signal corps for the campaign in Korea was aggravated by the fact that Korea had so few established communications facilities. The Mukden cable, a pre-World War II Japanese-built system, was still in operation but what was needed was more tactical communication. The shortage of signal units, a result of budget cuts, meant that in the summer of 1950 there was not one signal **battalion** in the **United States Army** to provide service to a **corps** headquarters. Line was laid and defended (Korean refugees cut the wire to tie up their bundles), and radio waves were bounced off mountain sides. After the victory at **Inchon**, Major General Spencer B. Akin (**Douglas MacArthur**'s signal officer during World War II), the chief signal officer was able to cope with the rapidly moving front, but then was again in a desperate situation as a result of the Chinese invasion. Field wire, radios, and terminal equipment were still in short supply as late as 1952.

SILVER STAR MEDAL. The **United States** third-highest award for bravery, it was awarded in the name of the president for gallantry in action against the enemy. Subsequent awards are indicated by an **oak leaf cluster** for the army and **gold star** for navy and marines.

SINO–SOVIET TREATY OF FRIENDSHIP AND ALLIANCE. Signed on 14 February 1950 the treaty, despite its name, was evidence of the growing disagreement between the **People's Republic of China** and the **Soviet Union. Mao Tse-tung** released some claims to territory and the Soviets pledged to come to China's aid if it was attacked by Japan or any nation working with **Japan**. The loan Mao anticipated was very small and did not meet the needs expected. When Mao entered the war, the Soviets did not provide the aid expected and ended up selling (not giving) arms and ammunition. There is evidence that President **Harry Truman**'s intervention in Korea was partly influenced by the desire to show that Joseph Stalin would not respond even if troops were landed on the Asian mainland.

SIXTEENTH CORPS (XVI). This was **United States corps** headquarters that was activated in **Japan** in 1951 but which never saw action in Korea.

SMALL ARMS, CHINESE PEOPLE'S VOLUNTEER ARMY. While based on Soviet designs, most of the arms carried by the **People's Republic of China** were manufactured in its own factories. The most heavily used was the Type 50 submachine gun, which was a nearly identical copy of the PPSh-41, carried by the **North Korean People's Army**.

SMALL ARMS, NORTH KOREAN PEOPLE'S ARMY. The **North Korean People's Army (NKPA)** was perhaps the best armed army in Korea. Within several months, however, because of the destruction of equipment and air raids, they were reduced to using **Soviet Union** army weapons that had been designed for World War II. The NKPA also used a great deal of captured American equipment. The primary weapons supplied were the Soviet-made PPSh-41 submachine gun, the Tokarev 7.62mm semi-automatic rifle, the 1944 7.62mm carbine, the type 99 long rifle, a Japanese-made bolt-action rifle, the PIRD-14.4mm anti-tank rifle, the Tokarev 7.62 pistol, and **bayonets**. Bayonet use was limited because such a large percentage carried submachine guns.

SMALL ARMS, UNITED NATIONS. By definition this is the weapon that can be carried and utilized by a single soldier. Many of the **United Nations** troops in Korea during the war carried weapons reflective of their own nation, but the vast majority were manufactured in the United States. Those supplied by the **United States** included the **M-1 Garand** M-11903 30-60 sniper rifle, the M-1 .30 caliber carbine, the M-1918 **Browning Automatic Rifle**, the M1911 .45 caliber pistol, and a variety of **bayonets**.

SMITH, OLIVER P. (1893–1977). A combat officer during World Wars I and II, he was assigned as commander of the Marine Corps School at Quantico. In 1948 he became assistant commandant of the **United States Marines** and assumed command of the **First Marine Division** in June 1950. He was involved in the **Inchon Landing**, the occupation of **Seoul**, and then the destructive battle at the **Chosin Reservoir**. His skillful use of **helicopters** aided the evacuation and saved numerous lives. His alleged quote, "Retreat Hell! We're just attacking in another direction," became a cry of defiance. He briefly assumed command of **IX Corps**, was promoted to lieutenant general, and became head of marine forces, Atlantic. He retired in 1955.

SMITH, WALTER BEDELL (1895–1961). General Bedell Smith was a major commander during World War II, ambassador to the **Soviet Union**, and in 1950 was named head of the **Central Intelligence Agency (CIA).** As director of the CIA, he was primarily responsible for its growth and the increasing complexity of its operations. In 1953 he resigned from the CIA to become undersecretary of state in the **Dwight D. Eisenhower** administration.

SON WON-IL (1908–1980). Admiral Son Won-il is credited with the founding of the **Republic of Korea's Navy**, having organized the Coastal Defense Army Unit in 1945. When war broke out, the admiral was at sea bringing home three patrol craft that had been purchased in the **United States**. During the latter part of the Korean War, he served as the defense minister for the **Republic of Korea**.

SORTIE. The term was used to identify one round-trip by one plane in any combination; for example, five sorties might be five planes on one trip, or one plane on five trips. During the Korean War the aircraft of the **United Nations** flew more than 1,040,708 sorties.

SOUTH AFRICA, UNION OF. This African Commonwealth nation sent a squadron of **F-51** Mustang fighters known as the "Flying Cheetahs." They flew as a part of the **Fifth United States Air Force** 18th Fighter Bomber Wing.

SOUTH KOREA. *See* REPUBLIC OF KOREA.

SOVIET UNION (UNION OF SOVIET SOCIALIST REPUBLICS). Maintaining the mistaken view that communism was both monolithic and international and believing that Soviet intentions were primarily in an expansion in Europe, the **United States** often misread the Soviet Union intentions and involvement. Certainly the Soviet Union, at least in the person of **Joseph Stalin**, was involved to some degree both in the decision to go to war and in maintaining the war once it was begun. Stalin did not prevent **Kim Il-Sung** from going to war even if he might not have been behind it. The absence of Soviet Union delegate to the **United Nations, Jacob Malik**, when the anti-invasion resolutions were being passed raised serious questions about aggressive intentions.

Joseph Stalin also conferred with Chinese premier **Mao Tse-tung** about the war and appeared to believe that the United States would not enter the conflict. The Korean War was not an attempt to expand international communism in Asia by military endeavor, nor was it a ploy to dislodge the United States from **NATO** commitments. It is also true that Soviet arms were supplied to some extent, and that it was this agreement that enabled the **People's Republic of China** to enter the war. Weapons and ammunition were made available, though the People's Republic of China was later charged for it. The decision to come to an agreement on the armistice was influenced by the death of Joseph Stalin and the desire on the part of Soviet leaders to return to the status quo.

Soviet Military Withdrawal from Korea. As his first act, newly elected **Kim Il-Sung** wrote both **Harry Truman** and **Joseph Stalin** asking them to withdraw their forces from Korea and recognize the **Democratic People's Republic of Korea**. Stalin recognized the DPRK on 19 September 1948 and announced the withdrawal of Soviet troops. The **Soviet Union** called upon the **United States** to do the same. The Truman administration was under a lot of pressure to withdraw and it accepted a provision of **National Security Council document 8/2**, which required removal of occupation forces by 30 June 1949.

SOVIET UNITED NATIONS SECURITY COUNCIL BOYCOTT. The **Soviet Union** delegate had been called back to Moscow for consultations in January 1950 after the seating of the **Republic of China** on the **United Nations Security Council**. He was, therefore, not present to vote on 25 June when the **United States** resolution was discussed and passed. Many historians suggest this indicates that the Soviet Union was not aware of the timing of the invasion.

SPECIAL OPERATIONS. The term refers to operations conducted against the **Democratic People's Republic of Korea** to cut supply lines, destroy communication, and tie down coastal defense personnel. Those involved included the 41st Independent Royal Marines, and both army and navy personnel who were dropped, carried, or deposited in the north for covert operations. Most of what would later be called "special operations" was conducted by the **partisans**.

SPENDER, PERCY C. (1897–1985). Australian ambassador to the **United States** during the Korean War and beyond, he was in favor of a Pacific pact much like **NATO** and saw entry into the Korean War as significant to the passage of a treaty. He supported the idea of sending Australian ground troops. The Australians would commit two **battal-**

ions. He agreed with **Great Britain** that to retaliate against the **People's Republic of China** was not wise, even though he and his government sided with the United States about not recognizing the government of the People's Republic of China. He would negotiate the **Australia–New Zealand–United States (ANZUS) Treaty**.

SPRING OFFENSIVE, 1951. On a line from just south of Kaesong on the east to Munsan and the **Imjin River** on the west the **Communist Chinese Forces** attacked on 22 April 1951, with 27 **divisions** along a 40-mile front. They struck **I, IX,** and **X Corps**, and three **Republic of Korea Army** divisions. The **United Nations** force was able to retreat carefully, holding the line to prevent the loss of **Seoul**, and to establish a new defensive line about 35 miles to the south. By 30 April the battle came to a close. The **United Nations**, under the command of Lieutenant General **James A. Van Fleet**, who assumed command on 11 April, had lost some essential territory and about 7,000 casualties. The People's Republic of China failed to capture Seoul and lost a reported 70,000 **casualties**. It was the largest battle of the Korean War.

SQUADRON. This was the basic administrative unit for aviation groups of the army, navy, marines, and air force and was composed of two or more division flights of aircraft, though not necessarily of the same make or type.

STAFF ORGANIZATION. In **United States** units during the Korean War the organization was based on an executive as chief of staff and four staff functions. Staff members, once identified, did not command troops. Beginning at the Pentagon or department level the functions were identified with somewhat expanded titles. G–1 was the adjunct, G–2 was the assistant chief of staff for intelligence and ranked as a major general; G–3 was called deputy chief of staff for operations at the major general rank; and G–4 was **logistics** and supply. At the **Joint Chiefs of Staff** level the functions were designated as J–1 (adjunct), J–2 (**intelligence**), J–3 (operations), and J–4 (logistic). At the division or corps level (army) the terms were G for general staff: G–1, G–2, G–3, and G–4. At the **battalion** and **regimental** level the second in command was the executive officer, followed by S–1 (adjunct), S–2 (intelligence), S–3 (operations and training), and S–4 (logistics and supply).

STALIN, JOSEPH (1879–1953). Stalin was the general secretary of the

Soviet Union's communist party from 1922 until his death and premier from 1941 to 1953. Stalin accepted the United States proposal on the division of Korea and remained open to unification until the Cold War began to heat up. In 1948 he ordered withdrawal of troops but left arms and advisers. Kim Il-Sung made a trip to Moscow seeking Russian aid and, while Stalin did not discourage the proposed invasion, he was very careful about the Soviet role in it. He withdrew his advisors so that none would be captured with the invading troops. Stalin defined the struggle as a civil war and was apparently concerned over escalation. He carefully distanced himself from what was happening there. He aided the People's Republic of China as it became involved by offering supplies but not troops. The stalemate at the Armistice table did not begin to break until after Stalin's death on 5 March 1953.

"STAND OR DIE" ORDER. On 29 July 1950 Lieutenant General Walton Walker, after meeting with General Douglas MacArthur, issued an order in which he stated that United States troops must hold their defensive positions at all costs. While the order has been interpreted in several ways, it must be seen as a statement that Eighth United States Army was expendable. The order, however, could not prevent the fact that the unit continually lost ground until forming a perimeter of defense around the port city of Pusan.

STATE DEPARTMENT. At this time, prior to the creation of a National Security Advisor, the Secretary of State was the primary advisor to the president on matters of foreign policy. During the Korean War Dean Acheson and his assistant for Far East affairs, Dean Rusk, were both hawks despite the continued charges against them that they were "soft on communism."

STATE–WAR–NAVY COORDINATING COMMITTEE 176/30. This was the 4 August 1947 report of the subcommittee to the State–War–Navy Coordinating Committee. It became basic policy until the 14 January 1948 approval of State–War–Navy Coordinating Committee 176/35. The basic recommendations were that the United States not pull out of Korea but that it should "liquidate" the costs in men and money without deserting Korea completely, The policy seems to have caught hold as the 1947 Korean Aid Bill was slashed providing $41 million for fiscal year 1948. On recommendation of George C. Marshall, a four-power meeting was called to establish Korean elections.

When the **Soviet Union** prevented this, he took the issue to the **United Nations (UN)** and put through UN Resolution, 14 November 1947.

STATE–WAR–NAVY COORDINATING COMMITTEE 176/35. This SWNCC statement, 14 January 1948, was **United States** policy until the emergence of **National Security Council** document 8. It was based on five points: the United States should reduce its commitment of men and money in Korea, the **Joint Chiefs of Staff** had little strategic interest in maintaining troops in Korea, the situation in Korea was untenable and the United States should find a way to pull out, the area in the south could not become self-sufficient, and the UN would hold elections there no later than 31 March 1948 to form a unified government. The report reaffirmed a unified independent Korea, but that the United States was not in a position to be accountable for that and ruled out any commitment to assistance beyond 31 December 1948.

STRATEGIC AIR COMMAND. *See* BOMBER COMMAND.

STRATEGIC AIRLIFT. *See* MILITARY AIR TRANSPORT SERVICE.

STRATEGY. Described as the use of resources to accomplish an established goal or end, it included military, economic, psychological, and political power focused on an identified mission. The assumption was that war and the military were but extensions of the political resource. War was usually considered three dimensional: tactical involved how battles were fought; operational was the use of a series of actions to complete a strategic end; and strategic was directed toward attainment of the political goals that led to the war.

STRATEGY, ALLIED. While not discounting the influence of the **Republic of Korea (ROK)**, **Great Britain**, and other contributing nations, the **United States** generally directed Allied strategy during the Korean War. Economically, it was able to enforce sanctions against nations that might have traded with the enemy. Diplomatically the United States was able to basically isolate the **Democratic People's Republic of Korea** and the **People's Republic of China (PRC)**. The opening of the war found the United States assuming an operational and strategic defensive with its immediate goals to slow and eventually contain the invading force. While there was unparalleled cooperation among the Allies, the united effort was not without difficulty and disagreement. Great Britain was particularly concerned by the United States aggressive attitude toward the PRC. Both sides were required to make adjustments and compromise. In September 1950 the Allies went on the offensive with the objectives changing to the liberation of the ROK and eventually the unification of Korea by force. When the PRC entered the war the Allied forces returned to containment. When containment was achieved in June of 1951 the war became an operational, tactical, and strategic defense that was content with a stalemate leading to the **Armistice**. *See also* STRATEGY, UNITED STATES.

STRATEGY, COMMUNIST. The communists' strategy appears to be far more simple than that of the **United Nations** or the **United States**. The policy throughout the war was the conquest of the **Republic of Korea** and they used every resource (political, economic, physiological, and military) to achieve this goal. Limited in both political and economic strength they turned to the military and psychological using every opportunity to weaken support from the home front and to sow dissatisfaction with the Allies. From the beginning the military strategy was operational offensive. Even while the communists were forced to withdraw during the advance on the **Yalu River**, and again with the stabilizing of the defensive line, the offensive goal never changed. By May or June of 1951 the military accepted the value of tactical defense but maintained the offensive goals through political and psychological efforts.

STRATEGY, UNITED STATES. Allied strategy was not always the same as that exercised by the **United States**. For the United States the early involvement committed the military to a defensive action designed, as in so many wars fought by the United States, to buy time for preparation. When the nation reached a point that it could bring its massive industrial and reserve strength into the fight, the strategy became that of destroying the enemy and liberating the **Republic of Korea**. After lapsing into the defensive mode during the **People's Republic of China** attack, the United States did not return to is usually strategic policy—to destroy the enemy and drive them from Korea—but maintained the defensive posture and sought to end the war by negotiations. This alteration, not entirely understood even today, forced a significant change in the way in which the United States conducted war.

Politically it reflected a decision to "contain" communism and not to attack in an effort to prevent an expanded war or even atomic warfare. Given time, men like **George F. Kennan** suggested, the ideology will die from within. The military response was the development of a *strategic defensive*, to frustrate expansion, and protect the status quo. Such a policy, the military understood, could never be conclusive. To end war by means of negotiation meant ending the war by compromise. In the United States this policy was never fully explained, nor was it accepted, and both the war and the president suffered a distinct loss of support. By many reasonable explanations the United States won the war in Korea because it stopped the invasion, contained communist expansion, and avoided a third world war. Unaware of what was happening to the traditional approach, America rejected the paradigm of Korea and thus found itself in the same position in the war in Vietnam.

STRATEMEYER, GEORGE E. (1890–1969). Lieutenant General Stratemeyer was a 1915 graduate of the United States Military Academy. During World War II he commanded the Army Air Force in China–Burma throughout the war. In April 1949 he took command of **Far East Air Force** and held that command when the Korean War began. Following a heart attack in May 1951 he relinquished his command to Lieutenant General **Otto P. Weyland** and in 1952 retired from the air force. He was a strong supporter of strategic bombing, believing it more important than close air–ground support.

SUBMARINES. United States Navy submarines were a part of the early response to the outbreak of the Korean War. A Korean War submarine was typically about 312 feet long, 27 feet wide, with a draft of 15 feet and powered by four diesel engines. The complement was seven officers and 70 enlisted men. Other than their customary task of screening naval forces, they performed reconnaissance, transported and supported clandestine raids by special forces, reconnoitered **Soviet Union** activities, and in general aided in the neutralization of enemy forces. The following are listed as participating in the Korean War: SS *Besugo, Blackfin, Blenny, Bluegill, Bugara, Cabezon, Caiman, Carp, Catfish, Charr, Diodon, Greenfish, Halfbeak, Menhaden, Perch, Pickerel, Pomodon, Queenfish, Remora, Ronquil, Sabalo, Scabbardfish, Sea Devil, Sea Fox Segundo, Stickleback, Tang, Tigrone, Tilefish, Tiru,* and *Volandor.*

SUBMARINE SEAFURIES. These planes entered service in 1941 as the Spitfire VB, converted with a hook and catapult spool. By the time of the Korean War the Mark XVII was in use. Considered a "delightful machine" by many flyers, it displayed excellent control harmony. It reached a speed of 398 miles per hour with a range of 400 miles. It was armed with four 20mm cannons and could carry a load of three 500-pound bombs.

SUIHO BOMBING ATTACK. In an effort to get the communists to accept the **Armistice** agreement, a massive air offensive was planned. Central to the attack was the huge 640,000 kilowatts dam located on the **Yalu River** northeast of Sinuiji. The **People's Republic of China (PRC)** used about 75 percent of the output for its industry. The **Joint Chiefs of Staff**, which had been reluctant to attack the dam because of the danger of increased PRC involvement, agreed to a raid on 19 June 1956. For three days the Suiho powerhouse was bombed. The raids were considered successful, but they did not change the communist position at the armistice talks. **Great Britain** claimed it had not been consulted about the raid and was upset with the decision.

SUKCHON. This was the site of one of two airborne operations of the **187th Airborne Regimental Combat Team.** In an effort to cut off the retreat of the **North Korean People's Army (NKPA)**, the force was dropped on 20 October 1950. One hundred and thirteen **C-119** and **C-47** transport aircraft were used. The drive did not manage to cut off the NKPA but did result in the taking of 3,818 **prisoners**. There were 111 **casualties**, more than one-third were accidents of the drop.

SUNG SHIN-LUN (1907–1990). A strong military leader who rose to prominence during the Chinese Civil War, he was named commissioner of the East China military and administrative committee. Rising to commander of the 9th Group Army of the **Chinese People's Volunteers** he gained a reputation as a hard fighter. His forces were some of the first into Korea and responsible for the Allied defeat at Chosin Reservoir. In summer 1952 he was named commander of the city of Shanghai.

SUPREME COMMANDER ALLIED POWERS (SCAP). Upon accepting the Japanese surrender General **Douglas MacArthur** was acting as the Supreme Commander Allied Powers. This command was activated to accept the formal surrender of **Japan** (on board the USS *Missouri*) and to command the Allied occupation forces in Japan.

SWEDEN. This country contributed military forces, the high in June 1951 at 162.

SWENSON, DAVID H. (1927–1950). On board the USS *Lyman K. Swenson*, Lieutenant (jg.) David H. Swenson was killed by fragments from communist shore fire at Wolmi-do. The accepted story was that he was killed on the ship named for his uncle Captain Lyman K. Swenson, who had been lost with the USS *Juneau* during World War II. Later investigation suggests the lieutenant's name was Swensen (with an e) and that a mistake in record keeping led to the confusion.

–T–

T-6 TEXAN (MOSQUITO). An advanced United States trainer that found considerable use during the Korean War as a forward observer-controlled aircraft spotting positions for **artillery** and bombardment.

T-BONE HILL, BATTLE OF. The fight began on 18 July 1952 as the Chinese launched a surprise attack on an outpost position on Hill 191 just south of T-Bone ridge. They were met by a combined force of the French Battalion and the United States 23rd Regiment. On the morning of 19 July, fierce fighting broke out along the ridge and continued, often with hand-to-hand fighting, until 23 July. When the primary attack failed, the Chinese engaged in attacks on several of the outposts, primarily Yoke and Eerie. The Chinese withdrew on 28 July but continued mortar and artillery bombardment on many of the ridge outposts.

TACTICAL AIRLIFT. *See* COMBAT CARGO COMMAND.

TACTICS. Primarily an expedient for achieving goals, it is generally used to discuss the organization of battle and the movement of troops for the successful completion of a combat mission. This is too broad a subject to be dealt with in a dictionary, but the identification of several innovations might be helpful in understanding the Korean War. One was General **Matthew Ridgway**, taking over after the long retreat from the Chosin Reservoir, who moved **Eighth United States Army** off the road and into the mountains. Two, **Operation Killer** and other related efforts were designed to kill the enemy rather than collect territory. Three, the **Communist Chinese Forces (CCF)** used a form of the "**human wave**" that in fact was simply frontal assaults that were psychologically, if not actually, effective. Four, the CCF reacted to air power by fighting primarily at night, withdrawing at dawn. Five, the communists operated by infiltration through the lines, cutting communication, and surrounding a unit so that when it attacked it did so from all directions, causing the **United States** to establish total perimeter defense. And, six, the most innovative tactic was the use of the **helicopter** to resupply troops in the field and for the movement of troops and the evacuation of wounded.

TAEBACK MOUNTAINS. Most significant of Korea's three mountain ranges, it runs north to south along the east coast. It separated **Eighth United States Army** and **Tenth Corps** during the **United Nations** advance in the latter part of 1950.

TAEGU, BATTLE OF. A highly embattled city and temporary capital of the **Republic of Korea**, it was under attack by the **North Korean People's Army (NKPA)** by late July 1950. It was essential to the United Nations as it formed the hinge along which a perimeter defense of Pusan could be built. Delayed by the **1st Cavalry Division** the NKPA finally crossed the Naktong River and by August were within 15 miles of the city. The government was moved again, this time to Pusan. The 27th Infantry battled the NKPA 13th Division at the "**Bowling Alley**," and the 23rd Infantry managed to stop the NKPA. A second attack struck in early September and General **Walton Walker** was in danger of losing Taegu. In a series of decisive attacks on Hill 314, a peak just seven miles north of Taegu, the NKPA was finally stopped and by 15 September was withdrawing. The last of the battle coincided with General **Douglas MacArthur**'s invasion at **Inchon** and **Eighth United States Army** breakout at **Pusan**.

TAEJON. The city of Taejon was located in central Korea, south of Seoul, along the **Kum River**. The advancing **Democratic People's Republic of Korea** forces reached the area in early July 1950. Because of its location, it played a major role in General **Walton Walker**'s first significant defense line in mid-July 1950.

    Taejon Agreement. This was an agreement reached with the **Republic of Korea** government, on 12 July 1950, where the **United States** was given exclusive jurisdiction over all U.S. military personnel. United States soldiers were not required to obey orders except from the American military. In return it was agreed that the United States military courts would have no jurisdiction over civilians.

Taejon, Battle of. *See* KUM RIVER, BATTLE OF.

Taejon, Command Center. Early in the war Taejon was the hub of the fighting. It was at the Taejon airstrip that Major General **William Dean** assumed command of the **United States Army** Forces in Korea replacing the General Headquarters, Advance Command and Liaison Group that had been in Korea since 1 July 1950. On 13 July 1950 **Eighth United States Army** established its headquarters in Taegu and took operational command of the war.

Taejon Declaration. On 15 July 1950, writing from the temporary capital at Taejon, President **Syngman Rhee** assigned the **Commander in Chief United Nations Forces**, General **Douglas MacArthur**, military control over all the land, sea, and air forces of the **Republic of Korea** for the duration of the conflict.

TAFT, ROBERT A. (1889–1953). This powerful Republican senator from Ohio was against **United States** imperialism and voted against the **North Atlantic Treaty Organization** because it expanded the president's power to commit United States troops without congressional action. Interestingly he favored President **Harry Truman**'s actions in Korea. He agreed with **Douglas MacArthur** and wanted troops from the **Republic of China** to be used in the Korean War but disagreed with MacArthur in that he was against using United States troops, or **nuclear weapons**, against the **People's Republic of China**. He sought the party nomination for president in 1948 and 1952 but failed and retired in June 1953.

TAILBOARD. *See* OPERATION TAILBOARD.

TAIWAN. Called **Formosa** during the Korean War period, it became the island stronghold of the **Republic of China**, then led by **Chiang Kai-shek** after the communist Chinese victory on the mainland. The island is separated from mainland **China** by the Taiwan Strait.

TANK. An armored self-propelled offensive vehicle with a revolving turret and at least one gun, usually mounted with one or more machine guns. The tanks, named for a description as a "water carrier" used to hide their manufacture, first appeared on the battlefield in 1916. *See* ARMOR; PATTON TANK; SHERMAN TANK.

TANK BATTALION. Each of the **infantry divisions** in **Japan** at the outbreak of war was authorized a heavy tank battalion. But only Company A of each battalion was equipped, and they were equipped with the light **Chaffee** reconnaissance tank. The **Republic of Korea** did not have tanks, so during the early stages of the Korean War the **North Korean People's Army** had the major advantage in **armor** support.

TASK ELEMENT. A subdivision of a **Task Group** usually composed of one or more ships with a specific short-term mission.

TASK FORCE. The term is used differently by the **United States Army** and the **United States Navy**. For the army it means an ad hoc unit, organized from a variety of units, to perform a specific mission or task. The unit usually carried the name of the officer in charge and was disbanded as soon as the mission was accomplished. For the navy task groups are semipermanent units created for a specific mission and might, like **Task Force 95 (Blockade and Escort Force)**, last for the duration of the war.

TASK FORCE 70. The fast carrier force served as a part of the preinvasion bombardments for the attacks on **Inchon, Pohang**, and **Wonsan** and the **Hungnam evacuation**.

TASK FORCE 77. The Seventh Fleet Strike Force was a combination of **United States, Australia, Canada**, and **New Zealand** warships that was a subordinate command of the **United States Navy Far East** and consisted of Task Force 77.1 Support Group, 77.2 Screening Group Destroyers, and 77.4 Fast Carriers of the Carrier Group. Task Force 77 operated primarily in the **Sea of Japan** and on the east coast of Korea. Task Force 77 initiated the first brief bombardment of the Korean War on 29 June 1959 when the USS *Juneau* fired on targets on the east coast of Korea.

TASK FORCE 90. The United States Amphibious Force (Far East) was the attack force at Inchon, Pohang, **Wonsan**, and **Hungnam** and provided covering fire for **United Nations** troops evacuating from Hungnam,

TASK FORCE 95. The designation of the **United Nations Blockade and Escort Force**, it provided gunfire support for the action at Inchon, Pohang, **Wonsan**, and the **Hungnam evacuation**. It established the **blockade** of Wonsan on 16 February 1950 that lasted until 27 July 1953, a siege of 861 days. The assigned tasks were the blockade of Korea, gunfire support for United Nations troops, bombardment, antimining exercises, escort, anti-submarine warfare, control of coastal fishing, and obtaining intelligence. *See also* TRAIN BUSTER CLUB.

TASK FORCE 96. This designated the Navy Forces Japan that provided patrol and **reconnaissance** support at Inchon, Pohang, **Wonsan**, and the **Hungnam evacuation**.

TASK FORCE FAITH. *See* TASK FORCE MACLEAN.

TASK FORCE MACLEAN/FAITH. Named for Colonel Donald Mac-Lean, commander of the 31st Infantry Regiment, **Seventh Division**, the task force was formed to relieve **First Marine Division** elements that were caught east of the **Chosin Reservoir**. The Task Force consisted of the Second and Third **Battalions** of the 31st, M-26 **Pershing tanks** of the regiment tank company, first battalion of the 32nd Infantry Regiment under Lieutenant Colonel Don C. Faith, the 57th Field Artillery Battalion, a platoon of eight quad-50s, and 40mm dusters from 15th Antiaircraft Battalion. Including **Republic of Korea** troops, there were about 3,200 soldiers. Relieving the Fifth Marine Regiment, the force took up positions east of the reservoir. His **Intelligence and Reconnaissance platoon**, sent out to scout the country, never came back. On the night of 27 November 1950 the **People's Republic of China** 80th Division struck the Task Force as three divisions of the **Communist Chinese Forces (CCF)** hit the marines west of the reservoir. Mac-Lean's defensive position was strung out. The First Battalion of the 31st took more than 100 casualties and the Second was not doing much better. His tanks were hit and several destroyed by the CCF using American 3.5-inch rockets. The CCF attack resumed on the night of 28–29 November and Donald MacLean withdrew into a perimeter. He was wounded and captured only to die in captivity.

Lieutenant Colonel William R. Reilly of the Third Battalion was severely wounded and so command fell to Lieutenant Colonel Don C. Faith. On 30 November Faith was ordered to fight south to the perimeter at Hagaru that was holding under the command of Colonel **Lewis B. "Chesty" Puller**. Faith, however, had more than 500 wounded and the temperature was dropping to 35 degrees below zero F. He found himself surrounded. Transferred from **Seventh Division** to **First Marine Division** control, the heavily pushed marines told them they had to take care of themselves. On the night of 30 November and 1 December the CCF attacked again and Faith suffered another 100 wounded. Faith put his wounded on trucks and moved south despite heavy CCF artillery and small-arms fire, and one case when U.S. Air Force planes mistakenly dropped napalm on his lead elements. Faith himself was wounded by a CCF grenade but he finally got the soldiers to Hudong only to find the regimental tank company that he assumed would cover them had been withdrawn. As the CCF hit them again Faith was killed (he would later be given the **Medal of Honor**) and many others were wounded. When it was over, only 385 of the original 3,200 had survived.

TASK FORCE SMITH. The first task force of United States troops to be committed to the war forming in Korea was named after its commander Lieutenant Colonel Charles B. Smith. It was composed of 440 soldiers drawn from several units. It consisted of First Battalion, 21st Infantry Regiment (less D company) of the **24th Infantry Division**, a recoilless rifle platoon from M Company with two 75mm rifles, Battery A of the 52nd Field Artillery Battalion (and its commander Lieutenant Colonel Miller O. Perry), and two 4.2 mortars. Assigned on 30 June 1950 they arrived in Korea on 1 July 1950 and took up positions near Taejon on 2 July. The task force relocated to a position north of Osan where it was hit on 5 July by elements of the **North Korean People's Army** 4th Division. The task force was accompanied by heavy **tanks**. The weapons Smith had available could not stop the Russian-built tanks. The task force held off the first wave of attack, but under the pressure of a second they began to withdraw. Disengagement was very difficult and the men began to move out individually. When they were able to reorganized in Taejon they recorded five officers and 148 men missing.

TASK GROUP. This term identified a subdivision of a **task force**, usually a unit of ships with a specific mission or assignment. During the Korean War, task groups were used for specific bombardment and support missions, often with a geographical designation.

TASK UNIT. One component of a **task group** or task element, usually a temporary designation for a specific mission. During the Korean War, task units were generally collected for bombardment or island invasion support missions.

TAYLOR, MAXWELL D. (1901–1987). A 1922 graduate of the Military Academy, General **Maxwell Taylor** was the commander of the 101st Airborne Division and jumped with them into Normandy on D-day. Later he served as superintendent of the United States Military Academy and as Army's G-3, chief of operations. He replaced General **James Van Fleet** as commander of **Eighth United States Army** in Korea. Aware of the political concerns and the pending negotiations, Taylor was reluctant to engage in extended combat or to take serious casualties. He eventually ordered the abandonment of both **Pork Chop Hill** and **Old Baldy**. He was appointed commander in chief, **Far East Command**. In May 1955 he followed General **Matthew B. Ridgway** as army chief of staff. He clashed with President **Dwight D. Eisenhower** over policies and retired. Later, under President John F. Kennedy he was recalled and appointed chair of the **Joint Chiefs of Staff**. During the Vietnam War he was Lyndon B. Johnson's appointment as ambassador to that country.

TENG HUA (1910–1980). He was the developer of the **Communist Chinese Forces** "night fight" and "near fight" that consisted of penetrating the lines after dark and attacking from all sides. As vice-commander of the **Chinese People's Volunteers Army** he was able, when that tactic began to lose impact, to alter **tactics** to the "underground China Wall," a tunnel system that provided a defensive line just north of the **38th Parallel**.

TENTH CORPS (X CORPS). Formed into a general headquarters, **Far East Command**, with a major general in command, it was originally a reserve building unit. It became the control headquarters for the **Inchon Landing** (composed of **First Marine Division** and **Seventh Infantry Division**). After the successful invasion at Inchon, General **Douglas MacArthur** kept X Corps as a separate command for the east coast invasion at **Wonsan**. It added the **Republic of Korea** I Corps and the **Third Infantry Division** for its move west and north. When the **People's Republic of China** entered the war, X Corps was ordered to retreat to **Hungnam**. Following the evacuation at Hungnam, X Corps became a part of **Eighth United States Army**. Command passed to Major General Clovis Byers and at the end of the war it was under Lieutenant General Isaac White.

THAILAND. The first Asian country to offer support for the Korean War,

Thailand sent a contingency, in July 1951, of one infantry **division** that was attached to the **United States Second Infantry Division**. This unit made a reputation in the defense of **Pork Chop Hill**. The 21st Infantry Regiment (renamed HM Queen Sirikit's Guard Unit) was attached to the **United States 24th Infantry Division**. In addition Thailand sent two corvettes, HMRTN *Bangpakon* and HMRTN *Prasae*, and units of the Royal Thai Air Force. Thailand suffered 136 dead and 496 wounded.

THIMAYYA, KADENERA SUBAYYA (1906–1965). He played a significant role in the **prisoner-of-war repatriation** as chair of the **Neutral Nations Repatriations Commission** (NNRC). Thimayya, known as "Thimmy" was a general in the **India** army and had been picked to head India's 5,000-person custodial force. Beginning in September 1953 he supervised the task of screening 22,600 communists and 359 **United Nations Command** prisoners who had declined being returned to the country of origin. The commission saw to it that the process was completed within the assigned eight-week period and dissolved itself on 1 February 1954.

THIRD INFANTRY DIVISION. The Third took part in the Champagne–Marne campaign of World War I earning the name the "Marne Division." It participated in 10 campaigns during World War II. When the Korean War broke out, the Third was scattered and two **battalions** stripped to build up the **First Cavalry Division** heading for Korea. The rebuilt division included the 65th Infantry (Puerto Rico) Division, the 9th, 10th, 39th, and 58th FA Battalion, the 64th Medium Tank Battalion, the Third Antiaircraft Artillery Battalion, the 10th Combat Engineers, and the Third Reconnaissance Company. After arriving in Korea on 20 August 1950, it was filled with thousands of Korean soldiers attached to the United States Army (KATUSA) and landed at **Wonsan** on 21 November 1950. The Third Division covered the withdrawal of **X Corps** from the **Chosin Reservoir** and the evacuation at **Hungnam**. Withdrawing by sea, the Third Division joined **Eighth United States Army** defensive line north of **Seoul**. It defended the **Imjin River** line during the **Communist Chinese Forces** spring offensive.

THIRD LOGISTICAL COMMAND. *See* KOREAN COMMUNICATIONS ZONE.

THIRTY-EIGHTH PARALLEL. Today it is the border between the

Democratic People's Republic of Korea and the **Republic of Korea**, but it was not intended to play that role. Selected as the occupation division between the **United States** and the **Soviet Union**, it was drawn as far north as the Army General Staff's Policy Section, Strategy and Planning Group, Operations Division felt the Russians would accept. **Dean Rusk**, then a colonel, claimed he was the one who selected this arbitrary demarcation line. The 190-mile line has no natural identifications: it crosses 12 rivers and 75 streams and dissects mountain ridges, highways, rail lines, and natural trails. Once it was established, however, the Soviet Union fortified the North Korea side of the line. When they rejected the call for national elections in 1947, and the **United Nations** held elections in the South, the 38th degree of north latitude became an international boundary.

Thirty-Eighth Parallel. This is the name of the magazine issued by the United States Korean War Commemoration Committee that sponsors and coordinates commemoration activities in the United States.

Thirty-Eighth Parallel, Crossing Decision. Following **Douglas MacArthur**'s victory at Inchon and the driving of the **North Korean People's Army (NKPA)** from the **Republic of Korea**, pressure to extend the war into the **Democratic People's Republic of Korea**, came to a head. Many advisors, including the **Joint Chiefs of Staff**, were encouraging President **Harry Truman** to finish the war and unify Korea under a single friendly government. President Truman made the decision to pursue the NKPA by 11 September 1950, even before the **Inchon Landing**. The passage of a **United Nations resolution of 7 October 1950**, designed to ensure stability in Korea, gave MacArthur whatever permission was needed, and he launched the offensive.

TRAIN. It is used in two different ways by the **United States** armed forces. First, it means a service force, or group of service elements, that provided logistical support. Second, it means the act of bringing a gun to bear on a given target.

TRAIN BUSTER CLUB. This honorary club of **Task Force 95** was organized in July 1952 by Captain H. E. Baker to identify and award those ships that had destroyed communist train(s) by sea-to-shore bombardment. Ships included (after the July starting date) HMCS *Crusader* with four; USS *Endicott* with three; USS *Orleck*, HMCS *Haida*, HMCS *Athabaskan*, USS *Pierce,* and HMS *Charity* with two each; and *Porter, Jaruis, Boyd, Trathen, Eversole, Kenya, Chandler, McCoy Reynolds, Car-*

mick, Maddox and *Piet Hein* with one each.

TRANSPORT AIRCRAFT. All transport aircraft used during the Korean War were propeller-driven. Transportation fell into two groups The first, which served inside the theater (tactical), was the Far East Air Force Combat Cargo Command (later to be called the 315th Air Division). The second was the intercontinental airlift (strategic) of the **Military Air Transport Service** (MATS). The planes used were the C-46 Commando and C-47 Skytrains flown by either **United States Air Force** personnel or **Royal Hellenic (Greek)** and Royal Thai Air Forces. The most common were C-54 Skymasters, C-119 Flying Boxcars, and later the giant C-124 Globemasters. MATS used the above planes but put more into service including C-97 Stratofreighters, C-118 Liftmasters, and C-121 Super Constellations. It also contracted with civilian aircraft.

TRIANGLE HILL, BATTLE OF. The hill (598) was part of a series of hills that were the object of **Operation Showdown**. The complex included Pike's Peak, Sandy Hill, and Jane Russell Hill on the right. The operation was to strengthen the defensive line held by United States **IX Corps** that ran north of Kumhwa. The **Communist Chinese Forces (CCF)** decided that the area was worth a fight and invested heavily. Segments of the **Seventh Infantry Division** moved forward and were soon fighting elements of the CCF 15th Army. The hill was taken on 15 October 1952. Then, on 30 October, the CCF was able to push the **Republic of Korea** off and to take, two days later, Jane Russell Hill. The conflict focused on Sniper Ridge a mile east, a part of the objective, and troops were able to capture it on 18 November, the fourteenth time the area had changed hands. The initial plan had expanded to take more than five weeks and resulted in more than 9,000 casualties.

TRIPARTITE MEETINGS. During November 1951 representatives from **France**, **Great Britain**, and the **United States** met in Paris on the subjects of **Australia**, Egypt, Germany, Iran, Korea, and the **North Atlantic Treaty Organization**. As far as Korea was concerned, the talks addressed the issue of monitoring a **cease-fire** once it was established. They feared that a demand for a strong inspection formula was not feasible but without it the United States was concerned that it would not be able to prevent a communist military offensive. After prolonged discussions, Great Britain and the United States considered preparing a statement saying that if the **People's Republic of China** broke the cease-fire it might well force the **United Nations Command** to bomb airfields in **Manchuria** or even order a naval **blockade** of the China coast. They also agreed that the statement should not be issued unless the **United Nations** was unable to negotiate for a strong inspection system. Britain was reluctant to agree to any plan that would commit them to a general blockade but was willing to consider a limited bombing of China in retaliation

TROOP SHIPS. *See* MILITARY SEA TRANSPORT SERVICE.

TRUCE TALK RESUMPTIONS (25 OCTOBER 1951). General **Matthew Ridgway** was not willing to resume talks at **Kaesong** because it was under control of the **Communist Chinese Forces**. The battle situation did not require any immediate resumption, according to Washington, and Ridgway was authorized to wait. Nevertheless continued pressure from **Great Britain** and the losses suffered by the **People's Republic of China** and the **Democratic People's Republic of Korea**, led both sides back to the table that had been moved, by agreement, to the village of **Panmunjom**.

TRUCE TALK RESUMPTIONS (26 APRIL 1953). **Joseph Stalin** died on 5 March 1953. On 15 March **Georgi Malenkov**, the new communistparty secretary, announced that the issues between the warring parties could be settled. On 28 March the communists accepted a **United Nations Command** proposal of 22 February for the exchange of sick and wounded **prisoners of war**. Chinese radio suggested on 30 March that prisoners should be sent to a neutral nation to ensure a proper and just **repatriation**. The **Soviet Union** and **Democratic People's Republic of Korea** both supported the idea. The **United States** agreed to the meeting of liaison officers and by 11 April an agreement on the exchange of sick and wounded had been worked out. The full group began meeting again on 26 April 1953.

TRUCE TALK SUSPENSION (23 AUGUST 1951). Claiming that **United Nations** planes bombed **Kaesong** (a United States plane did strafe Kaesong in error on 10 September 1951), the communists were upset because the **United Nations Command** would not consider the **38th Parallel** as the demarcation line, so they suspended talks.

TRUCE TALK SUSPENSION (8 OCTOBER 1952). The **United Na-**

tions suspended the truce talks at **Panmunjom** on 8 October 1952 after all further progress ground to a halt on **Agenda Item IV**, the repatriation of **prisoners of war**.

TRUMAN DOCTRINE. President **Harry S. Truman**'s Cold War policy is also referred to as "containment." Truman pushed through **Congress** the authority to wage the Cold War and to intervene in the civil affairs of nations in order to prevent the spread of communism. The policy was successfully defended in **United States** support for **Greece** and **Turkey** and again during the Berlin Air Lift.

TRUMAN, HARRY S. (1884–1973). Born and raised in Missouri, Harry S. Truman served with the Missouri National Guard in World War I. He became active in politics after the war and won election to Jackson County offices and in 1934 to the United States Senate. He was elected vice president, in 1944, primarily on the strength of his excellent reputation from the watchdog committee investigation of the defense industry, under President Franklin D. Roosevelt. After FDR's death Truman brought World War II to its end, made the decision to drop the atomic bomb on Japan, and authorized the use of **United States** aid to Greece and Turkey during the first stages of the Cold War .

He won election in his own right in 1948, worked through the Marshall Plan, committed the United States to a mutual defense treaty through the **North Atlantic Treaty Organization**, and accepted the recommendations of **National Security Council Document-68** that acknowledged America's responsibility to protect the world from communism. Seeing the **North Korean People's Army** invasion as a part of the planned takeover of the **Republic of Korea** and the expansion of international communism, Truman committed troops to Korea.

The American goals in Korea were never very clearly articulated and after the **People's Republic of China** intervention the national policy changed from driving the North Korean People's Army out and liberating the Republic of Korea to containment. The military outcome of this was difficult to implement and increasing disagreement between Truman and his field commander, **Douglas MacArthur**, led to MacArthur being fired. While the firing of General MacArthur was in order with Truman's view of the presidency, it was the last straw in Truman's political popularity. Truman decided not to run again and left office in January 1953.

Truman Fires Douglas MacArthur. President **Harry Truman** had never been greatly impressed with General **Douglas MacArthur**. From the beginning, the problem grew. MacArthur's insistence on making public statements that either criticized or detracted from the president's position added to the discomfort. MacArthur complained about the **Manchurian sanctuary**, about restraints on the use of **Republic of China** troops, the sidetracking of the presidential **cease-fire** proposal, and finally—after being told not to do so—MacArthur wrote his views to Representative **Joseph Martin** who read them on the floor of the United States House of Representatives. Truman signed the order of recall on 10 April 1951, and it was leaked to MacArthur before it was communicated officially. *See also* PRONUNCIAMENTO.

Truman's Address to Congress (19 July 1950). General **Douglas MacArthur** was calling for more divisions, and there was a shortage of soldiers, funds, and materials to fight the war. On the advice of Secretary of State **Dean Acheson** Truman asked **Congress** for new appropriations to fund the war. In his address he condemned the **Soviet Union** and the **Democratic People's Republic of Korea** and extended his promise to back the **United Nations**, bring about the neutralization of **Taiwan**, and support the Philippines and Indochina. As a result, and aided by a brief period of public support for the Korean War, Congress authorized an additional $11 billion and the increase of the military to 3.2 million people.

Truman's Atomic Bomb Press Conference. In a report to President **Harry Truman** the Pentagon suggested that it might, at some time, be necessary to use **nuclear weapons** to prevent American troops in Korea from being overrun. When the president met with the press on 30 November 1950 the **Communist Chinese Forces** had just entered the war and **United Nations** troops were in retreat. In responding to questions the president indicated that he would use every weapon necessary. When pushed by reporters he indicated that (contrary to the dictates of the Atomic Energy Act of 1946) the field officers would have charge of the use of such weapons. There was reaction from all over the world and **Great Britain** was so concerned that **Clement R. Attlee** came to meet with Truman. Truman did not act on the recommendations and turned his attention to the possibility of negotiations.

Truman's Proposed Cease-Fire Initiative. Taking advantage of **Eighth United States Army**'s success in regaining some military initiative, President **Harry Truman** sought to deliver a message to the communists saying that the **United Nations** was open to peace discussions, but if they did not enter negotiations the UN would pursue the war. The

Joint Chiefs of Staff told **Douglas MacArthur** of this plan on 20 March 1951, but before it could be implemented MacArthur issued his own ultimatum. The MacArthur threat was that the UN might well attack the **People's Republic of China**. This action was seen as defiant and most likely was one of the causes for MacArthur's dismissal. But, perhaps more important, it preempted the president's effort and slowed the process of negotiation.

Truman's Seizure of the Steel Plants. This happened after management rejected a union plan provided under arbitration with the Wage Stabilization Board. When management rejected the plan **Harry Truman**, acting as commander in chief, ordered Secretary of Commerce Charles Sawyer to seize and operate the nation's steel mills. The president felt the called strike might well have an immediate effect on the war in Korea. It was not a popular decision and 14 resolutions were introduced in **Congress** for his impeachment. On 2 June 1951 the Supreme Court voted 6–3 that the seizure was unconstitutional. After this, on 24 July 1951, Truman met with union and management and reached an agreement that favored the management position, and the mills went back into production.

Truman's Speech (1 September 1950). On this date President **Harry Truman** used radio and television to explain to the American people why the **United States** was in Korea. Using the fascist rise to power in 1930 as his analogy he affirmed that if the United States let the communists get away with it in Korea, they would do it again somewhere else. He blamed the **Soviet Union**, which he explained controlled the **Democratic People's Republic of Korea**. After outlining his various containment commitments around the world he said that the employment of troops in Korea was but another phase in the continuing struggle between imperialism and freedom. He acknowledged that the United States, along with the **Republic of Korea**, bore the greatest burden, but that the action was supported by the **United Nations**. As a result of this action Truman announced that the United States wanted to avoid a greater war with the Soviet Union, but listed as the nation's goals that the Republic of Korea be free, independent, and united. He closed with yet another affirmation that the United States must continue the fight against communism.

Truman's Statement (27 June 1950). This remarkable statement altered the **United States**, and probably world, history. In it Truman noted that the North Koreans had not withdrawn and that the attack on the South Koreans was evidence the **Soviet Union** would use military invasion to expand communism. He announced that he had ordered the Seventh Fleet to the Taiwan Strait to prevent the **People's Republic of China** from attacking and warned the **Republic of China** not to attack the mainland. In this statement he directed military assistance to the French fighting in Indochina (Vietnam), and he provided military aid to the Philippines that was fighting communist guerrillas. U.S. political leaders praised Truman's outspokenness.

TRUMAN–ATTLEE JOINT COMMUNIQUE. *See* ATTLEE, CLEMENT.

TRUMAN–EISENHOWER TRANSITION MEETING. After the 1952 election, President **Harry Truman**, President-elect **Dwight Eisenhower**, and their staffs met to discuss the Korean War. Truman offered to provide any information the new president might want and hoped to gain support for the **United States** position on the **cease-fire**. Truman wanted Eisenhower to make a statement of support in favor of the United States position on **prisoner-of-war repatriation**. Eisenhower refused and instead issued a public relations statement to announce the two had met and talked. The next day, however, 19 November 1952, Eisenhower released a statement suggesting that he favored non-forcible repatriation. Truman and Eisenhower did not meet again concerning Korea.

TRUMAN'S DECLARATION OF A NATIONAL EMERGENCY. The declaration of a national emergency activated statutory provisions that allowed the president to expand the armed forces and maintain the industrial base. It was also a psychological wake-up call in the case of the Korean War. Acting on staff advice, and following the victories of the **People's Republic of China** during December 1950, Truman declared the emergency on 16 December 1950. While he did not take full advantage of the economic powers the action gave him, it did serve the purpose of "doing something" in response to a war that was increasingly unpopular with the people of the **United States**.

TSAI CHENG-WEN (1915–   ). Major General Tsai Cheng-Wen was the chief negotiator of the Korean **Armistice** agreement on the communist side. During the Korean War he served as the primary liaison between the **Communist Chinese Forces** and the **North Korean People's Army (NKPA)**. He reported that the NKPA could not hold without air support and that a prolonged war would be disastrous for the **Democratic People's Republic of Korea**. When the time came he prepared the way for the involvement of the **Chinese People's Volunteers Army**. The difficulty with fighting in Korea, he reported, was the problems of translation and transportation.

TSARAPKIN, SEMYONG (1906–1984). He was the **Soviet Union**'s deputy permanent delegate on the **United Nations** Security Council. He took part in the discussions between Thomas J. Cory (**United States** delegate) and **Jacob A. Malik** that were preliminary to the **Kaesong** truce talks.

TSIANG TING-FU (1895–1965). During the Korean War Tsiang Ting-Fu was the permanent **Republic of China** delegate to the **United Nations**. Loyal to **Chiang Kai-shek**, though he was often seen as an alternative for him, he criticized the **United States** for not providing enough support for the **Republic of China**. He worked to get more Asian help for the fight in Korea and to maintain **Republic of Korea** representation in the UN. After the war, and during the last three years before his death, he was the Republic of China ambassador to the United States.

TUMEN RIVER. The flow of this river provides the border between the **Democratic People's Republic of Korea** and the **Soviet Union** and between the DPRK and eastern **Manchuria**. It moves for 324 miles from the mountains of central Korea and flows into the **Sea of Japan**.

TURKEY. The Turks were major contributors to the war effort in Korea. The Turkish Brigade (Turkish Army Command Force) provided, at the top strength, 5,455 soldiers and its own artillery units. The units joined **Eighth United States Army** in November 1950, fought the way through the invasion by **Communist Chinese Forces**, and became a part of the blocking force at **Kunu-ri**. Known by their allies as the "Terrible Turks," they were a tough hard-fighting unit. Famous for their **bayonet** charge against a CCF position in January 1951 that, it is said, led to General **Matthew B. Ridgway** ordering line units to fix bayonets. During the war 14,936 Turks served, 741 were killed in action, and 2,069 were wounded in action. The Turkish government did not award medals for valor but several members of the Turkish unit received awards from the United States government.

TWENTY-ONE-POWER UNITED NATIONS RESOLUTION. President **Harry Truman** wanted a **United Nations (UN)** resolution supporting the **United States** position on the voluntary **repatriation of prisoners of war**. The United States delegation was able to get 21 nations to support a resolution calling on the communists to accept the proposed voluntary repatriation of prisoners. The support failed, however, as the **V. K. Krishna Menon** proposal was seen as an alternative. A UN resolution, based on the Menon proposal, passed on 3 December 1952 and provided the framework for a settlement of this issue.

24TH INFANTRY DIVISION. Originally formed out of the Hawaiian Division, the 24th performed well during World War II and was on occupation duty in **Japan** when the Korean War broke out. The initial composition of the **division** was the 19th, 21st, and 34th Infantry Regiments; the 11th, 13th, 52nd, and 63rd Field Artillery; Company A 78th Tank Battalion; 26th Antiaircraft Battalion; the 3rd Engineer Battalion; and the 24th Reconnaissance Company. The division's 21st Infantry Regiment made up of **Task Force Smith** was the first to fight in Korea. The rest of the division was in Korea by 23 July and was nearly destroyed fighting a series of delaying actions at Osan, Cho'nan, the Kum River, and Taejon. Its commander, Major General **William F. Dean**, was taken prisoner.

It was strengthened on 8 August 1950 when M-46 Patton **tanks** replaced the Chaffee light tanks. On 31 August the Fifth Infantry Regiment and its 555th Field Artillery Battalion replaced the 34th. Survivors of the 34th were transferred to the 19th Infantry and the 21st Infantry. The division withdrew under heavy attacks by the **Communist Chinese Forces (CCF)** into positions south of **Seoul**. It counterattacked in March 1951 into the **Iron Triangle** and turned back the CCF **spring offensive**. After duty in the central sector of **Eighth United States Army** defensive line, it was transferred, in January 1952, to Japan and was replaced by the 40th Infantry Division. It returned to Korea in July 1953 to provide rear-area security but saw no additional combat. The "Victory Division" suffered 11,889 **casualties** and won both **United States** and **Republic of Korea Presidential Unit Citations.**

25TH INFANTRY DIVISION. Called the "Tropic Lightning Division," it was originally formed out of the Hawaiian Division. It fought in the Pacific during World War II. It was composed of the 27th and 35th Infantry Regiments; the black 24th Infantry Regiment; the 8th, 64th, 90th, and 159th Field Artillery; the 79th Tank Battalion; 21st and 159th Field Artillery; the 79th Tank Battalion; 21st Antiaircraft Artillery Battalion; the 65th Engineering Battalion; and the 25th Reconnaissance Company. Later in the war as integration moved through the army, the 24th Infantry Regiment and its 159th FA were disbanded and replaced with the 14th Infantry Regiment from Colorado with the 69th FA Battalion. It was on occupational duty in **Japan** when the Korean War broke out, and elements of the division were sent to the defense of the **Naktong perimeter** during early July. It took part at **Chongchon**, battles of **Iron Triangle**, and at Reno, Vegas, and Berlin outposts. It suffered 13,685 **casualties** and won two **Republic of Korea Presidential Unit Citations** and several **Distinguished Unit Citations**.

29TH REGIMENTAL COMBAT TEAM (RCT). Stationed on **Okinawa**, the RCT had only two of its three authorized **regiments**. The First and Third Battalions were ordered to Korea on 15 July 1950 and on 25 July committed to combat on the Naktong River line near Chinju. There it suffered heavy casualties and the First Battalion received a Presidential Unit Citation (United States). Eventually both battalions were integrated into the 25th Infantry Division.

TWINING, NATHAN F. (1897–1982). A graduate of the United States Military Academy at West Point in 1917 he transferred to the Army Air Service in 1923. In 1950 he became vice chief of staff and during the illness of the chief, General **Hoyt Vandenberg**, he represented the **United States Air Force** at **Joint Chiefs of Staff** meetings. He supported air power as the key to the United States future defense. He became the U.S. Air Force Chief of Staff on 30 June 1953.

–U–

UNIT AWARDS. *See* PRESIDENTIAL UNIT CITATIONS.

UNITED NATIONS. Formed in 1945 and located at Lake Success, New York, the United Nations had been involved with Korea since November 1947. At that time a nine-nation **UN Temporary Commission on Korea** was established to supervise elections and the formation of a new government. When the **Democratic People's Republic of Korea (DPRK)** launched its attack, Secretary-General **Trygve Lie** considered it an attack on the United Nations and thus supported the **United States** resolution to label the DPRK as the aggressor. On 26 June 1950 a resolution calling upon member nations to come to the aid of the **Republic of Korea** passed and on 7 July 1950 the United Nations passed a resolution making President **Harry Truman** the **executive agent** for the Security Council. When the **Soviet Union**'s delegate **Jacob Malik** returned to the Security Council with the veto. This ended Security Council directives, but the General Assembly continued to speak for the United Nations on Korea. The Korean War is considered the first UN war.

UNITED NATIONS ADDITIONAL MEASURES COMMITTEE. This group, a follow-up of the Collective Measures Committee, was composed of **Australia**, **Belgium**, Brazil, **Canada**, Egypt, **France**, **Great Britain**, the **Philippines**, **Turkey**, the **United States**, and Venezuela. The United States pushed for economic sanctions against the **People's Republic of China (PRC)**, but were opposed by Great Britain that did not want to push the PRC too far. On 14 May 1951 the group approved a United States proposal for embargos against China, and it was passed by the United Nations Political Committee 47–0. The resolution passed the General Assembly but made little difference, since most allied nations had already imposed such restrictions.

UNITED NATIONS AIR FORCES. Several nations contributed aircraft and pilots to the war in Korea. **Great Britain** supplied carrier-based Sea Furies, Seafires, and Fairey Fireflies. There were ground-based F-51 Mustangs of the **Royal Australian Air Force** and the **South African** Air Force Squadron. In addition the **Commonwealth** provided artillery spotter aircraft and three squadrons of Sunderland Flying boats. **Belgium** provided several DC-4 transports, **Greece** supplied eight C-47 Skytrain transports, and **Canada** and the Royal Thai Air Force provided air transports. The **Republic of Korea** had only 16 light planes, most of which were destroyed during the early days of the war. Once war began the ROKAF was provided with F-51 Mustangs. The records of these nations list 44,873 **sorties** flown at a cost of 152 aircraft.

UNITED NATIONS APPEAL FOR ADDITIONAL TROOPS. During December 1950 Secretary of State **Dean Acheson** began to approach other nations for additional troops for Korea. He was unable to secure any additional help. He asked **United Nations** Secretary-General **Trygve Lie**, who made numerous unsuccessful appeals. General **Matthew Ridgway** was not sure if additional troops were needed once the negotiations began, and the efforts changed from seeking more troops to increasing the capabilities of the **Republic of Korea Army**.

UNITED NATIONS CEASE-FIRE GROUP. The Political Committee of the **United Nations** General Assembly supported an Arab–Asian bloc resolution that sought to create a group to determine the basis for a **cease-fire**: Nasrollah Entezam of Iran, Lester B. Pearson of **Canada**, and Sir Benegal N. Rau of **India**. The **Communist Chinese Forces**, however, considered the group illegal and further efforts to come to an agreement were unsuccessful. The group was asked to establish a set of principles upon which a cease-fire might be negotiated, and they came up with five principles that, in time, the **People's Republic of China (PRC)** rejected on the grounds a cease-fire should precede a political discussion. Failure of peace talks led the United States to sponsor a resolution condemning the PRC as an aggressor. The 1 February 1951 resolution, however, also provided for a **United Nations Good Offices Committee,** based on the cease-fire group that was to continue to seek peaceful solution.

UNITED NATIONS CIVIL ASSISTANCE COMMAND, KOREA (UNCAC). This group was created to replace the **United Nations Korean Reconstruction Agency** that could not function well after the **People's Republic of China** entered the conflict. Early in 1951 the UNCAC was placed under **Eighth United States Army** to prevent disease and unrest in rear areas and to strengthen security within Korea. It provided food, shelter, and medical supplies to **refugees** for short-term relief and worked at reconstruction where possible. The group made an effort to decentralize the command structure with the **Republic of Korea** but with little success.

UNITED NATIONS COLLECTIVE MEASURES COMMITTEE. Created in November 1950 to suggest methods of establishing international peace, it recommended that member nations maintain armed forces to be used, when necessary, by the **United Nations**. The states involved were **Australia, Belgium,** Brazil, **Canada,** Egypt, **France, Great Britain,** Mexico, the **Philippines, Turkey,** the **United States,** and Venezuela. After the **Communist Chinese Forces** had pushed south of the **38th Parallel,** the United Nations resolution of 1 February 1951 branded the **People's Republic of China** the aggressor and established the **United Nations Additional Measures Committee.**

UNITED NATIONS COMMAND. At the request of the **United Nations** that had authorized a unified command in Korea on 7 July 1950 President **Harry S. Truman** designated General **Douglas MacArthur** as "Commanding General of the Military Forces" of the united command. This role, Commander in Chief United Nations Command, was added to MacArthur's other military responsibilities. The **Republic of Korea** on 24 July 1950 placed its military forces under the command of the United Nations. MacArthur added the **Far East Air Forces** and the **United States Naval Forces Far East** to the already identified **United States Army Forces Far East**. The General Headquarters United Nations Command and the General Headquarters **Far East Command** were basically the same. The United Nations Command was still in existence in the early 21st century, reporting its activities to the Security Council.

UNITED NATIONS COMMAND FINAL PRISONERS-OF-WAR SETTLEMENT PROPOSAL, 25 MAY 1953. Major General **William K. Harrison Jr.**, the senior **United Nations** delegate put forward this modified proposal on 25 May 1953. The **Neutral Nations Repatriation Commission (NNRC)** was to make its decision on repatriation by a majority vote, to hold non-repatriated **People's Republic of China** and **Democratic People's Republic of Korea** for 90 days, and if no solution was reached within 120 days, the prisoners were to be released or referred to the United Nations General Assembly. The NNRC was to release non-repatriated POWs and dissolve itself after 120 days if no other agreement was reached by political conference. The communists accepted the proposal, and it was signed on 8 June 1953. *See also* PRISONERS OF WAR.

UNITED NATIONS COMMISSION FOR THE UNIFICATION AND REHABILITATION OF KOREA (UNCURK). Following up on the victory after the successful **Inchon Landing**, the **United Nations (UN)** sought to move toward unification of Korea. This commission, created under the **United Nations Resolution of 7 October 1950**, consisted of representatives from **Australia**, Chile, **The Netherlands**, Pakistan, the **Philippines**, **Thailand**, and **Turkey**. While its immediate goal was to represent the United Nations in occupied territory, it was also charged with efforts to bring about a unified and independent democratic nation. On 12 October it was suggested that the UNCURK assume the government of all occupied territory in the **Democratic People's Republic of**

Korea. **Syngman Rhee** was angered but finally agreed to work toward a common goal. Nevertheless the tension remained as the UNCURK continued to interfere with what Rhee considered local politics. When the **People's Republic of China** entered the fight the question was moot. However, the commission continued until 1972 in the prolonged hope that the United Nations might have some influence in the unification.

UNITED NATIONS COMMISSION ON KOREA (UNCOK). The report of this commission, which was on duty along the **38th Parallel**, provided the evidence needed to convince the **United Nations** that the **Democratic People's Republic of Korea** had initiated the attack. The commission members had been in Korea between 9 and 23 June to investigate evidence of military buildups. It was very significant in the passage of the **United Nations Security Council Resolution, 25 June 1950**. *See also* UNITED NATIONS RESOLUTION, 12 DECEMBER 1948.

UNITED NATIONS GOOD OFFICES COMMITTEE. Established on 30 January 1951 and confirmed by **United Nations Resolution of 1 February 1951**, this was an effort to use the "good offices" of the United Nations to bring about a **cease-fire** in Korea.

UNITED NATIONS KOREAN RECONSTRUCTION AGENCY (UNKRA). This agency was established on 1 December 1950 by a **United Nations** resolution to help the Korean people rebuild from the effects of war. The UN recommended $250 million for immediate relief. To direct this program after the **People's Republic of China** intervention, the immediate task of the UNKRA was refocused in the **United Nations Civil Assistance Command**. The work of the body would establish the foundation for the economic growth and financial stability enjoyed by the **Republic of Korea**. *See also* UNITED NATIONS RESOLUTION, 1 DECEMBER 1950.

UNITED NATIONS NATIONAL ASSISTANCE. By January 1950, in response to the **United Nations** appeal, 49 nations had offered to help the **United Nations Command**. Those nations that actually provided material aid were: Argentina, Australia, Belgium, Bolivia, Brazil, Canada, Chile, Colombia, Costa Rica, Cuba, Denmark, Ecuador, El Salvador, Ethiopia, France, Great Britain, Greece, Iceland, India, Israel, Italy,

Lebanon, Liberia, Mexico, The Netherlands, New Zealand, Nicaragua, Norway, Pakistan, Panama, Paraguay, Peru, Philippines, Republic of China, South Africa, Sweden, Thailand, Turkey, Uruguay, and Venezuela.

UNITED NATIONS NAVAL SUPPORT. As in other commands, the **United States** provided the majority of the warships and personnel for the **United Nations** naval effort. The largest of the other contributions was the ships of **Great Britain**. Also an early supporter, **Australia** supplied one **carrier**, and five **frigates**. **New Zealand** sent two frigates and **Canada** four **destroyers**. Other nations made warships available including **Colombia** with two frigates, **France** one frigate, **The Netherlands** one destroyer, **Thailand** two frigates, and a hospital ship from **Denmark**. Once the war began the **Republic of Korea Navy**, while not technically a part of the United Nations, was put under operational control of the **United States Navy Far East**. At the beginning of the war they had available 15 motor **minesweepers**, an LST, and a frigate. Assigned to **blockade** operations and operating independently as **Task Group 96.7**, they were incorporated into **Task Force 95**, the **Blockade and Escort Force**.

UNITED NATIONS OFFENSIVE ACROSS THE THIRTY-EIGHTH PARALLEL. *See* THIRTY-EIGHTH PARALLEL CROSSING DECISION; UNITED NATIONS RESOLUTION, 7 OCTOBER 1950.

UNITED NATIONS PARTISAN INFANTRY (UNPIK). At one time the partisan strength reached almost 22,000. It was composed of Koreans from north of the **38th Parallel** who conducted raids behind the lines in either the **Democratic People's Republic of Korea** or the **People's Republic of China**. The **Eighth United States Army** provided food, shelter, and some equipment on a series of island bases. More than 200 Americans were involved in working with the partisans. The first "Green Berets" were involved in the partisan efforts. While of limited success, they did record a significant number of enemy casualties. In the main, however, the United States was not committed to unconventional warfare during the Korean period, and this limited the overall efficiency of the clandestine groups.

UNITED NATIONS PEACE OBSERVATION COMMISSION. *See* UNITED NATIONS UNITING FOR PEACE RESOLUTION, 3 NO-

VEMBER 1950.

UNITED NATIONS PRISONERS-OF-WAR ADMINISTRATION. As the early stages of the war progressed, the **United Nations Command** was unprepared for the large number of prisoners taken. On 16 September 1950 **Eighth United States Army** took control of **prisoners of war** and by November 1950 held about 137,000 prisoners. While the camps were harsh, there was little difficulty, until after the **Communist Chinese Forces** intervention. Fearing the large number of poorly controlled prisoners, General **Matthew Ridgway** ordered them combined into selected camps in **Operation Albany**. Most were moved to **Koje-do**, an island prison camp off the coast of **Pusan**. Because the **United Nations** could not provide adequate security **Republic of Korea** guards were used. In the camps communist leadership took over and the camps were well organized. The **Dodd–Colson incident**, where the camp commander was captured and forced to confess mistreatment of the prisoners, pushed Eighth United States Army to a more aggressive posture, which included separating prisoners of the **Democratic People's Republic of Korea** and the **People's Republic of China**. *See also* PRISONERS-OF-WAR CAMPS.

UNITED NATIONS RESOLUTION, 12 DECEMBER 1948. This resolution committed the **United Nations** to the survival of the **Republic of Korea**. It recognized the Republic of Korea as the only legitimate government on the peninsula and allowed its representatives to take part in United Nations decisions. It also set up the **United Nations Commission on Korea** (UNCOK) to oversee and verify the withdrawal of troops by the **United States** and **Soviet Union**. The resolution passed despite criticism by the Soviet Union. The resolution was a difficult one for many member nations because it alienated the Soviet Union and it increased the risk the United Nations would be involved in what many saw as a Korean civil war.

UNITED NATIONS RESOLUTION, 21 OCTOBER 1949. On 26 September 1949 the **United States**, the **Philippines**, **Australia**, and the **Republic of China** presented a resolution to maintain a commission in Korea to observe what was going on. The commission would observe, but it would also offer its services to negotiate between the **Republic of Korea** and the **Democratic People's Republic of Korea (DPRK)** on unification. The **United Nations** approved the resolution by a wide margin. After running into opposition from the DPRK, the commission asked for military observers to help monitor what was happening in Korea.

UNITED NATIONS RESOLUTION, 7 OCTOBER 1950. This gave the **United Nations Command** permission to cross the **38th Parallel** and pursue the **North Korean People's Army** in an effort to unify the Korean nation. In this case it was *ex post facto* since General **Douglas MacArthur** had already been authorized by the **Joint Chiefs of Staff** to move north.

UNITED NATIONS RESOLUTION, 1 DECEMBER 1950. It established the **United Nations Korean Reconstruction Agency** (UNKRA) that was to provide for relief and rehabilitation of Korea and to provide financial aid in that cause. It passed 51–0 with 5 abstentions. The agency was to consult with other nations concerning financial contributions.

UNITED NATIONS RESOLUTION, 14 DECEMBER 1950. This resolution emerged from the Arab–Asian effort and called for the creation of a three-person committee to determine the basis for a **cease-fire**.

UNITED NATIONS RESOLUTION, 1 FEBRUARY 1951. President **Harry Truman** was determined to achieve a condemnation of the **People's Republic of China (PRC)** after it entered the Korean War. On 20 January it proposed a resolution calling the PRC the aggressor. Several member nations, including **Great Britain**, indicated that they might not vote if it came to the Assembly, so the **United States** accepted two amendments that (when adopted) would keep open the efforts at a cease-fire and avoid immediate action by delaying the report of the **UN Additional Measures Committee** while the **UN Good Offices Committee** was making progress. The resolution passed, but **India** and Burma voted with the communist powers against it. *See also* UNITED NATIONS CEASE-FIRE GROUP.

UNITED NATIONS RESOLUTION, 18 MAY 1951. This created the **United Nations Additional Measures Committee**. *See also* UNITED NATIONS ADDITIONAL MEASURES COMMITTEE.

UNITED NATIONS SECURITY COUNCIL RESOLUTION, 25

JUNE 1950. This resolution was a diplomatic victory for the **United States** for it labeled the **Democratic People's Republic of Korea** as the aggressor and demanded an immediate cessation of hostilities. The **Soviet Union**, a member of the **Security Council**, was boycotting the meetings. The only serous resistance came from **Ales Babbler**, who abstained in Yugoslavia's vote. United Nations Secretary-General **Trygve Lie** was a strong source of support for the United States's resolution.

UNITED NATIONS SECURITY COUNCIL RESOLUTION, 27 JUNE 1950. This resolution came after evidence showed a full-scale attack on the **Republic of Korea**. It called upon member nations to come to the support of the Republic of Korea. Despite the fact that **Joseph Stalin** restricted **Jacob A. Malik**'s return to the **Security Council** to vote, the **Soviet Union** maintained that the vote was illegal because the **Republic of China** voted, and neither the **People's Republic of China** nor the Soviet Union had been in attendance. The motion passed 7–0 with Yugoslavia again abstaining, and **India** later announcing its support.

UNITED NATIONS SECURITY COUNCIL RESOLUTION, 7 JULY 1950. This resolution acknowledged a unified command for all **United Nations** forces in Korea with the **United States** acting as **executive agent**. The commander, General **Douglas MacArthur**, was authorized to use the United Nations flag to combine forces from various nations. Since it made few provisions for monitoring the situation, it left military command pretty much in the hands of the United States.

UNITED NATIONS SECURITY COUNCIL RESOLUTION, 8 NOVEMBER 1950. As a result of the **People's Republic of China**'s entrance into the war, the **United Nations** reversed itself and invited them to join in the discussions. On 8 November it passed a resolution calling on the People's Republic of China to withdraw its troops from Korea but this was vetoed by the **Soviet Union** on the grounds that the PRC was not involved in the discussion. The PRC delegation did get its chance, however, and addressed the council for several hours as delegate We Hsui-chuan condemned the **United States**.

UNITED NATIONS SERVICE MEDAL. *See* SERVICE MEDALS.

UNITED NATIONS TEMPORARY COMMISSION TO KOREA

(UNTCOK). This was established as a nine-nation commission to supervise elections to a Korean National Assembly. The **Soviet Union,** however, denied permission to enter the **Democratic People's Republic of Korea,** and so the election was only held in the **Republic of Korea.** In May 1948 a government was elected and the Republic of Korea was inaugurated on 15 August 1948.

UNITED NATIONS UNITING FOR PEACE RESOLUTION, 3 NOVEMBER 1950. The **United States** continued to be concerned about how to preserve the **United Nations** peacekeeping role when some nations, primarily the **Soviet Union,** used the veto. Several proposals were considered but **Great Britain** and **France** were both concerned with weakening the Security Council. After considerable behind-the-scenes effort and revamping the original proposal, the United States submitted, and the United Nations passed, the Uniting for Peace resolution. It had four major parts: one authorized the calling of the UN General Assembly within 48 hours of a conflict; another established a UN Peace Observation Commission to provide independent reports on current threats; a third was that each nation was asked to identify a portion of its military for use by the UN when requested by the Security Council or General Assembly; and fourth, a committee was to be formed on how to organize and use resources made available for the collective action.

UNITED STATES. While the war in Korea was fought under the flag of the **United Nations** it was, to a large measure, a war fought by the United States of America. While acknowledging the role of the **Republic of Korea**, more than 90 percent of the personnel and equipment from United Nations member nations came from the United States. It was, as well, the United States that provided most of the military strategy to fight the war, and the political justifications for not finishing it. When war broke out, the United States made every effort to support the effort but it was never really a popular war in America; that is, it provided no great causes, no dramatic phrase calling the nation to war, no specific goals to be achieved, and no ultimate victory to be celebrated.

UNITED STATES AIR FORCE. *See* AIR FORCE, UNITED STATES.

UNITED STATES ARMY. *See* ARMY, UNITED STATES.

UNITED STATES BOMBING OF A SOVIET AIRFIELD. Navigational error was the excuse given for this attack by two **United States** jet fighters when, on 8 October 1950, a **Soviet Union** airfield near Sukhaya Rechk was strafed. On 18 October the United States made a formal apology to the Soviet Union, offered to pay for the damage, and promised to discipline the pilots involved. No Soviet response was recorded.

UNITED STATES MARINES. *See* MARINES, UNITED STATES.

UNITED STATES NAVAL FORCES. *See* NAVY, UNITED STATES.

UNITED STATES NAVY. *See* NAVY, UNITED STATES.

UNITED STATES PRESIDENTIAL CITATION. *See* PRESIDENTIAL UNIT CITATIONS.

UNITED STATES–REPUBLIC OF KOREA, MUTUAL DEFENSE TREATY. A mutual security pact was agreed to as part of assuring **Syngman Rhee**'s cooperation with the **Armistice** agreement. Conditions in Korea had deteriorated to the point that the **United Nations Command** was considering **Operation Everready**, the overthrow of President Rhee. The Mutual Defense Treaty was signed on 8 August 1953. While it did not guarantee military aid, it did mean that the United States had accepted responsibility for the safety and security of the **Republic of Korea**. It is on the basis of this agreement that United States troops remain in Korea in the 21st century.

UNLEASHING OF (THE REPUBLIC OF) CHINA. On news of the attack by forces of the **Democratic People's Republic of Korea**, President **Harry Truman** took steps to protect **Taiwan** and to be sure the **Republic of China** maintained its neutrality during the war. This policy was the source of a great deal of criticism. Nevertheless on 2 February 1952, shortly after taking office, President **Dwight D. Eisenhower** released the Republic of China. That is, he informed his commands that the United States was no longer responsible for Taiwan security. While it may have appeased the right wing of the Republican Party, it did little to change conditions in either Taiwan or Korea.

UNSAN, BATTLE OF. The initial attack came on 2 November 1950 when forces of the **People's Republic of China** crossed the **Yalu River**

and, near Unsan, a crossroads village in the **Democratic People's Republic of Korea**, attacked and defeated the **Republic of Korea** II Corps, and brought **Eighth United States Army** to a halt. But instead of continuing the advance, the Communist Chinese Forces (CCF) halted, beginning what was to be a three-week lull in the fighting. Some historians suggest it was to give the United States time to reconsider its movement toward the Yalu. Others see the period of inactivity as the time required to complete moving CCF troops into line. The CCF halt bolstered General **Douglas MacArthur**'s belief that he could handle the situation and slowed the early consideration of potential truce talks.

URUGUAY. The government of Uruguay lacked the domestic support to send troops in support of the **United Nations** in Korea, but provided $2 million and 70,000 blankets.

USCGC (UNITED STATES COAST GUARD CUTTERS). *See* COAST GUARD, UNITED STATES.

USS (UNITED STATES SHIPS). The **United States** had more than 300 combat, auxiliary, and support ships in Korean waters during the war. While all rendered valuable service a few require further discussion. *See also ships by name.*

USS *AGERHOLM* (DD 826). United States **destroyer** of the Gearing class, she was commissioned on 20 June 1944. She displaced 3,479 tons, was 390 feet long, 40 feet wide with 60,000 horsepower and was armed with three 5-inch guns, three 3-inch guns on turrets, and two 3-inch guns. An element of the **Wonsan** bombardment and siege group, the destroyer was hit by shore batteries on 1 September 1952 near Kangsong and suffered damage and one casualty.

USS *ALFRED A. CUNNINGHAM* (DD 752). United States **destroyer** of the Sumner class, she was commissioned on 23 November 1944. With a displacement of about 2,890 tons she had a speed of 35 knots and carried a complement of 11 officers and 325 men, and was armed with six 5-inch guns. As a part of the **Wonsan** bombardment and siege group, she took part in the battle of the "buzz saw." The destroyer was hit on 19 September 1952 by shore fire near **Koje-do** with 18 **casualties**.

USS *ANTIETAM* (CF 36). Essex class United States **aircraft carrier**, commissioned on 28 January 1945, the *Antietam* served one tour of duty in Korea from October 1951 to March 1952. During that time she housed Air Group Fifteen that included the reserve units VF 831 and VF 837 (F9F), VF 713 (F4U), and VF 728 (Ads). She was one of the first to have the angled landing deck, at first 8 percent but then 10.5 percent. Known as the "Big O," she was later the featured carrier in the film *Task Force*.

USS *BADOENG STRAIT* (CVE 116). A "jeep" **carrier**, called either "bing bong" or "bing ding," she was a part of the Inchon support group and **Task Force 96.23**. The last of the "short hull" carriers was commissioned 26 November 1944. During her Korean tour she housed VMF 214 and VMF 323. Carrier **division** 96.8 was created around her, and the division supported the elements at **Pusan**, especially during the landing of the Marine Provisional Brigade. Between 18 August and 14 September 1950 she flew 671 **sorties** against enemy positions. She made a brief appearance at the **Wonsan** siege and supported the **Hungnam evacuation** by firing at the advancing communist forces.

USS *BARTON* (DD 722). A United States **destroyer** of the Sumner class, she displaced 2,890 tons, had a speed of about 35 knots, and carried 11 officers and 325 seamen. Armed primarily with six 5-inch guns, she was hit by shore fire on 10 August 1952 near **Wonsan** resulting in two **casualties**; then the following month she struck a **mine** on 16 September, 90 miles east of Wonsan, causing 11 casualties.

USS *BATAAN* (CVL). This United States light **carrier** served with Task Force 96.8. She should not be confused with Australia's **HMAS** *Bataan*, a **destroyer** on duty in Korean waters.

USS *BENEVOLENCE*. This U.S. hospital ship was recommissioned on 25 August 1950 in preparation for a tour in Korea. On her trials she collided with the SS *Mark Luchenbach* near San Francisco. The USS *Benevolence* sank with a loss of 18 sailors.

USS *BON HOMME RICHARD* (CV 31). Essex class United States **aircraft carrier**, commissioned on 26 November 1944, the *Bon Homme Richard* served two tours in Korea from May to November 1951, during which she was equipped with Air Group 102, consisting of four reserve squadrons, VF 781 (F9F), VF 783 and VF 874 (F4U), and VF

923 (AD); and from June to December 1952 with Air Group Seven, including VF 71 and VF 72 (F9F), VF 74 (F4U), and VF 75 (AD). She was known affectionately as "Bonnie Dick." She received a Presidential Unit Citation.

USS *BOXER* (CV-21). Essex class United States **aircraft carrier**, commissioned on 16 April 1944, she performed one of the war's earliest missions as she crossed the Atlantic with 145 badly needed F 51 prop aircraft in eight days and seven hours. The *Boxer* served three tours in Korea. Her first tour was from September to October 1950 with Air Group Two that included VF 21, VF 22, VF 63, VF 64 (**F4U**), and VF 65 (AD). Heading home the *Boxer* was recalled to aid in the support of the **Hungnam evacuation**. During her second tour in Korea, March to October 1951, she carried Air Group 101 and carried four reserve squadrons, VF 721 (**F9F**), VF 884, VF 791 (F4U), and VA 702 (AD). From May to July 1953 she served with Air Task Group One, with four squadrons: VF 52, VF 111, VF 151 (F9F), and VF 194 (AD). The *Boxer* was damaged on tour by fire and an explosion. She was an element of the **Inchon** and **Wonsan landings**.

USS *BRINKLEY BASS* (DD 887). United States **destroyer** of the Gearing class, she displaced 3,479 tons, was 390 feet long, 40 feet wide with 60,000 horsepower. She was armed with three 5-inch guns, three 3-inch guns on turrets, and two 3-inch guns. She served as a part of the **Wonsan** siege group and was hit by a shore battery on 22 May 1951 producing minor damage but causing eight casualties. On 24 March 1952 near Wonsan she sustained moderate damage and five casualties. She served during the **Hungnam evacuation**.

USS *BRUSH* (DD 745). This United States **destroyer** served with the first bombardment group to enter the Yellow Sea and was a part of the **Pusan** support group **Task Force**. She was the first United States ship to be mined and was badly damaged. The hit resulted in 36 wounded but the *Brush* made it back to Sasebo for repairs. She served with the first bombardment group and was hit on 15 May 1953 by shore battery near **Wonsan** with nine **casualties**. She served at the **Hungnam evacuation**.

USS *CHARLES S. SPERRY* (DD 697). This United States **destroyer** of the Sumner class had a displacement of about 2,890 tons and a speed of 35 knots. The primary armament was six 5-inch guns. She carried a complement of 11 officers and 325 men. The *Sperry* was hit by shore battery at Songin, 23 December 1950. The *Sperry*, along with the *Zeller* and the *St. Paul*, was involved in the evacuation of the **Third Infantry Division** from **Wonsan** and during the **Hungnam evacuation**.

USS *COLLETT* **(DD 730).** This United States Sumner class **destroyer** was commissioned in May 1944 and returned to service for the Korean War. With a displacement of about 2,890 tons, she had a speed of 35 knots and carried a complement of 11 officers and 325 men. The primary armament was six 5-inch guns. She first escorted ammunition ships from Japan to Korea in the early days of the war, was a part of the original bombardment group, and took part in the pre-invasion bombardment of Wolmi-do under the command of Commander Robert H. Close.

USS *DOUGLAS H. FOX* **(DD 779).** A United States **destroyer** of the Sumner class with a displacement of 2,890 tons and a speed of 35 knots, she carried a complement of 11 officers and 325 men. The primary armament was six 5-inch guns. The destroyer was hit by a shore battery near **Hungnam** 14 May 1952 that resulted in minor damage and two casualties.

USS *ENDICOTT* **(DMS 35).** An element of **Task Element 96.23**, she was hit by shore fire on 4 February 1952 near Songjin with no casualties. The *Endicott* was hit again near Chongjin on 7 April 1952 with no casualties and on 19 April 1952 near Songjin with no casualties. She was a member of **Task Force 95**'s **Train Buster Club** having destroyed three communist trains.

USS *ERNEST G. SMALL* **(DDR 838).** A United States **destroyer** of the Gearing class, she was commissioned 21 August 1945. She displaced 3,479 tons, was 390 feet long, and 40 feet wide with 60,000 horsepower. She was armed with three 5-inch guns, three 3-inch guns on turrets, and two 3-inch guns. The *Small* was hit by shore battery near **Hungnam** causing extensive damage and 27 casualties.

USS *ESSEX* **(CV-9).** This United States **carrier** was built at Newport News in February 1940 and recommissioned 1 February 1950 for service in the Korean War. The ship, known as "Oldest and Boldest," served three tours: August 1951 to March 1952; June 1952 to February 1953; and December 1953 to August 1954. During her time in Korea she maintained Air Carrier Groups 2 and 5.

USS *FRANK E. EVANS* (DD 754). United States Sumner class **destroyer** was commissioned on 3 February 1945. She had a displacement of about 2,890 tons, had a speed of 35 knots, and carried a complement of 11 officers and 325 men. The primary armament was six 5-inch guns. She was a part of the **Wonsan** siege group that was hit by a shore battery on 18 June 1951 and slightly damaged with four casualties. On 8 September 1952 she was nit near Tanchon with no casualties.

USS *GULL* (AMS 16). United States auxiliary motor **minesweeper** stationed at Pearl Harbor, she was sent to Korea in August 1950 and conducted the initial sweep of mines at **Chinnampo**. Hit by shore fire on 16 March 1953, she suffered two casualties. She was involved at the **Hungnam evacuation**.

USS *GURKE* (DD 783). United States **destroyer** of the Gearing class, she was commissioned on 12 March 1945. She displaced 3,479 tons, was 390 feet long, and 40 feet wide with 60,000 horsepower. She was armed with three 5-inch guns, three 3-inch guns on turrets, and two 3-inch guns. An element of the **Inchon** fire support group, she was hit by shore fire while bombarding near Songjin. She suffered minor damage and three casualties.

USS *HAYMAN* (DD 732). United States Sumner class **destroyer** commissioned on 16 June 1944, her primary armament was six 5-inch guns. She carried a complement of 11 officers and 325 men. The destroyer took a shell that hit six feet above the waterline on 8 September 1951, and again was hit again by shore batteries on 23 November 1951 near **Wonsan** with no casualties.

USS *HELENA* (CA 75). This United States **cruiser** served as one of the **Wonsan** bombardment and siege group. She was hit by short fire on 23 October 1951 causing four casualties and again on 31 July 1951 near **Wonsan** with minor damage and two casualties. Under the command of Captain Harold O. Larson, she was one of the first ships to use **helicopters** to spot artillery fire directed to on-shore targets.

USS *HENDERSON* (DD 785). This United States **destroyer** of the Sumner class was commissioned on 4 August 1945. With a displacement of about 2,890 tons, she had a speed of 35 knots and carried a complement of 11 officers and 325 men. The primary armament was six 5-inch guns. She was an element of the **Inchon** fire support group. On 23 February 1952, she was hit by shore batteries near **Hungnam** causing minor damage and no casualties. Hit again on 17 June 1953 by shore batteries near **Wonsan**, there was minor damage but no casualties.

USS *HERBERT J. THOMAS* (DDR 833). United States Gearing class radar picket **destroyer**, she displaced 3,479 tons, was 390 feet long, and 40 feet wide with 60,000 horsepower. She was armed with three 5-inch guns, three 3-inch guns on turrets, and two 3-inch guns. Part of the **Wonsan blockade** group, she was hit by shore based artillery on 12 May 1952 with no casualties.

USS *IOWA* (BB 61). This Iowa class United States **battleship** left for Korea in March 1952 where it replaced the **USS *Wisconsin***. She was the fourth battleship to serve in Korea. Displacing 54,700 tons, she was 888 feet long and 108 feet wide and could maintain a speed of 33 knots. She was armed with nine 6-inch guns, 20 5-inch guns, and carried a complement of 2,000. She served under Captain J. W. Cooper in a variety of bombardment missions along both coasts and made two visits to the siege at **Wonsan**.

USS *JAMES E. KYES* (DD 787). Gearing class United States **destroyer** commissioned on 8 February 1946, she displaced 3,479 tons, was 390 feet long, and 40 feet wide with 60,000 horsepower. She was armed with three 5-inch guns, three 3-inch guns on turrets, and two 3-inch guns. Identified as a part of Task Element 96.23, she was struck by shore fire on 19 April 1953 near **Wonsan** but there were no casualties. Later she was a part of the **Hungnam evacuation**.

USS *KEARSARGE* (CV 33). An Essex class United States **aircraft carrier** commissioned on 2 March 1946, she was recommissioned on 1 March 1952. The *Kearsarge* served in Korea from September 1952 to July 1953 during which time she housed air group 101 (later Air Group 14) including VF 11 with F2H fighters, VF 721 with F9Fs, VF 864 with F4Us, and VA 702 with Ads. She served later from July 1953 to January 1954 on the **Armistice** Patrol and was known as "Mighty K."

USS *KITE* (AMS 22). This United States auxiliary motor **minesweeper** with one officer and four enlisted men was hit when she was struck by 47 76mm shells from the shore batteries while sweeping at **Wonsan** on 19 November 1952.

USS *LAKE CHAMPLAIN* (CV 39). Essex class United States **aircraft carrier** commissioned on 3 June 45 and recommissioned on 19 September 1952, she was the last of the Essex class to be commissioned before the end of World War II. The *Lake Champlain* served one tour in Korea from June to October 1953 and had on board Air Group Four, including VF 22 and VF 62 (F2H2), VF 44 (**F4U**), and VA 47 (AD).

USS *LEONARD F. MASON* (DD 852). A Gearing class United States **destroyer**, she was commissioned on 28 June 1946. She was 390 feet long and 40 feet wide with 60,000 horsepower. She was armed with three 5-inch guns, three 3-inch guns on turrets, and two 3-inch guns. The *Mason* was a part of the **Wonsan** bombardment and siege group. She was struck near there by shore fire on 2 May 1952, but there were no casualties.

USS *LEWIS* (DE 535). This United States **destroyer** was hit by artillery from a communist shore battery near **Wonsan** on 21 October 1952 causing moderate damage and 8 casualties.

USS *LEYTE GULF* (CV 32). Essex class United States **aircraft carrier** commissioned on 11 April 1946, the *Leyte* served one tour in Korea from October 1950 to January 1951 during which she maintained Air Group Three with an unusual five squadrons: VF 31 and VF 32 (F9F), VF 33 and VF 34 (F4U), and VA 35 (AD). Known as "Leading Leyte," she served a series of bombardment and blockade missions and was deployed at **Hungnam**. She received the Presidential Unit Citation.

USS *MADDOX* (DD 731). This United States **destroyer** of the Sumner class was one of the first bombardment group to enter the Yellow Sea and an element of the **Pusan** support group, **Task Element 77.2**. The *Maddox* was involved in the **Wonsan** bombardment and siege group. She was hit by shore fire near Wonsan on 30 April 1952 with minor damage and no casualties, and again on 2 May 1953 near Wonsan with no casualties. She was involved in the **Hungnam evacuation**.

USS *MAGPIE* (AM 25). When this United States wooden-hull **mine-sweeper** was cleaning mines from **Wonsan** harbor under Lieutenant (jg) Warner Person, she struck a mine and on 29 September 1950 sank. Twelve of the crew were wounded but saved. The rest of the crew, 21 in all, was lost.

USS *MANSFIELD* (DD 728). A Sumner class United States **destroyer**, she was commissioned on 14 April 1944. With a displacement of about 2,890 tons, she had a speed of 35 knots and carried a complement of 11 officers and 325 men. The primary armament was six 5-inch guns. She was a part of the **Inchon** fire support group and later of the **Wonsan** bombardment and siege group under command of Commander E. H. Headland. She was mined and damaged, with five missing and 48 wounded, on 30 September 1950.

USS *MISSOURI* (BB 63). This Iowa class United States **battleship** arrived in Korea on 14 September 1950 after a full-speed 11,000-mile run from the **United States**. Displacing 54,700 tons, she was 888 feet long, 108 feet wide, and could maintain a speed of 33 knots. She was armed with nine 6-inch guns, 20 5-inch guns, and carried a complement of 2,000. At that time she was probably the most famous ship to miss the **Inchon Landing** but assisted in the breakout from **Naktong**. She also provided covering fire at **Hungnam** in support of the USS *Valley Forge* with the USS *Leyte Gulf* at Chongjin. She was the core of the fake amphibious landing at Kansong landing, part of the heavy bombardment group at Songjin (North Korea) 1950, was at **Wonsan** during the landing, and participated in the **Hungnam evacuation**. When she returned for refitting in April 1951, she had traveled 62,100 miles and had fired 2,895 16-inch shells and 8,043 5-inch shells.

USS *NEW JERSEY* (BB 62). An Iowa class United States **battleship** displacing 54,700 tons, she was 888 feet long and 108 feet wide and could maintain a speed of 33 knots. She was armed with nine 6-inch guns, 20 5-inch guns, and carried a complement of 2,000. She arrived on 17 May 1951, took part in the **Wonsan** siege, a series of bombardment missions at Chongjin, Kangnung, and during one heavy bombardment near Wonsan she was hit and seriously damaged by fire from a shore battery on 20 May 1951, resulting in four casualties

USS *ORISKANY* (CV 34). An Essex class United States **carrier** commissioned on 25 September 1950, the *Oriskany* served one tour in Korea from October 1952 to April 1953, at that time carrying Air Group 102 (later Air Group 12) with VF 781 and VF 783 (**F9F**), VF 874 (**F4U**), and VA 923 (AD). The ship played the fictional USS *Savo* in the movie *The Bridges of Toko-Ri*, and as herself in *Men of the Fighting Lady*.

USS *OSPREY* (AMS 28). This United States auxiliary motor **minesweeper** was hit by two shells from shore fire near **Wonsan** on 29 October 1951 resulting in considerable damage and one casualty; Sogin on 23 April 1952 with mild damage and no casualties; and again on 14 October 1952 near Kojo with four casualties. She was one of the most frequently hit minesweepers.

USS *PERKINS* (DDR 877). Gearing class United States **destroyer** commissioned on 4 April 1945. She displaced 3,479 tons, was 390 feet long, and 40 feet wide with 60,000 horsepower. She was armed with three 5-inch guns, three 3-inch guns on turrets, and two 3-inch guns. She was hit by shore fire near Koje-do on 13 October 1952, causing significant damage and 18 casualties.

USS *PHILIPPINE SEA* (CV 47). Essex class United States **carrier**, commissioned 11 May 46, the *Philippine Sea* served three tours in Korea. The first was August 1950 to March 1951 during which Air Group Eleven was assigned with VF 111 and VF 112 (**F9F**), VF 53 and VF 54 (**F4U**) and VA 55(AD). The second tour, January to August 1952 also with Air Group Eleven, included squadrons VF 112 and BF 113 (F9F), VF 114 (F4U) and VA 115 (AD). The third tour was from January to July 1953 with Air Group Nine, including VF 91 and VF 93 (F9F), VF 94 (F4U) and VA 95 (AD). She was laid down originally as Wright and known as "Phil Sea." An Atlantic Fleet carrier, she arrived in San Diego on 10 June 1950 after two months of effort. She was ordered out as the Korean War broke out, sailing on 5 July 1950 with her Air Group having not finished its training cycle. Ten days training was accomplished in the Hawaiian area. She received the **Presidential Unit Citation**.

USS *PIRATE* (AM 275). A United States steel hull **minesweeper**, she was cleaning mines from the harbor at **Wonsan** when she struck a mine and broke in two. She capsized and sank on 12 October 1950.

USS *PRINCETON* (CV-37). Essex class United States **aircraft carrier**

commissioned 18 November 1945, she was recommissioned 28 August 1950. The *Princeton* served three tours in Korea: December 1950 to August 1951 while carrying Air Group Nineteen that included VF 191 **(F9F)**, VF 192 and VF 193 **(F4U)**, and VA 195 (Ads). From June 1951 to 10 August 1951 of that tour she was home to Air Group Nineteen "X Ray" composed of VF 23 (F9F), VF 821 and VF 871 both reserve squadrons (F4U), and VF 34 (F4U). A second tour was from April to October 1952 where she again carried Air Group Nineteen with VF 191 (F9F), VF 192 and VF 193 (F4U), and VA 195 (Ads). The *Princeton*'s, third tour, March to July 1953, she carried Air Group Fifteen, including VF 152 (F4U), VF 153 and VF 154 (F9F), and VA 155 (Ads). She was originally planned to be named Valley Forge. Called "Sweet P," she set the record on 15 June 1953 for the most offensive **sorties** launched. She contributed 184 to the day's total of 910. She received the **Presidential Unit Citation**.

USS *ROWAN* (DD 782). This Gearing class United States **destroyer** was commissioned on 31 March 1945 and arrived in Korea in February 1952. She displaced 3,479 tons, was 390 feet long, and 40 feet wide with 60,000 horsepower. She was armed with three 5-inch guns, three 3-inch guns on turrets, and two 3-inch guns. She was a part of the **Wonsan** bombardment and siege group when she was hit by shore battery near Wonsan on 22 February 1952 causing minor damage but no casualties. She was hit again on 18 June 1953 by shore fire near Wonsan this time causing nine casualties.

USS *SAMUEL N. MOORE* (DD 747). United States Sumner class **destroyer** commissioned on 24 June 1944 with a displacement of about 2,890 tons, she had a speed of 35 knots and carried a complement of 11 officers and 325 men. The primary armament was six 5-inch guns. An element of the **Pusan** support group, Task Force 77, she was hit on 17 October 1951 by shore batteries near Hungnam with minor damage and three casualties. It took part in the **Hungnam evacuation**.

USS *SARSI* (ATF 111). This was a United States ocean-going tug. Typhoon Karen, which hit in August 1952, released more than 40 **mines** from their moorings, and they drifted out to sea. The *Sarsi*, working in the area, struck a mine and sank on 30 August 1952 with two casualties.

USS *SICILY* (CVE). A United States escort carrier, she arrived for Korean service 27 July 1950 and became a member of Task Group 96.8 in support of marine units. During this early phase her air group, VMF 323, flew 688 **sorties.**

USS *STICKELL* (DD 888). A Gearing class United States **destroyer**, she was an element of the **Wonsan** bombardment and siege group. She also joined the North Patrol (95.22) off Songjin on 16 May 1951, where she destroyed a bridge linking two tunnels. Finally she landed a party of **Republic of Korea** commandoes and occupied the island of Yondo to prevent its capture by **Communist Chinese Forces**.

USS *SWALLOW* (AMS 36). United States auxiliary motor **minesweeper**, she had steamed in from Honolulu at the beginning of the war and played a major role in the clearing of **Wonsan** Harbor prior to the landing of **X Corps**. She was hit three times by shore battery near Sognjin resulting in slight damage and no casualties.

USS *TAUSSIG* (DD 746). United States Sumner class destroyer commissioned on 20 May 1944 with a displacement of about 2,890 tons, she had a speed of 35 knots and carried a complement of 11 officers and 325 men. The primary armament was six 5-inch guns. She was a part of the **Pusan** support group Task Force 77 and **Task Element 96.23**. She was hit by shore fire on 17 March 1953 at **Wonsan** with no casualties recorded.

USS *VALLEY FORGE* (CV 45). This Essex class United States **aircraft carrier** was commissioned on 3 November 1946. She was just north of Hong Kong when she was called to duty as a part of the **Pusan** support group to serve four tours in Korea from June to November 1950 with Air Group Five including VF 51 and VF 52 **(F9F)**, VF 53 and VF 54 **(F4U)**, and VA 55 (AD). A second tour from December 1950 to June 1951 carried Air Group Two with VF 64, VF 24, VF 63 (F4U), and VA 65 (Ads). The third tour was from December 1951 to June 1952 during which she flew Air Task Group One with VF 52 and VF 111 (F9F), VF 653 a reserve squadron (F4U), and VF 194 (Ads). Her fourth tour ran from December 1953 to June 1953, carrying Air Group Five and including squadrons VF 51 and VF 52 (F9F), VF 92 (F4U), and VF 54 (Ads). When the war broke out the "Happy Valley" was well within cruising distance of Korea and, with Air Group Five aboard, was the number one carrier and jet-trained air group in the area. She was at the

Wonsan siege and the **Hungnam evacuation** and received the **Presidential Unit Citation**.

USS *WILTSIE* (DD 716). United States Gearing class **destroyer** commissioned on 12 January 1946, she displaced 3,479 tons, was 390 feet long, and 40 feet wide with 60,000 horsepower. She was armed with three 5-inch guns, three 3-inch guns on turrets, and two 3-inch guns. She was hit on 11 June 1953 by shore batteries at **Wonsan** but had no casualties. She fired on targets at Wonsan until a minute before the 2200 **Armistice** deadline.

USS *WISCONSIN* (BB 64). Iowa class United States **battleship** known by her crew as "Wishy," displaced 54,700 tons, was 888 feet long and 108 feet wide, and could maintain a speed of 33 knots. She was armed with nine 6-inch guns, 20 5-inch guns, and carried a complement of 2,000. She relieved the **USS *New Jersey*** and served in Korea for four months. On bombarding Kosong, she destroyed more than 50 percent of the city. She took part in a series of bombardment assignments on both coasts. On 16 March 1952 she was hit by shore battery near Songjin. The damage was small, but there were three casualties.

UTAH LINE. The United States **3rd**, **24th**, and **25th Divisions** launched Operation Dauntless on 11 April 1951 to extend the main defensive line and establish Utah Line. The objective was completed on 22 April 1951 at the cost of 95 killed and 1,056 wounded.

–V–

VAN FLEET, JAMES A. (1892–1992). A 1915 West Point graduate, he served in World Wars I and II, rising to the rank of major general in 1945. After serving as commander of Second Army, he was sent to Korea in 1951 to command **Eighth United States Army**. He successfully stopped the most ambitious **Communist Chinese Forces (CCF)** drive from 22 to 29 April and responded with a counterattack that drove the CCF across the **38th Parallel** and near **Iron Triangle** country. At this point it was decided that further advance was not necessary, and Van Fleet constructed the **Kansas** and **Wyoming Lines**. When the truce talks stalled in August 1951, Van Fleet, now promoted to full general, attacked and drove the CCF even farther into central Korea. When the truce talks started again, Van Fleet was ordered to stop. Deeply frustrated by the lack of political support and adequate supplies, and suffering from grief over the loss of his son shot down on a mission over North Korea, Van Fleet gave up his command and retired in April 1953. President **Dwight Eisenhower** later appointed him as a special ambassador to the Far East.

VANDENBERG, HOYT S. (1899–1954). A 1923 graduate of the Military Academy, he was instrumental in the development of the independent air force. He served for a year as director of the **Central Intelligence Agency** and later (1948) as chief of staff, **United States Air Force**. He was in this position during the Berlin Air Lift. When the **Democratic People's Republic of Korea** invaded, Vandenberg was not in favor of **United States** involvement, believing that it was a diversion. He changed his mind after a visit to Korea. He supported land forces but still cautioned against pushing the **People's Republic of China** or the **Soviet Union** too far. He was concerned about **Douglas MacArthur**, both in terms of his desire to widen the war and because the general did not seem able to use combined forces as needed. He supported **Harry Truman**'s decision to fire MacArthur. As the war continued he expanded his belief in interdiction and encouraged attacks on enemy resources. In April he joined the **Joint Chiefs of Staff** in advocating the bombing of previously off-limits targets and supported the idea of using **nuclear weapons**. He retired on 30 June 1953 and died a year later.

V-DEVICE. Some American medals can be awarded either for heroism or for meritorious service. To show that the award has been given for heroism, a metallic V-device is worn on the medal ribbon.

VENEZUELA. Serving as a member nation of the **United Nations Additional Measures Committee**, Venezuela was able to send medical supplies to Korea.

VETERANS OF THE KOREAN WAR. The more than six million Korean-era veterans returned to the United States to find their service was not well received. Five issues emerged that would make the Korean veteran's experience unique: one, the failure to obtain a victory in Korea was seen by the American people as a moral breakdown of the American soldier. The press was quick to suggest that the post-World War II soldier lacked courage, *esprit de corps*, discipline, and traditional American tough-mindedness. Two, those Americans who had been captured returned from their confinement with the cloud of "**brainwashing**" darkening their behavior and acceptance; three, the fact that 21 Americans chose to stay behind with their **People's Republic of China** captors, and the realization that no American **prisoner of war** had escaped from prisoner-of-war camps, suggested an unprecedented mark on the national character of those who served; four, the negative image—soldiers who did not win and who gave up too quickly—became the unflattering image of the Korean War veteran in popular films and literature; and five, the "less-than-proud" image of the Korean War veteran led **Congress** to provide only three-fourths of the benefits provided for World War II veterans and delayed the creation of a monument. It was the beginning of a national attitude that would be reflected among Vietnam War veterans.

As of June 2000, there were 3.9 million Korean War veterans. This number was down 21 percent from the 5 million in 1990. Korean War veterans make up about 16 percent of all veterans in the United States.

Veterans Association. Korean veterans are accepted as members in the basic associations for veterans: Veterans of Foreign Wars, American Legion, Disabled American Veterans, Catholic War Veterans, and Jewish War Veterans. The Korean War Veterans Association is the largest of the Korea-limited associations. There are also some unit associations, or campaign organizations such as Chosin Few for survivors of the **Chosin Reservoir Campaign**.

Veterans Compensation. Korean War veterans who were receiving service-connected compensations, as of the end of March 2002, were approximately 171,000. Of these, 69,000 are surviving spouses who receive benefits.

Veterans Education. About 18 percent of the Korean War era veterans had less than a high school education. Nearly 50 percent had some college. One of the unanswered questions about Korean War veteran responses is why a much smaller percentage of Korean veterans took advantage of the G.I. Bill educational offerings than did those of World War II.

VICKERS-SUPERMARINE SEA OTTER. A carrier-borne amphibian with a crew of four, used by **Great Britain**, it had a top speed of 132 miles per hour with a range of 725 miles. It was armed with three Vickers machine guns.

VYSHINSKII, ANDREI Y. (1883–1954). As the **Soviet Union**'s foreign minister from March 1949 to March 1953, he led the Soviet Union's position at the **United Nations** against **United States** involvement. In October 1950 he offered a **cease-fire** proposal that included the seating of the **People's Republic of China** in the UN. When **United Nations** forces crossed into **North Korea**, Vyshinskii charged the United States with using Japanese troops. He supported compulsory **repatriation** of prisoners and urged postponing the prisoner-of-war issue until after a cease-fire was reached. After **Joseph Stalin**'s death, he was named permanent representative to the UN, a position he held until his death.

–W–

WAIST OF KOREA. This describes the portion of Korea that is located in the area of the **Democratic People's Republic of Korea** where the width of the peninsula is less than 200 miles. The line runs from **Pyongyang** at the **Yellow Sea** to the city of **Wonsan** on the **Sea of Japan**. Early efforts at a **cease-fire**, proposed by **Great Britain** and **India**, were based on the **United Nations Command** stopping at this point.

WAKE ISLAND CONFERENCE. A one-day meeting held at Wake Island on 15 October 1950 between President **Harry S. Truman** and General of the Army **Douglas MacArthur**. President Truman's party consisted of General **Omar Bradley**, Secretary of the Army **Frank Pace**, Ambassadors **Philip Jessup** and **Averell Harriman**, and Assistant Secretary of State **Dean Rusk**. The primary discussion concerned victory in Korea and the possibility of the **People's Republic of China** intervention. In both cases MacArthur was optimistic. President Truman awarded him another **Distinguished Service Medal**. There was no official transcript of the meeting maintained.

WALKER, WALTON HARRIS (1889–1950). During World War II Lieutenant General Walton "Johnny" Walker commanded XX Corps under General George Patton. After the war he commanded Fifth Army and in 1948 he was assigned to Japan where he took command of **Eighth United States Army**. When war broke out he took Eighth United States Army to Korea and commanded it during the perimeter defense at **Pusan**. When **X Corps** invaded Inchon, his troops broke free and pushed to a line just south of the **38th Parallel**. After the decision to move into the **Democratic People's Republic of Korea**, Eighth United

States Army captured the capital of the Democratic People's Republic of Korea. He commanded Eighth United States Army through its pull-out and retreat following the involvement of the **People's Republic of China**. He was killed in a jeep accident on 23 December 1950 and was replaced by Lieutenant General **Matthew B. Ridgway**.

WAR CORRESPONDENTS. *See* CORRESPONDENTS; MEDIA; PRESS COVERAGE.

WAR CRIMES TRIALS. Many thought that because of the puppet nature of the **Democratic People's Republic of Korea** government any trial would have to place the blame for the war on the **Soviet Union**. A distinction was made in how war crimes were identified and General **Douglas MacArthur** was instructed to arrest and bring to trial any person who committed atrocities. But that was not the same as establishing blame for the military action. MacArthur discussed this with President **Harry Truman** at **Wake Island** suggesting that "war trials" did not work. While the "occupation plans" included the arrest of people involved in atrocities, there was no effort to conduct war trials. It was, as it turned out, hypothetical because the **United Nations Command** never united Korea.

WASHINGTON CONFERENCE. This was a series of meetings from 26 March to 7 April 1951 with ministers of foreign affairs of Latin America seeking aid. The Latin American countries had been supportive at the **United Nations** and continued to be in general, but failed to make many direct commitments. Most Latin American countries resented the **United States** failure to aid them after the World War II, particularly the lack of a local Marshall Plan. Only **Colombia** provided troops.

WEAPONS, PRIMARY COMMUNIST. Both the **People's Republic of China** and the **Democratic People's Republic of Korea** took advantage of captured **United States** weapons, securing enough weapons during the first 90 days to equip several divisions. The Chinese also had United States weapons (which they had captured) that had been sent to the **Republic of China** during and shortly after World War II. They also had a large amount of **Japanese** weapons. Still the majority of the weapons were from the **Soviet Union** and were, primarily, World War II weapons. They were the Russian 7.62 carbine, a bolt-action rifle made in 1944, and the Japanese 7.7mm Imperial Army Rifle. The communists, however, tended to favor submachine guns because the higher firepower was more effective in the hands of untrained troops; the "**burp gun**," the 7.62mm PPSh 41, which could be fired either full or semiautomatic, held 72 rounds and could fire 100 rounds per minute; the Tokarev 7.62mm semiautomatic rifle with flash suppresser and bipod; the Degtyarev 14.5mm anti-tank rifle (PTRD-1941) was used for long-range sniping. Each division of the **North Korean People's Army** was assigned 36. They were called "buffalo guns" by United Nations troops. Several varieties of machine guns were used, primarily the Coryunov heavy, which fired a 7.62mm and was wheel-mounted.

WEAPONS, PRIMARY UNITED STATES. The primary weapons used by the **United States** and Allied forces in Korea were those developed during World War II. Many of these had become obsolete. The primary weapons of the United States were the caliber .30 **M-1 (Garand) rifle**, a gas-operated, semiautomatic weapon weighing 9.5 pounds and which fired an 8-round clip with an effective range of 500 yards at 30 rounds per minute; the carbine, caliber .30, gas-operated weapon fired a lighter bullet than the M-1 and had a range of 300 yards and operated both as semiautomatic and automatic and carried a 15-round magazine; the pistol, caliber .45, 1911A-1, the standard sidearm, was effective at 25 yards and was semiautomatic; the **Browning Automatic Rifle (BAR)** fired the same .30 as the M-1, was semi-automatic and automatic, carried a 20-round clip, weighed 16 pounds, and could sustain fire at 500 rounds per minute; the .30 M-1919 A-3 (Light Machine Gun or LMG) that was air-cooled had a 32-round magazine, fully automatic, could sustain fire at 450 rounds per minute; the caliber .30, M 1917 A-1 (Heavy Machine Gun or HMG) water-cooled tripod-mounted; the .50 machine gun that weighed 82 pounds, was air-cooled, and could be fired at 575 rounds per minute at a range of 2,000 yards; the 3.5-inch **Rocket Launcher (Bazooka)** that fired a hollow-shaped charge, weighed 15 pounds and was rarely effective beyond 70 yards; the 57mm, 75 mm, and 205mm recoilless rifles developed blast from escaping gases without recoil (the 57mm could be shoulder fired) and fired regular shells with a flat trajectory. The 105mm was developed during the Korean War. The Allies also had available 60mm, 81mm, and 4.2 inch **mortars** usually carried by special weapons units. The 60mm, used by **infantry companies,** had a range of 1,500 yards. There was also the Quad .50, vehicle-mounted anti-personnel weapons that fired as many as 100,000 rounds per day and were used against massed troops. The Dual 40, originally an anti-craft weapon, was a vehicle-mounted Bofors 40mm automatic cannon used to support infantry.

WEBB, JAMES E. (1906–1992). Serving as under **secretary of state** under **Dean Acheson** from 1949, he complemented Acheson and President **Harry Truman** and listened to the both of them. He was present at the first **Blair House Meeting** and supported the joint recommendations of the **Departments of State** and **Defense**. He favored aid to the **Republic of Korea** and the evacuation of dependants but wanted to wait on the neutralization of **Taiwan**. Webb later became head of the National Aeronautics and Space Administration (NASA).

WEDEMEYER REPORT. On 18 September 1947 Lieutenant General Albert C. Wedemeyer made his report on his mission to Korea and the **People's Republic of China**. Turmoil in Korea and lingering criticism over the manner in which China policy had been formulated by the administration of **Harry Truman** led him to seek a method to withdraw from the Korean peninsula. He suggested that without aid from the **United States**, Korea would fall to the communists, and there would be immense repercussions in **Japan** and throughout Asia. The author also suggested that **Manchuria** should come under a **United Nations** trusteeship. The report, identified as top secret, was not available but during the controversy over the release of General **Douglas MacArthur**, the **State Department** published the portions dealing with China.

WEST, SIR MICHAEL (1905–1978). From 1952 to 1953 Sir Michael West commanded the **British Commonwealth Division** in Korea. The division was on the line most of the time. They fought with manpower shortages and friction between various Commonwealth units. To support his division he instituted a KATCOM program—Korean Argumentation Troops Commonwealth—after the American plan, **Korean Augmentation United States Army (KATUSA)**, where Korean soldiers were brought into the division.

WESTLAND DRAGONFLY. This was a service and utility **helicopter** that saw considerable service. Westland was licensed to build the Sikorsky 2.51 two-seat helicopter called Dragonfly HR.1. It had a speed of 91 miles per hour with very limited range. Used by United Nations forces, it was unarmed.

WEYLAND, OTTO P. (1902–1979). When the Korean War broke out, Lieutenant General Otto P. Weyland was assigned as vice-commander for operations **Far East Air Force**, and on Lieutenant General **George E. Stratemeyer**'s retirement assumed command of the **United States Far East Air Force**. He was in command during the effort to use air pressure strategy to bring the communists back to the negotiation table. Weyland was in favor of tactical interdiction and supported this approach in the controversy with the army, which preferred close air–ground support.

WHITE HORSE HILL, BATTLE OF. Hill 395 was on the front of the **Republic of Korea (ROK)** Ninth Division and was just five miles west of Chorwon. The hill guarded a main road and was necessary to control the Chorwon area. The **Communist Chinese Forces (CCF)** first hit Arrowhead (281) some two miles from White Horse in order to pin down the French Battalion and parts of the United States **2nd Infantry Division** there. Two battalions of the CCF 114th Division moved up against White Horse. Between 6 October and 8 October 1952 the hill changed hands four times. A break in the battle came on 12 October when the ROK 30th Regiment inflicted especially heavy casualties on the CCF. After losing nearly 10,000 men, the CCF pulled back on 15 October 1952.

WHITNEY, COURTNEY (1897–1969). A close personal friend of General **Douglas MacArthur**, he served in the military before resigning and opening a law practice in Manila. In September 1940 he returned to active duty and in 1941 went to the **Philippines** to organize MacArthur's secret service. In 1946 Whitney joined MacArthur's staff in Tokyo as head of the government sections and was a principal author of Japan's new constitution. When MacArthur was recalled, Whitney resigned from the army and served as MacArthur's press secretary during the congressional hearings. He was with MacArthur when the general died.

WILLOUGHBY, CHARLES A. (1892–1972). He entered the **United States Army** in 1910 as Adolph Charles Tscheppe–Wedenbach. He obtained his commission, changed his name, and served in Mexico and France, and as an instructor at the Command and Staff College in Fort Leavenworth, Kansas. It was there he met General **Douglas MacArthur**, who took him to the Philippines. A veteran of the campaigns at Bataan and Corregidor, he was serving as **G-2 (intelligence)** when the Korean War broke out. He was either unaware of the **People's Repub-**

lic of China's preparations for war or did not consider it important and identified the People's Republic of China **prisoners of war** as "stragglers." When General MacArthur was relieved of duty Major General Willoughby retired to become editor of the *Foreign Intelligence Digest.*

WILSON, CHARLES E. (1886–1972). A president of General Electric, he served President Franklin D. Roosevelt on the War Production Board during World War II. Called by President **Harry S. Truman** to head the newly created Office of Defense Mobilization, he worked to prepare the **United States** for a third world war while fighting a limited war in Korea. In one year the military budget increased from $15 to $60 billion. After clashing with **Harry Truman** over an increase pay package for the steel workers, he resigned in 1952. *See also* TRUMAN'S SEIZURE OF THE STEEL PLANTS.

WING. An organizational distinction used by the **U.S. Air Force, U.S. Navy**, and **U.S. Marine Corps**. An air force wing is commanded by a colonel and is composed of several **squadrons** commanded by a lieutenant colonel and organizationally subordinate to an air force (5th Air Force). An air force wing consisted of about 75 airplanes. The marine wing, during the Korean War, was commanded by a lieutenant general and was divided into two **Marine Aircraft Groups**. Each of the groups, commanded by a colonel, consisted of several squadrons. A navy wing was similar in organization to the air force wing, but was generally called a **Carrier Air Group**. It had about as many aircraft as an air force wing but was commanded by a navy commander.

WITHDRAWAL FROM THE DEMOCRATIC PEOPLE'S REPUBLIC OF KOREA. When the **People's Republic of China** sent the **Chinese People's Volunteers Army** across the **Yalu River** and attacked **United Nations** forces, the UN troops began to retreat. Despite the fierceness of the attack and the vulnerability of the troops, it was never a rout. On the west **Eighth United States Army** withdrew southward heading for defensive positions south of **Seoul**. Along the 200-mile retreat the **Second Infantry Division** provided, at a terrible cost, a protective barrier. On the east, **X Corps** retreated toward the port city of **Hungnam**. From there they reentered Korea near **Pusan**. During the latter part of December 1951 more than 100,000 United States and **Republic of Korea** troops were evacuated by the navy and 17,500 vehicles and over 90,000 refugees. *See also* HUNGNAM EVACUATION.

WOLMI-DO. A small fortified sentinel island guarding Inchon Harbor, it was held by the **North Korean People's Army** in September when the invasion of Inchon was planned. It was essential to first capture Wolmi-do. On 13 September 1950 the air and sea forces began the devastation of the island, and on 15 September the marines landed with little opposition.

WOMEN IN THE MILITARY. In 1950 the Women's Army Corps (WAC), Women in the Air Force (WAF), Women Accepted for Volunteer Emergency Service (WAVE), and Women Marines had about 22,000 people on active duty, more than 7,000 of them in nursing. Within two years this had grown to 46,000. During the war more than 600 nurses served in Korea, many of them in the **Mobile Army Surgical Hospitals** right on the edge of the battlefield. In September 1951 the Defense Advisory Committee on Women in the Armed Services (DACOWITS) was formed to serve the interests of women on active duty.

WŎN YONG-DUK (1907–1968). A medical doctor, he was involved in the education of officers and, when the war broke out, was given the command of the 5th Brigade. Later promoted to lieutenant general, he backed **Syngman Rhee** in the political crisis of 1952. After that he was named provost marshal of the **Republic of Korea** armed services. He was involved with Syngman Rhee in the release of the North Korean **prisoners of war**. *See also* RHEE, SYNGMAN (Rhee's Declaration of Martial Law).

WONJU, BATTLE OF. The **North Korean People's Army (NKPA)** reached Wonju, and the city fell on 5 July. The little city was important as a road and railroad hub and was the location of several actions. As the **Republic of Korea** forces were moving north after the breakout from **Pusan**, the NKPA withdrew and Wonju became the headquarters of the ROK II Corps. Retreating NKPA, cut off by the mountains, attacked the city killing most of the corps officers, five Americans, and more than 1,000 civilians before heading north. After the **People's Republic of China** became involved, the United States **2nd Division** held Wonju until the collapse of the ROK II Corps opened this flank and Lieutenant General **Matthew Ridgway** ordered Wonju abandoned. During **Operation Thunderbolt** in January 1951, the **Seventh Infantry Division** found Wonju deserted but the 7th was quickly under attack. The inability to supply its forces led the Communist Chinese Forces to withdraw. *See also* OPERATION THUNDERBOLT.

WONSAN. Eastern Korean port city and rail center located about 110 miles north of the **38th Parallel** in the **Democratic People's Republic of Korea**, its harbor was heavily mined and was the scene of a significant minesweeping effort that was the source of a large number of naval casualties. It was, beginning on 16 February 1951, placed under a siege that would turn out to be the longest in **United States** naval history: 861 days.

 Wonsan Landing. X Corps, having taken Inchon, was transported to the east coast for an invasion scheduled for 20 October 1950. The plan was to drive overland to **Pyongyang**, the capital of the **Democratic People's Republic of Korea**. The **Republic of Korea**, however, took Wonsan on 10 October 1950, and the enterprise was downgraded to an administrative landing. Held up by **mines**, the marines did not land until 25–27 October 1951. As the **Communist Chinese Forces** moved south following their attack, Wonsan was ordered evacuated and the navy brought out 3,834 military personnel, 1,146 vehicles, more than 10,000 tons of cargo, and 7,009 refugees. The city was abandoned on 7 December 1950.

 Wonsan, Mayor of. Beginning in May 1952 the prolonged siege of **Wonsan** led to the practice of calling the commander of **Task Force Unit 95**.2.1 the "Mayor of Wonsan." During this period those serving as mayor were Captain Warren E. Gladding, Captain Allan A. Ovrom, Commander Robert M. Hinckley, Commander Nels C. Johnson, Captain James B. Grady, Captain Milton T. Dayton, Commander Louis Lefelar, Captain Richard B. Levin, Captain Selby K. Santmyers, Commander Frederick M. Stiesberg, Captain Raymond D. Fusselman, Captain Walter E. Linaweaver, Commander Antoine W. Venne, Commander Colin J. MacKenzie, Captain Robert J. Ovrom, Captain Albert L. Shepherd, Captain Carl E. Buill, Captain Lester C. Conwell, Captain Dale Mayberry, Captain Harold G. Bowen, Commander Stephen W. Carpenter, Captain John C. Woelfel, Commander Edward J. Foote, Commander Donald F. Quigley, Commander Albert L. Gebelin, Captain Richard E. Myers, Captain Jack Maginnis, and Captain Carl. M. Dalton.

WOUNDED IN ACTION (WIA). More than 97,100 United States armed forces personnel were wounded during the Korean War. Some were wounded more than once, accounting for the 103,200 wounds listed.

WRONG, H. HUME (1894–1954). With a long history of political service, he was named **Canada**'s ambassador to Washington in 1946 and held that position until he was named under **Secretary of State** for external affairs in 1953. A strong supporter of the **United States** and of collective security he proposed a revision in the **United Nations** charter that would no longer allow the veto. He strongly endorsed Canada's decision to commit troops and was a participant in the Korean War briefing meetings. He spoke against the advance into **North Korea** and urged the United States to show caution and restraint in dealing with the **People's Republic of China**.

WYOMING LINE. Established by General **Matthew B. Ridgway**, it ran 20 miles north of the **Kansas Line** from which he intended to maintain contact with the enemy through the use of patrols. As Ridgway was convinced that the demarcation line would be determined by the positions of the armies, the decision was made to hold the Kansas Line. In order to protect it with outposts he wanted the **United Nations** position to hold as much of the Wyoming Line as possible. When the war ended the Kansas–Wyoming Line remained the essential position.

–X–

X CORPS. *See* TENTH CORPS.

XIE FANG (1908–1984). In June 1950 General Xie Fang was appointed chief of the 13th Group Army and then entered Korea as chief of staff of the **Chinese People's Volunteers Army**. He was a major force in the planning and execution of all of the **People's Republic of China** offensive actions. Of particular value was his effort at maintaining cooperation with the leaders of the **Democratic People's Republic of Korea (DPRK)**. When the **Armistice** talks began he was sent as a second delegate under Teng Hua. His influence was probably increased by the fact that the DPRK delegates often looked to him for guidance. After the armistice was signed he returned to the People's Republic of China, was promoted to major general, and was involved in military education.

XINAO. *See* BRAINWASHING.

XVI CORPS. *See* SIXTEENTH CORPS.

–Y–

YAK. This is the designation for the Soviet-built aircraft designed by Alexander S. Yakovlev for the Soviet Union Air Force. It went through 28 modifications, the first 15 of which appeared in the air forces of the **Democratic People's Republic of Korea** and the **People's Republic of China**. Primarily armed with one 20mm cannon and two 12.7mm machine guns, it carried two 220-pound bombs. It could reach a speed of 415 miles per hour.

YALU BRIDGE CONTROVERSY. When approaching the **Yalu River**, General **Douglas MacArthur** asked permission to bomb bridges over the Yalu River. He was denied for some time fearing that it would bring the **People's Republic of China**, and maybe even the **Soviet Union**, into the war. However, agreement was soon given and bombing of the bridges began. Some were destroyed, and it did seem to slow the flow of communist goods, though not all the bridges had been affected. And, as winter approached, the Yalu River froze. The primary influence seemed to have been in showing the People's Republic of China that the **United States** was a military threat to them.

YALU RIVER. The Yalu River provides the natural boundary between **North Korea** and **Manchuria**. It was the traditional invasion route into China and the symbol of Chinese defense. Even though President **Harry Truman** warned General **Douglas MacArthur** not to get too close, American troops actually reached the southern banks of the river.

YANG YU-CH'AN (1897–1975). Yang Yu-Ch'an replaced **John M. Chang** as the **Republic of Korea**'s ambassador to the **United States** in March 1951. While the **Armistice** talks were underway when he became involved, he was very much opposed to any treaty that would leave Korea divided. When it became obvious that the armistice agreement would be accepted, he announced that the Republic of Korea would continue the fight alone. He also suggested that the **United Nations** had betrayed Korea. He was appointed to the **Geneva Conference of 1954** that ended unsuccessfully.

YELLOW SEA. Located between the Korean peninsula and mainland China, it forms the western border of Korea. The sea is shallow, only about 140 feet deep, and subject to tidal ranges of 20 to 40 feet. The main port on the west is Inchon that serves **Seoul**, the capital of the **Republic of Korea** and **Chinnampo** (now called Nampo) that served the **Democratic People's Republic of Korea** capital at **Pyongyang**.

YI CHONG CH'AN (1916–1983). Major general and chief of staff of the **Republic of Korea Army**, he was later promoted to lieutenant general. During the political crisis over **Syngman Rhee**'s reelection, he was ordered to bring two divisions to the capital and refused on the grounds that the army should not be a political tool. Despite the fact the **United States** supported his decision, he was relieved as chief of staff and sent to the United States for further education.

YI HAK-GU (1920–1953). Soviet-trained officer during World War II and later chief of staff of the **North Korean People's Army** 13th Division, he was captured by the **United Nations Command** and as a colonel was the second highest ranking **prisoner of war**. He became a leader of the prisoners at **Koje-do** and was instrumental in the rebellion and the **Dodd–Colson incident**. He was repatriated after the **Armistice** and was purged shortly afterwards.

YI HYONG GUN [LEE HYUNG-KEJN] (1920–). Trained by the Japanese, he served with its army during World War II. When war broke out in Korea, Brigadier General Yi Hyong Gun was commander of the 2nd Division. Ordered to place his command so that it could counterattack, along with the United States **Seventh Division**, on 26 June 1950 he got in position but did not attack. Feeling that the situation was out of control, he withdrew his troops to the south. His action meant there were no means to block the advancing **North Korean People's Army**. However, Yi Hyong Gun went on to head the **Republic of Korea** Field Training Command, served as a delegate to the **cease-fire** negotiations and as the **Republic of Korea Army** chief of staff.

YI KWŎN-MU [LEE KWON MU] (1910–). The commander of the **North Korean People's Army** 4th Division, Major General Yi Kwŏn-Mu fought in World War II and the Chinese Civil War. After additional schooling in the **Soviet Union**, he returned as army chief of staff for the **Democratic People's Republic of Korea**. As head of the 4th Division he occupied the capital of the **Republic of Korea** and earned his division the name "Seoul Division." In 1950 he was named commander of NKPA II Corps, and in 1958, the chief of staff for the NKPA.

YI POM-SOK [LEE BUM SUK] (1900–1972). A strong supporter of a disciplined, racially pure, anti-communist youth force, he had earlier founded the Radical Youth Corps. He served as prime minister of the **Republic of Korea** and as defense minister prior to the Korean War but was forced out. Later he would exercise political influence in support of President **Syngman Rhee**'s shift to a presidential form of government. He became the focus of anti-Rhee forces and lost his bid for the vice presidency in 1952.

YI SANG-JO [LEE SANG CHO] (1915–1996). Born in what is now the Republic of Korea, he immigrated to China, fought as a unit commander with the Korean Volunteer Army in support of the **Chinese Communist Forces**, and became one of the founders of the **North Korean People's Army (NKPA)**. He was chosen as **Kim Il-Sung**'s ambassador to seek aid from the **People's Republic of China** when the NKPA was retreating into its own territory. He was the primary delegate to the peace negotiations and after the **cease-fire** served on the **Military Armistice Commission**. After the war he was purged by **Kim Il-Sung** and sought sanctuary in the **Soviet Union**. He lived there, received his Ph.D., and worked as a researcher.

YI SUNG-YOP (1905–1953). He served as the **Democratic People's Republic of Korea** minister of justice and, after the invasion, chair of the Seoul People's Committee, a position from which he engaged in secret **cease-fire** discussions with **Republic of Korea** leftists and the **United States**. The efforts failed and he lost power during conflicts between factions in the **North Korean Communist Party**. After the **Armistice** he was arrested and executed as an enemy of the state for working with the Americans to overthrow **North Korea**.

YIM, LOUISE (1899–1977). She was a highly successful educator and founder of Chung'ang Women's College and chancellor of Chung'ang University from 1953 to 1971. A close friend of **Syngman Rhee**, she served in his cabinet as an observer to the **United Nations** and in 1952 ran for vice president supporting Rhee but was not elected. She went on to become a member of the National Council for Reunification, a support organization with strong political ties.

YONGCHON, BATTLE OF. During the defense of the **Naktong Perimeter**, Yongchon played a strategic role because the transportation center it controlled was essential to United Nations defense along the line between Kyongju and Taegu. During the early hours of 5 September, the 15th **North Korean People's Army (NKPA)** launched its attack against the **Republic of Korea**. The center that was defending against tanks fell, and the NKPA soon occupied the city. It moved through the city and continued southeast toward Kyongju. The fighting was desperate with hand-to-hand fighting during which the city would change hands four times. On 10 September the **Republic of Korea** 8th Division mounted a counterattack that defeated the NKPA 15th Division and soon retook all the land it had lost. This defense is believed to have saved the United Nations line and allowed the later counteroffensive that followed the **Inchon Landing**. *See also* NAKTONG PERIMETER.

YOSU–SUNCH'ON REBELLION. Organized under communists within the 14th Regiment of the **Republic of Korea Army**, they rebelled on 19 October 1948, just two months after **Syngman Rhee**'s election. They took the city of Yosu where they killed those with known rightist leanings and members of the police. Rhee reacted immediately and by 23 October Sunch'on had been retaken. By 26 October hundreds of communists and suspected communists had been executed or imprisoned. As a result of the rebellion, the **United States** slowed their planned troop withdrawal.

YU JAI HYUNG (1921–). Brigadier General Yu Jai Hyung was commander 7th Division, **Republic of Korea Army**, in the Uijongbu corridor, the invasion route to **Seoul**. Without support he was unable to stop the **North Korean People's Army** advance, and the troops retreated into the hills. Promoted to major general, he commanded the ROK II Corps at the **Battle of Yongchon**. He was relieved for political reasons, in late October 1950, and then served with the **United Nations Command**'s delegation at the **Panmunjom** truce talks. After the war he served in a variety of capacities and became minister of defense in 1971.

YUGOSLAVIA. When war broke out in Korea, Yugoslavia, then a member of the **United Nations Security Council**, was in the difficult situation of trying to balance between preferred neutrality and upsetting the **United States**, and so abstained at the **United Nations** vote.

YUN CH'I-YŎNG (1898–1996). A strong supporter of President **Syng-**

man Rhee, he worked with Rhee until he was forced to resign over a disagreement Rhee had with Lieutenant General **John R. Hodge**, the **United States** occupational commander. After the outbreak of war he organized a volunteer corps that aided in the defense of **Pusan**. Later he worked with Americans in organizing clandestine operations into the **Democratic People's Republic of Korea**. He was opposed to the **Armistice** agreement. He later aided in the formation of the Democratic Republican party and served as mayor of **Seoul**.

–Z–

ZHOU ENLAI. *See* CHOU EN-LAI.

ZINCHENKO, CONSTANTIN E. (1909–   ). He was a representative of the **Soviet Union** who served as assistant secretary-general for Security Council Affairs at the **United Nations** from 1949 to 1952. He served as a conduit in establishing contact between the **United States** and the Soviet Union concerning peace talks. He left the UN under mysterious circumstances only to reappear some three years later as a journalist in Moscow.

ZONE OF INTERIOR (ZI). Used on official documents within the military to mean the **United States,** generally used to indicate time in the United States as opposed to time in the field.

ZORIN, VALERIAN A. (1902–1986). In October 1952 Zorin was appointed as **Jacob Malik's** replacement as the **Soviet Union**'s permanent delegate to the **United Nations**. He was the primary contact for **India**'s ambassador **Sarvepalli Radhakrishnan** during the period when India was proposing a peace plan.

Tanks from the 14th Tank Company preparing to move out in the snow

President Syngman Rhee, General William Dean, and General Mark Clark on Dean's release from three years as a POW

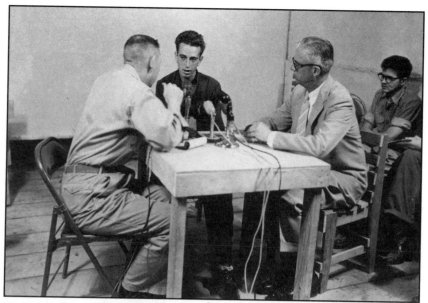

James Lucas and Robert Stevens interviewing Corporal Thompson at Freedom Village, 12 August 1953

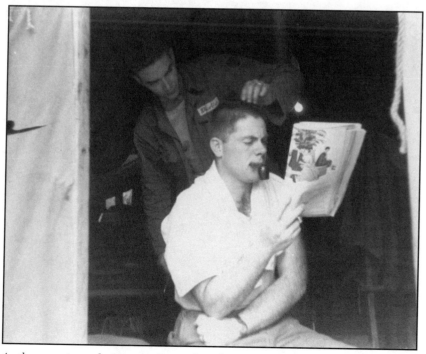

Author getting a haircut at Seventh Infantry Division rear

President-elect Dwight D. Eisenhower on his visit to Korea,
December 1952

Lower leg of the Chosin Reservoir called "Death Valley"

Pontoon bridge over the Han River, Korea 1952

USO entertainers performing on mobile stage for soldiers of the First Marine Division

Australian and British soldiers of the First Commonwealth Division at Kimpo Airfield

Appendix I
Casualties

Unit	Killed in Action	Wounded in Action
United States		
2nd Infantry Division	7,094	16,575
1st Marine Division	4,004	25,864
7th Infantry Division	3,905	10,858
1st Cavalry Division	3,811	12,086
24th Infantry Division	3,735	7,395
25th Infantry Division	3,048	10,186
3rd Infantry Division	2,160	7,939
Independent of divisions	1,432	—
Far East Air Force	1,200	368
5th Regt. Combat Team	867	3,188
45th Infantry Division	834	3,170
Naval Forces 7th Fleet	458	1,576
187th Regt. Combat Team	442	1,656
40th Infantry Division	376	1,457
1st Marine Air Wing	258	174

29th RCT was assigned to both 24th and 25th Division and counted above.

[*Battle Casualties of the Army*, 30 September 1954, U.S. Army]

Other Allied Nations		
Republic of Korea	59,000	291,000
British Commonwealth	1,263	4,817
United Nations members*	1,800	7,000

* Belgium, Colombia, Ethiopia, France, Greece, The Netherlands, the Philippines, Thailand, and Turkey

Appendix II
United Nations Commanders During the Korean War

Commanders in Chief of the United Nations Command
General Douglas MacArthur   23 July 1950–11 April 1951
General Matthew B. Ridgway   11 April 1951–12 May 1952
General Mark W. Clark   12 May 1952–27 July 1953

Commanding Generals of the Eighth United States Army
Lt. Gen. Walton H. Walker   13 July 1950–23 December 1950
Lt. Gen. Frank W. Milburn   23 December 1950–26 December 1950
Lt. Gen. Matthew B. Ridgway   26 December–10 April 1951
Lt. Gen. James A. Van Fleet   11 April 1951–10 February 1953
Lt. Gen. Maxwell D. Taylor   11 February 1953–27 July 1953

Commanding Generals Far East Air Force
Lt. Gen. George E. Stratemeyer   26 April 1949–21 May 1951
Lt. Gen. Earle E. Partridge   21 May 1951–1 June 1951
Maj. Gen. O. P. Weyland   1 June 1951–27 July 1953

Commanders of the Far East Naval Forces
Vice Admiral C. Turner Joy   26 August 1949–4 June 1952
Vice Admiral R. P. Briscoe   4 June 1952–27 July 1953

Commanding Generals of the 5th Air Force
Lt. Gen. Earle E. Partridge   6 October 1948–21 May 1951
Maj. Gen. Edward J. Timberlake   21 May 1951–1 June 1951
Maj. Gen. Frank F. Everest   1 June 1951–30 May 1952
Lt. Gen. Glenn O. Barcus   30 May 1952–31 May 1953
Lt. Gen. Samuel E. Anderson   31 May 1953–27 July 1953

Commanders of United States Seventh Fleet
Vice Admiral Arthur D. Struble   6 May 1950–28 March 1951
Vice Admiral H. H. Martin   28 March 1951–3 March 1952
Vice Admiral R. P. Briscoe   3 March 1952–20 May 1952
Vice Admiral J. J. Clark   29 May 1952–27 July 1953

Commanding Generals of the United States I Corps

Maj. Gen. John B. Coulter	August 1950–11 September 1950
Maj. Gen. Frank W. Milburn	11 September 1950–19 July 1951
Maj. Gen. John W. O'Daniel	19 July 1951–29 June 1952
Maj. Gen. Paul W. Kendall	29 June 1952–11 April 1953
Maj. Gen. Bruce C. Clarke	11 April 1953–27 July 1953

Commanding Generals of the United States IX Corps

Maj. Gen. Frank W. Milburn	10 August 1950–12 September 1950
Maj. Gen. John B. Coulter	12 September 1950–31 January 1951
Maj. Gen. Bryant E. Moore	31 January 1951–23 February 1951
Maj. Gen. Oliver Smith (MC)	24 February 1951–5 March 1951
Maj. Gen. William F. Hoge	5 March 1951–24 December 1951
Maj. Gen. Willard G. Wyman	24 December 1951–31 July 1952
Maj. Gen. Joseph P. Cleveland	31 July 1952–9 August 1952
Maj. Gen. Reuben E. Jenkins	9 August 1952–27 July 1953

Commanding Generals of United States X Corps

Maj. Gen. Edward M. Almond	26 August 1950–15 July 1951
Maj. Gen. Clovis E. Byers	15 July 1951–5 December 1951
Maj. Gen. Williston B. Palmer	5 December 1951–12 August 1952
Maj. Gen. I. D. White	15 August 1952–27 July 1953

Commandants of the Marine Corps

General Clifton B. Cates	1 January 1948–31 December 1951
General Lemuel C. Shepherd Jr.	1 January 1952–27 July 1953

Chiefs of Staff of the Republic of Korea Army

Maj. Gen Chae Byung Dok	10 April 1950–30 June 1950
Lt. Gen. Chung Il Kwon	30 June 1950–23 June 1951
Maj. Gen. Lee Chong Chan	23 June 1951–23 July 1952
Lt. Gen Paik Son Yup	23 July 1952–5 May 1953

Bibliography

For many years there was surprisingly little written about the Korean War. It never seemed to capture the imagination of either scholars or the popular press. Considered "forgotten" by many, it has not been forgotten as much as ignored. In the last decade of the 20th century the amount of material has increased and some fine work has been done both on the history of the Korean War and the related questions of causes and effects. Thus this bibliography, which still must be very selective, tends to reflect works that have appeared since the 1980s. It consists of books, articles, and dissertations that relate directly to the subject. All the titles here are available in English; though a good many of them are translations. Since United States relations with Korea go back as far as the 1860s, a few works about these early concerns are included yet most deal with the period between World War II and the signing of the cease-fire in 1953.

Certainly the primary difficulty with understanding the Korean War is the unavailability of archival materials in the Democratic People's Republic of Korea, People's Republic of China, and to some limited degree the former Soviet Union. The cooling of the Cold War has opened up many sources and a number of these are available through the work of Kathryn Weathersby and the Woodrow Wilson Cold War Center. Captured North Korean documents can be located in National Archives, Accession Group 242, in the Far East Command Files.

Another difficulty with conducting Korean War research is that while many nations participated in the war, only a few have made the effort to preserve, or to publish, materials dealing with their contribution to the war. The exception is Great Britain, which has produced several well-documented narratives of Commonwealth participation. Commonwealth records are generally available through the Liddell Hart Center for Military Archives at Kings College, London, or the Royal Commission for Historical Manuscripts in London. The New Zealand Archives at Wellington is also useful. The Public Archives of Ottawa, Canada, or the Historical Section Department, Department of External Affairs (Ottawa) is available though their records are still being organized. The Australian Department of National Defence houses that nation's record. The contribution of most other countries has generally been ignored or, if available, consists of a single book or a few articles. As much as possible some source has been provided for each nation involved.

Archival records of the United States involvement in the Korean War are scattered in a variety of academic, military, private, and governmental collections. The list is long and the travel involved exhaustive. The prime locations are the Library of Congress, Washington; the Center for Military History, Washington; the United States Army Military History Institute, Carlisle Barracks, Pennsylvania; Air University Library, Maxwell Air Force Base, Alabama; the Marine Corps Historical Center, Washington; the Gillman Library (National Security Archives) Washington University; Combat Studies Institute at Fort Leavenworth, Kansas; and Naval Historical Center, Washington. Of particular help is the Center for the Study of the Korean War, Graceland University, Independence, Missouri, campus that holds one of the largest libraries on the Korean War.

Primary materials concerning the role of the presidents involved can be located at the Harry S. Truman Presidential Library in Independence, Missouri, and the Dwight D. Eisenhower Presidential Library in Abilene, Kansas. Also significant are the Douglas MacArthur Memorial Library, Norfolk, Virginia; Modern Military Branch, National Archives; and Butler Library, Columbia University, New York. The official records of the United Nations are held at Lake Success, New York. Microfilm copies are available at major governmental depositories including the Combined Arms Research Library at the Command and Staff College, Fort Leavenworth, Kansas.

Oral histories are particularly helpful in understanding the fighting of the Korean War. Oral histories can be located at the Butler Library, Columbia University, New York; the United States Army Eighth Army Historical Office's Korean War Project, Washington; and the Foreign Affairs Oral History Project, Lauinger Library, Georgetown University.

General histories can be most helpful, especially for the beginner, and there are several fine works available. Among these are T. R. Fehrenbach, *This Kind of War* (1963, 2001); Clay Blair, *The Forgotten War: America in Korea 1950–1953* (1987); Harry J. Middleton, *The Compact History of the Korean War* (1965); David Rees, *Korea: The Limited War* (1970); James L. Stokesbury, *A Short History of the Korean War* (1988); Isidor F. Stone, *The Hidden History of the Korean War* (1988); and John Toland, *In Mortal Combat: 1950–1953* (1991).

Several good documentary collections are available. Thomas H. Etzold and John L. Gaddis, *Containment: Documents on American Policy and Strategy, 1945–1950* (1978); *Records of the Joint Chiefs of Staff, Part 2: 1946–53: Meetings of the Joint Chiefs of Staff* (1980), and Paul M. Edwards, *The Korean War: A Documentary History* (2000).

For an overall view of what was going on diplomatically and politically a good source is Bruce Cumings, *Liberation and the Emergence of Separate Regimes* (1981) and the *Roaring of the Cataract* (1990); or David Detzer, *Thunder of the Captains: The Short Summer in 1950* (1977).

Two or three battles or events have drawn considerable attention and produced some excellent studies. Among these are the invasion at Inchon harbor discussed in Robert D. Heinl, *Victory at High Tide: The Inchon–Seoul Campaign* (1968) and Michael Langley, *Inchon Landing: MacArthur's Last Triumph* (1979). The defensive action at the Naktong (Pusan) Perimeter is well covered in W. Uzal Ent, *Fighting on the Brink: Defense of the Pusan Perimeter* (1996). The fight at Chosin Reservoir is expertly discussed in Eric M. Hamel, *Chosin: Heroic Ordeal of the Korean War* (1981) and Lynn Montross and Nicholas Canzona, *The Chosin Reservoir Campaign* (1957). The Hungnam evacuation is covered in detail in Glenn, Cowart, *Miracle in Korea: The Evacuation of X Corps from the Hungnam Beachhead* (1992).

There is still much to be written about the hill war that continued for nearly two years and most resembled World War I. One fine example of what can be done is S. L. A. Marshall, *Pork Chop Hill: The American Fighting Man in Action, Korea, Spring* (1953/1956).

The navy played a vital role but has received little attention by scholars. The best works are still the early efforts of naval officers: Malcolm Cagle and Frank A. Manson, *The Sea War in Korea* (1957); and James A. Field Jr., *History of United States Naval Operations* (1962). Two later works that have provided good coverage are Charles Cole, *Korea Remembered: Enough of a War* (1995), and the dissertation "A Study of the United States Navy's Minesweeping Efforts in the Korean War" (1993).

The marine's role has been well documented. Among the best is Robert D. Heinl, *Soldiers of the Sea: The United States Marine Corps, 1775–1962* (1962).

The air force, new and untried as a separate command, was very active. In many respects it is the best-known arm to serve in Korea. Three fine volumes record this role: Robert F. Futrell, *The United States Air Force in Korea, 1950–1953* (1983); James T. Stewart, *Airpower: The Decisive Force in Korea* (1957); and Wayne Thompson and Bernard C. Nalty, *Within Limits: The U.S. Air Force and the Korean War* (2000).

Works written on any of the many special operations that took place in Korea have been slower in coming out. In some cases the accounts are based on information considered, until recently, to be secret. There are several, but three are particularly informative. They are William B.

Breuer, *Shadow Warriors: The Covert War in Korea* (1996); Edward Evanhoe, *Darkmoon: Eighth Army Special Operations in the Korean War* (1995); and Ben Malcolm, *White Tigers: My Secret War in North Korea* (1995).

History is as much analysis as it is narrative and some very fine analysis of the Korean War has appeared in the past few years. Of these half a dozen draw special attention. James Cotton and Ian Neary, editors, *The Korean War in History* (1989) provide a good general view of the Korean War and its impact on history. David R. McCann and Barry S. Strauss, editors, *War and Democracy: A Comparative Study of the Korean War and the Peloponnesian War* (2001) offer an excellent look at the situation when a democracy goes to war. Rosemary Foot gives several insightful opportunities in "Making Known the Unknown War: Policy Analysis of the Korean Conflict in the Last Decade," *Diplomatic History* 15 (Summer 1991): 411–13; *Substitute for Victory: The Politics of Peacemaking and the Korean War* (1990); and *The Wrong War: American Policy and the Dimensions of the Korean Conflict, 1950–1953* (1985).

This bibliography is arranged by subject and alphabetically within subjects. The items are not cross-referenced, as items can be easily located under subject headings within the dictionary. Author's names are presented in the English manner with last names first. Some Chinese and Korean names cannot be separated and so are listed as spoken, which is the common identification. In one or two cases technical exactness has been ignored in order to make the bibliography more useable. For example the recoilless rifle, while actually an infantry weapon, is listed in artillery.

In the past decade a significant number of World Wide Web sites have been created. Many of them are excellent sources, and provide a lot of information. As with all Internet sites, care must be taken as to the source of the information. The following are some of the most helpful sources:

The Korean War Veteran Association (www.kwva.org) is the site of the official veterans organization.

The Korean War. net (www.KoreanWar.net) is a non-profit organization that is recognized by the U.S. Department of Defense.

The Cold War International History Project (cwilp.si.edu/default.htm) supports and records major releases of historical information held by a wide variety of governments.

Canadians in Korea runs the site that provides information about Canada's role. (www.vac-acc.gc.ca/historical/koreanwar/korea.htm)

In anticipation of the 50th anniversary of the Korean War the Department of Defense, Korean War Commemoration Committee (korea50.army.mil) was established as the official public access.

For the People's Republic of China's point of view the Korean War FAQ was established (centurychina.com/history/krwarfaq.html) and has a lot of information.

The People's Korea (www.korea-np.cojp./pk) provides the official view of the Democratic People's Republic of Korea.

For information dealing with American prisoners of war/ missing in action the Coalition of Families of Korean & Cold War POW/MIAs is very helpful (www.coalitionoffamilies.org).

Contents

I. General Accounts

A. BIBLIOGRAPHIES

Association of Asian Studies. *Cumulative Bibliography of Asian Studies 1941–1965: Subject Bibliography,* four volumes. Boston: G. K. Hall Publishing, 1970–1972.

Backus, Robert L., comp. *Russian Supplement to the Korean Studies Guide.* Berkeley: Institute of International Studies, University of California, 1958.

Blanchard, Carroll H. Jr. *Korean War: Bibliography and Maps of Korea.* Albany, N.Y.: Korean Conflict Research Foundation, 1964.

Brune, Lester H. *The Korean War: Handbook of the Literature and Re-*

search. Westport, Conn.: Greenwood Press, 1996.

Burns, Richard D. *Harry S. Truman: A Bibliography of His Times and Presidency.* Wilmington, Del.: Scholarly Resources, 1984.

Chung Yong Sun. *Korea: A Selected Bibliography.* Kalamazoo, Mich.: Korean Research and Publications, 1965.

Coletta, Paolo E. *An Annotated Bibliography of American Naval History.* Frederick, Md.: University Press of America, 1988.

Cresswell, Mary Ann, and Carl Berger. *United States Air Force History: An Annotated Bibliography.* Washington, D.C.: Office of Air Force History, 1971.

Edwards, Paul M. *The Inchon Landing, Korea, 1950: An Annotated Bibliography,* Westport, Conn.: Greenwood Press, 1994.

———. *The Korean War: An Annotated Bibliography.* Westport, Conn.: Greenwood Press, 1998.

———. *The Pusan Perimeter, Korea: An Annotated Bibliography.* Westport, Conn.: Greenwood Press, 1998.

Ginsburgs, George. *Soviet Works on Korea, 1945–1970.* Los Angeles: University of Southern California Press, 1973.

Henthorn, William E., comp. *A Guide to Reference and Research Materials on Korean History.* Honolulu: East–West Center, 1968.

Higham, Robin, and Jacob W. Kipp, eds. *Military History Bibliographies.* New York: Garland, 1993.

Horak, Stephan M., ed. *Russia, the USSR and Eastern Europe: A Bibliographic Guide to English Language Publications, 1964–1974.* Littleton, Colo.: Libraries Unlimited, 1978.

———. *Russia, the USSR and Eastern Europe: A Bibliographic Guide to English Language Publications, 1979–1980.* Littleton, Colo.: Libraries Unlimited, 1982.

Hutson, Susan Moiffman. *McCarthy and the Anti-Communist Crusade: A Selected Bibliography.* Los Angeles: California State University Press, 1979.

Hyatt, Joan, comp. *Korean War, 1950–1953: Selected References.* Maxwell Air Force Base, Ala.: Air University Library, 1990.

Imperial War Museum Library. *The War in Korea, 1950–1953: A List of Selected References.* London: War Museum Library, 1961.

Kim Hn-Kyo, and Hong Kyoo Park. *Studies on Korea: A Scholar's Guide.* Honolulu: University of Hawaii Press, 1959.

Kuehl, Warren F., and Nancy M. Ferguson, eds. *The United States and the United Nations: A Bibliography,* Political Issues Series. Los Angeles: California State University, 1981.

Lee Chong-Sik. "Korea and the Korean War." *In Soviet Foreign Relations and World Communism*, ed. Thomas Hammond. Princeton, N.J.: Princeton University Press, 1965.

McFarland, Keith D. *The Korean War: An Annotated Bibliography*. New York: Garland, 1986.

Millett, Allan R., and B. Franklin Cooling III. *Doctoral Dissertations in Military History*. Manhattan: Kansas State University Library, 1972.

Moss, William. *Archives in the People's Republic of China: A Brief Introduction for American Scholars and Archivists*. Washington, D.C.: Smithsonian Archives, 1993.

O'Quinlivan, Michael, and James S. Santelli. *An Annotated Bibliography of the United States Marines in the Korean War*. Washington, D.C.: Historical Branch G-3, Headquarters United States Marines, 1970.

Paige, Glen. "A Survey of Soviet Publications on Korea, 1950–1956." *Journal of Asian Studies* (7 August 1958): 579–94.

Rasor, Eugene L., ed. *General Douglas MacArthur, 1888–1964: Historiography and Annotated Bibliography*. Westport, Conn.: Greenwood Press, 1994.

Robinson, Mary Ann, comp. *The Home Front and War in the Twentieth Century*. Colorado Springs, Colo.: United States Air Force Academy, 1982.

Roos, Charles, comp. *A Bibliography of Military Medicine Relating to the Korean Conflict, 1950–1956*. Washington, D.C.: National Library of Medicine, 1957.

Seeley, Charlotte Palmer, comp. *American Women in the U.S. Armed Forces: A Guide to the Records of Military Agencies in the National Archives Relating to American Women*. Washington, D.C.: National Archives, 1992.

B. DICTIONARIES

Effenberger, David. *A Dictionary of Battles*. New York: Crowell, 1967.

Gailey, Harry A. *Historical Dictionary of the United States Marine Corps*. Lanham, Md.: Scarecrow Press, 1998.

Kohn, George Childes. *Dictionary of Wars: Revised Edition*. New York: Facts on File, 1999.

Matray, James I. *Historical Dictionary of the Korean War*. Westport, Conn.: Greenwood Press, 1991.

Newell, Clayton R. *The United States Army: A Historical Dictionary*. Lanham, Md.: Scarecrow Press, 2002.

Noel, John V., and Edward L. Beach. *Naval Terms Dictionary*. Annapolis, Md.: Naval Institute Press, 1988.

Quick, John. *Dictionary of Weapons and Military Terms*. New York: McGraw-Hill, 1973.

Sandler, Stanley. *The Korean War: An Encyclopedia*. New York: Garland, 1995.

Spiller, Roger J., ed. *Dictionary of American Military Biography*. Westport, Conn.: Greenwood Press, 1984.

Summers, Harry G. Jr. *Korean War Almanac*. New York: Facts on File, 1990.

Terry, Michael Robert. *Historical Dictionary of the United States Air Force and Its Antecedents*. Lanham, Md.: Scarecrow Press, 1999.

Tucker, Spencer C., ed. *Encyclopedia of the Korean War: a Political, Social, and Military History*. Santa Barbara, Calif.: ABC–CLIO, 2000.

Wedertz, Bill. *Dictionary of Naval Abbreviations*. Annapolis, Md.: Naval Institute Press, 1984.

C. CHRONOLOGIES AND GENERAL RESOURCES

Allard, Dean, and Betty Bern, eds. *U.S. Naval History Sources in the Washington Area and Suggested Research Subjects*. Washington, D.C.: Government Printing Office, 1970.

American University. *U.S. Army Handbook for Korea*. Washington, D.C.: Government Printing Office, 1958.

Brimmer, Brenda. *A Guide to the Use of United Nations Documents (Including References to Specialized Agencies and Special UN Bodies)*. Dobbs Ferry, N.Y.: Oceana Publications, 1962.

A Chronicle of Principal Events Relating to the Korean Question, 1945–1954. Peking: World Culture, 1954.

Cooney, David M. *A Chronology of the U.S. Navy, 1775–1965*. New York: Watts, 1965.

Edwards, Paul M. *The Korean War: A Documentary History*. Malabar, Fla.: Krieger Press, 2000.

Efenberger, David. *A Dictionary of Battles*. New York: Crowell, 1967.

Frank, Benis M. *Marine Corps Oral History Collection Catalogue*. Washington, D.C.: United States Marine History and Museum Division, 1989.

Geselbracht, Raymond H., and Anita M. Smith. *Guide to the Historical Materials in the Harry S. Truman Library*. Independence, Mo.: H. S. Truman Library, 1995.

Hajnal, Peter I. *Guide to United Nations Organization, Documentation, and Publishing.* Dobbs Ferry, N.Y.: Oceana Publications, 1974.

Jessup, John Jr., *An Encyclopedic Dictionary of Conflict and Conflict Resolution, 1945–1996.* Westport, Conn.: Greenwood Press, 1998.

Jessup, John E. Jr., and Robert W. Coakley, eds. *A Guide to the Study and Use of Military History.* Washington, D.C.: Center of Military History, 1979.

Kuehl, Warren, ed. *Dissertations in History: An Index to Dissertations Completed in History Departments of United States and Canadian Universities.* Lexington: University of Kentucky Press, 1972.

Moss, William. *Archives in the People's Republic of China: A Brief Introduction for American Scholars and Archivists.* Washington, D.C.: Smithsonian Archives, 1993.

National Historical Publications Commission. *Directory of Archives and Manuscript Repositories.* Washington, D.C.: Government Printing Office, 1978.

Neutral Nations Repatriation Commission. *Korea: Reports and Selected Documents.* New Delhi: India Press, 1954.

Records of the Joint Chiefs of Staff: Part II, The Far East, 1946–1953. Frederick, Md.: University Publications, 1980.

Sanders, Staley, ed. *The Korean War: An Encyclopedia.* New York: Garland, 1994.

Wickman, John E., ed. *Historical Materials in the Dwight D. Eisenhower Library.* Abilene, Kans.: Eisenhower Library, 1984.

D. ATLASES

Blanchard, Carroll H. Jr. *An Atlas of the War in Korea 1950–1953.* "The Pusan Perimeter," volume 2. Albany: State University of New York, 1972.

Esposito, Vincent J., ed. *The West Point Atlas of American Wars,* two volumes. New York: Praeger, 1959.

Griess, Thomas E. *Atlas of the Arab–Israeli Wars, The Chinese Civil War, and the Korean War.* New York: Avery Publishing, 1986.

Hartman, Tom, and John Mitchell. *A World Atlas of Military History 1945–1984.* New York: Facts on File, 1984.

Keegan, John, and Andrew Wheatcroft. *Areas of Conflict: An Atlas of Future Wars.* New York: Simon and Schuster, 1986.

Zaichikov, V. T. *Geography of Korea.* New York: Institute of Public Relations, 1951.

E. OFFICIAL HISTORIES

Appleman, Roy E. *U.S. Army in the Korean War: South to the Naktong, North to the Yalu.* Washington, D.C.: Government Printing Office, 1961.

Cagle, Malcolm, and Frank Manson. *The Sea War in Korea.* Annapolis, Md.: Naval Institute Press, 1957.

Cagle, Malcolm, Frank Manson, and Walter Karig. *Battle Report: The War in Korea,* volume IV. New York: Rinehart, 1952.

Chinese People's Liberation Army, Academy of Military Science. *A Military History of the Anti-U.S. Air-Korea War.* Peking: Foreign Publishing, 1988.

Cowdrey, Albert E. *The Medic's War.* Washington, D.C.: Government Printing Office, 1987.

Field, James A. *History of United States Naval Operations: Korea.* Washington, D.C.: Government Printing Office, 1962.

Futrell, Robert F. *The United States Air Force in Korea: 1950–1953,* Washington, D.C.: Government Printing Office, 1983.

Hermes, Walter G. *U.S. Army in the Korean War: Truce Tent and Fighting Front.* Washington, D.C.: Government Printing Office, 1966.

Miller, John Jr., Owen J. Carrol, and Margaret E. Tackley. *Korea: 1951–1953.* Washington, D.C.: Government Printing Office, 1956.

Montross, Lynn, and Nicholas A. Canzona. *The East–Central Front: U.S. Marine Operations in Korea: 1950–1953,* volume IV, Washington D.C.: Government Printing Office, 1962.

O'Neill, Robert. *Australia in the Korean War,* two volumes. Canberra: Australian War Memorial and the Australian Government Publishing Service, 1981, 1985.

Reister, Frank A. *Battle Casualties and Medical Statistics: U.S. Army Experience in the Korean War.* Washington, D.C.: The Surgeon General, 1973.

Sawyer, Robert K. *Military Advisors in Korea: KMAG in Peace and War,* Army Historical Series. Washington, D.C.: Center of Military History, 1962.

Schnabel, James. *The United States Army in the Korean War, Policy and Direction: The First Year.* Office of the Chief of Military History: Government Printing Office, 1972.

Wood, Herbert Fairlie. *Official History of the Canadian Army: Strange Battleground. The Operations in Korea and Their Effects on the Defense of Canada.* Ottawa: Ministry of National Defense, 1966.

F. KOREAN HISTORY, CULTURE, AND BACKGROUND

Bunge, Frederica M., ed. *North Korea: A Country Study.* New York: The American University, 1981.

Hatada, Takashi. *A History of Korea.* New York: ABC–CLIO, 1969.

Hongkee. *Korea: Her History and Culture.* Seoul, Republic of Korea: Office of Public Information, 1959.

Jin Kim Seong. *Handbook of Korea.* Seoul: Korean Ministry of Culture and Information, 1978.

Lee Ki-bail. *A New History of Korea.* Cambridge, Mass.: Harvard University Press, 1984.

McCune, George M., and Arthur L. Grey. *Korea Today.* Cambridge, Mass.: Harvard University Press, 1950.

McCune, Shannon. *Korea's Heritage: A Social and Regional Geography.* New York: E. Tuttle Company, 1956.

Nalty, Bernard C., and Truman Stonebridge. "Our First Korean War." *American History Illustrated* 2, no. 5 (1967): 10–19.

Oberdorfer, Don. *The Two Koreas: Contemporary History.* New York: Basic Books, 1999.

Tae Hung Ha. *Folk Customs and Family Life.* Seoul: Korean Information Services, 1958.

II. Origins of the Korean War

A. COLD WAR RELATIONS, 1865–1951

Baldwin, Frank, ed. *Without Parallel: The American–Korean Relationship since 1945.* New York: Pantheon, 1974.

Bell, Coral. "Korea and the Balance of Power." *Political Quarterly* 25, no. 1 (1954): 17–29.

Beloff, Max. *Soviet Policy in the Far East 1944–1951.* New York: Oxford University Press, 1953.

Blum, Robert, and Doak Barnett, eds. *The United States and China in World Affairs.* New York: McGraw-Hill, 1996.

Borton, Hugh. "Korea under American and Soviet Occupation, 1945–1947." In *Survey of International Affairs,* ed. Arnold Toynbee, London: Oxford University Press, 1952.

Buite, Russell D. "'Major Interests': American Policy toward China, Taiwan, and Korea, 1945–1950." *Pacific Historical Review* 473 (August 1978): 425–51.

Cho Soon Sung. *Korea in World Politics, 1940–1950: An Evaluation of American Responsibility.* Berkeley: University of California Press, 1967.

Cumings, Bruce. *The Roaring of the Cataract, 1947–1950.* Princeton, N.J.: Princeton University Press, 1981.

The East-Asian Crisis, 1945–1951: The Problem of China, Korea, and Japan: Papers. London: International Centre for Economics and Related Disciplines, London School of Economics, 1982.

Fisher, Louis. *Russia, America, and the World.* New York: Harper and Brothers, 1961.

Goncharov, Sergei N., John W. Lewis, and Xue Litai, *Uncertain Partners: Stalin, Mao, and the Korean War.* Stanford, Calif.: Stanford University Press, 1993.

Gordenker, Leon. *The United Nations and the Peaceful Unification of Korea: The Politics of Field Operations, 1947–1950.* The Hague: Marinue Nijhoff, 1959.

Harding, Harry, Yuan Ming, and Pei-ching Ta Hsueh, eds. *Sino–American Relations, 1945–1955: A Joint Reassessment of a Critical Decade.* Washington, D.C.: Scholarly Resources, 1989.

Iriye, Akira. *The Cold War in Asia: A Historical Introduction.* Englewood Cliffs, N.J.: Prentice-Hall, 1974.

Kim Joungwoon Alexander. *Divided Kingdom: The Politics of Development, 1945–1972.* Cambridge, Mass.: Harvard University Press, 1975.

McCauley, Mary. *Soviet Politics 1917–1991.* London: Oxford University Press, 1992.

McCune, George M. and Arthur L. Grey Jr. *Korea Today.* Cambridge, Mass.: Harvard University Press, 1950.

Meade, E. G. *American Military Government in Korea.* New York: King's Crown, 1951.

Mehnert, Klaus. *Peking and Moscow.* New York: G. P. Putnam's Sons, 1963.

Okonogi, Masao. "The Domestic Roots of the Korean War." In *The Origins of the Cold War in Asia*, ed. Yonosuke Nagai and Akira Iriye. New York: Columbia University Press, 1971.

Oliver, Robert T. *Why War Came in Korea.* New York: Fordham University, 1950.

Poole, Peter A. *China Enters the United Nations.* New York: Franklin Watts, 1974.

Ree, Erik Van. *Socialism in One Zone: Stalin's Policy in Korea, 1945– 1947.* New York: St. Martin's Press. 1989.

Stairs, Denis. *The Diplomacy of Constraint: Canada, The Korean War, and the United States.* Toronto: University of Toronto Press, 1974.

U.S. Department of State. *The Conflict in Korea: Events Prior to the Attack on June 25, 1950.* Washington, D.C.: Government Printing Office, 1951.

Wiltz, John Edward. "Did the United States Betray Korea in 1905?" *Pacific Historical Review* 44 (August 1985): 243–70.

Woodrow Wilson Cold War Center. *Cold War Flashpoints.* Princeton, N.J.: Woodrow Wilson Cold War Center, 1995.

———. *The Cold War in the Third World and the Collapse of Détente in the 1970s.* Princeton, N.J.: Woodrow Wilson Cold War Center, 1997.

B. ORIGINS AND CAUSES OF THE WAR

Acheson, Dean. "Act of Aggression in Korea." *Department of State Bulletin* 23 (10 July 1950): 43–46.

———. "Crisis in Asia: An Examination of U.S. Policy." *Department of State Bulletin* 22 (1950): 111–18.

Ahn, Chon. *The Study on the Day of the Outbreak of War: A Critique on the Inducement Theory of the War.* Seoul: Kwa Hak Fyo Yuk Sa, 1993.

"Aims and Objectives in Resisting Aggression in Korea." *Department of State Bulletin* 23 (11 September 1950): 407–10.

"Authority of the President to Repel the Attack in Korea." *Department of State Bulletin* 23 (1950): 43–50.

Berger, Carl. *The Korean Knot: A Military Political History.* Philadelphia: University of Pennsylvania Press, 1968.

Berstein, Barton J. "New Light on the Korean War." *International History Review* 3, no. 2 (April 1981): 256–77.

———. "The Week We Went to War: American Intervention in the Korean Civil War," *Foreign Service Journal* 54, no. 1(January 1977): 6–9, 33–35, and 54; no. 2 (February 1977): 8–16, 33–35.

Bo Yibo. "The Making of the Lean-to-One-Side Decision." trans. Ahai Qiang. *Chinese Historians* 5 (spring 1992): 57–62.

Brands, H. W. *The Devil We Knew: Americans and the Cold War.* New York: Oxford University Press, 1987.

Chen Jian. "China's Road to the Korean War." *Working Paper, Cold War History Project.* Washington, D.C.: Woodrow Wilson Cold War Center, 1995–96.

———. "The Sino–Soviet Alliance and China's Entry into the Korean

War." Washington, D.C.: Woodrow Wilson Cold War Center, 1991.

Cho Li San. "Kim Started War." *New York Times* (6 July 1990): A5.

Cho Soon-sung. *Korea in World Politics, 1941–1950: An Evaluation of American Responsibility.* Berkeley: University of California, 1967.

Chung Dae-Hwa. "How the Korean War Began." trans. Karunakar Gupta, *China Quarterly* 52 (October/December 1972): 699–712.

Connally, Thomas. *My Name Is Tom Connally.* New York: Crowell, 1954.

Cumings, Bruce. *The Origins of the Korean War: Liberation and the Emergence of Separate Regimes 1945–1947.* Princeton, N.J.: Princeton University Press, 1981.

Dean, Vera M. "Justification of War." *Foreign Policy Bulletin* 31, no. 15 (January 1952): 5–6.

Deane, Hugh. "Korea, China, and the United States: A Look Back." *Monthly Review* 46, no. 9 (1955): 20.

Detzer, David. *Thunder of the Captains: The Short Summer in 1950.* New York: Crowell, 1977.

Dresser, Robert B. *How We Blundered into [the] Korean War and Tragic Future Consequences.* New York: Committee for Constructive Government, 1950.

George, Alexander L. *U.S. Reaction to North Korean Aggression.* Santa Monica, Calif.: Rand Corporation, 1954.

Golden, Eric. "The President, the People, and the Power to Make War." *American Heritage* 21, no. 3 (1970): 28–35.

Gorcharov, Sergei N. "Stalin's Dialogue with Mao Zedong." *Journal of Northeast Asia Studies* 10, no. 4 (winter 1991–1992): 45–76.

Gupta, Karunakar. "How Did the Korean War Begin?" *China Quarterly* 52 (October/December 1972): 699–716.

Heichal, Gabriella T. "Decision Making during the Crisis: The Korean War and the Yom Kippur War." Ph.D. Georgetown: George Washington University, 1984.

Hitchock, Wilbur W. "North Korea Jumps the Gun." *Current History* (20 March 1951): 136–44.

Ho, Chong-ho, Sok-hui Kang, and Tae-ho Pak. *The U.S. Imperialists Started the Korean War.* Pyongyang, Korea: Foreign Languages Publishing House, 1993.

Hunt, Michael H. "Beijing and the Korean Crisis, June 1950–June 1951." *Political Science Quarterly* 107, no. 3 (fall 1992): 453–78.

Jung, Young Suk. "A Critical Analysis on the Cause of the Korean War." *Journal of Asiatic Studies* 15, no. 1 (1972): 85–94.

Kim, Chull Baum, and James Matray, eds. *Korea and the Cold War: Divi-*

sion, Destruction and Disarmament. Claremont, Calif.: Regina Books, 1993.

Lowe, Peter. *The Origins of the Korean War.* London: Longman, 2000.

Matray, James. *The Reluctant Crusade: American Foreign Policy in Korea, 1941–1950.* Honolulu: University of Hawaii Press, 1985.

Merrill, John. *Korea: The Peninsular Origins of the War.* Newark: University of Delaware Press, 1988.

Paige, Glen D. *The Korean Decision: June 24–30, 1950.* New York: Free Press, 1968.

———. *1950: Truman's Decision: The United States Enters the Korean War.* New York: Chelsea, 1970.

Pelz, Stephen E. *America Goes to War, Korea, June 24–30, 1950: The Politics and Process of Decision.* Washington, D.C.: The Woodrow Wilson Cold War Center, 1979.

———. "When the Kitchen Gets Hot, Pass the Buck: Truman and Korea in 1950." *Reviews in American History* (6 December 1978): 548–55.

Pritt, Denis N. *New Light on Korea.* London: Labour Monthly, 1951.

Sho, Jin Chull. "The Role of the Soviet Union in Preparation for the Korean War." *Journal of Korean Affairs* (3 January 1974): 3–14.

Simmons, Robert R. *The Strained Alliance: Peking, P'yongyang, Moscow, and the Politics of the Korean Civil War.* New York: Free Press, 1975.

Smith, Beverly. "The White House Story: Why We Went to War in Korea." *Saturday Evening Post* (10 November 1951): 22–23, 76–77, 80–88.

Stueck, William Whitney. *The Road to Confrontation.* Chapel Hill: University of North Carolina Press, 1981.

Thornton, Richard C. *Odd Man Out: Truman, Stalin, Mao, and the Origins of the Korean War.* Novato, Calif.: Presidio, 2000.

"United States Submits 'Conclusive Proof' of Captured Army Orders." *United Nations Bulletin* (15 June 1951): 578–79.

Warner, Albert L. "How the Korean Decision Was Made." *Harper's* (June 1951): 99–106.

Weathersby, Kathryn. "Attack or Not to Attack? Stalin, Kim Il Sung, and the Prelude to War." *Woodrow Wilson Cold War Center Bulletin* 5 (spring 1995): 1, 2, 9.

———. "Soviet Aims in Korea and the Origins of the Korean War, 1945–1950: New Evidence from Russian Archives," Working Paper 8. *Woodrow Wilson Cold War Center Bulletin* (2 January 1993).

———. "The Soviet Role in the Early Phase of the Korean War: New

Documentary Evidence." *Journal of American–East Asian Relations* 4 (winter 1993): 425–58.

C. CHINESE INTERVENTION IN THE KOREAN WAR

Hoyt, Edwin P. *The Day the Chinese Attacked: Korea 1950.* New York: McGraw-Hill. 1990.

Huo, Hwei-ling. "A Study of the Chinese Decision to Intervene in the Korean War." Ph.D. New York: Columbia University, 1989.

Kim, Ho Joon. "Why China Goes to War: Risk-Taking Factors and Patterns of Crisis Behavior: Three Comparative Case Studies." Ph.D. Georgetown: George Washington University, 1996.

Weathersby, Kathryn, trans. "New Findings on the Korean War." *Woodrow Wilson Cold War Center Bulletin* 3 (fall 1993) 1, 14–18.

Whiting, Allen. *China Crosses the Yalu: The Decision to Enter the Korean War.* New York: Macmillan, 1960.

Xiaobing, Li, and Glenn Trancy, trans. "Mao's Telegrams during the Korean War, October–December 1950." *Chinese Historians* 5 (fall 1992).

———. "Mao's Dispatch of Chinese Troops to Korea: Forty-Six Telegrams, July–October 1950." *Chinese Historians* 5 (spring 1992): 63–86.

Yufan, Hao, and Zhai Zhihai. "China's Decision to Enter the Korean War: History Revisited." *China Quarterly* 12 (March 1990): 94–115.

Zagoria, Donald S. "Mao's Role in the Sino–Soviet Conflict." *Pacific Affairs* (summer 1974): 139–53.

Zelman, Walter A. *Chinese Intervention in the Korean War.* Berkeley: University of California, 1967.

Zhang, Shu Guang. *Mao's Military Romanticism: China and the Korean War, 1950–1953.* Lawrence: University of Kansas Press, 1995.

Zhang, Xi. "Peng Dehuai and China's Entry into the Korean War." trans. Jian Chen. *Chinese Historians* 6, no. 1 (spring 1993): 1–30.

III. Nations Involved in the Korean War

A. UNITED NATIONS

"Aid from U.N. to U.S. Forces Will Stay Small." *U.S. News and World Report* 29 (18 August 1950): 24.

"Events in Korea Deepen Interest in United Nations." *Department of State Bulletin* 23 (18 September 1950): 450–51.

Farley, Miriam S. "The Korean Crisis and the United Nations." In *State of Asia*, ed. Lawrence Rogers. New York: Alfred A. Knopf, 1951.

Hillen, John. *Blue Helmets: The Strategy of UN Military Operations.* New York: Brassey's, 2000.

"Review of Security Council Action in Defense of Korea." *Department of State Bulletin* 23, no. 8 (18 September 1950): 451–54.

Yoo, Tae-ho, *The Korean War and the United Nations.* Belgium: University of Louvain Press, 1965.

B. INVOLVED NATIONS

1. Commonwealth Nations

a. Australia

Bartlett, Norman. *With the Australians in Korea.* Canberra: Australian War Memorial, 1954.

Cooper, Alastair. "At the Crossroads: Anglo–Australian Naval Relations, 1945–1960. *Journal of Military History* 58, no. 4 (October 1994).

Gallaway, Jack. *The Last Call of the Bugle: The Long Road to Kapyong.* St. Lucia, Australia: University of Queensland Press, 1994.

McCormack, Gavan. *Cold War Hot War: An Australian Perspective on the Korean War.* Sydney: Hale and Iremonger, 1983.

Odgers, George. *Across the Parallel: The Australian 77 Squadron with the United States Air Force in the Korean War.* London: Heinemann, 1952.

Wilson, David. *Lion over Korea: 77 Fighter Squadron RAAF, 1950–1953.* Canberra: Banner Books, 1994.

b. Canada

Barris, Ted. *Deadlock in Korea: Canadians at War, 1950–1953.*Toronto: Macmillan Canada, 1999.

Canada, Army Headquarters, General Staff Historical Section. *Canada's Army in Korea: A Short Official History.* Ottawa: Queen's Printer, 1956.

———. *Canada's Army in Korea: The United Nations Operations, 1950–1953, and Their Aftermath.* Ottawa: Queen's Printer, 1956.

Coad, B. A. "The Land Campaign in Korea." *Journal Royal United Service Institution* 97 (February 1952): 1–14.

Evans, Paul, and B. Michael Frolic, eds. *Reluctant Adversaries: Canada and the People's Republic of China, 1949–1970.* Toronto: University of Toronto Press, 1991.

Greisler, Patricia. *Valour Remembered: Canadians in Korea.* Ottawa: Department of Veterans Affairs, 1982.

McDougall, C. C. "Canadian Volunteers Prepare for Combat." *Soldiers* 6 (June 1951): 54–57.

McGuire, F. R. *Canada's Army in Korea.* Ottawa: Historical Section, Army General Staff, 1956.

McNair, Charles T. "The Royal Canadian Navy in Korea." *Army Information Digest* (6 November 1951): 50–53.

Melady, John. *Korea: Canada's Forgotten War.* Toronto: Macmillan, 1983.

Meyers, Edward. *Thunder in the Morning Calm: The Royal Canadian Navy in Korea, 1950–1955.* St. Catharines, Ontario: Vanwell, 1991.

Stairs, Denis. "Canada and the Korean War: The Boundaries of Diplomacy." *International Perspective* 6 (1972): 25–32.

———. *The Diplomacy of Constraint: Canada, the Korean War, and the United States.* Toronto: University of Toronto Press, 1974.

Thorgrimsson, Thor and E. C. Russell. *Canadian Naval Operation in Korean Waters, 1950–1953.* Ottawa: Department of National Defence, Canadian Forces, Headquarters Naval Historical Section, 1965.

Wood, Herbert Fairlie. *Official History of the Canadian Army: Strange Battleground: The Operations in Korea and Their Effect on the Defence Policy of Canada.* Ottawa: Ministry of National Defence, 1966.

c. New Zealand

McGibbon, Ian. *New Zealand and the Korean War.* New York: Oxford University Press, 1992.

New Zealand, Department of External Affairs. *New Zealand and the Korean Crisis.* Wellington: Owen, 1950.

16 Field Regiment: Royal New Zealand Artillery, 1950–1954. No publisher, 1954.

d. United Kingdom including Commonwealth Division

Barclay, C. N. *The First Commonwealth Division: The Story of British Commonwealth Land Forces in Korea, 1950–1953.* Aldershot, England: Gale & Polden, 1954.

Carew, Tim. *Korea: The Commonwealth at War*. London: Cassell, 1967.

Cassels, Sir James H. "The Commonwealth Division in Korea." *Journal Royal United Service Institution* 98 (August 1953): 362–72.

Cosgrove, Peter J. *The Commonwealth Military Perspective of Commonwealth Division Operations in Korea 1950–1953*. Quantico, Va.: Marine Corps Command and Staff College, 1979.

Cunningham–Boothe, Ashley, and Peter Farrar. *British Forces in the Korean War*. London: The British Korean Veterans Association, 1988.

Davis, S. J. *In Spite of Dungeons*. London: Hodder and Stoughton, 1955.

Dayal, Shiv. *India's Role in the Korean Question*. New Delhi, India: Chand, 1959.

Eaton, Hamish B. *Something Extra: 28 Commonwealth Brigade, 1951–1974*. Edinburgh: Pentland Press, 1993.

Farrar-Hockley, Anthony. *The British Part in the Korean War*, two volumes. London: Her Majesty's Stationery Office, 1990, 1995.

———. *The Edge of the Sword*. London: Frederick Muller, 1954.

Gaston, Peter. *Thirty-Eighth Parallel: The British in Korea*. Glasgow: A. D. Hamilton, 1976.

Gogate, Rajaram V. "How India Looks at Korea." *Korean Study* 2 (1953): 7–8.

Grey, Jeffrey. *The Commonwealth Armies and the Korean War: An Alliance Study*. New York: Manchester University Press, 1988.

Hennessy, Peter. *Never Again: Britain, 1945–1951*. London: Jonathan Cape, 1992.

Landsdown, John R. P. *With the Carriers in Korea: The Fleet Air Arm Story, 1950–1953*. Worcester: Square One, 1992.

Linklater, Eric. *Our Men in Korea*. London: Her Majesty's Stationery Office, 1952.

MacDonald, Callum. *Britain and the Korean War*. Oxford: Basil Blackwell, 1990.

Malcolm, George I. *The Argylls in Korea*. London: Nelson, 1952.

McGregor, P. M. J. "History of No. 2 Squadron, SAAF in the Korean War." *Military History Journal* 42 (June 1978): 82–89.

Moore, Dermont M. "SAAF in Korea." *Militia* 4 (1980): 24–34.

Murti, Bhaskaria. *India's Stand on Korea*. New Delhi, India: Congress Party in Parliament, 1953.

Ovendale, Ritchie. *The English-Speaking Alliance: Britain, the United States, the Dominions, and the Cold War, 1945–1951*. London: Allen and Unwin, 1985.

Pratt, Sir John. *Korea: The Lie That Led to War*. London: Britain China

Friendship Association, 1951.

Prince, Stephen. "The Royal Navy's Contribution to the Korean War." *Journal of Strategic Studies* 17 (June 1994): 94–120.

The Royal Ulster Rifles in Korea. Belfast: William Mullan, 1953.

Royle, Trevor. *War Report.* Edinburgh: Mainstream, 1987.

Smurthwaite, David, and Linda Washington. *Project Korea: The British Soldier in Korea 1950–1953.* London: National Army Museum, 1988.

Steinberg, Blema S. "The Korean War: A Case Study in Indian Neutralism." *Orbis* 8 (winter 1965): 937–54.

Thomas, Peter. *41 Independent Commando Royal Marines, Korea 1950–1952.* Portsmouth: Royal Marines Historical Society, 1990.

Whiting, Charles. *Battleground Korea: The British in Korea.* Stroud, England: Sutton, 1999.

Wybrow, Robert J. *Britain Speaks Out.* London: Macmillan, 1989.

2. *United States*

a. General

Colithier, Marcel. "Latin America and the Korean Crisis." MA. Baton Rouge: Louisiana State University, 1984.

Cooling, B. Franklin. "Allied Interoperability in the Korean War." *Military Review* 63 (June 1983): 26–52.

DeVaney, Carl N. "Know Your Allies." *Military Review* (March 1953): 11–19.

Fox, William J. *Inter-Allied Co-Operation During Combat Operations.* Washington, D.C.: Office of the Chief of Military History, Department of the Army, 1952.

Loesch, Robert J. "Korean Milestones: 1950–1953." *Soldiers* 8 (September 1953): 57.

War History Editing Committee. *The Participation of UN Forces.* Seoul: South Korean Defense Ministry, 1980.

b. United States Air Force

Ambody, Francis J. "Skynights, Nightmares, and MiGs." *American Aviation Historical Journal* 34 (winter 1989): 308–13.

———. "We Got Ours at Night: The Story of the Lockheed F-94 Starfire in Combat." *American Aviation Historical Journal* 27, no. 2 (1982): 148–50.

Baer, Bud. "Three Years of Air War in Korea." *American Aviation* (6 July 1953): 20–21.

Blunk, Chester I. *"Every Man a Tiger:" The 731 USAF Night Intruders over Korea:* Manhattan, Kans.: Sunflower University Press, 1987.

Brown, David. *The Seafire: The Spitfire That Went to Sea.* Annapolis, Md.: Naval Institute Press, 1989.

Burning, John R. *Crimson Sky: The Air Battle for Korea.* New York: Brassey's Press, 1999.

Cleveland, William M. *Mosquitos in Korea.* New York: Mosquito Association, 1991.

Crane, Conrad C. *American Air Power Strategy in Korea, 1950–1953.* Lawrence: University Press of Kansas, 2000.

Dorr, Robert, John Lake, and Warren Thompson. *Korean War Aces.* London: Osprey Aerospace, 1995.

Dorr, Robert, and Warren Thompson. *The Korean Air War.* Osceola, Wis.: Motorbooks International, 1994.

Farmer, James A., and M. J. Strumwasser. *The Evolution of the Airborne Forward Air Controller: An Analysis of Mosquito Operations in Korea.* Santa Monica, Calif.: Rand, 1967.

Futrell, Robert F. *The United States Air Force in Korea: 1950–1953,* Washington, D.C.: Government Printing Office, 1983.

Goldberg, Alfred, ed. *History of the United States Air Force, 1907–1957:* Princeton, N.J.: Van Nostrand, 1957.

Hightower, Charles D. *The History of the United States Air Force Airborne Forward Air Controllers in World War II, the Korean War, and the Vietnam Conflict.* Fort Leavenworth, Kans.: Army Command and General Staff College, 1984.

Jackson, Robert. *Air War over Korea.* New York: Scribner's, 1973.

Kropf, Roger K. "The U.S. Air Force in Korea: Problems That Hindered the Effectiveness of Air Power." *Airpower* (spring 1990).

Landsdown, Josh. *With the Carriers in Korea: The Sea and Air War in South East Asia.* London: Merrill, 1997.

Launius, Roger D. *Task Paper in Airlift History.* Washington, D.C.: Office of History, Military Airlift Command, 1998.

Mark, Edward. *Aerial Interdiction: Air Power and Land Battles in Three American Wars.* Washington D.C.: Center for Air Force History, 1994.

Scutts, Jerry. *Air War over Korea.* London: Arms and Armour, 1982.

Sherwood, John Darrell. *Officers in Flight Suits: The Story of American Air Force Fighter Pilots in the Korean War.* New York: New York University Press, 1996.

Stewart, James T. *Air Power: The Decisive Force in Korea.* Princeton, N.J.: Van Nostrand and Company, 1957.

Strawbridge, Dennis, and Nannette Kahn. *Fighter Pilot Performance in Korea.* Chicago, Ill.: University of Chicago Press, 1955.

Teschner, Charles G. "The Fighter-Bomber in Korea." *Air University Quarterly Review* 7 (summer 1954): 71–80.

Thompson, Warren and Jack C. Nicholls. *Korea: The Air War 1950–53.* Osprey Aerospace, 1956.

Thompson, Wayne, and Bernard C. Nalty. *Within Limits: The U.S. Air Force and the Korean War.* Washington, D.C.: Air Force History Program, 2000.

Thyng, Harrison R. "Air-to-Air Combat in Korea." *Air University Quarterly Review* 6 (summer 1953): 40–45.

Warnock, A. Timothy. *The USAF in Korea: A Chronology, 1950–1953.* Washington, D.C.: Air Force History Program, 2000.

Winnefeld, James A., and Dana J. Johnson. *Joint Air Operations: Pursuit of Unity in Command and Control, 1942–1991.* Annapolis, Md.: Naval Institute Press, 1993.

c. United States Army

Alexander, Belvin. *Korea: The First War We Lost.* New York: Hippocrene, 1986.

Appleman, Roy E. *Disaster in Korea: The Chinese Confront MacArthur.* College Station, Tex.: Texas A&M University Press, 1989.

——. *East of the Chosin: Entrapment and Breakout in Korea, 1950.* College Station, Tex.: Texas A&M University Press, 1987.

——. *Escaping the Trap: The U.S. Army X Corps in Northeast Korea, 1950.* College Station, Tex.: Texas A&M University Press, 1990.

——. *Ridgway Duels for Korea.* College Station, Tex.: Texas A&M University Press, 1990.

——. *U. S. Army in the Korean War: South to the Naktong, North to the Yalu.* Washington, D.C.: Government Printing Office, 1961.

Black, Robert W. *Rangers in Korea.* New York: Ivy Books, 1989.

Crossland, Richard B., and James T. Currie. *Twice the Citizen: A History of the United States Army Reserves, 1908–1983.* Washington, D.C.: Office of the Chief of Military History, Army Reserve, 1984.

Daily, Edward L. *MacArthur's X Corps in Korea: Inchon to the Yalu, 1950.* Paducah, Ky: Turner Publishing, 1999.

Gugeler, Russell A., ed. *Combat Actions in Korea.* Washington, D.C.:

Combat Forces Press, 1954.

Hermes, Walter G. *U.S. Army in the Korean War: Truce Tent and Fighting Front*. Washington, D.C.: Government Printing Office, 1966.

Marshall, S. L. A. *Military History of the Korean War*. New York: F. Watts, 1963.

Mossman, Billy C. *U.S. Army in the Korean War: Ebb and Flow*. Washington, D.C.: Office of the Chief of Military History, Department of the Army, 1990.

Schnable, James F. *U.S. Army in the Korean War: Policy and Direction: The First Years*. Washington, D.C. : Office of the Chief of Military History, Department of the Army, 1972.

Stanton, Shelby. *America's Tenth Legion: X Corps in Korea*. Novato, Calif.: Presidio Press, 1989.

Wilkinson, Allen B. *Up Front Korea*. New York: Vantage Press, 1967.

d. United States Coast Guard

Price, Scott T. *The Forgotten Service in the Forgotten War: The U.S. Coast Guard's Role in the Korean Conflict*. Annapolis, Md.: Naval Institute Press, 2000.

e. United States Marines

Alexander, Joseph, and Merrill Barlett. *Sea Soldiers in the Cold War: Amphibious Warfare, 1945–1991*. Annapolis, Md.: Naval Institute Press, 1995.

Ballenger, Lee. *The Outpost War: U.S. Marines in Korea,* volume I. New York: Brassey's, 2000.

Bartlett, Tom. "The Fabulous, Frozen Fighting First." *Leatherneck* 63 (December 1980): 16–21.

Blakeney, Jane. *Heroes, U.S. Marine Corps, 1861–1955*. Washington, D.C.: Blakeney Publishers, 1957.

Campigno, A. J. *A Marine Division in Nightmare Alley*. New York: Comet Press Books, 1958.

Dockery, Charles. "Marine Air over Korea." *Marine Corps Gazette* 69 (December 1985): 38–42.

Dockery, Kevin. *Seals in Action*. New York: Avon Books, 1991.

Doll, Thomas E. *USN/USMC over Korea: Navy and Marine Corps Air Operations over Korea*. Carrollton, Tex.: Squadron/Signal, 1988.

Drysdale, Douglas B. "41 Commando." *Marine Corps Gazette* (August

1951).

Fails, William R. *Marines and Helicopter, 1946–1973.* Washington, D.C.: Headquarters, Marine Corps, 1978.

Giusti, Ernest H. *The Mobilization of the Marine Corps Reserve in the Korean Conflict.* Washington, D.C.: Historical Branch, G-2, Division Headquarters, U.S. Marine Corps, 1967.

Greer, Andrew. *The New Breed: The Story of the U.S. Marines in Korea.* New York: Harper & Row, 1952.

McClellan, Thomas L. "Operation Bumblebee: How the U.S. Marine Corps Developed Airmobile Tactics during the Korean War." *USA Aviation Digest* (June 1988): 38–44.

Meid, Pat, and James M. Yinglin. *Operations in West Korea.* Washington, D.C.: U.S. Marine Corps Historical Branch, 1972.

Millett, Alan R. *Semper Fidelis: The History of the United States Marine Corps.* New York: Macmillan, 1980.

Montross, Lynn. *Cavalry of the Sky: The Story of the U.S. Marine Combat Helicopters.* New York: Harper, 1954.

Montross, Lynn, Hubard D. Kuokka, and Norman W. Hicks. *The East-Central Front; U.S. Marine Operations in Korea: 1950–1953,* volume IV, Washington, D.C.: Government Printing Office, 1962.

Moskin, J. Robert. *The U.S. Marine Corps Story.* New York: McGraw-Hill, 1977.

Owens, Joseph R. *Colder than Hell: A Marine Rifle Company at Chosin Reservoir.* Annapolis, Md.: Naval Institute Press, 1996.

Parker, William D. *A Concise History of the United States Marine Corps, 1775–1969.* Washington, D.C.: History and Museum Division, Headquarters, U.S. Marine Corps, 1970.

Rawlins, Eugene W. *Marines and Helicopters, 1946–1962.* Washington, D.C.: History and Museum Division, Headquarters, U.S. Marine Corps, 1976.

Simmons, Edwin. H. *The United States Marines, 1775–1975.* New York: Viking Press, 1976.

f. United States Navy

Beach, Edward L. *The United States Navy: 200 Years.* New York: Henry Holt, 1986.

Cagle, Malcolm, Frank A. Manson, and Walter Karig. *Battle Report: The War in Korea,* volume IV. New York: Rinehart, 1952.

Cagle, Malcolm W., and Frank A. Manson. *The Sea War in Korea.* Annapolis, Md.: Naval Institute Press, 1957.

polis, Md.: Naval Institute Press, 1957.

Carrison, Daniel J. *The United States Navy*. New York: Praeger Library, 1969.

Cole, Charles F. *Korea Remembered: Enough of a War*. Las Cruces, N.M.: Yucca Tree Press, 1995.

Coletta, Paolo E. *The American Naval Heritage in Brief*. Washington, D.C.: University Press of America, 1981.

———. "The Defense Unification Battle, 1947–1950: The Navy." *Prologue* 7, no. 1 (1975): 6–17.

———. *The United States Navy and Defense Unification: 1947–1953*. East Brunswick, N.J.: Associated University Presses, 1981.

Field, James A. *History of United States Naval Operations: Korea*. Washington, D.C.: Government Printing Office, 1962.

Freidman, Norman. *Carrier Air Power*. Annapolis, Md.: Naval Institute Press, 1981.

———. *U. S. Destroyers: An Illustrated Design History*. Annapolis, Md.: Naval Institute Press, 1982.

Hallion, Richard P. *The Naval Air War in Korea*. Baltimore, Md.: The Nautical and Aviation Publishing Company of America, 1986.

Hooper, Edwin B. *The Navy Department: Evolution and Fragmentation*. Washington, D.C.: Naval Historical Foundation, 1978.

———. *United States Navy Power in a Changing World*. New York: Praeger, 1988.

Hoyt, Edwin. *Carrier Wars*. New York: McGraw-Hill, 1989.

Isenberg, Michael T. *The United States Navy in an Era of Cold War and Violent Peace, 1945–1962*. New York: St. Martin's Press, 1993.

Keegan, John. *The Price of Admiralty: The Evolution of Naval Warfare*. New York: Penguin Books, 1988.

Lott, Arnold S. *Most Dangerous Seas*. Annapolis, Md.: Naval Institute Press, 1986.

Melia, Tarama Moser. *"Damn the Torpedoes": A Short History of the U.S. Naval Mine-Countermeasures, 1777–1991*. Washington, D.C.: Department of the Navy: Naval Historical Center, 1991.

Muir, Malcolm. *The Iowa Class Battleships: Iowa, New Jersey, Missouri, Wisconsin*. New York: Blandford Press, 1987.

Naval Institute. *To Use the Sea: Readings in Seapower and Maritime Affairs*. Annapolis, Md.: Naval Institute Press, 1973.

Pawlowski, Gareth L. *Flat-Tops and Fledglings: A History of American Aircraft Carriers*. South Brunswick, N.J.: A. S. Barnes, 1971.

Potter, Edward B., ed. *Sea Power: A Naval History*. Annapolis, Md.: Naval Institute Press, 1981.

Reilly, John C. Jr. *Operational Experience of Fast Battleships: World War II, Korea, Vietnam.* Annapolis, Md.: Naval Institute Press, 1989.

Ryan, Paul B. *First Line of Defense: The U. S. Navy since 1945.* Stanford, Calif.: Hoover Institution Press, 1981.

Terzibaschitsch, Stefan. *Escort Carriers and Aviation Support Ships of the U.S. Navy.* Annapolis, Md.: Naval Institute Press, 1981.

Uhlig, Frank Jr. *How Navies Fight.* Annapolis, Md.: Naval Institute Press, 1994.

Watson, Bruce W. *The Changing Face of the World's Navies 1945 to Present.* New York: Brassey's, 1991.

3. Republic of Korea

Braitsch, Fred Jr. "The Korean Marine Corps." *Leatherneck* 36 (1953): 30–33.

Hall, Thomas A. "KMAG and the 7 ROK Division." *Infantry* 79 (November/December 1989): 18–23.

Holly, David C. "The ROK Navy: Reorganization after World War II with U.S. Aid: Its Record during the Korean Conflict." *Naval Institute Proceedings* 78 (November 1952): 1218–25.

Kubloin, H. "The ROK Navy." *Naval Institute Proceedings* (October 1953): 1134–35.

Lucas, Jim Griffing. *Our Fighting Heart: The Story of the Republic of Korea.* Washington, D.C.: Korean Pacific Press, 1951.

The Ministry of National Defense, The Republic of Korea. *The History of the United Nations Forces in the Korean War,* five volumes. Seoul, South Korea: Ministry of National Defense, 1972–1975.

United States Operations Research Office. *Integration of ROK Soldiers into the U.S. Army Units (KATUSA).* Washington, D.C.: Government Printing Office, 1990.

4. Japan

Auer, James. *The Postwar Rearmament of Japanese Maritime Forces, 1945–1971.* New York: Praeger, 1973.

Cheong, Sung-hwa. *The Politics of Anti-Japanese Sentiment in Korea.* Westport, Conn.: Greenwood Press, 1991.

Drifte, Reinhard. "Japan's Involvement in the Korean War." In *The Korean War in History.* ed. James Cotton and Ian Neary. Atlantic Highlands, N.J.: Humanities Press International, 1989.

Kawai, Kazuo. *Japan's American Interlude*. Chicago, Ill.: University of Chicago Press, 1960.

Kosaka, Masataka. *100 Million Japanese: The Postwar Experience*. Tokyo: Kodansha, 1972.

Lauren, Paul Gordon, and Raymond Wylie, eds. *Destinies Shared*. Boulder, Colo.: Westview Press, 1989.

Nagi, Yonosuke, and Akira Kriye, eds. *The Origins of the Cold War in Asia*. New York: Columbia University Press, 1977.

Nimmo, William, ed. *The Occupation of Japan: The Impact of the Korean War*. Norfolk, Va.: General Douglas MacArthur Foundation, 1960.

5. Allied Nations

Brecher, Michael. *Israel, The Korean War and China: Images, Decisions, and Consequences*. Jerusalem Academic Press: Hebrew University, 1974.

Crocker, Isabel. *Burma's Foreign Policy and the Korean War*. Santa Monica, Calif.: Rand, 1958.

Danisman, Basri. *Situation Negative!* The Hague: International Documentation and Information Centre, 1973.

Daskalopoulos, Ioannis. *The Greeks in Korea*. Washington, D.C.: Department of the Army, Office of the Assistant Chief of Staff for Intelligence, 1988.

Davison, Daniel P. "The Colombian Army in Korea: A Study of Integration." MA. Vermillion: University of South Dakota, 1958.

DeVaney, Carl N. "Know Your Allies." *Military Review* 32, no, 12 (1953): 11–19.

Ensslen, R. F. Jr. "Numbah One Shot." *Army* (August 1957): 30–35.

Fanning, Anne K. "Turkish Military in the Korean War: MA. Lubbock: Texas Tech University, 1993.

Galbraith, C. "Colombian Participation in the Korean War." MA. Gainesville: University of Florida, 1973.

Gallego, Manuel. *The Philippine Expeditionary Force to Korea: Before the Eyes of the Law*. Manila: No publisher, 1950.

Jensen, Peter K. "The Turkish Military Contribution to the United Nations Command in the Korean War, 1950–1953." MA. Princeton, N.J.: Princeton University, 1978.

Jimenez, Ernesto T., ed. *These Are Your Boys—The Avengers*. Tokyo: International Printing, 1954.

Martin, Harold H. "The Greeks Know How to Die." *Saturday Evening Post* 224 (1951): 26–27, 83–84.

———. "Who Said the French Won't Fight?" *Saturday Evening Post* 223 (1951): 19–21, 107–8.

Ozselcuk, Musret. "The Turkish Brigade in the Korean War." *International Review of Military History* 46 (1980): 253–72.

Ramsey, Russell W. "The Colombian Battalion in Korea and Suez." *Journal of Inter-American Studies and World Affairs* 9, no. 4 (October 1967): 541–60.

Royal Netherlands Navy, Historical Section, Naval Staff. "On the Way from Tread." *Naval Institute Proceedings* (September 1952): 966–71.

Skordiles, Komon. *Kagnew: The Story of the Ethiopian Fighters in Korea.* Tokyo: Radio Press, 1954.

Vilasanta, Juan F. *Dateline Korea: Stories of the Philippine Battalion.* Bacolod City, Philippines: Naleo, 1964.

6. Communist Nations

a. General

Meyers, Samuel M., and Albert D. Biderman. *Mass Behavior in Battle and Captivity: The Communist Soldier in the Korean.* Chicago, Ill.: University of Chicago Press, 1962.

Sega, Julius. *A Study of North Korean and Chinese Soldiers' Attitudes toward Communism, Democracy, and the United Nations.* Chevy Chase, Md.: Operations Research Office, Johns Hopkins University Press, 1954.

b. Democratic People's Republic of Korea

Atkins, E. L., H. P. Griggs, and Roy T. Sessums. *North Korean Logistics and Methods of Accomplishment.* Chevy Chase, Md.: Johns Hopkins University Press, 1951.

Bermudez, Joseph. *North Korean Special Forces.* Annapolis, Md.: Naval Institute Press, 1998.

Cumings, Bruce. "Kim's Korean Communism." *Problems of Communism* 23 (1974): 27–41.

Kahn, Lessing A., et al. *A Study of North Korean and Chinese Soldiers' Attitudes toward the Korean War.* Chevy Chase, Md.: Johns Hopkins Press, 1952.

Koon, Woo Nam. *The North Korean Communist Leadership, 1945–1965.* Birmingham: University of Alabama Press, 1974.

Paige, Glenn D. *The Korean People's Democratic Republic.* Stanford, Calif.: Hoover Institution, 1966.

Park, Gap-dong. *The Korean War and Kim Il-Sung.* Seoul: Baram gwa-Mulyol, 1990.

United States Army Forces Far East, General Staff. *Materiel in the Hands of or Possibly Available to the Communists Forces in the Far East.* APO: Army Forces Far East, 1953.

Yang, Key P. "The North Korean Regime, 1945–1955." MA. Washington, D.C.: American University, 1958.

c. People's Republic of China

Bueschel, R. M. *Communist Chinese Air Power.* New York: Praeger, 1968.

Chang, Gordon H. *Friends and Enemies: The United States, China, and the Soviet Union, 1948–1972.* Stanford, Calif.: Stanford University Press, 1990.

Chang, Tao-Li. *Why China Helps Korea.* Bombay: People's Publishing House, 1951.

Chen, Jian. *China's Road to the Korean War: The Making of the Sino–American Confrontation.* New York: Columbia University Press, 1996.

Cheng, J. Chester. "The Dynamics of the Chinese People's Liberation Army: Regularization and Revolutionization, 1949–1959." *Military Review* 54 (May 1974).

Chilimuniya, Aurosimov, and Shihu-ku-li-the-tzu. *Chinese Communist General Principles of Army Group Tactics.* Manila: General Headquarters, Far East Command, Military Intelligence Section, General Staff, 1951.

Chinese Tactics and Lessons Learned. APO: Headquarters, 2 Infantry Division, United States Army, 1952.

Clegg, Arthur. *No War with China.* London: Communist Party, 1951.

Corr, Gerald H. *The Chinese Red Army.* New York: Schocken Books, 1974.

Fairbanks, John K., ed. *The Chinese World Order.* Cambridge, Mass.: Harvard University Press, 1954.

Farrar–Hockley, Anthony. "A Reminiscence of the Chinese People's Volunteers in the Korean War." *China Quarterly* 98 (June 1984): 287–304.

George, Alexander L. *The Chinese Communist Army in Action: The Korean War and Its Aftermath.* New York: Columbia University Press, 1967.

Gittings, John. *The Role of the Chinese Army.* New York: Oxford University Press, 1967.

Griffith, Samuel B. *The Chinese People's Liberation Army.* New York: McGraw-Hill, 1967.

Hanrahan, Gene Z. "The People's Revolutionary Military Council in Communist China." *Far Eastern Survey* 23 (May 1954).

Headquarters, United States Army Forces, Far East (advanced), Office of the Assistant Chief of Staff, G-2. "Chinese Communist Army and North Korean Army Logistics and Class Supply." *USAFFE Intelligence Digest* 6 (April 1956): 49–68.

Hinton, Harold C. *China's Turbulent Quest.* Bloomington: Indiana University Press, 1972.

Hoyt, Edwin. *The Day the Chinese Attacked: Korea, 1950.* New York: McGraw-Hill, 1990.

Niessal, A. "The Army of Communist China." *Military Review* 35 (June 1955).

O'Ballance, Edgar. *The Red Army of China: A Short History.* New York: Praeger, 1963.

Riggs, Robert B. *Red China's Fighting Hordes.* Harrisburg, Penn.: The Military Service Publishing, 1952.

Roe, Patrick. *The Dragon Strikes: China and the Korean War, June–December 1950.* Novato, Calif.: Presidio, 2000.

Scalapino, Rogert A., and Chong-sik Lee. *Communism in Korea.* Berkeley: University of California, 1972.

Schwartz, Benjamin I. *Communism and China: Ideology in Flux.* Cambridge, Mass.: Harvard University Press, 1968.

Segal, Gerald. *The Great Power Triangle.* London: Macmillan, 1982.

Spurr, Russell. *Enter the Dragon: China's Undeclared War against the United States in Korea, 1950–1951.* New York: Newmarket Press, 1988.

Stueck, William. *The Korean War: An International History.* Princeton, N.J.: Princeton University Press, 1995.

Thomas, R. C. W. "The Chinese Communist Forces in Korea." *Military Review* 32 (February 1953).

Weller, Donald. *Chinese Communist Strategic and Tactical Doctrine.* No publisher, 1964.

Whiting, Allen. *China Crosses the Yalu: The Decision to Enter the Ko-*

rean War. Stanford, Calif.: Stanford University Press, 1960.

Whitson, William W. *The Chinese High Command*. New York: Praeger, 1973.

Xu, Yan. "The Chinese Forces and Their Casualties in the Korean War: Facts and Statistics." *Chinese Historians* 6, no. 2 (fall 1993).

Zhai, Qiang. *The Dragon, the Lion, and the Eagle: Chinese–British–American Relations 1949–1958.* Kent, Ohio: Kent State University Press, 1994.

Zhang Xi. "Peng Dehuai and China's Entry into the Korean War." *Chinese Historians* 6, no. 1 (spring 1993): 1930.

Zhanu, Shuguang, and Chen Jian, eds. *Chinese Communist Foreign Policy and the Cold War in East Asia: Documentary Evidence*. Chicago: Imprint Publications, 1994.

d. Soviet Union

Body, Alexander J. *The Soviet Air Force since 1918*. London: Macdonald and Jane's, 1977.

Cohen, Stephen. *Rethinking the Soviet Experience*. New York: Oxford University Press, 1985.

Halliday, Jon. "Air Operations in Korea: The Soviet Side of the Story." In *A Revolutionary War,* ed. William J. Williams. Chicago: Imprint Publications, 1993.

Jan, Ji Bao. "China's Policies toward the Soviet Union and the United States before and in the Korean War." MA. Portland, Oregon: Portland State University, 1995.

Khrushchev, Nikita. *Khrushchev Remembers and Khrushchev Remembers, The Last Testament,* trans. Strobe Talbott. Boston: Little Brown, 1974.

Lee, William T., and Richard F. Staar. *Soviet Military Policy since World War II.* Stanford, Calif: Stanford University Press, 1986.

Lineer, Thomas A. "Evolution of Cold War Rules of Engagement: The Soviet Combat Role in the Korean War." MA. Fort Leavenworth, Kans.: Command and General Staff College, 1993.

Mosley, Philip. *The Kremlin and World Politics: Studies in Soviet Policy and Action.* New York: Random House, 1960.

Smorchkow, Aleksandr. "Heroic Pilot Recalls His Days in Korea." *Moscow International Broadcast Service.* 11 June 1990 trans. In FBIS SOV 90–121 (22 June 1990).

Ulam, Adam. *The Communists: The Story of Power and Lost Illusions:*

1948–1991. New York: Charles Scribner's, 1991.

Weathersby, Kathryn, trans. "New Finding on the Korean War." *Woodrow Wilson Cold War Center Bulletin* 3 (fall 1993) 1, 14–18.

———. "Soviet Aims in Korea and the Origins of the Korean War, 1945–1950: New Evidence from the Archives." *Woodrow Wilson Cold War Center Bulletin* (November 1993b).

———. "The Soviet Role in the Early Phase of the Korean War: New Documentary Evidence." *Journal of American-East Asian Relations* 2, no. 4 (winter 1993): 425–58.

Zaloga, Steven J. "The Russians in MiG Alley." *Air Force Magazine* 74, no. 2 (February 1991): 74–77.

IV. Narrative (General) Studies of the War

Acheson, Dean. *The Korean War.* New York: Norton, 1971.

Alexander, Bevin. *Korea: The First War We Lost.* New York: Hippocrene, 1986.

Appleman, Roy E. *Disaster in Korea: The Chinese Confront MacArthur.* College Station, Tex.: Texas A&M University Press, 1989.

———. *Escaping the Trap: The U.S. Army X Corps in Northeast Korea, 1950.* College Station, Tex: Texas A&M University Press, 1990.

———. *Ridgway Duals for Korea.* College Station, Tex.: Texas A&M University Press, 1990.

Bachrach, Deborah. *The Korean War.* San Diego, Calif.: Lucent Books, 1991.

Berger, Carl. *The Korean Knot: A Military–Political History.* Philadelphia: University of Pennsylvania Press, 1968.

Blair, Clay. *The Forgotten War: America in Korea 1950–1953.* New York: Times Books, 1987.

Bong-yon, Choy. *Korea: A History.* Rutland, Vt.: Charles E. Tuttle, 1971.

Burchett, Wilfred G. *This Monstrous War.* Melbourne, Australia: Waters, 1953.

Catchpole, Brian. *The Korean War.* New York: Carroll & Graf Publishers, 2000.

Confrontation in Asia: The Korean War. West Point, N.Y.: Department of History, United States Military Academy, 1981.

Edwards, Richard. *The Korean War.* Hove, England: Wayland, 1988.

Fehrenbach, T. R. *This Kind of War: A Study in Unpreparedness.* Washington, D.C.: Brassey's, 1963.

Fincher, Ernest. *The War in Korea*. New York: Franklin Watts, 1981.

Forty, George. *At War in Korea*. New York: Bonanza Books, 1985.

Gardner, Lloyd. *The Korean War*. Chicago: Quadrangle Books, 1972.

Gay, Martin, and Kathlyn Gay. *The Korean War*. New York: Twenty-First Century Books, 1996.

Goulden, Joseph. *Korea: The Untold Story of the War*. New York: Times Books, 1982.

Halliday, Jon, and Bruce Cumings. *Korea: The Unknown War*. New York: Pantheon Books, 1988.

Hankuk, Jon Jang Sa. *History of the Korean* War, five volumes. Seoul: Hangrim Publishing, 1990–1992.

Hastings, Max. *The Korean War*. New York: Simon & Schuster, 1987.

Hickey, Michael. *The Korean War: The West Confronts Communism*. New York: Overlook Press, 2000.

Hoyt, Edwin P. *The Bloody Road to Panmunjom*. New York: Stein & Day, 1985.

Kaufman, Burton I. *The Korean War: Challenges in Crisis, Credibility, and Command*. Philadelphia: Temple University Press, 1997.

Kurland, Gerald. *The Korean War*. New York: Samhar Press, 1973.

Lawson, Don. *The United States in the Korean War*. New York: Abelard, 1964.

Leckie, Robert. *Conflict: The History of the Korean War, 1950–1953*. New York: Putnam, 1962.

MacDonald, Callum A. *Korea: The War before Vietnam*. New York: Free Press, 1986.

Middleton, Harry J. *The Compact History of the Korean War*. New York: Hawthorn, 1965.

O'Ballance, Edgar. *Korea 1950–1953*. London: Faber, 1969.

Osgood, Robert. *Limited War: The Challenge to American Strategy*. Chicago, Ill.: University of Chicago Press, 1957.

Paik, Son-Yup. *From Pusan to Panmunjom*. Washington, D.C.: Brassey's, 1992.

Rees, David. *Korea: The Limited War*. New York: St. Martin's Press, 1970.

———. *The Korean War: History and Tactics*. New York: Crescent Books, 1984.

Ridgway, Matthew B. *The Korean War: History and Tactics*. Garden City, N.Y.: Doubleday, 1967.

Stokesbury, James L. *A Short History of the Korean War*. New York: William Morrow, 1988.

Stone, Isador F. *The Hidden History of the Korean War*. New York: William Morrow, 1988.

Stueck, William. *The Korean War: An International History*. Princeton, N.J.: Princeton University Press, 1995.

Taylor, Maxwell D. *The Uncertain Trumpet*. New York: Harper, 1959.

Toland, John. *In Mortal Combat: 1950–1953*. New York: William Morrow and Company, 1991.

Whelan, Richard. *Drawing the Line: The Korean War, 1950–1953*. Boston: Little Brown, 1990.

V. Military Battles, Campaigns, and Operations

A. GENERAL

Coleman, J. D. *Wonju: The Gettysburg of the Korean War*. Washington, D.C.: Brassey's, 2000.

Flint, Roy K. "Task Force Smith and the 24 Division." In *America's First Battles 1776–1965,* ed. Charles E. Heller, and William A. Stofft. Lawrence: University Press of Kansas, 1986.

Marshall, Samuel L. A. *The River and the Gauntlet: Defeat of the Eighth Army by the Chinese Communist Forces, November 1950, in the Battle of the Chongchon River, Korea*. New York: William Morrow, 1953.

Pratt, Sherman W. *Decisive Battles of the Korean War: An Infantry Company Commander's View of the War's Most Critical Engagements*. New York: Vintage Press, 1992.

Stanton, Shelby L. *America's Tenth Legion: X Corps in Korea, 1950*. Novato, Calif.: Presidio Press, 1989.

Tallent, Robert W. "Street Fight in Seoul." In *The Leatherneck: An Informal History of the U.S. Marines,* ed. Karl Schuon. New York: Watts, 1993.

Tapplet, R. D., and R. E. Whipple. "Darkhorse Sets the Pace." *Marine Corps Gazette* 37 (June–July 1950): 14–23, 44–50.

Tate, James H. "The First Five Months." *Army Information Digest* (March 1951): 40–48.

Thompson, Reginald. *Cry Korea*. London: MacDonald and Company, 1957.

B. DECISION TO CROSS THE 38TH PARALLEL

Grey, A. L. Jr. "The Thirty-Eighth Parallel." *Foreign Affairs* (April 1951).

LaFeber, Walter. "Crossing the 38th: The Cold War in Microcosm." In *Reflections on the Cold War,* ed. Lynn H. Miller, and Ronald W. Pruesen. Philadelphia: Temple University Press, 1974.

Matray, James I. "Truman's Plan for Victory: National Self-Determination and the Thirty-Eighth Parallel Decision in Korea. *Journal of American History* 66 (September 1979): 314–33.

McCune, S. "The Thirty-Eighth Parallel in Korea." *World Politics* 1 (1949).

Sandusky, Michael C. *America's Parallel.* Alexandria, Va.: Old Dominion Press, 1983.

C. PUSAN

Canzona, Nicholas A. "Marines Land at Pusan: August 1950." *Marine Corps Gazette* 69 (August 1985): 42–46.

Ent, W. Uzal. *Fighting on the Brink: Defense of the Pusan Perimeter.* Paducah, Ky: Turner Publishing, 1996.

Hoyt, Edwin P. *The Pusan Perimeter: Korea, 1950.* New York: Stein and Day Publishers, 1984.

Montross, Lynn. "The Pusan Perimeter: Fight for a Foothold." *Marine Corps Gazette* 35 (June 1951): 30–39.

Tallent, Robert W. "Pusan–A Stop Enroute." *Leatherneck* 33 (1950): 14–17.

D. INCHON AND SEOUL

Banks, Charles L. "Inchon to Seoul: Service in Action." *Marine Corps Gazette* 35, no. 5 (May 1951): 20–21.

Halloran, B. F. "Inchon Landing." *Marine Corps Gazette* 56 (September 1972): 25–32.

Heinl, Robert D. Jr. "Inchon: The Beachhead for Professionals." *Marine Corps Gazette* 69 (September 1985): 3–6.

———. "The Inchon Landing: A Case Study in Amphibious Planning." *Naval War College Review* 39 (summer 1967): 51–72.

———. *Victory at High Tide: The Inchon–Seoul Campaign.* Philadelphia: Lippincott, 1968.

Langley, Michael. *Inchon Landing: MacArthur's Last Triumph.* New York: Times Books, 1979.

Larew, Karl G. "Inchon Invasion Not a Stroke of Genius or Even Necessary." *Army* 38 (December 1988): 15–20.

Lavine, Harold. "Inchon: 'A Helluva Gamble' that Paid Off." *Newsweek* 36, no. 13 (25 September 1950): 25.

Mamaux, David H. *Operation CHROMITE: Operational Art in a Limited War.* Fort Leavenworth, Kans.: United States Army Command and Staff College, 1987.

Montross, Lynn. "The Inchon Landing: Victory over Time and Tide." *Marine Corps Gazette* 35 (July 1951): 26–35.

Mortensen, Roger. *Inchon and the Strategy of the Indirect Approach.* Maxwell Air Force Base, Ala.: Air Command and Staff College, Research Report, 1977.

Pirnie, Bruce R. "The Inchon Landing: How Great Was the Risk?" *Joint Perspective* 3 (summer 1982): 86–97.

Rogers, John S. *The Battle for Seoul: An Overview of Marine and Enemy Forces Used.* No publisher, 1982.

Sheldon, Walt. *Hell or High Water: MacArthur's Landing at Inchon.* New York: Macmillan, 1968.

Smith, Lynn D. "A Nickel after a Dollar: MacArthur's Daring Plan for the Invasion of Inchon." *Army* 20 (September 1970): 24.

Tallent, Robert W. "Inchon to Seoul." *Leatherneck* 34 (1951): 12–17.

Utz, Curtis A. *Assault from the Sea: The Amphibious Landing at Inchon.* Washington, D.C.: Naval History Center, Department of Navy, 1994.

E. CHOSIN

Chong, Anson, and Charles Joseph Hilton. *Chosin, The Untold Story.* Honeoye, N.Y.: International Association, 1993.

Condit, Kenneth W., and Ernest H. Giusti. "Marine Air at the Chosin Reservoir." *Marine Corps Gazette* 36 (July–August 1952).

Craig, Berry. *The Chosin Few: North Korea, November–December 1950.* Paducah, Ky.: Turner Publishing, 1989.

Hammel, E. M. *Chosin: Heroic Ordeal of the Korean War.* New York: Vanguard Press, 1981.

Hopkins, William B. *One Bugle, No Drums: The Marines at Chosin Reservoir.* Chapel Hill, N.C.: Algonquin, 1986.

Montross, Lynn, and Nicholas Canzona. *The Chosin Reservoir Campaign.* Washington, D.C.: United States Marine Corps Headquarters, 1957.

F. HUNGNAM

Cowart, Glenn C. *Miracle in Korea: The Evacuation of X Corps from the*

Hungnam Beachhead. Columbus: University of South Carolina Press, 1992.

Cowings, John S., and Kim Nam Che. *Twelve Hungnam Evacuees.* Headquarters: Eighth United States Army, 1975.

Doyle, James H., and Arthur J. Mayer. "December 1950 at Hungnam." *Naval Institute Proceedings* 80 (December 1954): 1337–40.

Gilbert, Bill. *Ship of Miracles.* Chicago: Triumph Books, 2000.

G. WONSAN

Kinney, Sheldon. "All Quiet at Wonsan." *Naval Institute Proceedings* 80 (August 1954): 859–67.

Phillips, Richard B. "The Siege of Wonsan." *Army Information Digest* 8 (November 1953): 39–47.

H. HILL WAR

Barker, A. J. *Fortune Favours the Brave—The Battle of the Hook, Korea, 1953.* London: Leo Cooper, 1974.

Green, Carl R. *The Korean War Soldier at Heartbreak Ridge.* Mankato, Minn.: Capstone Press, 1991.

Gugeler, Russell A. "Attack along a Ridgeline." *Combat Forces Journal* 4, no. 10 (May 1954): 22–27.

Hinshaw, Arned. *Heartbreak Ridge.* New York: Praeger, 1988.

Marshall, S. L .A. *Operation Punch and the Capture of Hill 440: Suwon, Korea, February 1951.* Chevy Chase, Md.: Johns Hopkins University Press, 1952.

———. *Pork Chop Hill: The American Fighting Man in Action, Korea, Spring 1953.* New York: William Morrow, 1956.

Martin, Harold H. "The Epic of Bloody Hill." *Saturday Evening Post* 223 (1950): 50–54, 59–60.

Russell, William C. *Stalemate & Standoff: The Bloody Outpost War.* DeLeon Springs, Fla: W. Russell, 1993.

———. *Ten Days at White Horse.* Arlington, Va.: No publisher, 1988.

I. TASK FORCE SMITH

Cannon, Michael. "Task Force Smith: A Study in (un)Preparedness and (ir) Responsibility." *Military Review* 68, no. 2 (February 1988): 63–74.

Colon, William. "Task Force Smith." *Infantry* 70 (January–February

1980): 35–37.

Davies, William J. *Task Force Smith: A Leadership Failure.* Carlisle Barracks, Penn: United States Army War College, 1992.

Delay and Withdrawal: Task Force Smith and the 24 Division, 5–9 July 1950. APO: Eighth United States Army, 1990.

J. SPECIAL OPERATIONS

Beaumont, Roget A. *Military Elites.* Indianapolis, Indiana: Bobbs-Merrill, 1974.

Breuer, William B. *Shadow Warriors: The Covert War in Korea.* New York: Wiley, 1996.

Davidson, W. Phillips, and Jean Hungerford. *North Korean Guerilla Units.* Santa Monica, Calif.: Rand, 1951.

Evanhoe, Ed. *Darkmoon: Eighth Army Special Operations in the Korean War.* Annapolis, Md.: Naval Institute Press, 1995.

Hass, Michael. *In the Devil's Shadow: U.N. Special Operations during the Korean War.* Annapolis, Md.: Naval Institute Press, 2000.

Kemp, Robert F. *Combined Operations in the Korean War.* Carlisle Barracks, Penn: United States Army War College, 1989.

Malcolm, Ben S. *White Tigers: My Secret War in North Korea.* Washington, D.C.: Brassey's, 1995.

Paschall, Rod. *A Study in Command and Control: Special Operations in Korea, 1951–1953.* Carlisle Barracks, Penn.: United States Army Military History Institute, 1988.

UN Partisan Forces in the Korean Conflict, 1951–1952: A Study in Their Characteristics and Operations. Tokyo: Military History Detachment, 1954.

VI. Uniforms, Medals, Ribbons, and Citations

Above and Beyond: A History of the Medal of Honor from the Civil War to Vietnam. Boston: Boston Publishing Company, 1987.

Archambault, Alan H. *Soldiers of the Korean War.* Gettysburg, Penn.: Thomas Publications, 2000.

Borts, Lawrence H., and Frank C. Foster. *Medals of America Presents United States Military Medals, 1939 to Present.* Fountain Inn, S.C.: Medals of America Press, 1995.

Ingraham, Kevin R. *Honors, Medals, and Awards of the Korean War.* Binghamton, N.Y.: Prospect Press, 1993.

Jacob, Bruce. *Korean's Heroes: The Medal of Honor Story.* New York: Lion, 1958.

Johnson, Robbie. *Canadian War Service Badges 1914–1954.* Surrey, British Columbia: Johnson Books, 1995.

Jordon, Kenneth N. *Forgotten Heroes: 131 Men of the Korean War Awarded the Medal of Honor, 1950–1953.* Atglen, Penn.: Schiffer Publications, 1995.

The Military Ribbons of the United States Army, Navy, Marines, Air Force, and Coast Guard: A Complete Guide to Correct Ribbon Wearing. Fountain Inn, S.C.: Medals of America Press, 1995.

Stanton, Shelby L. *Korean War Order of Battle.* Washington, D.C.: Government Printing Office, 1999.

———. *U.S. Army Uniforms of the Korean War.* Harrisburg, Penn.: Stackpole, 1992.

United States Army, Far East Command, *Uniform, Insignia, Equipment [of the] North Korean Army.* Tokyo: Far East Command, 1953.

Warnock, Timothy A., *Combat Medals, Streamers, and Campaigns.* Washington, D.C.: Office of Air Force History, 1990.

VII. Intelligence

Karalekas, Ann. *History of the Central Intelligence Agency.* Laguna Hills, Calif.: Aegean Park Press, 1977.

Milano, James U., and Patrick Brogan. *Soldiers, Spies, and the Rat Line.* New York: Brassey's, 2000.

Nichols, Donald. *The North Korean Intelligence Organization.* No publisher, 1956.

Willoughby, Charles A. *Intelligence in War: A Brief History of MacArthur's Intelligence Service, 1941–1951.* Tokyo: Dai-Nippon Printing Company, 1959.

VIII. Logistics

A. GENERAL

Ammunition Shortages in the Armed Services. Washington, D.C.: Congressional Record, Senate, 83rd Congress, 1st Session, 1953.

Atkins, E. L., H. P. Griggs, and Roy T. Sessums. *North Korean Logistics and Methods of Accomplishment.* Chevy Chase, Md.: Johns Hopkins University Press, 1951.

Bunker, William B. "Organization for an Airlift." *Military Review* 31 (April 1951): 25–31.

Bykofsky, Joseph. *Battlefield Mobility: Pooled Motor Transport in a Combat Support Role.* Washington, D.C.: Department of the Army, 1958.

Correa, Edward L. *Logistics and the Chinese Communist Intervention during the Korean Conflict (1950–1953).* Carlisle Barracks, Penn: United States Army War College, 1986.

Flanagan, William J. "Korean War Logistics: The First Hundred Days." *Army Logistics* 18 (March–April 1986): 34–38.

Huston, James A. "Korean Logistics." *Military Review* 36, no. 2 (February 1957): 18–32.

———. *The Sinews of War: Army Logistics.* Washington, D.C.: Government Printing Office, 1966.

Launius, Roger. "MATS and the Korean Airlift." *Airlift* 12 (summer 1990): 16–21.

Martin, John G. *It Began at Imphal: The Combat Cargo Story.* Manhattan, Kans.: Sunflower University Press, 1988.

O'Brien, M. J. *Trans-Pacific Airlift in Support of Army Operations, July 1950–June 1952.* Chevy Chase, Md.: Johns Hopkins University Press, 1955.

Shrader, Charles. *Communist Logistics in the Korean War.* Westport, Conn.: Greenwood Press, 1995.

Shreve, Robert O. *Combat Zion Logistics in Korea.* Chevy Chase, Md.: Johns Hopkins University Press, 1951.

Walker, Stanley L. "Logistics of the Inchon Landing." *Army Logisticians* (July–August 1981): 34–38.

Wilson, John B. *Army Lineage Series: Armies, Corps, Divisions, and Separate Brigades.* Washington, D.C.: Government Printing Office, 1987.

B. MEDICAL AND CASUALTIES

Apel, Otto, and Pat Apel. *MASH: An Army Surgeon in Korea.* Louisville: University of Kentucky, 1999.

Best, Robert J. *Study of Battle Casualties among Equivalent Opposing Forces, Korea, September 1950.* Chevy Chase, Md.: Johns Hopkins University Press, 1953.

Bower, Warner F. "Evacuating Wounded from Korea." *Army Information Digest* 5. no. 12 (December 1950): 47–54.

Bradbury, William C., Samuel M. Meyers, and Albert Biderman. *Mass Behavior in Battle and Captivity: The Communist Soldier in the Korean War.* Chicago, Ill.: University of Chicago Press, 1968.

Cleaver, Frederick W. *U.S. Army Battle Casualties in Korea.* Chevy Chase, Md.: Johns Hopkins University Press, 1956.

Cowdrey, Albert E. "Germ Warfare and Public Health in the Korean Conflict." *Journal of the History of Medicine and Allied Sciences* 39 (1984).

———. *The Medic's War.* Washington, D.C.: Government Printing Office, 1987.

Day, William W. *The Running Wounded: A Personal Memory of the Korean War.* Riverton, Wyo.: Big Ben Press, 1990.

Engle, Eloise. *Dawn Mission: A Flight Nurse in Korea.* New York: John Day, 1962.

Hume, Edgar E. "United Nations Medical Service in the Korean Conflict." *Military Surgeon* 109 (1951): 91–95.

Sams, Crawford F. *Medic.* Carlisle Barracks, Penn.: United States Army Military History Institute, 1986.

Watts, John C. *Surgeon at War.* London: Allen, 1955.

Weintraub, Stanley. *War in the Wards: Korea's Unknown Battle in a Prisoner-of-War Hospital Camp.* Garden City, N.Y.: Doubleday, 1964.

White, William L. *Back Down the Ridge.* New York: Harcourt Brace, 1953.

C. TRANSPORTATION AND TROOP MOVEMENT

Arnold, Chris. *Steel Pots: A History of Army Headgear.* New York: James Bender. 1997.

Gough, Terrence J. *Army Mobilization and Logistics in the Korean War: A Research Approach.* Washington, D.C.: Center of Military History, 1987.

Huston, James A. *Guns and Butter, Powder and Rice: U.S. Army Logistics in the Korean War.* Selinsgrove, Penn.: Susquehanna University Press, 1989.

———. *The Sinews of War: Army Logistics 1775–1953.* Washington, D.C.: Chief of Military History, 1966.

Stanton, Shelby. *U.S. Army Uniforms of the Korean War.* Harrisburg, Penn.: Stackpole, 1992.

D. CONSCRIPTION, DRAFT, AND RESERVES

Archambault, Alan H. *Soldiers of the Korean War*. Gettysburg, Penn.: Thomas Publications, 2000.

Benson, Lawrence R. "The USAF's Korean War Recruiting Rush—And the Great Tent City at Lackland Air Force Base." *Aerospace Historian* 25 (1978): 61–73.

Berebitsky, William. *A Very Long Weekend: The Army National Guard in Korea 1950–1953*. Shippensburg, Penn.: White Mane Publishing, 1996.

Boettcher, Thomas D. *First Call: The Making of the Modern U. S. Military, 1945–1953*. Boston: Little Brown, 1992.

Coggins, Thomas M. "Replacements Are Coming." *Marine Corps Gazette* 37 (1953): 50–54.

Crossland, Richard B., and James T. Currie. *Twice the Citizen: A History of the United States Army Reserve, 1908–1983*. Washington, D.C.: Office of the Chief, Army Reserve, 1984.

Flynn, George Q. "The Draft and College Deferments during the Korean War." *Historian* 50 (May 1988): 369–85.

Giusti, Ernest H. *The Mobilization of the Marine Corps Reserve in the Korean Conflict*. Washington, D.C.: Historical Branch, G-2, Division Headquarters, U.S. Marine Corps, 1967.

Hershey, Lewis B. "Mobilization of Manpower." *Quartermaster Review* 30 (1950): 4–5, 144–47.

Jones, James C. "Recall." *Leatherneck* 34 (1951): 14–21.

McQuiston, I. M. "History of the Reserves since the Second World War." *Journal of Military History* 23 (spring 1959): 23–27.

Moenk, Jean R. *Training During the Korean Conflict, 1950–1954*. Fort Eustis, Va.: United States Army Transportation Training Center, 1962.

Seals, Billy R. *Evolution of Military Manpower Policy: The Korean War*. Maxwell Air Force Base, Ala.: Air War College, 1975.

IX. Weapons (All Participants)

A. GENERAL

Bellene, E. F. "Wonder Weapon" *Combat Forces Journal* 3, no. 4 (November 1952): 28–30.

"Building Our Military Power." *Army Information Digest* 5, no. 9 (1950): 3–10.

Cox, William. *Report on the Use of Body Armor in Combat, Korea, February 1952–July 1952.* Washington, D.C.: Government Printing Office, 1952.

B. ARMOR

Baker, Roger. *USMC Tanker's Korea.* Oakland, Ore.: Elderberry, 2001.
Batchelor, John H., and Kenneth MacKey. *Tank: A History of the Armored Vehicle.* New York: Charles Scribner's Sons, 1970.
Brodie, Bernard, and Fawn Brodie. *From Crossbow to H-Bomb.* New York: Dell Publishing, 1962.
Cary, James. *Tanks and Armor in Modern Warfare.* New York: Franklin Watts, 1968.
Chamberlain, Peter, and Cris Ellis. *The Sherman: An Illustrated History of the M4 Medium Tank.* New York: Arco, 1969.
Crow, Duncan, and Robert J. Icks. *Encyclopedia of Tanks.* London: Chartwell, 1975.
Dougherty, Jack D. "Logistical Support of Armored United in Korea: A Research Report." Fort Knox, Ky.: Armored School, 1952.
Dunstan, Simon. *Armour of the Korean War, 1950–1953.* London: Osprey Publishing, 1982.
———. *Tank War in Korea.* London: Arms and Armour Press, 1985.
Hunnicutt, R. P. *Pershing: A History of the Medium Tank T20 Series.* Berkeley, Calif.: Feist Publications, 1971.
Johnson, Ellis A. *Armored Warfare in the Eight Army in Korea.* Fort Monroe, Va.: Chief of Army Field Forces, 1951.
Liddell Hart, B. H. (two volumes). *The Tanks.* London: Cassell, 1959.
Milsom, John. *Russian Tanks, 1900–1970; The Complete Illustrated History of Soviet Armoured Theory and Design.* London: Arms and Armour Press, 1970.
Orgokiewicz, Richard M. *Armoured Forces: A History of Armoured Forces and Their Vehicles.* New York: Arco Publishing, 1970.

C. ARTILLERY

Bell, E. V. H. "The 4.2 Mortar in Korea." *Combat Forces Journal* 3, no. 5 (December 1952): 27–29.
Cocklin, Robert F. "Artillery in Korea." *Combat Forces Journal* 2 (August 1951): 22–27.
Foss, Christopher F. *Artillery of the World* (revised edition). New York:

Charles Scribner's Sons, 1976.

Garn, Phil R. "75mm Recoilless Rifle in Korea." *Combat Forces Journal* 2, no. 9 (April 1952): 23–25.

Manchester, William. *The Arms of Krupp 1587–1968*. Boston: Little Brown, 1968.

Owens, Richard W. "AA Makes the Team." *Combat Forces Journal* 3, no. 10 (May 1953): 27–29.

D. CHEMICAL AND BIOLOGICAL

Bellene, E. F. "Wonder Weapon." *Combat Forces Journal* 4 (November 1952): 28–30.

Burchett, Wilfred G. *This Monstrous War*. Melbourne, Australia: Waters, 1953.

Endicott, Stephen L. "Germ Warfare and the 'Plausible Denial': The Korean War 1952–1953." *Modern China* 5, no. 1 (January 1979): 79–104.

Enoch, Kenneth, and John S. Quinn. *Statements by Two Captured U.S. Air Force Officers on Their Participation in Germ Warfare in Korea*. Peking: Chinese People's Committee for World Peace, 1952.

Warner, Denis. *The Germ Warfare Hoax: How It Was Fabricated*. Seoul: United Nations Korean War Allies Association, 1977.

E. MINES

Knight, Charlotte. "Men of the Mine Sweepers." *Collier's* 128, no. 19 (10 November 1951): 13–15, 66–68.

List, William F. *History of the First USS* Dextrous*: With Collateral Notes on Minesweepers, Minesweeping, and Collateral Events*. Linthicum, Md.: W. F. List, 1994.

Lott, Arnold S. *Most Dangerous Sea*. Annapolis, Md.: Naval Institute Press, 1959.

McCaull, Julian. *The Hinge*. New York: Alcyhone Publications, 1984.

Meacham, James. "Four Mining Campaigns: An Historical Analysis of the Decisions of the commander." *Naval War College Review* 19 (June 1967): 75–129.

Melia, Tamara Moser. *"Damn the Torpedoes": A Short History of U.S. Naval Mine Countermeasures, 1777–1991*. Washington, D.C.: Naval Historical Center, 1991.

F. NUCLEAR

Anders, Roger M. "The Atomic Bomb and the Korean War: Gordon Dean and the Issue of Civilian Control." *Military Affairs* 52 (January 1988): 1–6.

Bachrach, Bernard. *Nuclear Arms*. New York: Greenhaven Press, 1984.

Betts, Richard K. *Nuclear Blackmail and Nuclear Balance*. Washington, D.C.: Brookings Institution, 1987.

Botti, Timothy. *The Long Wait: The Forging of the Anglo–American Nuclear Alliance, 1945–1968*. Westport, Conn.: Greenwood Press, 1987.

Bundy, McGeorge. *Danger and Survival: Choices about the Bomb in the First Fifty Years*. New York: Random House, 1988.

Calingaert, Daniel. "Nuclear Weapons and the Korean War." *Journal of Strategic Studies* 11, no. 2 (June 1988): 177–202.

Dingman, Roger. "Atomic Diplomacy during the Korean War." *International Security* 13, no. 3 (winter 1988–1989): 61–89.

Foot, Rosemary J. "Nuclear Coercion and the ending of the Korean Conflict." *International Security* 13, no. 3 (winter 1988–1989): 92–112.

Friedman, Edward. "Nuclear Blackmail and the End of the Korean War." *Modern China* 1, no. 1 (January 1975): 75–91.

Harken, Gregg. *The Winning Weapon: The Atomic Bomb in the Cold War*. New York: Knopf, 1981.

Kissinger, Henry A. *Nuclear Weapons and Foreign Policy*. New York: Harper and Brothers, 1957.

Ryan, Mark A. *Chinese Attitudes toward Nuclear Weapons: China and the United States during the Korean War*. London: An East Gate Book, 1989.

Snyder, Jack. *Atomic Diplomacy in the Korean War*. Washington, D.C.: Pew Charitable Trusts, 1993.

Spaight, J. M. "Korea and the Atomic Bomb." *Journal Royal United Service Institution* 95 (November 1950): 566–70.

Trachtenburg, Marc. "A 'Wasting Asset': American Strategy and the Shifting Nuclear Balance, 1949–1954." *International Security* 13, no. 3 (winter 1988–1889): 5–49.

Wheeler, Michael O. *Nuclear Weapons and the Korean War*. McLean, Va.: Center for National Security Negotiations, 1994.

G. PLANES

Barker, E. L. "The Helicopter in Combat." *Naval Institute Proceedings*

77, no. 11 (November 1951): 1207–22.

Brown, David. *The Seafire: The Spitfire That Went to Sea.* Annapolis, Md.: Naval Institute Press, 1989.

Dorr, Robert. *F-86 Sabre: History of the Sabre and the FJ Fury.* Osceola, Wis.: Motorbooks International, 1993.

Evans, Douglas K. *Sabre Jets over Korea: A Firsthand Account.* Blue Ridge Summit, Penn.: TAB Books, 1984.

Kitchens, John W. "Cargo Helicopters in the Korean Conflict." *United States Army Aviation Digest* 41, no. 10 (October 1992) and 41, no. 11 (November 1992).

Milesh, Robert. *Excalibur III: The Story of the P-51 Mustang.* Washington, D.C.: National Air and Space Museum Press, 1978.

Tillman, Barrett. *Corsair: The F4U in World War II and Korea.* Annapolis, Md.: Naval Institute Press, 1979.

Vader, John. *Spitfire.* New York: Ballantine Books, 1969.

H. SHIPS

Faltum, Andrew. *The Essex Aircraft Carriers.* New York: The Nautical and Aviation Publishing Company of America, 1996.

Friedman, Norman. *U.S. Destroyers: An Illustrated Design History.* Annapolis, Md.: Naval Institute Press, 1982.

Muir, Malcolm. *The Iowa Class Battleships: Iowa, New Jersey, Missouri, Wisconsin.* New York: Blandford Press, 1987.

I. SMALL ARMS

Ezell, Edward Clinton. *Small Arms of the World: A Basic Manual of Small Arms.* Mechanicsburg, Penn.: Stackpole Books, 1983.

Hogg, Ian V., and John Weeks. *Military Small Arms of the 20th Century.* Northfield, Ill.: DBI Books, 1985.

Marshall, S. L. A. *Infantry Operations and Weapons Usage in Korea* London: Greenhill Books, 1988.

Owens, J. I. H., ed. *Brassey's Infantry Weapons of the World, 1950–1975.* New York: Bonanza Books, 1979.

X. Media, Propaganda, and Censorship

A. PRESS

Aronson, James. *The Press and the Cold War*. Indianapolis, Indiana: Bobbs-Merrill, 1970.

Cleary, Thomas J. "Aid and Comfort to the Enemy." *Military Review* 48 (August 1968): 51–55.

Cronin, Mary M. "An Analysis of Wartime Agenda: The Korean War Reporting of Marguerite Higgins." Talk given to Association for Education in Journalism, 1990, Boston, Massachusetts: Emerson College, 1990.

Dorn, Frank. "Briefing the Press." *Army Information Digest* 6 (1951): 36–41.

Ehrhart, W. D., and Philip K. Jason, eds. *Retrieving Bones: Stories and Poems of the Korean War*. New Brunswick, N.J.: Rutgers University Press, 1999.

Erwin, Ray. "Censorship, Communications Worry 200 K-War Correspondence." *Education Public* 83 (1950): 7, 44.

Higgins, Marguerite. *War in Korea: The Report of a Woman Combat Correspondent*. Garden City, N.Y.: Doubleday, 1951.

Kahn, Ely J. *The Peculiar War: Impressions of a Reporter in Korea*. New York: Random House, 1952.

Lande, Nathaniel. *Dispatches from the Front: News Accounts of American Wars 1776–1991*. New York: Henry Holt, 1995.

Moeller, Susan D. *Shooting War: Photography and the American Combat Experience*. New York: Basic Books, 1991.

Smith, Howard. "The BBC Television Newsreel and the Korean War." *Historical Journal of Film, Radio, and Television* 8 (1988): 227–52.

Winnington, Alan. *I Saw the Truth in Korea: Facts and Photographs That Will Shock Britain!* London: People's Press, 1950.

B. PROPAGANDA

Daugherty, William E. *Evaluation and Analysis of Leaflet Program in the Korean Campaign, June–December 1950*. Chevy Chase, Md.: Johns Hopkins University Press, 1951.

Daugherty, William, and M. Janowitz. *A Psychological Warfare Casebook*, Chevy Chase, Md.: Johns Hopkins University Press, 1958.

Kahn, Lessing, and Julius Segal. *Psychological Warfare and Other Fac-*

tors Affecting the Surrender of North Korean and Chinese Forces.
Washington, D.C.: Government Printing Office, 1953.

Maynard, Richard A. *Propaganda on Film: A Nation at War.* Rochelle
Park, N.J.: Hayden, 1975.

McLaurin, R., ed. *Military Propaganda: Psychological Warfare and Operations.* New York: Praeger, 1982.

Mossman, Billy. *EUSAK Combat Propaganda Operations, 13 July 1950–
September 1952.* Far East United States Army Forces: 3 Historical
Detachment, n. d.

Pease, Stephen E. *Psywar: Psychological Warfare in Korea, 1950–1953.*
Harrisburg, Penn.: Stackpole, 1992.

Suid, Larry H., and David Culbert. *Films and Propaganda in American: A
Documentary History.* Westport, Conn.: Greenwood Press, 1991.

Toplin, Robert Brent, ed. *Hollywood as Mirror: Changing Views of "Outsiders" and "Enemies" in American Movies.* Westport, Conn.: Greenwood Press, 1993.

C. LITERATURE AND FILM

Aichinger, Peter. *The American Soldier in Fiction, 1860–1963.* Ames:
Iowa State University Press, 1975.

Axelsson, Arne. *Restrained Response: American Novels of the Cold War
and Korea, 1945–1962.* Westport, Conn.: Greenwood Press, 1990.

Biskind, Peter. *Seeing Is Believing: Film and Politics in the 1950s.* New
York: Pantheon Books, 1983

Brock, Garland. *War Movies.* New York: Facts on File, 1987.

Brunner, Edward. *Cold War Poetry.* Urbana: University of Illinois Press,
2000.

Butler, Lucius A., and Chaesoon T. Youngs. *Films for Korean Studies.*
Honolulu: Center for Korean Studies, 1978.

Cleveland, Les. *Dark Laughter: War in Song and Popular Culture.* Westport, Conn.: Praeger, 1994.

Cumings, Bruce. *War and Television.* London: Verso, 1992.

Edwards, Paul M. *A Guide to Films on the Korean War.* Westport, Conn.:
Greenwood Press, 1997.

Ehrhart, W. D., ed. "I Remember: Soldier–Poets of the Korean War." *Literature and the Arts* 9, no. 2 (fall/winter 1997).

Fussell, Paul, ed. *The North Book of Modern War.* New York: Norton,
1991.

Kagan, Norman. *The War Film.* New York: Pyramid Publications, 1974.

Lande, Nathaniel. *Dispatches from the Front: News Accounts of American Wars, 1776–1991.* New York: Henry Holt, 1995.

Maynard, Richard A. *Propaganda on Film: A Nation at War.* Rochelle Park, N.J.: Hayden, 1975.

Serling, Rod. *Patterns: Four Television Plays with the Authors' Personal Commentaries.* New York: Simon, 1957.

Suid, Larry H. *Guts and Glory: Great American War Movies.* Reading, Mass.: Addison-Wesley, 1978.

Virilio, Paul. *War and Cinema.* trans. Patrick Camiller. London: Verso, 1989.

West, Phillip, and Suh Ji-moon, eds. *Remembering the Forgotten War.* London: M. E. Sharpe, 2001.

Wilson, Keith. *Graves Registry and Other Poems.* New York: Grove Press, 1969.

D. ORAL HISTORY

Berry, Henry. *Hey, Mac, Where Ya Been?* New York: St. Martin's Press, 1988.

Breece, Katharine A. *Memories: A Collection of Korean Conflict Oral Histories from Veterans and Others.* Arlington, Va.: Yorktown High School, 1993.

Chancey, Jennie Ethell, and William R. Forstchen. *Hot Shots: An Oral History of the Air Force Combat Pilots of the Korean War.* New York: William Morrow, 2000.

Gardam, John. *Korean Volunteer: An Oral History from Those Who Were There.* Burnstown, Ontario: General Store Publishing House, 1994.

Knox, Donald. *The Korean War, Pusan to Chosin: An Oral History.* San Diego: Harcourt, 1985.

Knox, Donald, and Alfred Coppel. *The Korean War: Uncertain Victory.* New York: Harcourt Brace Jovanovich, 1998.

Tomedi, Rudy. *No Bugles, No Drums: An Oral History of the Korean War.* New York: John Wiley and Sons, 1993.

Wilson, Arthur, and Norman Strickbine. *Korean Vignettes Faces of War.* Portland, Ore.: Artwork, 1996.

XI. RESPONSE AND RECREATION

A. HOME FRONT

Bodner, John. *Remaking American: Public Memory, Commemoration, and Patriotism in the Twentieth Century.* Princeton, N.J.: Princeton University Press, 1991.

Brune, Lester H. "Guns and Butter: The Pre-Korean War Dispute over Budget Allocation." *American Journal of Economics and Sociology* 48, no. 3 (July 1989): 357–72.

Caridi, Ronald J. *The Korean War and American Politics: The Republican Party as a Case Study.* Philadelphia: University of Pennsylvania Press, 1969.

Chester, Edwards W. *Radio, Television, and American Politics.* New York: Sheed and Ward, 1969.

Diggins, John R. *The Proud Decades: America in War and in Peace, 1941–1960.* New York: Norton, 1988.

Foot, Rosemary. *The Wrong War.* Ithaca, N.Y.: Cornell University Press, 1985.

Gietschier, Steven P. "Limited War and the Home Front: Ohio during the Korean War" MA. Kent, Ohio: Ohio State University, n. d.

Goldman, Eric. *The Crucial Decade, 1945–1955.* New York: Knopf, 1956.

Halberstam, David. *The Fifties.* New York: Villard Books, 1993.

Harper, Alan D. *The Politics of Loyalty: The White House and the Communist Issue, 1946–1952.* Westport, Conn.: Greenwood Press, 1969.

Heller, Francis, ed. *The Korean War: A 25-Year Perspective.* Lawrence: Regents Press of Kansas, 1977.

Herzon, Frederick D., John Kincaid, and Verne Dalton. "Personality & Public Opinion: The Case of Authoritarianism, Prejudice, & Support for the Korean and Vietnam Wars." *Polity* 11 (fall 1978).

Hickman, Bert. *The Korean War and United States Economic Activities, 1950–1952.* New York: National Bureau of Economic Research, 1955.

Holsingwe, M. Paul. *War and American Popular Culture: A Historical Encyclopedia.* Westport, Conn.: Greenwood Press, 1999.

Horne, Gerald. *Communist Front? The Civil Rights Congress, 1946–1956.* Cranbury, N.J.: Associated University Presses, 1998.

Judd, Walter H., "The Mistakes That Led to Korea." *Reader's Digest* 57, no. 343 (November 1950): 51.

Levantrosser, William F., ed. *Harry S. Truman: The Man from Independ-*

ence. Westport, Conn: Greenwood Press, 1986.

Miller, Douglas, and Marion Novak. *The Fifties: The Way We Really Were.* Garden City, N.Y.: Doubleday, 1977.

Niebuhr, Reinhold. *The Irony of American History.* New York: Scribner, 1952.

Paige, Glenn. *The Korean Decision: June 24–30, 1950.* New York: Free Press, 1968.

Paterson, Thomas G., ed. *Cold War Critics: Alternatives in American Foreign Policy in the Truman Years.* Chicago: Quadrangle Books, 1971.

Porter, David. *People of Plenty: Economic Abundance and the American Character.* Chicago, Ill.: University of Chicago Press, 1954.

Richardson, Elmo. *The Presidency of Dwight D. Eisenhower.* Lawrence: Regents Press of Kansas, 1991.

Rose, Lisle. *The Cold War Comes to Main Street.* Lawrence: University of Kansas Press, 1999.

Suchman, Edward A., Rose K. Goldsen, and Robin M. William Jr. "Attitudes toward the Korean War." *Public Opinion Quarterly* 17 (summer): 1953.

———. "Student Reaction to Impending Military Service." *American Sociological Review* 18 (June 1953).

Thomas, James A. "Collapse of the Defensive War Argument." *Military Review* 53 (May 1973).

Whitney, Richard W. "Mobilizing Public Opinion." *Military Review* 30 (March 1951).

B. CONGRESS

Barber, James., comp. *Political Leadership in American Government.* Boston: Little Brown, 1964.

Bond, Jon R., and Richard Fleischer. "Are There Two Presidencies? Yes, But Only for Republicans." *Journal of Politics* 50 (1985): 747–67.

Bone, Hugh A. "Western Politics and the 1952 Election." *Western Political Quarterly* 4 (March 1951): 93–99.

Burns, James MacGregor. "The Case for the Smoke-Filled Room" *New York Times Magazine* (15 June 1952): 144–50.

Caridi, Ronald J. "The G.O.P. and the Korean War." *Pacific Historical Review* 37, no. 4 (1968): 423–43.

Carpenter, Ted Galen. "'United States' NATO Policy at the Crossroads: The 'Great Debate of 1950–1951.'" *International History Review* 8, no. 3 (August 1986): 345–516.

Craig, Richard B. *The Bracero Program: Interest Groups and Foreign Policy*. Austin: University of Texas Press, 1971.

Davidson, Roger H., and Richard C. Sachs. *Understanding Congress: Research Perspectives*. Washington, D.C.: Government Printing Office, 1991.

Davidson, Roger, and Richard Baker, eds. *First among Equals: Outstanding Senate Leaders of the Twentieth Century*. Washington, D.C.: Congressional Quarterly, 1991.

DeGrazia, Alfred. *The Western Public and Beyond*. Stanford, Calif.: Stanford University Press, 1954.

Fetzer, James. "Senator Vandenberg and the American Commitment to China, 1945–1950." *Historian* 36 (February 1974): 283–303.

Fisher, Louis. *Constitutional Conflict between Congress and the President*. Princeton, N.J. : Princeton University Press, 1985.

Goldman, Eric F. *The Crucial Decade: American 1945–1955*. New York: Knopf, 1956.

Hartmann, Susan M. *Truman and the 80th Congress*. Columbia: University of Missouri Press, 1971.

Hoyt, Edwin C. "The United States Reaction to the Korean Attack: A Study of the Principles of the UN Charter as a Factor in American Policy Making." *American Journal of International Law* 55, no. 1 (January 1961): 45–76.

Kaufman, Natalie H. *Human Rights, Treaties, and the Senate: A History of Opposition*. Chapel Hill: University of North Carolina, 1990.

Kepleyk, David R. "The Senate and the Great Debate of 1951." *Prologue* 14 (winter 1982): 213–26.

Koen, Ross Y. *The China Lobby in American Politics*. New York: Octagon Books, 1974.

LaPalombara, Joseph G. "Pressure, Propaganda, and Political Action in the Election of 1950." *Journal of Politics* 14 (May 1952): 308–9.

Martin, Joe. *My First Fifty Years in Politics*. New York: McGraw-Hill, 1960.

Mayhew, David. *Party Loyalty among Congressmen: The Differences between Democrats and Republicans, 1947–1962*. Cambridge, Mass.: Harvard University Press, 1966.

Neuberger, Richard E. "Congress and the Fair Deal: A Legislative Balance Sheet." *Public Policy* 5 (1954): 349–81.

Paterson, Thomas G., ed. *Cold War Critics: Alternatives in American Foreign Policy in the Truman Years*. Chicago: Quadrangle Books,

1971.

Peirce, Neal, R. *Politics in America, 1945–1966.* Washington, D.C.: Congressional Quarterly Service, 1967.

Piper, J. Richard. "Presidential–Congressional Power Prescriptions in Conservative Political Thought since 1933." *Presidential Studies Quarterly* 21 (winter 1991): 35–54.

Rourke, John. "Congress and the Cold War." *World Affairs* 139 (spring 1977).

Smith, Beverly. "He Makes the Generals Listen." *Saturday Evening Post* 224, no. 37 (1951): 20–21, 134–38.

Spitzer, Robert J. *President and Congress: Executive Hegemony at the Crossroads of American Government.* Philadelphia: Temple University Press, 1993.

Truman, David. *The Congressional Party: A Case Study.* New York: Wiley, 1959.

C. COMMUNISM AT HOME

American Business Consultants. *Red Channels: The Report of Communist Influence in Radio and Television.* New York: American Business Consultants, 1950.

Bayles, Edwin R. *Joe McCarthy and the Press.* Madison: University of Wisconsin Press, 1981.

Carr, Robert Kenneth. *The House Committee on Un-American Activities.* New York: Octagon Books, 1979.

Caute, David. *The Great Fear: The Anti-Communist Purge under Truman and Eisenhower.* New York: Simon and Schuster, 1978.

Donner, Frank. *The Un-Americans.* New York: Ballantine, 1961.

Freeland, Richard M. *The Truman Doctrine and the Origins of McCarthyism: Foreign Policy, Domestic Politics, and Internal Security, 1946–1948.* New York: Knopf, 1976.

Fried, Richard R. *Nightmare in Red: The McCarthy Era in Perspective.* New York: Oxford University Press, 1991.

Griffith, Robert, and Athan Theoharis, eds. *The Specter: Original Essays on the Cold War and the Origins of McCarthyism.* New York: New Viewpoints, 1974.

Latham, Earl. *The Communist Conspiracy in Washington: From the New Deal to McCarthy.* Cambridge, Mass.: Harvard University Press, 1966.

Purifoy, Lewis. *Harry Truman's China Policy: McCarthyism and the Diplomacy of Hysteria, 1947–1951.* New York: New Viewpoints, 1976.

Theoharis, Athan. *Seeds of Repression: Harry S. Truman and the Origins of McCarthyism.* Chicago: Quadrangle Books, 1971.

Thompson, Francis H. *Frustration of Politics: Truman, Congress, and the Loyalty Issue 1945–1953.* Rutherford, N.J.: Fairleigh Dickinson University Press, 1979.

D. PUBLIC OPINION

Adler, Selig. *The Isolationist Impulse: Its Twentieth Century Reaction.* New York: Abelard, 1957.

Buckley, Gary S. "American Public Opinion and the Origins of the Cold War: A Speculative Reassessment." *Mid-America* 60 (January 1978): 35–42.

Erskine, Hazel. "The Polls: Is War a Mistake?" *Public Opinion Quarterly* 34, no. 1 (1970): 134–50.

Herzon, Frederick D. "Personality and Public Opinion: The Case of Authoritarianism, Prejudice, and Support for the Korean and Vietnam Wars." *Polity* 11, no. 1 (1978): 92–113.

Modigliani, Andre. "Hawks and Doves, Isolationism and Political Distrust: An Analysis of Public Opinions on Military Policy." *American Political Science Review* 66, no. 3 (1972): 960–78.

Muller, John E. "Trends in Popular Support for the Wars in Korea and Vietnam." *American Political Science Review* 65, no. 2 (1971): 358–75.

Toner, James H. "American Society and the American Way of War: Korea and Beyond." *Parameters* 11, no. 1 (1981): 79–90.

E. HISTORIOGRAPHY

Cook, Glenn S. "Korea: No Longer the Forgotten War." *Journal of Military History* 56 (July 1992): 489–92.

Cotton, James, and Ian Neary. *The Korean War in History.* Atlantic Highlands, N.J.: Humanities Press International, 1989.

Gaddis, John Lewis. "The Emerging Post-revisionist Synthesis on the Origins of the Cold War" and "Responses." *Diplomatic History* 7 (summer 1983): 171–204.

Ha, Yong Sun, ed. *New Approaches to the Study of Korean War: Beyond Traditionalism and Revisionism.* Seoul: NaNam, 1990.

Halliday, Jon. "What Happened in Korea? Rethinking Korean History 1945–1953." *Bulletin of Concerned Asian Scholars* 5, no. 3 (1973).

Okinshevich, Leo. comp. *United States History and Historiography in Postwar Soviet Writing, 1945–1970: A Bibliography.* Santa Barbara, Calif.: ABC–CLIO, 1976.

Park, Hong-Kyu. "Korean War Revisited–Survey of Historical Writing." *World Affairs* 137 (spring 1975).

Swartout, Robert, J. "American Historians and the Outbreak of the Korean War: An Historiographical Essay." *Asian Quarterly* (1979): 65–77.

Unger, Irwin. "The New Left and American History: Some Recent Trends in United States Historiography." *American Historical Review* 72 (July 1967): 1237–63.

West, Philip. "Interpreting the Korean War." *American Historical Review* 94 (February 1989): 80–96.

XII. Women and Minorities

A. WOMEN IN THE MILITARY

Alsmeyer, Marie Bennett. *The Way of the Waves: Women in the Navy.* Conway, Ark.: Hamba Books, 1981.

Campbell, D'Ann. *Women at War with America: Private Lives in a Patriotic Era.* Cambridge, Mass.: Harvard University Press, 1984.

Curtin, Ann. "Army Women on Active Duty." *Army Information Digest* 8, no. 6 (1953): 22–30.

Day, Francis Martin, Phyllis Spence, and Barbara Ladouceur. *Women Overseas: Memories of the Canadian Red Cross Corps.* Vancouver, B.C.: Ronsdale Press, 1998.

Douglas, Deborah G. *United States Women in Aviation: 1940–1985.* Washington, D.C. Smithsonian Institution Press, 1990.

Ebbert, Jean, and Marie-Beth Hall. *Crossed Currents: Navy Women from WWI to Tailhook.* Washington, D.C.: Brassey's, 1993.

Keller, Nor Okja. *Comfort Women.* New York: Penguin Books, 1999.

May, Elaine Tyler. *Pushing the Limits: American Women, 1940–1961.* New York: Oxford University Press, 1994.

Mitchell, Brian. *Weak Link: The Feminization of the American Military.* Washington, D.C.: Regnery Gateway, 1989.

Omori, Frances. *Quiet Heroes: Navy Nurses of the Korean War 1950–1953, Far East Command.* St. Paul, Minn.: Smith House Press, 2000.

Soderbergh, Peter A. *Women Marines in the Korean War Era.* Westport, Conn.: Greenwood Press, 1994.

Stemlow, Mary V. *A History of the Woman Marines, 1946–1977.* Washington, D.C.: U.S. Marine History and Museums Division, 1986.

Stiehm, Judith H. *Army and the Enlisted Woman.* Philadelphia: Penn.: Temple University Press, 1989.

Willenz, June A. *Women Veterans: American's Forgotten Heroines.* New York: Continuum Publishing, 1963.

B. MINORITIES AND THE KOREAN WAR

Ansel, Raymond B. *From Segregation to Desegregation: Blacks in the U.S. Army 1703–1954.* Carlisle Barracks, Penn.: United States Army War College, 1990.

Balmforth, E. E. "Getting Our ROKs Off." *Combat Forces Journal* 1, no. 7 (February 1951): 22–25.

Banks, Samuel L. "The Korean Conflict." *Negro History Bulletin* 36, no. 3 (1973): 131–32.

Dalfiume, Richard M. *Desegregation of the Armed Forces: Fighting on Two Fronts, 1939–1953.* Columbia: University of Missouri Press, 1969.

Davis, Lenwood O., and George Hill, comps. *Blacks in the American Armed Forces 1776–1983.* Westport, Conn.: Greenwood Press, 1985.

Dedziak, Mary. "Desegregation as a Cold War Imperative." *Stanford Law Review* 41 (November 1988): 61–120.

Foner, Jack D. *Blacks and the Military in American History.* New York: Praeger, 1974.

Gropman, Alan. *The Air Forces Integrates 1946–1964.* Washington, D.C.: Center for Air Force History, 1985.

MacGregor, Morris J. Jr. *Integration of the Armed Forced, 1940–1965.* Washington D.C.: Center of Military History, 1981.

Marshall, Thurgood. *Report on Korea: The Shameful Story of the Court Martials of Negro GIs.* New York: National Association for the Advancement of Colored People, 1951.

Martin, Harold H. "How Do Our Negro Troops Measure Up?" *Saturday Evening Post* 23 (16 June 1951): 30–31.

Nalty, Bernard D. *Strength for the Fight: A History of Black Americans in the Military.* New York: Free Press, 1986.

Rishell, Lyle. *With a Black Platoon in Combat: A Year in Korea.* College Station, Tex.: Texas A&M University Press, 1993.

Shaw, Henry I., and Ralph W. Donnelly. *Blacks in the Marine Corps.* Washington, D.C.: History and Museum Division, Headquarters, United States Marine Corps, 1975.

Skaggs, D. C. "The KATUSA Experiment: The Integration of Korean National into the U.S. Army, 1950–1953." *Journal of Military History* 38, no. 2 (April 1974): 53–58.

University Publications of America. *Papers of the NAACP, Part Nine, Discrimination in the U. S. Armed Forces, 1918–1955.* Frederick, Md.: University Publications of America, 1989.

XIII. Autobiography, Biography, and Memoirs

A. COMMUNIST

Domes, Juergen. *Peng Te-huai: The Man and the Image.* Stanford, Calif.: Stanford University Press, 1985.

Koon Woo Nam. *The North Korean Communist Leadership, 1945–1965.* Birmingham, Ala.: University of Alabama Press, 1974.

Mao Tse-tung. *Mao: An Anthology of His Writing.* Denver, Colo.: Mentor Books, 1972.

———. *On the People's Democratic Dictatorship.* Peking: Foreign Language Press, 1967.

Osanka, Franklin Mark, ed. *Modern Guerrilla Warfare: Fighting Communist Guerrilla Movement, 1941–1961.* New York: Free Press, 1962.

Peng Dehuai. *Memoirs of a Chinese Marshall (1898–1974).* Beijing: Foreign Languages Publishing, 1984.

Schram, Stuart. *Mao Tse-tung.* New York: Simon & Schuster, 1966.

B. UNITED NATIONS

Goodrich, Leland M. *Korea: A Study of United States Policy in the United Nations.* New York: Council on Foreign Relations, 1956.

Gordenker, Leon. *The United Nations and the Peaceful Unification of Korea: The Politics of Field Operations, 1947–1950.* The Hague: Nijhoff, 1959.

Jessup, Philip. *The Birth of Nations.* New York: Columbia University Press, 1974.

Kaushik, Ram P. *The Crucial Years of Non-Alignment: USA, the Korean War, and India.* New Delhi, India: Kumar, 1972.

Lie, Trygve. *In the Cause of Peace: Seven Years with the United Nations.* New York: Macmillan, 1954.

Riggs, Robert E. *Politics in the United Nations: A Study of United States Influence in the General Assembly.* Westport, Conn: Greenwood Press,

1984.

Stairs, Denis. "The United Nations and the Politics of the Korean War." *International Journal* (Canada) 25, no. 2 (1970): 302–20.

Stoesssinger, John G. *The United Nations and the Superpowers*, New York: Random House, 1970.

Yoo, Tae-Ho. *The Korean War and the United Nations: A Legal and Diplomatic Historical Study.* Louvain: Librarie Desbarax, 1967.

C. UNITED STATES/ALLIES

Acheson, Dean. *Present at the Creation: My Years at the State Department.* New York: Norton, 1969.

Allen, Richard C. *Korea's Syngman Rhee: An Unauthorized Portrait.* Rutland, Vt.: Tuttle, 1960.

Ferrell, Robert H., ed. *The Autobiography of Harry S. Truman.* Boulder: Colorado Associated University Press, 1980.

Gilbert, Martin. *Never Despair: Winston S. Churchill 1945–1965.* London: Heinemann, 1988.

Griffith, Thomas. *MacArthur's Airman: General George C. Kenney and the War in the Southwest Pacific.* Lawrence: University of Kansas Press, 1998.

Hisson, Walter H. *George F. Kennan: Cold War Iconoclast.* New York: Columbia University Press, 1989.

Mahher, William A. *Shepherd in Combat Boots; Chaplain Emil Kapuan of the First Cavalry Division.* Shippensburg, Penn.: Burd Street Press, 1997.

Manchester, William. *American Caesar: Douglas MacArthur, 1880–1964.* Boston: Little Brown, 1978.

Oliver, Robert T. *Syngman Rhee: The Man behind the Myth.* New York: Dodd Mead, 1955.

Pogue, Forrest C. *George C. Marshall: Statesmen, 1945–1959.* New York: Viking-Penguin, 1987.

Schaller, Michael. *Douglas MacArthur: The Far East General.* New York: Oxford University Press, 1989.

D. LEADERSHIP

Acheson, Dean, and Arthur H. Vandenberg Jr., "From Doubt to Leadership: Senator Arthur Vandenberg." In *Political Leadership in American Government*, comp. James D. Barber. Boston: Little Brown, 1964.

Ambrose, Stephen E. *Eisenhower,* two volumes. New York: Simon and Schuster, 1983, 1984.

Blumenson, Martin. *Mark Clark.* New York: Jonathan Cape, 1985.

Bundy, McGeorge, "The Private World of Robert Taft." *Reporter* (11 December 1951): 37–39.

Burns, James MacGregor. *President Government: The Crucible of Leadership in America.* Englewood Cliffs, N.J.: Prentice-Hall, 1965.

Clark, Mark W. *From the Danube to the Yalu.* New York: Harper, 1954.

Collins, J. Lawton. *Lightning Joe: An Autobiography.* Baton Rouge: Louisiana State University Press, 1979.

————. *War in Peacetime: The History and Lessons of Korea.* Boston: Houghton Mifflin, 1969.

Davis, Burke. *Marine! The Life of Lt. Gen. Lewis (Chesty) Puller, USMC (Ret.).* Boston: Little Brown, 1962.

James, D. Clayton. *The Years of MacArthur: Triumph and Disaster 1945–1964.* Boston: Houghton Mifflin, 1985.

Leary, William, ed. *MacArthur and the American Century.* Lincoln: University of Nebraska Press, 2001.

MacArthur, Douglas. *Reminiscences.* New York: McGraw-Hill, 1964.

Manchester, William. *MacArthur: American Caesar.* New York: Dell, 1979.

Perret, Geoffrey. *Old Soldiers Never Die: The Life of Douglas MacArthur.* New York: Random House, 1996.

Puryear, Edgar F. *American Generalship: Character Is Everything in Command.* Novato, Calif.: Presidio, 2000.

Senate Joint Committee on Armed Services and Foreign Relations. *Military Situation in the Far East: Hearings to Conduct an Inquiry into the Military Situation in the Far East and the Facts Surrounding the Relief of General of the Army Douglas MacArthur from His Assignments in That Area.* Washington, D.C.: 82d Cong., First Sess, 5 volumes, 1951.

Smith, Jean Edward. *Lucius D. Clay.* New York: Henry Holt, 1990.

Smith, Robert. *MacArthur in Korea: The Naked Emperor.* New York: Simon and Schuster, 1982.

Soffer, Jonathan M. *General Matthew B. Ridgway: From Progressivism to Reagansim, 1895–1993.* Westport, Conn.: Greenwood Press, 1998.

Spainer, John W. *The Truman–MacArthur Controversy and the Korean War.* Cambridge, Mass.: Belknap Press at Harvard University, 1959.

Taylor, John. *General Maxwell Taylor: The Sword and the Pen.* Garden City, N.Y.; Doubleday, 1989.

Taylor, Maxwell D. *Swords and Plowshares*. New York: Norton, 1972.
Weintraub, Stanley. *MacArthur's War: Korea and the Undoing of an American Hero*. New York: Free Press, 2000.
Whitney, Courtney. *MacArthur: His Rendezvous with History*. New York: Knopf, 1956.

XIV. Armistice (Cease-Fire) Negotiations

Berstein, Barton J. "Syngman Rhee: The Pawn As Rook—The Struggle to End the Korean War." *Bulletin of Concerned Asian Scholars* 10, no. 1 (1978).
Bullen, Roger. "Great Britain, the United States and the Indian Armistice Resolution on the Korean War, November 1952." In *Aspects of Anglo–Korean Relations*, International Studies. London: International Centre for Economics and Related Disciplines, London School of Economics, 1981.
Dille, John. *Substitute for Victory*. Garden City, N.Y.: Doubleday, 1954.
Foot, Rosemary. *A Substitute for Victory: The Politics of Peacemaking at the Korean War Armistice Talks*. Ithaca, N.Y.: Cornell University Press, 1990.
Goldhamer, Herbert. *The 1951 Korean Armistice Conference: A Personal Memoir*. Santa Monica, Calif.: Rand Corporation, 1994.
Goodman, Allen E. *Negotiating While Fighting: The Diary of Admiral C. Turner Joy at the Korean Armistice Conference*. Stanford, Calif.: Hoover Institution Press, 1978.
Ikles, Fred C. *Every War Must End*. New York: Columbia University Press. 1999.
Joy, C. Turner. *How Communists Negotiate*. New York: Macmillan, 1955.
Kirkbride, Wayne A. *Panmunjom: Facts about the Korean DMZ*. Elizabeth, N.J.: Hollym, 1994.
Niksch, Larry A. *The Korean Armistice Negotiations*. Washington, D.C.: Library of Congress, 1967.
The Team behind the Armistice: The Story of the Support Group UNCMAC, Munsan-ni, Korea. United States: Support Group, TI & E Office, 1954.
The Truth of the Panmunjom Incident. Pyongyang, Korea: Foreign Languages Publishing, 1976.
Vatcher, William H. Jr. *Panmunjom: The Story of the Korean Military Negotiations*. New York: Praeger, 1958.
Yi, Chong-gun. *Panmunjom*. Pyongyang, Korea: Foreign Languages Pub-

lishing, 1986.

XV. Prisoners of War

Biderman, Albert D. "Communist Attempts to Elicit False Confessions from Air Force Prisoners of War." *Bulletin New York Academy of Medicine* 33 (1957): 616–25.

———. "The Image of Brainwashing." *The Public Opinion Quarterly* 26, (winter 1962): 54–63.

———. *March to Calumny: The Story of American POWs in the Korean War.* New York: Macmillan, 1963.

Bradbury, William C. *Determinants of Loyalty and Disaffection in Chinese Communist Soldiers during the Korean Hostilities: An Explanatory Study.* Washington, D.C.: Georgetown University, 1956.

Bunker, Gerald E. *The Question of Repatriation of Prisoners of War and the Korean Peace Talks: Historical, Political, and Legal Aspects.* Cambridge, Mass.: Harvard University Press, 1963.

Carmelite Nuns, Seoul. *Carmel and the Korean Death March.* Flemington, N.J.: St. Teresa's Press, 1984.

Crosbie, Philip. *March Till They Die.* Dublin: Browne and Nolan, 1956.

Dean, William F., and William L. Worden. *General Dean's Story.* New York: Viking, 1954.

Deane, Philip. *I Was a Captive in Korea.* New York: Norton, 1953.

Drummond, S. "Korea and Vietnam: Some Speculations about the Possible Influences of the Korean War on American Policy in Vietnam." *Army Quarterly Defense Journal* 97 (1968): 65–71.

Finletter, Thomas K. "The Meaning of Korea." *Army Information Digest* 9 (September 1951): 3–8.

Hansen, Kenneth K. *Heroes behind Barbed Wire.* Princeton, N.J.: Van Nostrand, 1957.

Hunter, Edward. *Brainwashing in Red China: The Calculated Destruction of Men's Minds.* New York: Vanguard Press, 1951.

Jolidon, Laurence. *Last Seen Alive: The Search for the Missing POWs from the Korean War.* Austin, Tex.: Ink-Slinger Press, 1995.

Kinkead, Eugene. *In Every War But One.* New York: Norton, 1959.

Lech, Raymond B. *Broken Soldier: American Prisoners of War in North Korea.* Chelsea, Mich.: Scarborough House, 1991.

Meyers, Samuel M., and William C. Bradbury. *The Political Behavior of Korean and Chinese Prisoners of War in the Korean Conflict: A Historical Analysis.* Washington, D.C.: George Washington University,

1958.

Sanders, H. J. *Analysis of the Korean War Prisoner-of-War Experience.* Springfield, Va.: Monroe, 1974.

Schein, Edgar H. *A Psychological Follow-up of Former Prisoners of War of the Chinese Communists.* Cambridge: Massachusetts Institute of Technology, 1960.

Tosi, George. *The Parallel Exchange.* New York: Carlton Press, 1987.

Tsouras, Peter G., and Timothy R. Lewis. *The Transfer of the U.S. Korean POWs to the Soviet Union.* Washington, D.C.: United States Department of State, 1993.

United States Department of the Army, Pamphlet 30–101. *Communist Interrogation and Exploitation of Prisoners of War.* Washington, D.C.: Government Printing Office, 1956.

Voelkel, Harold. *Behind Barbed Wire in Korea.* Grand Rapids, Mich.: Zondervan, 1953.

White, William L. *The Captives of Korea: An Unofficial White Paper on the Treatment of War Prisoners.* Westport, Conn.: Greenwood Press, 1977.

Zeller, Larry. *In Enemy Hands: A Prisoner in North Korea.* Louisville: University of Kentucky Press, 1991.

XVI. Commentary and Analysis of the Korean War

"Analysis of Issues by Korean Commission." *United Nations Bulletin* 9, no. 1 (October 1950): 301–4.

Bailey, Sydney D. *The Korean Armistice.* New York: St. Martin's Press, 1992.

Barclay, C. N. "Lessons of the Korean Campaign." New York: *Brassey's Annual* (1954): 122–33.

Barham, Pat, and Frank Cunningham. *Operation Nightmare: The Unvarnished Truth about America's Betrayal in Korea and the United Nations.* Los Angeles, Calif.: Sequoia University Press, 1953.

Bennett, Bruce W. *Two Alternative Views of War in Korea: The North and South Korea Revolutions in Military Affairs.* Santa Monica, Calif.: Rand, 1995.

Best, Robert J. *The Structure of a Battle: Analysis of a UN–NK Action North of Taegu, Korea, September 1950.* Chevy Chase, Md.: Johns Hopkins University Press, 1954.

Bhagat, B. S. "Military Lessons of the Korean War." *Journal Royal United Service Institution* (January–April 1952): 5–21.

Brooks, Robert O. *Russian Airpower in the Korean War: The Impact of Tactical Intervention and Strategic Threat on United States Objectives.* Maxwell Air Force Base, Ala.: Air University, 1964.

Cagle, Malcolm W. "Inchon: The Analysis of a Gamble." *Naval Institute Proceedings* 80 (1954): 47–51.

Carter, Gregory A. *Some Historical Notes on Air Interdiction in Korea.* Santa Monica, Calif.: Rand, 1966.

Casey, Charles E. *In Memory—Lest We Forget: Korean War 1950–1954, KIA and MIA and Others.* Plattsmouth, Neb.: Potter Offset Print, 1993.

Chen, Jian. "China's Changing Aims During the Korean War, 1950–1951." *The Journal of American East Asian Relations* 1 (spring 1992): 8–41.

Chinnery, Philip D. *Korean Atrocity! Forgotten War Crimes, 1950–1953.* Annapolis, Md.: Naval Institute Press, 2000.

Christensen, Thomas. "Threats, Assurances, and the Last Chance for Peace: The Lessons of Mao's Korean War Telegrams." *International Security* 17 (summer 1992): 122–54.

Cohen, Eliot A., and John Gooch. *Military Misfortunes: The Anatomy of Failure in War.* New York: Free Press, 1990.

Cottrell, Alvin J., and James E. Dougherty. "The Lessons of Korea: War and the Power of Man." *Orbis* 2 (spring 1958): 39–64.

Crowe, Clarance. *An Analysis of the Inchon–Seoul Campaign.* Maxwell Air Force Base, Ala.: Air University, 1983.

Deagle, Edwin A. Jr. "The Agony of Restraint: Korea, 1951–1953." Ph.D. Cambridge, Mass.: Harvard University, 1970.

DeWeerd, Harvey A. "Lessons of the Korean War." *Yale Review* 40 (summer 1951): 592–603.

———. "Strategic Surprise in the Korean War." *Orbis* 6, no. 3 (fall 1963): 435–52.

Donovan, Robert J. *Nemesis: Truman and Johnson and the Coils of War in Asia.* New York: St. Martin's Press, 1984.

Fishel, Wesley R., and Alfred H. Hausrath. *Language Problems of the U.S. Army during the Hostilities in Korea.* Chevy Chase, Md.: Johns Hopkins University Press, 1958.

Fondarcaro, Steve. *A Strategic Analysis of U.S. Special Operations during the Korean Conflict, 1950–1953.* Fort Leavenworth, Kans.: United States Army Command and General Staff College, 1988.

Foot, Rosemary. *The Wrong War: American Policy and Dimensions of the Korean Conflict 1950–1953.* Ithaca, N.Y.: Cornell University Press, 1985.

Friedman, Edward, and Mark Selden. *America's Asia: Dissenting Essays on Asian–American Relations.* New York: Random House, 1971.

Ha, Youn Sun, ed. *New Approaches to the Study of Korean War: Beyond Traditionalism and Revisionism.* Seoul: Na Nam, 1990.

Hansen, Kenneth. *Heroes behind Barbed Wire.* Princeton, N.J.: Van Nostrom, 1957.

Heller, Francis H. *The Korean War: A 25-Year Perspective.* Lawrence: Regents Press of Kansas, 1977.

Hughes, Paul D. *Battle in the Rear: Lessons from Korea.* Fort Leavenworth, Kans.: United States Army Command and General Staff College, 1968.

Jervis, Robert. "The Impact of the Korean War on the Cold War." *Journal of Conflict Resolution* 24 (December 1980): 563–92.

Kim, Nam G. *From Enemies to Allies: The Impact of the Korean War on U. S.–Japanese Relations.* San Francisco: International Scholastic Studies, 1997.

Kim, Sam Kyu. *History of the Korean War: Reevaluation of Modern History.* Tokyo: Korean Hyoronsha, 1967.

King, O. H. P. *Tail of the Paper Tiger.* Caldwell, Idaho: Caxton Printers, 1961.

Kriebel, P. Wesley. "Unfinished Business—Intervention under the U.N. Umbrella: America's Participation in the Korean War, 1950–1953." In *Intervention of Abstention: The Dilemma of American Foreign Policy.* ed. Robin D. Higham. Lexington: University Press of Kentucky, 1975.

Lee, Suk Jung. *Ending the Last Cold War: Korean Arms Control and Security in Northeast Asia.* Brookfield, Vt.: Dartmouth Publishers, 1997.

Liem, Channing. *The Korean War: An Unanswered Question.* Albany, N.Y.: Committee for a New Korean Policy, 1992.

Marshall, Samuel L. A. *Battlefield Analysis of Infantry Weapons, Korean War.* Cornville, Ariz.: Desert Publications, 1984.

Martin, John G. *It Began at Imphal.* Manhattan, Kans.: Sunflower University Press, 1988.

Ministry of Information. *The Origins and Truth of the Korean War: An Analysis of False Perspectives by Revisionists.* Seoul: No publisher, 1990.

Nagai, Yonosuke. "The Korean War: An Interpretative Essay." *The Japanese Journal of American Studies* 1 (1981): 151–74.

Oliver, Robert T. *Syngman Rhee and American Involvement in Korea, 1942–1952: A Personal Narrative.* Seoul: Panmun, 1978.

Poats, Rutherford. *Decision in Korea.* New York: McBride, 1954.

Ra, Hong-Yk. *The Unfinished War: Korea and the Great Power Politics 1950–1990*. Seoul: Jenyewon, 1994.

Rayburn, Robert. *Fight the Good Fight: Lessons from the Korean War*. Pasadena, Calif.: Courant, 1956.

Rush, Eugene J. *Military Strategic Lessons Learned from the Korean Conflict as They Related to Limited Warfare*. Carlisle Barracks, Penn.: United States Army War College, 1974.

Srivastava, M. P. *The Korean Conflict: Search for Unification*. New Delhi: Prentice-Hall of India, 1982.

Tarpley, John F. "Korea: 25 Years Later." *Naval Institute Proceedings* 104 (1978): 50–57.

Weathersby, Kathryn, trans. "New Findings on the Korean War." *Woodrow Wilson Cold War Center Bulletin* 3 (fall 1993): 1, 14–18.

Williams, William J., ed. *A Revolutionary War: Korea and the Transformation of the Postwar World*. Chicago: Imprint Publications, 1993.

Wint, Guy. *What Happened in Korea: A Study in Collective Security*. London: Batchworth, 1954.

XVII. Postwar

Brooks, Robert O. *Russian Airpower in the Korean War: The Impact of Tactical Intervention and Strategic Threat on United States Objectives*. Maxwell Air Force Base, Ala.: Air University, 1964.

Kim, Nam G. *From Enemies to Allies: The Impact of the Korean War on U.S.–Japan Relations*. San Francisco: International Scholastic Studies, 1997.

King, O. H. P. *Tail of the Paper Tiger*. Caldwell, Idaho: Caxton Printers, 1961.

Korea and the Cold War: Division, Destruction, and Disarmament. Claremont, Calif.: Regina books, 1993.

Mayers, David A. *Cracking the Monolith: U.S. Policy against the Sino–Soviet Alliance, 1949–1955*. Baton Rouge: Louisiana State University Press, 1986.

Srivastava, M. P. *The Korean Conflict: Search for Unification*. New Delhi: Prentice-Hall of India, 1982.

"We Weren't Permitted to Win in Korea." *U.S. News & World Report* 37 (3 September 1954): 81–84.

Williams, William J., ed. *A Revolutionary War: Korea and Transformation of the Postwar World*. Chicago: Imprint Publications, 1993.

Worden, William. "We Won Back Korea—And We're Stuck With It."

Saturday Evening Post 223 (1950): 31, 153.

About the Author

Paul M. Edwards received his Ph.D. at the University of St. Andrew, Scotland, and has taught at the university level for more than 30 years. He is currently director of The Center for the Study of the Korean War, located at the Independence, Missouri, campus of Graceland University. Dr. Edwards is the author of more than a dozen books including *The Korean War: A Documentary History* (2000), *Hermit Kingdom: Poems of the Korean War* (1995), and *To Acknowledge a War* (2001).